The F.

FO

ANNUAL 1979-80

Macdonald and Jane's . London and Sydney

ISBN: 0354 09085 2

COVER PHOTOGRAPH:

Dagenham's Reggie Harris is squeezed out by Kettering defenders Richard Dixey (5), Sean Suddards (6) and Billy Kellock in the F.A. Trophy semi-final first leg which resulted in a 0–0 draw.

Published by Queen Anne Press,
Macdonald and Jane's Publishing Group Limited,
Paulton House,
8 Shepherdess Walk,
London, N1 7LW

Typeset, printed and bound in Great Britain by
C. Nicholls & Company Ltd.
The Philips Park Press, Manchester

F.A. NON-LEAGUE FOOTBALL ANNUAL 1979-80

Editorial Committee: The Editor, E. G. Powell (Chairman of the F.A. Publications Committee) and Adrian Titcombe (F.A. Competitions Secretary).

Advisory Committee: John Bowles (*Exchange Telegraph*) Steve Clark, Peter Grove, Glen Kirton (F.A.), Barry Lenton, Dave Milsted, Bill Mitchell, Neil Scott (*Daily Telegraph*), Gregory Tesser, Jim Voiels and Paul Brady.

Editor: Following a career in senior amateur football in which he scored over 100 goals with Corinthian Casuals, Kingstonian, Dulwich Hamlet and the R.A.F., Tony Williams became joint editor of *The Amateur Footballer*. This was followed by a spell as managing editor of Jimmy Hill's *Football Weekly*, *Sportsweek* and *Monthly Soccer* before he became the co-founder and compiler of *Rothmans Football Yearbook*, and undertook four years of promotional work for Rothmans on the four sponsored leagues. He now edits the *F.A. Cup Review*, produces programmes for F.A. games not played at Wembley, is soon to edit the new F.A. quarterly magazine, *F.A. Today*, and runs a football promotions company.

Editorial Office: 130 High Street, Hungerford, Berkshire.

CONTENTS

EDITORIAL

The exciting progress made in non-league football during the last year is described in detail elsewhere in this book, but the significance of the featured innovations must be clear for all to see. Last year the friendly and welcoming spirit of most clubs outside the highly-commercial Football League was mentioned in the first editorial, but while the social aspect of football must always be appreciated, the non-league game is undoubtedly becoming progressively more competitive every season.

The Semi-Professional Internationals have produced a new elite band of players in the senior leagues and already Eamonn O'Keefe has signed for Everton, Trevor Peake for Lincoln City, and Jim Arnold is playing for Blackburn Rovers.

It will be fascinating to watch the progress of the Alliance Premier League as the ex-Southern and N.P.L. clubs fight for supremacy and settle down to new travelling habits.

Office Cleaning Services have opened up a new world for the leagues with their very competitive knock-out cup, and while the leagues are fighting for prestigious victories, their member clubs also realise that their ever-increasing wage bills make success an absolute necessity with lucrative cup runs a priority as the pressures of non-league football continue to increase. As the game is more commercially orientated, success is vital and in this atmosphere the traditional spirit of non-league football may be affected. So while the non-league game continues to become more exciting and professional, let's hope that its character doesn't change.

If a football follower wants to see high-class football he will go to a First Division match, but the vast number of people associated with non-league football have chosen this level of the game because it is friendly, personal, and satisfying. We must all be careful to appreciate the progress made, to continue to become more efficient and professional and never to lose sight of the importance of a competitive spirit, but the traditional character of non-league football and its clubs must always be fostered, for this is its real attraction and strength.

NON-LEAGUE REVIEW

No one involved in non-league football can say that the 1978-79 season was uneventful! A semi-professional international tournament was introduced by the Football Association and once again international caps became available for the best players in England at this level; Office Cleaning Services sponsored an exciting new inter-league knock-out cup competition which helped to bring all the best players in the country together in very competitive surroundings; the 'Alliance' took shape as 13 Southern and seven Northern Premier League clubs qualified to join the new league which was to become the first competition of its kind to cover the whole country geographically; and, despite a long and hard winter which affected the competitions, both the F.A. Trophy and F.A. Vase finals attracted record attendances.

The season started with congratulations being offered to Wigan Athletic who went into the Football League, and what a good season it was for these new boys in Division Four! Wigan gradually climbed into a challenging position just under the top four, while Wimbledon clinched a promotion spot in only their second campaign. Incidentally, the ex-Southern League club have a chairman, vice-chairman and secretary who all came from Isthmian League clubs, as well as manager Dario Gardi, who was a Sutton United player for many years!

Spurs held

The F.A. Cup produced its normal share of intriguing battles in the earlier rounds and two 'outsiders' found their way through to the prestigious Third Round. Altrincham landed an exciting away Tie with Tottenham Hotspur without previously having had to face Football League opposition, while Maidstone United were also asked to travel – but for them it was practically a local derby at Charlton. The chance of both semi-professional clubs forcing replays was most improbable, but this was the outcome of two memorable Cup Ties.

At The Valley, the Southern League club's fine achievement was overshadowed by the rather pathetic sight of two Charlton colleagues, both talented goalscorers in their own right, showing their frustration with their poor form, possible personal rivalry and certainly Maidstone's coolness, by exchanging blows and being sent off. Eventual victory in the replay can in no way have compensated for the poor form and publicity suffered by the Kent League club since this incident.

At White Hart Lane, not even the pugnacious attitude of skipper King could detract from an amazingly mature team performance by Altrincham. Having weathered the expected early onslaught only to concede a goal from a penalty, it looked as if the First Division side should record a very comfortable victory. However, the Ardiles-King confrontation settled down to become a very intriguing personal battle to watch, and indeed the N.P.L. club, with their confident attitude allied to their considerable skill, gradually convinced themselves that this was a game that was within their grasp. Their attacks were more positive and, as the game reached the last quarter, 'The Robins' were well on top and deserved their equaliser. If they hadn't been playing a First Division club they would, in similar circumstances, have found no difficulty in sweeping aside opposition that had degenerated into a spiritless and disorganised team. The match ended in a draw, but a replay was a triumph. However, Spurs did not make the same mistakes again and they showed a far more determined attitude to record a 3-0 win at Maine Road.

The season began to settle down, with a few outsiders emerging as formidable challengers to the favourites in the senior competitions. In the Berger Isthmian League, Croydon, Dulwich Hamlet and Barking – three clubs relying on youthful squads – were making inroads into the normal dominance of the experienced Enfield, Wycombe Wanderers and Dagenham, although 'The Champions' were still most people's favourites to retain the title. Worcester City and Maidstone United seemed to have the edge on Bath City, Telford United and Kettering in the Southern League, while Mossley had quickly come to the front ahead of Altrincham and Boston United, the pre-season favourites, in the Northern Premier

League. After their glorious Cup run in 1977-78 Blyth Spartans were highly-fancied in the Northern League, but it was Bishop Auckland who made the early running with Spennymoor United and Consett just behind. Of course the action wasn't all at the top, because places in the new 'Alliance' were being fought for by middle of the table clubs in the Southern and Northern Premier Leagues who could qualify only by recording adequate league positions over two seasons of football.

N.P.L Trophy traditions

As the terrible winter weather heralded a rather depressing start to 1979, senior clubs without any league aspirations turned to the Cups for a little excitement and possible success. The F.A. Trophy has become an extremely high-powered competition which can only be won by a top quality club possessing skill, sound tactics and a complete dedication to success. The pre-season favourites probably included Blyth, Enfield, Altrincham, Runcorn and Bath City, but only the Northern Premier League clubs had any tradition in the competition. All the F.A.'s national knock-out cup competitions lost continuity because of the weather but some spectacular results were still achieved.

When the last 16 clubs were known, only three of the Northern Premier League's Trophy specialists were still in contention, but when the semi-finalists qualified, there were still two of them left, but the clubs – Stafford Rangers and Runcorn – were drawn together! Runcorn, semi-finalists for the third time in four years, did at least record their first Trophy semi-final goal but, having lost by a goal at home they drew the away match and consequently lost the Tie at Stafford, with their leading goalscorer forced to take over in goal and the Stafford winner coming from a deflection!

In the other semi-final two normally high-scoring and attractive sides produced only a single goal between them in their two semi-final legs and this was scored by Kettering to give Mick Jones's team their just reward for an impressive Trophy record throughout the competition. Any club who can eliminate Scarborough 3-0, Maidstone United 2-0, Enfield 0-0, 3-0 and Dagenham 0-0, 1-0 deserves to play at Wembley.

8

In recent Trophy finals, Dagenham had thrown away a victory which was within their grasp when allowing Scarborough's substitute to disrupt their defensive concentration late in the game, and Leatherhead had never been allowed into their stride by Altrincham. It was now Kettering's chance to prove that the South could add 'steel' to their undoubted ability to entertain with cultured football. (Kettering had three of the Southern League's top four goalscorers who had scored 77 goals between them.) It is now history that the game went according to the expected form. Some excellent flowing football from Kettering floundered on a rock hard and solidly packed Stafford defence, before a superbly executed break from defence created a chance that was finished off by Wood in as professional a manner as it was fashioned. The game continued in the same pattern with Kettering flitting about like moths around a bulb but never realising their potential. In contrast Stafford Rangers always looked latently dangerous, and it was no real surprise when Wood, who conserved his energy for use in the area where it mattered most, seized on a half chance to rifle home an excellent opportunist goal. Although it was said that possibly the better team had lost – was it really true?

The Northern Premier League has produced a never-ending supply of clubs capable of winning the most important non-League competition, in a stadium with an atmosphere that demands strong nerves and character to merit success. They do this season after season and their recipe for success must surely be right for the competition. All credit therefore should go to Stafford Rangers and the Northern Premier League.

The F.A. Trophy attendance last season was 32,000 and, while the experts will attribute this to either the fact that the game was played the week after the F.A. Cup Final or that two well-organised and well-supported clubs contested the game, I feel very strongly that the hard work and dedication of the Football Association and its competitions secretary, Adrian Titcombe, in particular had a great deal to do with the success of the occasion.

Adrian can afford to feel equally pleased with the F.A. Vase competition this season for, once again, as in every pre-

9

vious final, the attendance figures broke the previous record. Billericay became undisputed kings of the competition when recording their third victory in four years, and the hat-trick by striker Young must have been one of the best ever seen at Wembley. A firm header, a well-timed volley and a beautifully executed 25-yard 'chip' would have made even Kevin Keegan proud. Almondsbury Greenway didn't set Wembley alight on the day but their appearance at the great stadium was a just reward for four seasons of consistent F.A. Vase performances. They provided perhaps the most spectacular result of the season's competition when they beat Southern League Gosport Borough 4-3 after trailing 0-3 10 minutes from full time in the fifth round.

New champions

On the League front, new champions emerged to take three of the main League titles throughout the country. Only Spennymoor United of the Northern League retained their championship, and this only after a thrilling finish with Bishop Auckland and Consett. They also won the Durham Senior Cup for the fifth time in the last seven years. Mossley won their League and Cup double in the Northern Premier League; Worcester City, following a good F.A. Cup run, held off Kettering in the Southern Premier; and Barking were rewarded for their relentless attacking policy throughout the season with a memorable first Isthmian championship. As they also won the very competitive London Senior Cup and reached the second round of the F.A. Cup, manager Eddie McCluskey and his young squad had good reason to feel pleased with themselves. One of the most exciting championship battles was in the Western League where Frome Town stormed through the second half of the season to beat Bideford at the last moment, and Falmouth Town relinquished their title for the first time since joining the League. The Cheshire County League had another successful campaign in which the top six of the Premier Division again proved they were capable of challenging the best in the country, and Horwich R.M.I. were rewarded with the championship after a superb season. The extremely exciting Division

One promotion battle saw 10 aspiring clubs fighting it out until the last two weeks of the season, and the extension of the League was obviously a great success.

Midland pyramid?

The Midlands must surely present the ideal area in which a natural progressive pyramid could be set up for non-league clubs. The top of the pyramid will be discussed in an Alliance article elsewhere in this book, but the lower progression depends on the attitudes of the regional leagues and on negotiations with the Football Association. There is no doubt that all clubs should be encouraged to reach up for their own particular ceiling and, if clubs want to challenge for Football League status, they presumably attempt to work their way through the Premier Divisions that feed the Alliance.

The Berger Isthmian League, with three divisions in the home counties, gives most clubs sufficient scope to satisfy their ambitions. At the top such well-equipped clubs as Wycombe Wanderers and Dulwich do not appear to aspire to League football, while possibly the ambitious Enfield and Dagenham may consider moving on in the future. The healthy promotion and relegation system has seen the very progressive and impressively-equipped Harlow Town and Harrow Borough change places with the famous Kingstonian and Leytonstone clubs. Ilford, with money to invest following the sale of their ground, have merged with Leytonstone, a club needing financial backing, and hopefully they will enjoy a happy future together. This merger meant that only Southall were relegated to Division Two from whence local rivals Farnborough Town and Camberley Town will try their luck in Division One, while Billericay Town join Barton Rovers and Dorking Town as Isthmian new boys.

If ever a whole League rose to a challenge then it could be said that the Southern League lifted themselves to fight off the threatened take over in the South of England by the vastly improved Berger Isthmian League clubs.

In the O.C.S. Knock-Out Cup, Barry Watling (Maidstone United) with Barry Lloyd (Yeovil Town) and Mick Jones (Kettering Town) brought together a spirited squad of players at a time when end of season injuries and unavail-

11

ability made selection difficult. A full review of the competition can be found elsewhere in this book, but the Southern League's triumph, without conceding a goal, produced a number of heroes who were rewarded with England squad places – Brian Thompson and Brian Parker (Yeovil Town), John Watson (Wealdstone), Trevor Peake and Brendan Phillips (Nuneaton Borough) and Neil Merrick, who played extremely well in the final but who wasn't selected for England training. The Northern Premier League never really hit top form in the final at Yeovil but they featured with the Northern League in a superb semi-final. Next season it is hoped that eight leagues will be involved to compete in the O.C.S. competition and will be able to play their cup Ties throughout the season. O.C.S. should be congratulated on this fine sponsorship which has helped England find its best non-league players and has given non-league football a very special tournament indeed. Howard Wilkinson and Keith Wright, who looked after the England team in such a professional and talented way that they earned the admiration and respect of all involved with the squad, were generous in their appreciation of O.C.S.'s efforts on behalf of English non-league football. The organisation of the host clubs matched the initiative shown by the Football Association in inaugurating the competition, and everyone who attended could hardly fail to have been impressed.

Certainly, non-league football has achieved a great deal, but in closing may I leave you with a very important question: are you really supporting the game in the best ways possible. If your club is knocked out of its national tournament, do you encourage club members to support the Trophy or Vase finals? If your league is playing an important O.C.S. Cup Tie, will you support it because these sponsored competitions rely on good attendances to make all the efforts worthwhile? Do you support the England semi-professional international and the F.A. XI trial games because you believe representative football is good for non-league football?

As I visit clubs all over the country, I hear so many people complaining about the lack of interest, glamour and publicity concerning the non-league game. We can honestly say that more has now been done to rectify this situation than ever before, but support and appreciation will ensure the improvement continues.

The Non-League Football Fellowship which is being launched hopes to foster all the interests and good ideas that this type of football encourages. Whether you join it or not, please remember it will be the amount of enthusiasm and encouragement shown by you that will decide whether the game at this level continues to progress in the same way as it has done in the last year.
Tony Williams

AFFILIATED ASSOCIATIONS

Amateur Football Alliance: W. P. Goss, Room 33, 3rd Floor, 6 Langley Street, London, W.C.2 (01-240 3837)

English Schools F.A.: General Secretary, 4a Eastgate Street, Stafford, ST16 2NN (Stafford 51142)

Oxford University: Sir Harold Thompson, C.B.E., St John's College, Oxford

Cambridge University: S. Ashton, St Catherine's College, Cambridge

Army: Maj. A. Dobson, M.B.E., Army F.A., Ministry of Defence (A.S.C.B.), Clayton Barracks, Aldershot, Hants (Aldershot 24431 ext 2571)

Royal Air Force: S/Ldr. M. G. T. Standing, 'Kersey', Milton Lawns, Chesham Bois, Amersham, Bucks (Amersham 7914 – home; 01-845 2300 ext 363 – business)

Royal Navy: Lt. Cdr. H. A. Sheppard, RN Sports Office, H.M.S. Nelson, Portsmouth, PO1 3HH (Portsmouth 22351 ext 22671)

F.A. NON-LEAGUE FOOTBALL ANNUAL AWARDS 1978-79

TEAM OF THE YEAR: BARKING
Manager: Eddie McCluskie

Berger Isthmian League champions; London Senior Cup winners; 2nd Rnd F.A. Cup

SPECIAL MERIT AWARD: WORCESTER CITY
Manager: 'Nobby' Clarke

Southern League champions; 2nd Rnd F.A. Cup

NON-LEAGUE 'F.A. CUP' AWARD: ALTRINCHAM

FIVE PERSONALITIES OF THE SEASON 1978-79

**JIM ARNOLD (STAFFORD RANGERS)
TONY JENNINGS (ENFIELD)
BILLY KELLOCK (KETTERING TOWN)
CHRIS TUDOR (ALMONDSBURY GREENWAY)
HOWARD WILKINSON (ENGLAND MANAGER)**

During the coming season the above clubs and personalities will be presented with mementoes and commemorative pennants for their clubhouses.

MERIT AWARD for clubs at F.A. Vase level: **BILLERICAY TOWN,** for their third F.A. Vase victory at Wembley in front of a record crowd, and for winning the Kingsmead Athenian League championship for the second successive season.

F.A. Challenge Trophy

F.A. CHALLENGE TROPHY REVIEW

There are, unfortunately, no prizes for losers but, on this occasion, it seems appropriate to open a review of last season's Challenge Trophy with a reference to Runcorn who, for the third time in four years, failed to reach Wembley at the semifinal stage. Their conquerors, Stafford Rangers, also knocked them out in 1976 with a goal from the penalty spot, while in 1978 they drew at Altrincham only to lose on their own ground. Last season they were once again dogged by misfortune when their 'keeper Lloyd suffered a broken leg at an early stage on their home territory, forcing them to put leading scorer Whitbread in goal instead for the 2-1 defeat. Having fallen further behind at Stafford, Runcorn battled back for a draw but could not grab the all-important aggregate equaliser. In the circumstances, the usual condolences of 'there's always next year' had a somewhat hollow ring.

In the other semi-final, Dagenham, runners-up in 1977, failed to convert their chances in the goalless home leg and the following week, amidst scenes of wild enthusiasm, Kettering booked their Wembley place with a Kellock goal while their goalkeeper, Lane, distinguished himself as the Isthmian side piled on the pressure.

The exemption system for the Trophy, taking account as it does of the performances both in the competition and in the senior leagues, means that the stronger clubs do not appear until the Third Qualifying Round or First Round Proper. The early rounds are not, however, without noteworthy performances. Barking in successive Ties put out Clacton Town 7-0 and Chelmsford City 10-2, while Horwich RMI accounted for two Northern League sides, Whitley Bay and Ashington. The two Isthmian Division One neighbours, Wembley and Harrow Borough, dented Southern League pride by defeating Premier clubs Barnet and AP Leamington respectively.

The entry of the first exempted batch of clubs saw some of the fancied teams suffer rude shocks. Telford United failed against Eastwood Town, while Harrow Borough put paid to Gravesend and Northfleet who had just given Wimbledon a fright in the Cup. Yeovil Town gave a clear warning of their potential with their 8-1 walloping of Merthyr Tydfil, and Horwich continued to embarrass the Northern League by knocking out Tow Law.

The Competition Proper soon provided upsets of its own as Bath City went down to Minehead, Marine disposed of Bangor City and King's Lynn edged out Redditch United, their supposed betters in the Southern League. Nevertheless, the biggest shock came with the defeat of the holders, Altrincham, at home to Cheltenham. It may be that they were suffering the effects of their fine efforts against Spurs the week before, but the West Country side's victory was made even more noteworthy since they were forced to play their leading scorer Dave Lewis as an emergency goalkeeper. It was, however, the end of the road for Harrow (at Hayes) and Horwich (at Spennymoor).

It is at the Second Round stage that the competition really comes alight with the first open Draw which always produces exciting pairings. Enfield, who had declared that winning the Trophy was their number one priority, went to Northwich to win 3-1 and Kettering triumphed over Scarborough, those most stubborn of opponents, by winning 3-0. The previous season's semi-finalists, Spennymoor, went down to Witton Albion, while Boston United thumped Worcester City 4-0. Wycombe Wanderers made an abortive trip to Blyth and returned to draw before finally gaining a convincing 3-0 home win.

For the Northern Premier League to have only three representatives in the last 16 was, to say the least, unusual and these Northern teams were further reduced as the draw sent Boston United to Stafford and a 2-0 defeat. Runcorn could not score at home to Margate but managed two goals in the replay. Enfield thrust Cheltenham aside 4-0, and Bishop Auckland struggled through a huge fixture backlog to eliminate Enderby. Leatherhead suffered a rare home defeat against Yeovil, Wycombe also lost likewise to Hayes, who enjoyed their best-ever Trophy run, and Dagenham needed three attempts to subdue Witton Albion. Kettering emphasised their good form, beating Maidstone 2-0.

The quarter-finals were all contested by an old 'professional' club against an ex-Amateur Cup rival, with the outcome a 3-1 win for the 'pros'. The lone 'amateur' victory came for Dagenham when they won 2-0 at home to Yeovil. Hayes lost by the odd goal in three at Runcorn, with all the goals coming in the last five minutes. The other two Ties went to replays, with Stafford finishing off the weary Bishop Auckland side at home, but Kettering travelled to Enfield for a surprisingly comfortable 3-0 victory.   *Adrian Titcombe*

17

F.A. CHALLENGE TROPHY 1978-79

PRELIMINARY ROUND

Bootle	4	Connahs Quay Nomads		1
Kirkby T.	1	Skelmersdale U.		0
Colwyn Bay	1	Oswestry T.		0
Alfreton	1	Bridlington Trin.		3
Boston	2	Spalding U.		0
Heanor T.	1	Alvechurch		3
Arnold	1 1	Stourbridge	1	0
Eastwood (Hanley)	1 0	Bedworth U.	1	1
Bilston	2	Moor Green		1
Eastwood T.	6	Belper T.		1
Darlaston	1	Tamworth		0
Clacton T.	3	Gorleston		0
Harwich & Parkeston	4	Sudbury T.		0
Hertford T.	6	Chesham U.		1
Corby T.	1	St Albans C.		0
Maidenhead U.	3	Aylesbury U.		2
Dunstable	1	Wokingham T.		1
Epsom & Ewell	1 1	Hounslow	1	0
Clapton	4	Aveley		0
Walton & Hersham	1 0 1	Corinthian-Casuals	1 0	2*
Hornchurch	2	Hampton		0
Wembley	2	Met. Police		1
Ilford	2	Addlestone		1
Finchley	0	Crawley T.		1
Ashford T.	3	Bromley		1
Medway	0 1	Ramsgate	0	0
Folkestone & Shepway	3	Sheppey U.		1
Tonbridge AFC	2	Sittingbourne		0
Fareham T.	3	Andover		0
Basingstoke T.	2	Welton R.		1
Glastonbury	1	Clevedon T.		3
Paulton R.	1	Salisbury		2
Mangotsfield PF	2	Shepton Mallet T.		1
Cinderford T.	0	Barry T.		1
Trowbridge T.	2 2	Gloucester C.	2	1
Dawlish	1 1	Bridgwater T.	1	2
Bridport	2	Tiverton T.		3

FIRST QUALIFYING ROUND

Horden CW	2	Durham C.		0
Prestwich Heys	2	Gateshead		5
Emley	1 4	Penrith	1	1
Tow Law T.	1	W. Auckland T.		0
Whitley Bay	1	Horwich RMI		4
Mexboro T.	1	Droylsden		2
South Bank	0	Darwen		4
Barrow	2	Billingham Syn.		1
Evenwood T.	0	Accrington Stan.		2

18

Shildon	0 1	Bridlington Trin.	0 2
Radcliffe Boro'	2	Ferryhill Ath.	1
N. Shields	0 3	Netherfield	0 1
Bootle	3	Pwllheli & Dist.	1
Kirkby T.	2	St Helens T.	1
New Brighton	0 2	S. Liverpool	0 3
Burscough	1	Rhyl	0
Colwyn Bay	0	Formby	2
Boston	2	Ashton U.	0
Nantwich T.	0	Stalybridge Celtic	2
Witton Alb.	2	Middlewich Ath.	1
Long Eaton U.	2	Worksop T.	0
Leek T.	1	Mossley	2
Sutton T.	2	Hyde U.	0
Louth U.	2 4	Eastwood T.	2 3
New Mills	1	Buxton	2
Enderby T.	2	Sutton Coldfield T.	1
Darlaston	0	AP Leamington	1
Corby T.	0	Lye T.	2
Dudley T.	2 2	Bedworth U.	2 1
Arnold	4	Wellingboro' T.	2
Highgate U.	1 2	Bilston	1 3
Harrow Boro'	5	Ware	3
Cambridge C.	2 0 1	Wealdstone	2 0*2*
Leytonstone	1 2 0	Boreham Wood	1 2*4 †
Wisbech T.	1 2 2	Chelmsford C.	1 2** 3**†
Wembley	1 3	Barnet	1 2
Clapton	2 1	King's Lynn	2 3
Harlow T.	1 1	Harwich & Parkeston	1 0
Dunstable	1	Hayes	2
Barking	7	Clacton T.	0
Milton Keynes C.	1	Lowestoft T.	0
Hertford T.	0	Tilbury	1
Croydon	5	Epsom & Ewell	0
Woking	2 3 0 1	Waterlooville	2 3 0†† 0***
Maidenhead	1 1	Kingstonian	1 0
Dulwich Hamlet	1	Carshalton Ath.	0
Bognor Regis T.	3	Ashford T.	1
Folkestone & Shepway	3	Crawley T.	1
Tonbridge AFC	2	Fareham T.	1
Corinthian-Casuals	3 2	Basingstoke T.	3 1
Medway	2	Horsham	1
Mangotsfield PF	0	Redditch U.	2
Trowbridge T.	1 1	Barry T.	1 4
Alvechurch	2 1	Witney T.	2 2
Clevedon T.	0	Weston-s-Mare	3
Bridgend T.	0	Llanelli	2
Ton Pentre	0	Oxford C.	3
Salisbury	1 4	Tiverton T.	1 0
Bridgwater T.	3	Poole T.	1
Frome T.	1 2	Taunton T.	1
Bideford		Dorchester T.	1 1

*at Wealdstone † at Leytonstone ** at Wisbech †† at Waterlooville
*** at Woking

SECOND QUALIFYING ROUND

Emley	1 1		Gateshead	1 2
Bridlington Trin.	1 2		North Shields	1 0
Darwen	1 2		Tow Law T.	1 7
Horden CW	0 2		Radcliffe Boro'	0 1
Burscough	2		Barrow	3
Droylsden	0		Accrington Stan.	1
Horwich RMI	3		Ashington	0
Mossley	2 3		Formby	2 2*
Buxton	1 2		S. Liverpool	1 0
Bootle	0		Witton Alb.	3
Stalybridge Celtic	4		Kirkby T.	0
Arnold	0		Eastwood T.	3
Bilston	1		Sutton T.	5
Boston	3		Bedworth U.	0
Enderby T.	1 4		Long Eaton U.	1 2†
Wealdstone	1		Harlow T.	2
King's Lynn	2		Ilford	1
Barking	10		Chelmsford C.	2
Corinthian-Casuals	0		Wembley	4
Harrow Boro'	2		AP Leamington	1
Southall & Ealing Boro'	0		Oxford C.	1
Hayes	2		Milton Keynes C.	1
Boreham Wood	3 1		Tilbury	3 2
Tonbridge AFC	2		Dulwich Hamlet	3
Medway	0		Maidenhead U.	1
Croydon	3		Folkestone & Shepway	1
Bognor Regis T.	1 0		Woking	1 2
Barry T.	2		Weston-s-Mare	1
Lye T.	1 0		Witney T.	1 1
Llanelli	1		Redditch U.	4
Bridgwater T.	1 1		Salisbury	1 2
Taunton T.	3		Dorchester T.	2

at Southport   † at Enderby

THIRD QUALIFYING ROUND

Tow Law T.	1 0		Horwich RMI	1 6
Frickley Ath.	1		Barrow	2
Bishop Auckland	4		Willington	0
Bridlington Trin.	1		Chorley	3
Stalybridge Celtic	1 3		Mossley	1 2
Workington	2 0		Goole T.	2 3
Accrington Stan.	6		Gateshead	1
Horden CW	0		Consett	1
Eastwood T.	1		Telford U.	0
Burton Alb.	1 0		Grantham	1 1
Enderby T.	1 1 3		Boston	1 1 0*
Macclesfield T.	0 1		Witton Alb.	0 3
Buxton	1 2		Gainsborough Trin.	1 3
Hednesford T.	0		Northwich Vic.	2

20

King's Lynn	2	Sutton T.	1
Hayes	1	Hitchin T.	0
Hillingdon Boro'	2	Bishop's Stortford	0
Wembley	0	Dover	3
Woking	0 1	Tilbury	0 0
Harrow Boro'	2	Gravesend & Northfleet	0
Sutton U.	4	Walthamstow Ave.	0
Harlow T.	1 1	Croydon	1 0
Staines T.	1	Hastings U.	2
Dulwich Hamlet	1	Barking	2
Margate	4	Dartford	1
Cheltenham T.	4	Banbury U.	2
Maidenhead U.	1	Minehead	2
Salisbury	0	Taunton T.	2
Bromsgrove R.	0	Witney T.	2
Redditch U.	3	Barry T.	0
Oxford C.	1	Kidderminster Harriers	4
Yeovil T.	8	Merthyr Tydfil	1

at Worksop

'ALL SPORTS INTERNATIONAL NEWSPAPER' GOALSCORING CUP

The above trophy was presented to the Football Association to be awarded to the club that won by the most goals its North v South friendly match on the eve of the F.A. Trophy final. In the event of a tie, the club who scored the most goals would be acknowledged the winner.
Maidstone United (S.L.) 1   Lancaster City (N.P.L.) 2
Wycombe Wanderers (B.I.L.) 0 Altrincham (N.P.L.) 1
Harrow Borough (B.I.L.) 1   Burscough (C.C.) 1
Addlestone (S.L.) 0   Marine (C.C.) 0
The Cup was won by Lancaster City.

21

STAFFORD RANGERS 2
Wood 2
19th May at Wembley

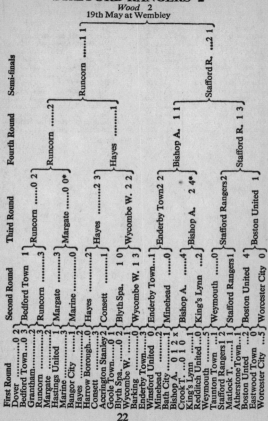

First Round	Second Round	Third Round	Fourth Round	Semi-finals
Dover 0 2				
Bedford Town...0 3	Bedford Town 1			
Grantham........2		Runcorn 0 2		
Runcorn 3	Runcorn 3		Runcorn 2	
Margate 2	Margate 3			Runcorn 1 1
Hastings United 1		Margate 0 0*		
Marine 3	Marine 0			
Bangor City 1				
Hayes 2	Hayes 2			
Harrow Borough..0		Hayes 2 3		
Consett 3	Consett 1		Hayes 1	
Accrington Stanley2				
Goole Town......0 1	Blyth Spa. 1 0			
Blyth Spa. 0 2		Wycombe W. 2 2		
Wycombe W. 1	Wycombe W. 1 3			
Barking 3				
Enderby Town....0	Enderby Town...1			
Winsford United .2		Enderby Town2 2		
Minehead 2	Minehead 0		Bishop A. 1 1	
Bath City 1				
Bishop A. ...0 1 2 x	Bishop A. 4	Bishop A. 2 4*		
Crook T. ...0 1 0				Stafford R. ...2 1
King's Lynn 1	King's Lynn ...2			
Redditch United..0				
Weymouth 5	Weymouth 0			
Taunton Town ...1		Stafford Rangers2		
Stafford Rangers 2	Stafford Rangers 1		Stafford R. 1 3	
Matlock T. ...1 1				
Atherstone Town..1	Boston Unted 4			
Boston United ...2		Boston United 1		
Eastwood Town ...0	Worcester City 0			
Worcester City ...5				

KETTERING TOWN 0
attendance 32,000

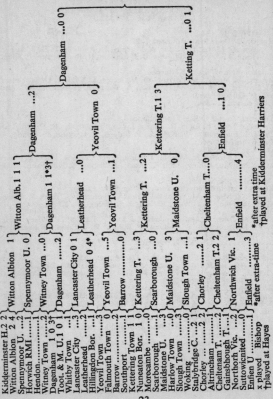

Final
Dagenham ...0 0
Ketting T. ...0 1

Semi-finals
Dagenham ...2
Yeovil Town 0
Kettering T.1 3
Enfield ...1 0

Quarter-finals
Witton Alb. 1 1 1
Dagenham 1 1*3†
Leatherhead ...0
Yeovil Town ...1
Kettering T. ...2
Maidstone U. 0
Cheltenham T ...0
Enfield ...1 0

Round 2
Witton Albion 1
Spennymoor U. 0
Witney Town ...0
Dagenham 1 1*3†
Lancaster City 0 1
Leatherhead 0 4*
Yeovil Town ...5
Barrow 0
Kettering Town 1 0
Scarborough ...0
Maidstone U. 3
Slough Town ...1
Chorley 2 1
Cheltenham T.2 2
Northwich Vic. 1
Enfield 4

Round 1
Kidderminster H.2 4
Witton Albion 2 4
Spennymoor U. ...2
Horwich RMI 1
Hendon...........1
Witney Town ...2
Dagenham 1 0 3†
Toot. & M. U.1 0 1
Whitby Town ...1
Lancaster City ...3
Leatherhead ...2
Yeovil Town ...3
Falmouth Town ...2
Southport ...1
Kettering Town 1 1
Nuneaton Bor. ...0
Morecambe 0
Scarborough ...3
Maidstone U. ...3
Harlow Town ...3
Slough Town ...0
Woking ...1
Stalybridge C. ...2
Chorley 2 1
Altrincham ...1
Cheltenham T. ...2
Gainsbrough T. ...1
Northwich Vic. ...2
Sutton United ...0
Enfield 1

*after extra time
†played at Kidderminster Harriers
*after extra time
x played   Bishop
†played at Hayes

23

F.A. CHALLENGE TROPHY

QUARTER FINALS / SEMI-FINALS
MATCH DETAILS

QUARTER FINALS

Runcorn 2 Hayes 1 (attendance 1,102)
Runcorn: G. Lloyd, T. Rutter, A. Murphy, D. Rylands, P. Duff, A. King, P. Wilson, M. Scott, B. Whitbread, J. Kenyon, K. Barnes; sub. P. Spencer (used).
Goalscorers: M. Scott, K. Barnes.
Hayes: A. Jarrett, A. Carrington, V. Akers, L. Craker, G. Bartlett, M. McGovern, P. Morrissey, R. Wiles, A. Tottman, D. Hatton, R. Nelson; sub. G. Gilbert (used).
Goalscorer: V. Akers.

Kettering Town 1 Enfield 1 (attendance 3,278)
Kettering Town: F. Lane, R. Ashby, J. Lee, F. Easthall, R. Dixey, S. Suddards, J. Flannagan, W. Kellock, P. Phipps, R. Clayton, N. Evans; sub. L. Hughes (not used).
Goalscorer: P. Phipps.
Enfield: T. Moore, M. Wright, J. Tone, T. Jennings, K. Elley, T. Gibson, M. O'Sullivan, J. Knapman, K. Searle, J. Bishop, S. King; sub. T. Bass (used).
Goalscorer: K. Searle.
Replay: Enfield 0 Kettering Town 3 (attendance 1,634)
Enfield: T. Moore, M. Wright, J. Tone, T. Jennings, K. Elley, R. Howell, M. O'Sullivan, T. Gibson, K. Searle, J. Bishop, S. King; sub. T. Bass (used).
Kettering Town: F. Lane, R. Ashby, J. Lee, F. Easthall, R. Dixey, S. Suddards, J. Flannagan, W. Kellock, P. Phipps, R. Clayton, N. Evans; sub. L. Hughes (not used).
Goalscorers: R. Clayton 2, N. Evans.

Bishop Auckland 1 Stafford Rangers 1 (attendance 811)
Bishop Auckland: H. Garrow, J. McDonald, L. Rutherford, A. Young, K. Hills, A. Suggett, T. Waugh, M. Gooding, T. Sword, B. Coulson, K. Brown; sub. K. Blair (used).
Goalscorer: K. Hills.
Stafford Rangers: J. Arnold, F. Wood, C. Nixon, J. Sargeant, B. Seddon, R. Ritchie, W. Secker, S. Chapman, A. Wood, M. Cullerton, C. Chadwick; sub. P. Marsden (used).
Goalscorer: J. Sargeant.
Replay: Stafford Rangers 3 Bishop Auckland 1 (attendance 2,241)
Stafford Rangers: J. Arnold, F. Wood, C. Nixon, J. Sargeant, B. Seddon, R. Ritchie, W. Secker, S. Chapman, A. Wood, M. Cullerton, P. Marsden; sub. T. Neal (not used).
Goalscorer: M. Cullerton 3.
Bishop Auckland: H. Garrow, J. McDonald, L. Rutherford, A. Watson, R. Hills, K. Parker, T. Waugh, M. Gooding, T. Sword, B. Coulson, A. Suggett; sub. K. Brown (not used).
Goalscorer: T. Sword.

Dagenham 2 Yeovil Town 0 (attendance 1,792)
Dagenham: I. Huttley, P. Wellman, P. Gilbert, J. Dunwell, D. Bond, D. Moore, M. Harkins, J. Borland, N. Fox, R. Kidd, T. Horan; sub. R. Harris (used).
Goalscorer: J. Dunwell 2.
Yeovil Town: B. Parker B. Thompson, A. Cottle, B. Jones, T. Cotton, M. Harrison, S. Morrall, D. Platt, C. Green, N. Piper, J. Clancy; sub. K. Leigh (used).

SEMI-FINALS

First Leg: Runcorn 1 Stafford Rangers 2 (attendance 2,386)
Runcorn: G. Lloyd, T. Rutter, N. Kenwright, D. Rylands, P. Duff, A. King, P. Wilson, M. Scott, B. Whitbread, J. Kenyon, K. Barnes; sub. P. Spencer (used).
Goalscorer: M. Scott.
Stafford Rangers: J. Arnold, F. Wood, C. Nixon, J. Sargeant, B. Seddon, R. Ritchie, W. Secker, S. Chapman, A. Wood, M. Cullerton, P. Marsden; sub. R. Jones (not used).
Goalscorers: A. Wood, (1 o.g.).

Second Leg: Stafford Rangers 1 Runcorn 1 (attendance 3,584)
Stafford Rangers: J. Arnold, F. Wood, C. Nixon, J. Sargeant, B. Seddon, R. Ritchie, W. Secker, S. Chapman, A. Wood, M. Cullerton, C. Chadwick; sub. R. Jones (not used).
Goalscorer: M. Cullerton.
Runcorn: B. Fitzgerald, T. Rutter, A. Murphy, D. Rylands, P. Duff, A. King, P. Wilson, M. Scott, B. Whitbread, P. Spencer, K. Barnes; sub. J. Kenyon (used).
Goalscorer: P. Wilson.

First Leg: Dagenham 0 Kettering Town 0 (attendance 3,079)
Dagenham: I. Huttley, P. Wellman, T. Scales, J. Dunwell, D. Bond, D. Moore, M. Harkins, J. Borland, N. Fox, R. Harris, T. Horan; sub. P. Gilbert (used).
Kettering Town: F. Lane, R. Ashby, J. Lee, F. Easthall, R. Dixey, S. Suddards, J. Flannagan, W. Kellock, P. Phipps, R. Clayton, N. Evans; sub. L. Hughes (not used).

Second Leg: Kettering Town 1 Dagenham 0 (attendance 6,829)
Kettering Town: F. Lane, R. Ashby, J. Lee, F. Easthall, R. Dixey, S. Suddards, J. Flannagan, W. Kellock, P. Phipps, R. Clayton, N. Evans; sub. L. Hughes.
Goalscorer: W. Kellock.
Dagenham: I. Huttley, P. Wellman, T. Scales, J. Dunwell, D. Bond, D. Moore, M. Harkins, J. Borland, N. Fox, R. Kidd, T. Horan; sub. J. Holder (used).

F.A. CHALLENGE TROPHY FINALS
1977-78

1970 (*Attendance:* 28,000)
Macclesfield Town   2 (Lyons, Fidler B.)   **Telford United   0**
Macclesfield Town: Cooke; Sievwright, Bennett, Beaumont, Collins, Roberts; Lyons, Fidler B., Young, Corfield, Fidler D.
Telford United: Irvine; Harris, Croft, Flowers, Coton, Ray, Fudge, Hart, Bentley, Murray, Jagger.

1971 (*Attendance:* 29,500)
Hillingdon 2 (Reeve, Bishop) **Telford United 3** (Owen, Bentley, Fudge)
Hillingdon: Lowe; Batt, Langley; Higginson, Newcombe, Moore, Fairchild, Bishop, Reeve, Carter, Knox.
Telford: Irvine; Harris, Croft, Ray, Coton, Carr, Fudge, Owen, Bentley, Jagger, Murray.

1972 (*Attendance:* 24,000)
Stafford Rangers 3 (Williams (2) Cullerton (1)) **Barnet 0**
Stafford Rangers: Aleksic; Chadwick, Clayton, Sargeant, Aston, Machin, Cullerton, Chapman, Williams, Bayley, Jones.
Barnet: McClelland; Lye, Jenkins, Ward, Embrey, King, Powell, Ferry, Flatt, Easton, Plume.

1973 (*Attendance:* 23,000)
Scarborough 2 (Leask, Thompson) **Wigan Athletic 1** (Rogers) (a.e.t.)
Scarborough: Garrow; Appleton, Shoulder, Dunn, Siddle, Fagan Donoghue, Franks, Leask (Barmby), Thompson, Hewitt.
Wigan Ath.: Reeves, Morris, Sutherland, Taylor, Jackson, Gillibrand, Clements, Oates (McCunnell), Rogers, King, Worswick.

1974 (*Attendance:* 19,000)
Dartford 1 (Cunningham) **Morecambe 2** (Richmond, Sutton)
Dartford: Morton; Read, Payne, Carr, Burns, Binks, Light, Glozier, Robinson (Hearne), Cunningham, Halliday.
Morecambe: Coates; Pearson, Bennett, Sutton, Street, Baldwin, Done, Webber, Roberts (Galley), Kershaw, Richmond.

1975 (*Attendance:* 21,000)
Matlock Town 4 (Oxley, Dawson, T. Fenoughty, N. Fenoughty)
    Scarborough 0
Matlock Town: Fell; McKay, Smith, Stuart, Dawson, Swan, Oxley, Fenoughty N., Scott, Fenoughty T., Fenoughty M.
Scarborough: Williams; Hewitt, Pettit, Dunn, Marshall, Todd, Houghton, Woodall, Davidson, Barmby, Aveyard.

1976 (*Attendance:* 21,000)
Scarborough 3 (Woodall, Abbey, Marshall pen) **Stafford Rangers**
(Jones 2) (after extra time)
Scarborough: Barnard; Jackson, Marshall, Dunn, Ayre, Donoghue, Dale,
Woodall, Abbey, Hilley.
Stafford Rangers: Arnold; Ritchie, Richards, Sargeant, Seddon, Morris,
Chapman, Lowe, Jones, Hutchison, Chadwick.

1977 (*Attendance:* 20,500)
Dagenham 1 (Harris) **Scarborough 2** (Dunn pen, Abbey)
Dagenham: Huttley; Wellman, Currie P., Dunwell, Moore, Currie W.,
Harkins, Saul, Fox, Harris, Holder.
Scarborough: Chapman; Smith, Marshall (Barmby), Dunn, Ayre, Deere,
Aveyard, Donoghue, Woodall, Abbey, Dunn.

1978 (*Attendance:* 20,000)
Altrincham 3 (Heathcote, Johnston, Rogers) **Leatherhead 1** (Cook)
Altrincham: Eales; Allan, Crossley, Bailey, Owens, King, Morris, Heath-
cote, Johnston, Rogers, Davison (Flaherty).
Leatherhead: Swannell; Cooper, Eaton, Davies, Reid, Malley, Cook,
Salkeld, Kelly, Baker, Doyle (Bailey).

CLUB RECORDS BEFORE ABOLITION
OF F.A. AMATEUR CUP 1969-74

	69–70	70–71	71–72	72–73	73–74	Total
Macclesfield T. (N.P.L.)	W	Q–F	Q–F	1	S–F	21
Telford U. (S.L.)	F	W	S–F	1	2	21
Stafford Rangers (N.P.L.)	2	1	W	S–F	Q–F	19
Buxton (N.P.L.)	2	Q–F	Q–F	3	3	16
Hillingdon Boro' (S.L.)	Q–F	F	3	2	1	16
Chelmsford (S.L.)	S–F	2	3	Q–F	1	15
Morecambe (N.P.L.)	1	—	3	Q–F	W	15
Scarboro' (N.P.L.)	2	2	2	W	3	15
Wigan Ath. (N.P.L.)	2	3	3	F	1	15
Barnet (S.L.)	S–F	1	F	1	1	14
Dartford (S.L.)	2	1	Q–F	1	F	14
Bangor C. (N.P.L.)	3	3	1	Q–F	2	13
Bedford T. (S.L.)	1	2	2	Q–F	Q–F	13
Grantham (S.L.)	3	1	Q–F	2	3	13
Yeovil T. (S.L.)	1	S–F	S–F	1	1	13
Romford (S.L.)	3	2	1	3	3	12
Stourbridge (W.M./S.L.)	2	Q–F	1	3	2	12
Weymouth (S.L.)	3	2	1	2	Q–F	12
Burton Alb. (S.L.)	Q–F	3	2	1	1	11
Bromsgrove R. (S.L.)	3	2	2	1	2	10
Hereford U. (S.L.)	2	S–F	3	—	—	10

$W = 7, F = 6, S–F = 5, Q–F = 4$

COMPLETE CLUB RECORDS 1969-78

	69-70	70-71	71-72	72-73	73-74	74-75	75-76	76-77	77-78	78-79	TOTAL
Scarborough	2	2	W	W		F	W	W	2	2	38
Stafford Rangers	2	2	W	S-F	Q-F	S-F	F	2	Q-F	W	37
Bedford T.	1	1	2	Q-F	2	1	2	2	1		29
Telford Utd.	F	W	2	2	2	3	2	2	3		27
Wigan Ath.	2	3	3	F	W	2	3	Q-F	1	1	27
Morecambe T.	1		1	2	2	2	1	2	3	1	26
Macclesfield T.	W	Q-F	3	Q-F	S-F	2	3	Q-F	1	1	25
Hillingdon Boro'	Q-F	1	3	1	1	2	W	3	2	1	25
Matlock T.	3	2	1	2	Q-F	W	3	F	Q-F	2	25
Weymouth		2		2	1	S-F	3	2	1	4	25
Dagenham	1	S-F		1	1	1	2	2	Q-F		23
Yeovil T.	Q-F	3	S-F	1	2	Q-F	1	2	1	1	22
Burton Alb.	3	3	2	1	1	1	1	2	3		22
Bangor C.	3	1	Q-F	2	2	2	1	1	2	1	21
Dartford	1	Q-F	Q-F	3	1	1	1		1	2	20
Grantham	2	2	1	3	3	2	1	3	S-F		20
Buxton	3		Q-F	3	3	3		1	1	1	18
Romford							1	1	S-F	S-F	18
Runcorn									W	2	18
Wimbledon	Q-F	3	1	2	1	Q-F	1	1	1	1	18
Worcester C.	3	3	3	2	2	1	1	3	1	2	18
Bromsgrove R.	2	2	2	2	1	1	S-F	1	1		17
Chelmsford	S-F	1		1	1	1	Q-F	Q-F	W	1	17
Altrincham		1	3	2	1	1	1		2	2	17
Chorley						1	2	1	1	1	16
Barnet	S-F	1	3			1		1	1	2	15

W = 7, F = 6, S-F = 5, Q-F = 4.

28

CLUB RECORDS AFTER ABOLITION OF F.A. AMATEUR CUP 1974-1978

W=7, F=6, S–F=5, Q–F=4.

	74–75	75–76	76–77	77–78	78–79	TOTAL
Scarborough (N.P.L.)	F	W	W	1	2	23
Dagenham (B.I.L.)	Q–F	3	F	Q–F	S–F	22
Stafford Rangers (N.P.L.)	1	F	2	2	W	18
Runcorn (N.P.L.)	–	S–F	3	S–F	S–F	18
Matlock (N.P.L.)	W	3	3	3	1	17
Bedford Town (S.L.)	S–F	Q–F	1	Q–F	2	16
Enfield (B.I.L.)	3	S–F	1	2	4	15
Altrincham (N.P.L.)	1	–	S–F	W	1	14
Leatherhead (B.I.L.)	2	2	1	F	3	14
Goole Town (N.P.L.)	Q–F	2	3	3	1	13
Weymouth (S.L.)	3	2	Q–F	2	2	13
Slough Town (B.I.L.)	–	3	S–F	2	2	12
Tooting & Mitcham (B.I.L.)	1	Q–F	3	3	1	12
Wigan Athletic (N.P.L.) ...	Q–F	3	2	3	–	12
Morecambe (N.P.L.)..........	2	3	Q–F	1	1	11
Burton Albion (S.L.)	S–F	2	2	1	–	10
Hendon (B.I.L.)	1	2	3	3	1	10
Atherstone (S.L.)	1	3	2	3	1	10

**ALL GENUINE FOLLOWERS OF THE GAME
OUTSIDE THE FOOTBALL LEAGUE
SHOULD BENEFIT FROM**

[THE NON-LEAGUE FOOTBALL FELLOWSHIP

The aims of The Fellowship are to promote non-league football, support the Football Association in their bid to increase awareness of the F.A. Trophy, F.A. Vase and semi-professional internationals, help the game's sponsors and build a nationwide family of non-league football supporters and give them information and help from the Fellowship. Membership of The Fellowship costs £3.00 for the 1979-80 season, and members will receive a badge, membership card, a newsletter at least four times a year, and The Fellowship staff will attempt to give any information requested by members in connection with non-league football.

The newsletter will give information on such matters as:
semi-professional internationals * sponsored competitions
nationwide league news * fund raising schemes
personalised club products * club shops
programme collecting * programme swaps
programme fairs * general club news
F.A. Trophy news * F.A. Vase news
semi-professional international overseas supporters tours
– club tours
F.A. Trophy and Vase Wembley Finals – eve of match friendlies
and post-match Fellowship socials
travel advice in U.K. or abroad * pen friends
Special information on non-league periodicals and discounts
for Fellowship members in subscription for non-league
periodicals.

* * * * *

It is hoped that a nationwide network of N.L.F.F. club co-ordinators will be set up (in association with club secretaries) to help entertain visiting members at non-league matches throughout the season.

Please enrol me as a member of The Non-League Football Fellowship and send me my membership badge, card and regular newsletter.

I enclose the annual membership fee of £3.00
Name: Club supported:
Address:
Tel no:
Would you be willing to act as an N.L.F.F. co-ordinator at your club?
Yes/No
Cheques should be made out to The Non-League Football Fellowship and sent to The Non-League Fellowship, 130 High Street, Hungerford, Berkshire.

F.A. TROPHY FINAL

Stafford Rangers (1) 2 (Wood 2)   **Kettering (0) 0**
Attendance: 32,000

For the first year ever, the Trophy final was played after the Cup final and the pairing of two well-supported clubs brought a record gate of 32,000. The form which had taken Kettering to runners-up spot in the Southern League encouraged many people to tip them to break the N.P.L. hold, although there was concern for the fitness of Lee and Phipps. Stafford had already lost the services of Nixon since the semi-final, but felt half the side's 1976 Wembley experiences might prove useful.

In the event, the early exchanges suggested that Kettering's wounded team members had made full recoveries, with Phipps catching the eye with his positive running on and off the ball, and Lee managing a couple of long-range efforts. Stafford looked dangerous on the occasional counter-attack, but after 20 minutes Arnold had to spread himself in front of Dixey who lifted his shot over from six yards. The thirtieth minute saw Easthall's shot hit the bar after Arnold had foiled a fine run by Phipps and, although the Kettering goal had one or two scares, their fluent passing movements meant Stafford striker Wood saw more action in his own half. However, after 34 minutes a swift Stafford raid saw the lively Cullerton make ground on the right before Wood met his squared pass in his stride and scored comfortably from near the penalty spot. Not surprisingly, Kettering's rhythm was disturbed and doubtless they went in at half-time feeling somewhat unlucky.

Immediately after the restart Wood headed just over the bar, but the general pattern saw Kettering pressing forward against a resolute defence in which the powerful Seddon was prominent. In the sixty-fourth minute, Stafford's grip tightened as Cullerton won a fierce tussle for the ball which ran loose to Wood, who again beat Lane without fuss. Kettering's attacks now lacked penetration and Wood twice came close to his hat-trick as Stafford became only the second club to win the Trophy more than once.

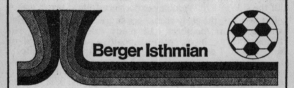

F.A. Challenge Vase

Like all other sporting competitions, the Vase lost its way somewhat after Christmas as the Arctic weather took a firm grip of the country. It was difficult to assess true form, particularly in the North, as midweek fixtures often meant weakened teams had to take the field. However, there were still many regulars amongst the survivors as well as the newcomers the Vase brings forth each year.

One innovation of the 1978-79 season was the entry of two Channel Island clubs who were prepared to subsidise their opponents in order to extend their competitive experience. Both First Tower United (Jersey) and St Martin's (Guernsey) won two Ties before being paired by the Draw – a match which was won by the Guernsey side for a Third Round trip to Gosport, who proved just too strong for them.

The 'big guns' are, of course, exempted from the first two rounds but those clubs starting out in the Preliminary include many who believe it will be their year to establish themselves amongst the elite. Certainly, Forest Green must have had high hopes after putting 12 goals past Avon Bradford but Northern Alliance champions Brandon United, who had been hotly tipped, had their dreams shattered by Norton CCT at Brandon's home ground. The First Round saw the convincing defeat of Midland Counties top team, Brigg Town, by Hall Road Rangers, while Newport IOW notched seven and Cheshunt six.

The first of the favourites to fall were Hungerford Town, semi-finalists in 1978, who went down by the odd goal in seven at home to Alton Town. The holders, Blue Star, defeated Wearside rivals, Wingate, but the other finalists, Barton Rovers, needed extra time against Wootton Blue Cross, as did Billericay at home to Rainham. Almondsbury Greenway, however, scored five goals against earlier high scorers,

33

Forest Green. Vase stalwarts Friar Lane OB and Farnborough Town both had single-goal away victories, while Irthlingborough Diamonds, Haringey Borough and Burnham all progressed without a hitch. Surprisingly, March Town United, who reached the First Round Proper in the F.A. Cup, lost to Histon.

Blue Star relinquished their hold on the Vase in the Third Round when they were defeated 4-2 by Whickham, who now included two of the Wembley winners in their side. The only other casualty amongst the fancied clubs was Burnham, whom the Draw unkindly sent to Barton. However, perhaps the biggest shock was Anstey Nomads' 7-0 hammering of Halesowen who had already defeated Telford in the Cup. Billericay made their intentions plain, putting five past Epping, while Cheshunt brought their three-round tally to 16.

By the time the Fourth Round is reached, there are no 'soft touches' left and it was therefore, surprising to note the number of away victories including Barton, Farnborough, Almondsbury Greenway and Eastbourne United, all of whom faced tricky fixtures. In fact, there were no real upsets in the round but Shepshed Charterhouse drew attention to themselves with their defeat of Skegness Town. Both the challengers from the North-east, Whickham and Seaham CW Red Star, needed replays to put them into the last 16.

The Fifth Round provided probably the most amazing match of the whole competition when Almondsbury trailed Gosport Borough 0-3 in their replay with only a quarter of an hour remaining. Almost unbelievably they pulled back the three goals and snatched the winner in extra time. Farnborough showed their power at Cheshunt, winning 4-0, and Barton and Billericay likewise travelled for victory. The battle of the North-east went to Whickham while Willenhall Town dismissed Irthlingborough.

The eight quarter-finalists naturally have very real ambitions of a Wembley appearance and, for this reason, the Sixth Round often presents a test of players' nerves. Whickham entertained Willenhall in their third Vase Tie in eight days and their home advantage was probably the deciding factor in the 3-2 victory. Billericay made full use of their Vase experience to win by the only goal at Eastbourne, but their old rivals,

34

Farnborough, were well beaten at Almondsbury who thus reached the last four for the second successive year. Shepshed established themselves as serious contenders with their 3-2 extra time victory at Barton, earning themselves a semi-final Tie against Billericay.

The 1976 and 1977 winners, Billericay, took a 2-0 lead at home but were pulled back in the return. However, the replay at Cambridge saw Billericay's best display of the season as they booked their Wembley place 2-0. Many pundits doubted whether Almondsbury's single goal at home to Whickham would be sufficient for the trip to the North-east, but a superb defensive performance earned them a 1-1 draw for a 2-1 aggregate win.

Adrian Titcombe

F.A. CHALLENGE VASE 1978-79

PRELIMINARY ROUND

Home		Away	
Darlington RA	3	Wallington	1
Ryhope CW	2	Whickham	3
Carlisle C.	1	Billingham Soc.	3
Brandon U.	0	Norton CC1	0
Peterlee Newtown	1	Carlisle Spar.	2
Heaton Stannington	2	Boys Welfare	1
Boldon CA	2	Smith's Dock	2
Wallsend T.	4	Guisboro' T.	1
Seaham CW RS	0	Washington	3
Pickering T.	1	Sunderland Pyrex	5
Wingate	0	Eppleton CW	1
Teesside Poly.	0	Little Lever	2
Wren Rovers	6	O. Blackburnians	2
Nelson	5	Stork	0
Leyland Motors	5	Newton	0
Waterloo Dock	6	Blackpool Mechs.	1
Salford Ams.	3	Whalley Range Am.	1
Lytham	0	N. Withington	1
Wythenshawe Ams.	0	Hoylake Ath.	1
Prescot BI	1	Kidsgrove Ath.	4
East Chorlton Am.	0	Heswall	2*
Linotype	2	Chadderton	0
Glossop	3	Ossett T.	6
BSC Parkgate	0	Clitheroe	0
Thackley	1	Bradley Rgrs.	0
Harrogate T.	1	Normanby PW	3
Fryston Colliery	1	North Ferriby U.	1
Guiseley	2	Bentley Vic.	3
Birkenshaw R.	1	Hatfield Main	0
Brook Sports	3		

Home		Away	
Yorkshire Am.	1	Gainsboro' Utd.	2
Hall Road Rgrs.	3	Ashby Inst.	1
Immingham T.	3	Refford T.	4
Ruston Sports	0	Pilkington Rec.	2
Rawmarsh Welfare	4	Barton T.	2
Skegness T.	2	Kiverton Pk.	0
Oakham U.	1	Ruston Bucyrus	0
Thringstone		Newfoundpool WMC	3
Norton Woodseats	3	Staveley Wks.	2*
Shepshed Ch'house	5	Carrvale U.	3
Clay Cross Wks.	2	Paget Rgrs.	1*
Long Eaton Grange	2	Tividale	0
Walsall Sportsco	1	Oadby T.	2*
Solihull Boro'	0	Hinckley T.	2
Wednesfield Soc.	5	GKN Sankey	2
Boldmere St Michaels	0	Long Buckby	2
+Coventry Sporting	1	Brierley Hill	
Willenhall T.	1	Desboro' T.	1
Knowle	0	Coleshill T.	4
Walsall Wood	0	Northfield T.	0*
Rothwell T.	1	Valley Sports Rugby	0
Ely C.	3	Leverington	2
Stowmarket	2	Holbeach U.	2*
Holt U.	6	Beccles	2
Soham T. Rgrs.	0	Bungay T.	1
March T. U.	0	Norwich Union	0
Chatteris T.	3	Watton U.	3
Melton T.	0	Mirrlees Blackstone	2
Royston T.	3	Diss T.	4
Felixstowe T.	0	Maldon T.	0*

Stratford T.	0	Bicester T.	2
Eaton Bray U.	0	N'hampton Spencer	1*
Knebworth	2	Olney T.	0
Stansted	2	Langford	3
Letchworth GC	8	Huntingdon U.	1*
Wolverton & BR	2	Hemel Hempstead	2
Sandy Alb.	4	Sun Sports	2
Cheshunt	0	Potton U.	1
Tiptree U.	0	Haverhill R.	1
Leggatts OB	1	Baldock T.	1
Hatfield T.	1	Thame U.	6
Wootton Blue X	3	RR Engines	2*
Sawbridgeworth	1	Arlesey R.	4
Witham T.	3	Eynesbury R.	1
Pirton	3	Saffron Walden T.	1
Chingford	0	Selby	3
Vauxhall Motors	4	Edgware	0
Heybridge Swifts	1	Braintree & Crittall	1
Wallingford T.	3	Harefield U.	1
Tansley	3	Stotfold	1
Willesden	3	Didcot T.	2
Harpenden T.	1	Shillington	0
Woodford T.	3	Kingsbury T.	1
Norsemen	3	Swanley T.	4*
Windsor & Eton	2	Eton Manor	0
Ford U.	0	Whyteleafe	0
††W. Wickham	0	Darenth Heathside	2
Erith & Belvedere	2	LB of Greenwich	0
Bracknell T.	0	Malden Vale	1
Thatcham T.	2	BAC (Weybridge)	2
Chalfont St Peter	0	Banstead Ath.	1
Civil Service	3	Frimley Green	1
Malden T.	1	Feltham	0
Flackwell Heath	1	Chertsey T.	4
Ulysses	1	Egham T.	3*
Kew Assoc.	2 3	Marlow	2 1

Cobham	1	Shoreham	1
Steyning	0	Horsham YMCA	1
O. Salesians	1	Camberley T.	0
Dartford Glentworth	5	Canvey Island	4*
Crockenhill	6	Crown & Manor	2
E. Grinstead	2	Whitstable T.	2 3
Faversham T.	5	Sidley U.	1
Bexley	1	Welling U.	1
Herne Bay	3	Hythe T.	4
Wigmore Ath.	2	Merstham	3
Ringmer	1	Three Bridges	2
Dorking T.	2	Southwick	1
Tunbridge Wells	1	Horley T.	0
Littlehampton T.	2	Bexhill T.	1
Worthing	1	Farnham T.	0
Newport IOW	5	Selsey	0
Brading T.	4	Swanage & Herston	2
Chichester C.	1	Cowes	2
Alton T.	3	Swaythling	1
First Tower U.	1	Havant T.	3
Brockenhurst	0	Sholing Sports	3
Fleet T.	1	St Martins	0
Amesbury	0	Wantage T.	0 0 2**
Clandown	6	Larkhall Ath.	0 0
Ledbury T.	2	Wilton R.	5
Pegasus Jnrs.	0	W. Midlands Police	2
Worrall Hill	1	Fairford T.	3
Malmesbury Vic.	1	Shortwood U.	1
Calne T.	0	Radstock T.	1
Sharpness	3	Chippenham T.	1
Cirencester T.	0 1	Bristol St George	0 2
Ilminster T.	1	Port of Bristol	3
Westbury U.	1	Odd Down	0*
Peasedown Ath.	4	Glenside St Gabriels	1 3
Bristol Manor Farm	1	Keynsham T.	1
Stonehouse	1	Clanfield	2

Home		Away		Home		Away	
Forest Green R.	12	Avon Bradford	1	Faversham T.	1 4	Ringmer	1 0
Brixham U.	3	Ottery St Mary	1	Swanley T.	3	Herne Bay	0 0
Exmouth T.	0	Holsworthy	1	Whitstable T.	1	Tunbridge Wells	2 0
Coggeshall T.	2	Bowers U.	1	W. Wickham	1	Tansley	0

* after extra time; † w.o. for Coventry Sporting as Long Buckby withdrew; ** at Bath City. †† at Dareth Heathside F.C.;

FIRST ROUND

Home		Away		Home		Away	
Wingate	1	Gresley R.	0	Newfoundpool WMC	1		
Carlisle Spar.	2	Walsall Sportsco	4*	Knowle	3		
Billingham Soc.	1	Oldbury U.	3	Shepshed Ch'house			
Heaton Stannington	1	Coventry Sporting	2	Gornal Ath.	4		
Norton CCT	3	Northfield T.	2	Armitage	2		
Whickham	4	Kidsgrove Ath.	1	Bridgnorth T.	2		
Guiseley	0	Willenhall T.	1	W. Midlands Police	3		
Leeds Poly.	0	Evesham U.	2	Anstey Nomads	1		
Harrogate T.	1	RC (Warwick)	5	Brierley Hill All.	0*		
Irlam T.	1 1	Melvern T.	1 0	Astwood Bank	1		
Fleetwood T.	3	Moreton T.	3	Wednesfield Soc.			
Linotype	2	Halesowen T.	4 3	Ledbury T.	4 1		
Lytham	2	Felixstowe T.	3	Watton U.	0		
Salford Ams.	3	Soham T. Rgrs.	2	Beccles			
Waterloo Dock	4	CNSOBU	0	Stowmarket	1		
Brook Sports	1	Haverhill R.	0	Royston T.	1		
Norton Woodseats	1 1	Vauxhall Motors	6 0	March T. U.	1		
N. Withington	1 2	St Neots T.	0	Shillington	6		
Appleby FA	2	Pirton	0	Bicester T.	1		
Ossett T.	2	Northampton Spencer	1	Berkhamsted T.	2		
Bentley Vic.	2	Stansted	0	Baldock T.	4		
Hall Road Rgrs.	5	Rushden T.	2 2	Ely C.	0		
Clipstone Welfare	0	Histon	2	Ampthill T.	2 0		
Rawmarsh Welfare	2	Wootton Blue X	3	Olney T.	1		
Bourne T.	0	Thame U.	0	Letchworth GC	3		
Skegness T.	5	Arlesey T.	1	Wolverton T. & BR	0		
Hinckley T.	2	Kidlington	1	Amersham T.	2		
Rothwell T.	0 1	Witham T.	0	Basildon U.	4		
Long Eaton Grange	0 3						

38

FA Cup / FA Vase preliminary results (two match columns per block)

Home		Away	
Brightlingsea U.	1	Rainham T.	1
Leyton-Wingate	2	Heybridge Swifts	3
Coggeshall T.	1	Bowers U.	2
Faversham T.	1	Ringmer	4
Swanley T.	1	Herne Bay	3
Whitstable T.	1	Tunbridge Wells	2
W. Wickham	0	Tansley	6
Crockenhill	0	Cheshunt	1
Selby	3	Woodford T.	0
Banstead Ath.	3	Whyteleafe	3
Dartford Glentworth	0	Grays Ath.	2
Hoddesdon T.	3	Welling U.	0
Sun Sports	4	Kew Assoc.	1
Willesden	4	Ruislip Manor	3
Feltham	1	Cray Wanderers	1*
Civil Service	1	Redhill	2
Merstham	3	LB of Greenwich	0
Uxbridge	3	Chessington U.	0
Arundel	4	Alton T.	1
First Tower U.	4	Littlehampton T.	2

Home		Away	
Amesbury	1	St Martins	2*
Sholing Sports	0	Newbury T.	1
Worthing	7	Brading T.	0
Newport IOW	7	Chichester C.	0
Malden Vale	4	Dorking T.	0
Ash U.	0	Shoreham	3
Steyning	1	Egham T.	3
Camberley T.	4	Wallingford T.	1
Windsor & Eton	2	Chertsey T.	0
BAC (Weybridge)	1	Chobham	2
Abingdon T.	0	Hazels	0
Larkhall Ath.	2	Peasedown Ath.	1
Worrall Hill	3	Bristol St George	0
Clanfield	3	Cadbury Heath	2*
Westbury U.	3	Shortwood U.	2*
Forest Green R.	0	Yate T.	1
Sharpness	3	Westland-Yeovil	1*
Radstock T.	2	Keynsham T.	2
Illogan RBL	1	Exmouth T.	1
Ilminster T.	3	Brixham U.	3

after extra time.

SECOND ROUND

Home		Away	
Blue Star	2	Wingate	2
Seaham CW RS	4	Annfield Plain	4
Washington	1	Boldon CA	1
Whickham	1 3	Darlington RA	3
Thackley	4	Fleetwood T.	1 0
Prescot T.	4	Hallam	3
Lytham	0	Salford Ams.	0
Ossett Alb.	2	Waterloo Dock	1
Leeds Ashley Road	2	Linotype	2
Norton Woodseats	4	Irlam T.	4

Home		Away	
Ossett T.	1	Tadcaster Alb.	0
Gainsboro' U.	1	Winterton R.	2
Appleby FA	3	Hall Road Rgrs.	1
Lincoln U.	1	Brook Sports	3
Retford T.	1 0	Kidsgrove Ath.	1
Frecheville Com.	3	Bentley Vic.	0
Sheffield	0	Congleton T.	4
Shepshed Ch'house	1	Armitage	0
Wigston Fields	2	Skegness T.	1
Rushden T.	1 2	Newfoundpool WMC	1

Bourne T. 2 – 1 Stamford
Coventry Sporting 0 – 1 Friar Lane OB
Wednesfield Soc. 2 – 2 Long Eaton Grange
Paget Rgrs. 1 – 1 Hinckley Ath.
Anstey Nomads 0 – 2 Blakenall
RC Warwick 0 – 1 Irthlingboro' Dia.
Willenhall T. 3 – 1 Walsall Sportsco
Halesowen T. 5 – 3 Malvern T.
Buckingham T. 0 – 7 Bicester T.
CNSOBU 2 – 1 Soham T. Rgrs.
Felixstowe T. 0 – 1 Coggleshall T.
Egham T. 3 – 4 Leyton-Wingate
Barton R. 2 – 1* Wootton Blue X
Feltham 0 – 3* Epping T.
Hoddesdon T. 4 – 1* Royston T.
St Neots T. 2 – 3* Letchworth GC
Arlesey T. 0 – 1 Kempston R.
Selby 2 – 2 Camberley T.
Tring T. 0 – 0 Ruislip Manor
Berkhamsted T. 2 – 3 Burnham
Billericay T. 2 – 1* Rainham T.
Baldock T. 0 – 5 Cheshunt

E. Ham U. 1 – 0 Basildon U.
Grays Ath. 1 – 0 Swanley T.
Windsor & Eton 2 – 1 Banstead Ath.
Kew Assoc. 1 – 5 Haringey Boro'
Molesey 0 – 2 Malden Vale
Amersham T. — 2 Farnboro' T.
BAC (Weybridge) 1 – 0 Uxbridge
Abingdon T. 1 – 3 Newbury T.
Eastbourne U. 3 – 1 Faversham T.
Mersham 1 – 2 Alma Swanley
Eastbourne T. 1 – 2 Tunbridge Wells
Redhill 0 – 1 W. Wickham
Newport IOW 4 – 0 Gosport Boro'
Worthing — 0 Ash U.
St Martins 1 – 4 First Tower U.
Hungerford T. 3* – 1 Alton T.
Clanfield 1 – 2 Worrall Hill
Westbury U. 2 – 0 Peasedown Ath.
Almondsbury Grnway 5 – 1 Forest Green Rovers
Exmouth U. 3 – 0 Ilminster T.
Westland-Yeovil 1* – 4* Keynsham T.
Histon 5 – 1 March T. U.

* after extra time

Mancunian Products

Official suppliers to the Football Association of ties, badges and 'honours' caps for the England international teams.
For further information for your own club requirements contact:

    Barry Chaytow,
    Manchester Tie and Scarf
    Co Ltd, Morton Street,
    Middleton, Manchester.
    (Telephone: 061-654 8304)

F.A. CHALLENGE VASE - BILLERICAY TOWN'S THIRD WIN

BILLERICAY TOWN 4
Young 3, Clayden
28th April at Wembley

Third Round	Fourth Round	Fifth Round	Sixth Round	Semi-finals
Felixstowe T. ...4 1				
Soham Town R. 4 3	Soham T. R. 1			
Arlesey Town 0		Leyton-W. ...0*0		
Leyton-Wingate...2	Leyton-Wingate..2			
Clanfield 0			Eastbourne U. ...0	
Camberley T. 3	Camberley T. ..1			
Eastbourne U. 0		Eastbourne U.0 2		
Alma Swanley 0	Eastbourne U. ..2			
Alton Town 1*				Billericay T.2 0 2
Worthing 2	Worthing 5			(at home in first leg)
Peasedown Ath. ..2		Worthing 1		
Ilminster Close ...1	Peasedown Ath. 2			
Billericay Town ..5			Billericay T. 1	
Epping Town 0	Billericay T. ...2			
Royston Town 1		Billericay T. ...2		
Histon 1	Royston T. 0			
Friar Lane OB.....4*				replay at Cambridge City
Sheffield 2	Friar Lane OB ..1			
Hinckley Ath. 0		Friar Lane OB...2		
Wednesfield Soc. ..3	Hinckley Ath. ...0			
Haringey Bor. 3			Barton Rovers 2*	
Tring Town 1	Haringey Bor. ..1			
Barton Rovers 2*		Barton Rovers .4		
Burnham 1	Barton Rovers ..2			
Norton W seats ..1				Shepshed C.020
Shepshed C. 7	Shepshed C. 1			
Skegness T. 3		Shepshed C. ...4		
Bourne Town......2	Skegness T. 0			
Bentley Vic. 2			Shepshed C. 3	
Boldon CA........0	Bentley Vic. ...0			
Leeds Ashley Rd. 1 2		Winterton R. ...2		
Winterton R. ...1 3	Winterton R. ...2			

42

ALMONDSBURY GREENWAY 1
Price
attendance 17,500

```
Gosport B. ......3
St. Martins ......1
                    Gosport B. ......4
Tunbridge Wells 0*2*
Uxbridge ......0 1
                                        Gosport B. ...1*3
Windsor & Eton ...4
Newbury Town ...2
                    Tunbridge Wells 2
Westland-Yeovil ...0
Almondsbury G. ...2
                                                            Almondsbury G. 3
Rushden Town ...3
Bicester Town ...0
                    Windsor & E. ...0
Cheshunt ......5
East Ham U. ...1*
                                        Almondsbury 1 4
Molesey ......0
Grays Athletic ...0
                    Almondsbury G. 2
West Wickham ...2*2
Farnborough T. ...2 3
                                                                                Almondsbury 1 1
                    Bicester Town ...0                                          (at home in
Thackley ......1 2*                                                             first leg)
Lytham ......1 1
                                        Cheshunt ......0
Blue Star ......4
Whickham ......4
                    Cheshunt ......2
Seaham CWRS ...4
Ossett Town ......0
                                                            Farnborough T. 1
Ossett Albion......0
Prescot Town......2
                    Molesey ......2
Lincoln United 1 3
Appleby F. A. 1 0
                                        Farnborough T. 4
Retford Town ...1
Willenhall T. ......3
                    Farnborough T. 4
St. Neots Town ...0
Irthlingborough D. 4
                                                                                Whickham 0 1
Anstey Nomads...7
Halesowen Town 0

                    Lytham ......2 0
                                        Whickham ......5
                    Whickham ...2 2
                                                            Whickham ......3
                    Seaham CWRS 3
                                        Seaham CWRS 2
                    Prescot Town...1 1
                                                                                Whickham
                    Lincoln United ...2
                                        Willenhall T. ...2
                    Willenhall T. ......3
                                                            Willenhall T. ...2
                    Irthlingbor. D. ..2
                                        Irthlingbor. D. 1
                    Anstey Nomads...1
```

*after extra time

43

F.A. CHALLENGE VASE

QUARTER FINALS / SEMI-FINALS
MATCH DETAILS

QUARTER FINALS

Whickham 3 Willenhall 2 (attendance 1,223)
Whickham: I. Robson, A. Scott, T. Callaghan, M. Chapman, G. Cook, D. Hunter, L. Stokoe, D. Callaghan, W. Cawthra, I. Diamond, J. Nesbitt; sub. R. McKenzie (not used).
Goalscorers: M. Chapman (pen.), J. Nesbitt.
Willenhall: V. Sharrard, J. Newell, R. Dams, T. Evans, R. Heath, B. Fox, M. Whitehouse, M. Drury, G. Matthews, B. Beresford, K. Haynes; sub. C. Martin (used).
Goalscorers: G. Matthews, B. Beresford.

Barton Rovers 2 Shepshed Charterhouse 3 (attendance 934)
Barton Rovers: K. Blackwell, G. Evans, S. Norris, R. Cox, J. Downard, A. Tomkins, A. Dunn, P. Fossey, C. Jarvis, S. Turner, D. Harnaman; sub. P. Smith (used).
Goalscorer: S. Turner 2.
Shepshed Charterhouse: N. Hodges, D. Blockley, P. Mitchell, R. Wilcox, M. Kendrick, A. Straker, K. Jones, M. Hollis, J. Pawley, A. Gould, D. Kirby; sub. A. Turner (used).
Goalscorers: R. Wilcox (pen.), K. Jones, D. Kirby.

Eastbourne United 0 Billericay Town 1 (attendance 1,570)
Eastbourne United: N. Field, P. Stephens, R. Upton, A. Noakes, R. Shepherd, K. Warner, N. Ivemy, D. Boon, J. Kemp, J. Daubney, R. Saunders; sub. D. Smith (used).
Billericay Town: P. Norris, P. Blackaller, W. Bingham, P. Whettell, S. Bone, J. Reeves, J. Pullin, P. Scott, F. Clayden, D. Young, D. Groom; sub. C. Harle (not used).
Goalscorer: W. Bingham.

Almondsbury Greenway 3 Farnborough Town 1 (attendance 412)
Almondsbury Greenway: R. Hamilton, P. Bowers, R. Scarrett, M. Sullivan, C. Tudor, D. Wookey, P. Bowers, J. Shehean, A. Kerr, D. Butt, S. Price; sub. B. Kilbaine (not used).
Goalscorers: P. Bowers, J. Shehean, D. Butt.
Farnborough Town: T. Hammond, T. Davies, H. Richardson, S. Ramayon, J. McHale, J. Harley, R. Hill, T. Waughman, D. Sheedy, R. Saunders, A. Gunn; sub. A. Vooght (not used).
Goalscorer: J. Harley.

SEMI-FINALS

First Leg: Billericay Town 2 Shepshed Charterhouse 0 (attendance 2,223)
Billericay Town: P. Norris, G. Sullivan, W. Bingham, P. Whettell, S. Bone, J. Reeves, J. Pullin, P. Scott, F. Clayden, D. Young, D. Groom; sub. A. Russ (not used).
Goalscorers: W. Bingham, J. Reeves.

Shepshed Charterhouse: J. Hodges, D. Blockley, P. Mitchell, M. Hollis, M. Kendrick, A. Straker, K. Jones, R. Wilcox, J. Pauley, A. Gould, D. Kirby; sub. A. Turner (not used).

Second Leg: Shepshed Charterhouse 2 Billericay Town 0 (attendance 2,532)
Shepshed Charterhouse: J. Hodges, D. Blockley, P. Mitchell, R. Wilcox, M. Kendrick, A. Straker, K. Jones, M. Hollis, J. Pawley, A. Gould, A. Turner; sub. G. Corcoran (used).
Goalscorers: J. Pawley, A. Gould.
Billericay Town: P. Norris, A. Russ, W. Bingham, P. Whettell, S. Bone, J. Reeves, J. Pullin, P. Scott, F. Clayden, D. Young, D. Groom; sub. C. Knott (used).
Replay: Billericay Town 2 Shepshed Charterhouse 0 (attendance 1,600)
Billericay Town: P. Norris, M. Carrigan, W. Bingham, P. Whettell, S. Bone, J. Reeves, J. Pullin, P. Scott, F. Clayden, D. Young, D. Groom; sub. T. Fearey (not used).
Goalscorer: F. Clayden 2.
Shepshed Charterhouse: J. Hodges, D. Blockley, P. Mitchell, R. Wilcox, M. Kendrick, A. Straker, C. Brookes, M. Hollis, J. Pawley, A. Gould, D. Kirby; sub. G. Corcoran (used).

First Leg: Almondsbury Greenway 1 Whickham 0 (attendance 1,012)
Almondsbury Greenway: R. Hamilton, P. Bowers, R. Scarrett, M. Sullivan, C. Tudor, D. Wookey, P. Bowers, J. Shehean, A. Kerr, D. Butt, S. Price; sub. B. Kilbaine (not used).
Goalscorer: A. Kerr.
Whickham: I. Robson, A. Scott, T. Callaghan, M. Chapman, G. Cook, E. Wilson, L. Stokoe, D. Callaghan, W. Cawthra, I. Diamond, J. Nesbitt; sub. A. Simpson (used).

Second Leg: Whickham 1 Almondsbury Greenway 1 (attendance 2,126)
Whickham: I. Robson, A. Scott, T. Callaghan, M. Chapman, G. Cook, E. Wilson, L. Stokoe, D. Callaghan, W. Cawthra, I. Diamond, J. Nesbitt; sub. A. Simpson (used).
Goalscorer: J. Nesbitt.
Almondsbury Greenway: R. Hamilton, P. Bowers, R. Scarrett, M. Sullivan, C. Tudor, D. Wookey, P. Bowers, J. Shehean, A. Kerr, D. Butt, S. Price; sub. B. Kilbaine (not used).
Goalscorer: S. Price.

F.A. CHALLENGE VASE FINALS

1974–75 (*Attendance:* 10,000)
Epsom 1 (*Wales*) **Hoddesdon 2** (*Sedgwick 2*)
Epsom: Page, Bennett, Webb, Wales, Worby, Jones, O'Connell, Walker, Tuite, Eales, Lee.
Hoddesdon: Gulvin, Green, Hickey, Maybury, Stevenson, Wilson, Bishop, Picking, Sedgwick, Nathan, Schofield.

1975–76 (*Attendance: 12,000*)
Billericay T. 1 Stamford 0 (*after extra time*)
Billericay: Griffiths, Foreman, Bone, Payne, Pullin, Coughlin, Geddes, Aslett, Clayden, Scott, Smith.
Stamford: Johnson, Kwiatkowski, Marchant, Crawford, Downs, Hird, Barnes, Walpole, Smith, Russell, Broadhurst.

1976–77 (*Attendance: 15,150*)
Billericay T. 1 (*Clayden*) Sheffield 1 (*Coughlan own goal*) (*after extra time*)
Billericay: Griffiths, Payne, Pullin, Coughlan, Bone, McQueen, Woodhouse, Aslett, Clayden, Scott, Wakefield.
Sheffield: Wing, Gilbody, Lodge, Hardisty, Watts, Skelton, Kay, Travis, Pugh, Thornhill, Haines. Strutt came on as sub for Hardisty.
REPLAY AT NOTTINGHAM FOREST (*Attendance: 3,482*)
Billericay T. 2 (*Aslett, Woodhouse*) Sheffield 1 (*Thornhill*)
Billericay: Griffiths, Payne, Pullin, Whettell, Bone, McQueen, Woodhouse, Aslett, Clayden, Scott, Wakefield.
Sheffield: Wing, Gilbody, Lodge, Strutt, Watts, Skelton, Kay, Travis, Pugh, Thornhill, Haines.

1977–78 (*Attendance: 16,391*)
Blue Star 2 (*Dunn, Crumplin*) Barton Rovers 1 (*Smith*)
Barton Rovers: Blackwell, Stephens, Crossley, Evans, Harris, Dollimore, Dunn, Harnaman, Fossey, Turner, Smith.
Blue Star: Halbert, Feenan, Thompson, Davidson, Dixon, Benyon, Diamond, Callaghan, Crumplin, Storey, Dixon.

'ALL SPORTS INTERNATIONAL NEWSPAPER' GOAL SCORING CUP

The above trophy was presented to the Football Association to be awarded to the club that won by the most goals its North v South friendly match on the eve of the F.A. Vase final. In the event of a tie the club who scored the most goals would be acknowledged the winner.
Barton Rovers (S.L.M.) 4   Leyton-Wingate (K. Ath.) 0
Darenth Heathside (L. Spartan) 0   Chadderton (Manchester) 0
The Cup was won by Barton Rovers.

F.A. VASE FINAL

Billericay Town (2) 4 (Young 3, Clayden)
Almondsbury Greenway (0) 1 (Price)   *Attendance:* 17,500

The Challenge Vase is probably the only Wembley final that could pair two such contrasting opponents as Billericay Town and Almondsbury Greenway. Billericay, appearing in their third final, were well accustomed to the big occasion and were renowned for their thorough pre-match preparations. Almondsbury, the defeated semi-finalists in 1978, usually played in front of a handful of spectators and believed football to be fun. One of their victims described them as the most unprofessional side they had met, although what could be less professional than losing?

Perhaps predictably, the Essex side were first into their stride and mounted a number of promising attacks, one of which forced Hamilton, the 'keeper, to push the ball over his crossbar from Bingham. At the other end, Kerr was demonstrating his skill without any great support from his Almondsbury colleagues but, after 12 minutes, Billericay went ahead as Clayden's header back across the goal gave Young the chance to nod the ball past the stranded Hamilton. Thus encouraged, the favourites always looked likely to increase their lead and, after 33 minutes, Clayden found himself shunned near the Almondsbury penalty spot to glide in Scott's free kick. As the pressure mounted, the Bristol side were doubtless relieved to avoid further disaster before half-time.

Four minutes after the restart, Price pounced to reduce the deficit as Norris lost Shehean's shot. The scorer now began to show his true form and, with Kerr, set out to test the Billericay defence in which Bone was playing a captain's role. The revival lasted until the seventieth minute, when a right-wing corner was met by Young at the far post with a spectacular overhead kick. Almondsbury still refused to capitulate despite the hobbling Tudor's exit and the completion of Young's hat-trick as he ran from the half-way line to chip the advancing Hamilton. After Billericay had received the Vase from Ron Greenwood, the England manager, a record crowd of 17,500 were enthusiastic in showing their approval of the efforts of both teams in an open and entertaining contest.

47

ROTHMANS FOOTBALL YEARBOOK 1979-80
Edited by Jack Rollin

The tenth edition of the most successful yearbook ever published.

1000pp £5.50 hardback £3.75 limp bound

ROTHMANS BOOK OF FOOTBALL LEAGUE RECORDS 1888-89 TO 1978-79
Ian Laschke

How to settle who won which game and when. The book contains the result of every Football League match since 1888-89.

352pp £10.00 hardback (available from November)

PLAYFAIR FOOTBALL ANNUAL 1979–80
Edited by Peter Dunk and Lionel Francis

The hugely successful pocket-sized guide to the football season

256pp 80p paperback

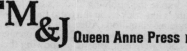

M&J Queen Anne Press

CHALLENGE CUP REVIEW

Statistics would seem to indicate that the 1978–79 season was not an outstanding one for non-leaguers in the Challenge Cup. There were only two survivors in the Third Round Proper compared with six the previous season, and neither of these were able to emulate Blyth Spartans' success which is, admittedly, not very surprising. Nevertheless, both Maidstone United and Altrincham made their mark before their exit. Maidstone's performance in holding Second Division Charlton Athletic at the Valley has been largely overshadowed by their opponents' problems, but it is worth remembering that the Southern League side led for a long period before the sendings-off. Charlton's increased determination saw them through in the replay but only by the odd goal in three.

Altrincham, the Trophy holders, faced a formidable task at Tottenham but they were not satisfied simply to share in a big pay day and used the occasion to promote their Football League ambitions. The jokes about the 'Alty' players learning Spanish soon faded as skipper John King had a number of early confrontations with the World Cup hero, Ardiles, although it was a foul on the latter which brought about Taylor's penalty to give Spurs the lead. However, the expected landslide did not materialise and Altrincham grew in confidence so that Johnson's equaliser six minutes from time was fully deserved. The replay could not take place at Moss Lane since the enormous interest generated would have jeopardised crowd safety and the First Division side were therefore spared the claustrophobic atmosphere they must have been dreading. Despite the majority of the crowd of almost 30,000 cheering for the underdogs, the Spurs players were obviously determined to avoid further ignominy and eventually ran out 3–0 winners.

Thus this season's non-league challenge was over by mid-January, although a number of clubs were able to reflect on earlier triumphs and near misses. Maidstone dismissed Exeter City 1–0 in the Second Round while the First Round produced two marvellous results. Pride of place was claimed by Worcester City, who proved their worth in a 2–0 victory over Plymouth Argyle – the first of two Cup shocks for Malcolm Allison! However, whilst Worcester had the home advantage, the unfancied Cheshire Leaguers, Droylsden, had to travel to Rochdale for their act of giant-killing. Their 1–0 win should have been better rewarded by the Draw which paired them with Altrincham.

Runcorn seemed to do the hard work in gaining a 1–1 draw at Chester, only to be swamped 5–0 on their own ground. Similarly, last season's heroes, Blyth Spartans, drew at York City's home ground before going down gallantly 5–3 in front of their own supporters. Weymouth led Aldershot until the later stages of the original match but they too disappointed at home in the replay. Gravesend's 0–0 draw with the Fourth Division leaders, Wimbledon, included a penalty save by 'keeper Smelt and the replay at Plough Lane went into extra time before the non-leaguers conceded the winning goal.

The Second Round saw Worcester draw at Newport and come close to winning the replay, only conceding a freak equaliser in the last minute of proper time and a second goal in extra time. One of the season's most stirring matches was between Woking from the Isthmian League, and Swansea City, riding high in Division Three, who eased to a two-goal lead before Woking battled back for a 2–2 draw. The replay took place on one of the first frosty pitches which were to become so commonplace and the home side had not found their feet before Swansea were two goals up. A brave rally pulled one back but the Welsh side led 3–1 at the interval. However, Woking refused to lie down and die, scoring a second and then a third, as their supporters roared them on. The result was in the balance as the match went into extra time before the Woking side's legs gave way from the effort and Swansea added two late goals to win 5–3.

One of the more surprising qualifiers for the First Round Proper was the Town and Country League side, March Town United, who travelled to Division Three Swindon and gained great credit in their 2–0 defeat. The Draw did not, in general, deal kindly with the non-league clubs and in several cases it was probably home advantage that saw the League side through as Stafford Rangers (at Hull) and Boston

United (at Tranmere) and Hitchin (at Bournemouth) all
went down 2–1. Nuneaton Borough disappointed, losing
2–0 at home to Crewe, while Leatherhead's draw with Colchester was followed by an emphatic 4–0 away defeat in the
replay.   *Adrian Titcombe*

NON-LEAGUE CLUBS IN F.A. CUP
3rd ROUND 1970-71 TO 1978-79

Year	*Club and league*	*Lost to*
1970-71	Yeovil Town (S.L.)	Arsenal (h) (3rd)
1970-71	Wigan Athletic (N.P.L.)	Manchester City (a) (3rd)
1970-71	Barnet (S.L.)	Colchester Utd. (h) (3rd)
1970-71	Rhyl (Ches.)	Swansea City (a) (3rd)
1971-72	Hereford United (S.L.)	West Ham United (a) (4th). After replay. Beat Newcastle United (h) (3rd). After replay
1971-72	Blyth Spartans (N.)	Reading (a) (3rd) in replay
1971-72	Boston United (N.P.L.)	Portsmouth (h) (3rd)
1972-73	Barnet (S.L.)	Queen's Park Rangers (h) (3rd) replay
1972-73	Chelmsford (S.L.)	Ipswich Town (h) (3rd)
1972-73	Margate (S.L.)	Tottenham Hotspur (h) (3rd)
1973-74	Boston United (N.P.L.)	Derby County (h) (3rd). After replay
1973-74	Hendon (I.L.)	Newcastle Utd. (Watford) (3rd) After 3rd replay
1973-74	Grantham (S.L.)	Middlesbrough (h) (3rd)
1973-74	Altrincham (N.P.L.)	Blackburn Rovers (h) (3rd)
1973-74	Alvechurch (W. Mid.)	Bradford City (a) (3rd)
1974-75	Leatherhead (I.L.)	Leicester City (a) (4th) (conceded ground advantage). Beat Brighton (a) (3rd)
1974-75	Wimbledon (S.L.)	Leeds United (at Selhurst Park) (4th). After replay. Beat Burnley (a) (3rd)
1974-75	Stafford Rangers (N.P.L.)	Peterborough Utd. (h) (4th). Beat Rotherham Utd. (a) (3rd). After replay
1974-75	Wycombe Wanderers (I.L.)	Middlesbrough (a) (3rd). After replay
1974-75	Altrincham (N.P.L.)	Everton (Old Trafford) (3rd). After replay
1975-76	Tooting & Mitcham (I.L.)	Bradford City (a) (4th). Beat Swindon (h) (3rd). After replay
1975-76	Scarborough (N.P.L.)	Crystal Palace (h) (3rd)
1976-77	Northwich Victoria (N.P.L.)	Oldham Athletic (Maine Road, Manchester) (h) (3th). Beat Watford (h) (3rd)

1976-77 Wimbledon (S.L.)	Middlesbrough (a) (3rd). After replay
1976-77 Matlock Town (N.P.L.)	Carlisle Utd. (a) (3rd)
1976-77 Kettering Town (S.L.)	Colchester Utd. (h) (3rd)
1977-78 Blyth Spartans (N.)	Wrexham (Newcastle) (5th) in replay Beat Stoke City (a) (4th)
1977-78 Enfield (I.L.)	Blyth Spartans (a) (3rd)
1977-78 Scarborough (N.P.L.)	Brighton & H.A. (a) (3rd)
1977-78 Tilbury (I.L.)	Stoke City (a) (3rd)
1977-78 Wealdstone (S.L.)	Queen's Park Rangers (a) (3rd)
1977-78 Wigan Athletic (N.P.L.)	Birmingham City (a) (3rd)
1978-79 Altrincham (N.P.L.)	Tottenham Hotspur (Maine Road, Manchester) (3rd). After replay
1978-79 Maidstone United (S.L.)	Charlton Athletic (h) (3rd) in 3rd replay

1977–78 *was the best season for non-league clubs with six, in the 3rd Rnd, and Blyth Spartans appearing in the 6th Rnd Draw.*

SEMI-PROFESSIONAL
INTERNATIONAL TOURNAMENT

The first English semi-professional international caps have now been awarded. The gap between the glamorous but at times rather unreal 'amateur' days has been bridged, and hopefully we can look forward to a new and exciting English international squad representing their country with distinction at semi-professional level for years to come.

To produce a team worthy of representing its country in a quarter of a season was the difficult task handed to the F.A. regional coaches, Howard Wilkinson and his assistant, Keith Wright. Howard was already one of Mr Greenwood's 'team', but there was a great deal more than personal pride at stake. If the administration, coaching and the end product – the team performance – were considered successful, a whole new world of football might be opened up, giving new opportunities to ambitious club players and coaches in non-league football. Aided by the excellent O.C.S. Inter-League Cup, most of the prospective 'caps' were brought together in their league sides where very competitive representative match conditions prevailed.

The F.A. Trophy finalists were obviously busy preparing for Wembley, but one training weekend was enjoyed by a large shadow squad at Barton Rovers' excellent ground, where the players soon realised that their managers meant business! Following the Trophy and O.C.S. finals the England squad was selected. Kettering's dashing striker, Peter Phipps, was unable to accept his invitation due to his wife expecting their first child at the time of the internationals, and reserve defender, Kenny Hill of Maidstone, just missed the final selection, but a powerful squad met at Lilleshall on the Sunday, four days before the first-ever official semi-professional international.

The squad comprised of: *Goalkeepers:* Jim Arnold (Stafford R.); Brian Parker (Yeovil T.); *Defenders:* Brian Thompson (Yeovil T.); Gordon Simmonite (Boston U.); Jeff Lee (Kettering); John Davison (Altrincham); Tony Jennings (En-

53

field); Dave Adamson (Boston U.); Trevor Peake (Nuneaton B.); *Mid-field players:* Brendan Phillips (Nuneaton B.); Keith Houghton (Blyth S.); John Watson (Wealdstone); Stuart Chapman (Stafford R.); Nick Ironton (Barking); *Forwards:* Eamonn O'Keefe (Mossley); Les Mutrie (Blyth S.); Barry Whitbread (Runcorn); Roy Clayton (Kettering).

Two other excellent choices were to complete what turned out to be a very happy and highly professional team – Alan Smith, the Blackpool physiotherapist, and Doctor Tabour.

Following well-organised and efficient training victories against Barton Rovers, Moor Green and Telford, the team had taken shape, and Howard Wilkinson nominated Tony Jennings, the very experienced Enfield captain, as England's first semi-professional skipper. Tony's ability to read a game and organise his side during a match is just what any manager needs and, although one of only a few southerners in the squad, he earned the unanimous praise and respect of all his colleagues during their week together.

Howard's team contained few surprises. Jim Arnold, a safe and highly successful goalkeeper for many years, just edged out the equally efficient Brian Parker. Brian Thompson, an outstanding Geordie defender from Yeovil with pace and attacking flair, and John Davison, Altrincham's ex-U.A.U. left-sided player, played on the flanks in the back four. Trevor Peake, whose determination and rock hard defensive qualities had shown him to be an outstanding ball winner in the middle of the back, partnered Tony Jennings, while the mid-field had an interesting blend of differing talents. On the right, Brendan Phillips linked brilliantly with his full-back Thompson and striker O'Keefe and built many a well-organised and controlled attack. He was also always aware of goal chances, but the tournament's top scorer turned out to be Boston United's Dave Adamson. Dave is better known as a defender but, given a central mid-field role – as an anchor man in reality – to give stability, he proceeded to crash home two penalties and an excellent set piece header from Davison's corner via a touch on from Mutrie, to collect a hat-trick against Scotland. On the left, the midfield position was shared by Blyth's rangy Keith Houghton whose power in the air and danger going forward was replaced in the second match for the steady graft of John Watson – probably the most consistent player in the O.C.S. tournament. Both players did well in England shirts and no doubt they will be challenging each other and reserve Nicky Ironton for the position again next season. Up front a fine balance between the tall elegant Les Mutrie, the equally skilful and very mobile Barry Whitbread, and the explosive attacking qualities of the stocky Eamonn O'Keefe who usually patrolled the right flank, proved to be just right.

Gordon Simmonite came on as substitute full-back in both matches so the unlucky squad members, apart from Brian Parker, were three men who had at least had the consolation of playing at Wembley two weeks earlier. They were Jeff Lee and Roy Clayton of Kettering and Stuart Chapman of Stafford Rangers, but their loyalty and general contribution to the happy week was greatly appreciated.

The two games provided a complete contrast. Scotland, a team selected from their Football League Division Two and Junior football, just hadn't had time to prepare and were swamped by the English organisation. Apart from Adamson's hat-trick, Les Mutrie intercepted a bad clearance by the Scottish goalkeeper to score, and Barry Whitbread won possession just outside the opposition's penalty area to register a good individual goal.

The Dutch, however, having overcome by 3-0 a rather volatile Italian under-21 team which had two players sent off, brought their all-amateur team to the final as a squad that had played a great deal together. Their fine understanding was apparent in the first half when the game hung very finely in the balance, but in the second half England completely controlled the proceedings and ground the opposition down with a display of well-organised, skilful team football.

The winning goal came 15 minutes from the end and was another set piece. A long in-swinging corner deceived both the goalkeeper and central defenders to land snugly on the head of little Eamonn O'Keefe, whose one-yard header was probably the most important goal of his life. Needless to say, Dave Adamson was the one on hand to make sure it went over the line.

Celebrations were the order of the day, and after Barney

55

Mulrenan, the chairman of the Football Association's representative match committee, had presented the cup, a group of very proud Englishmen took a long time to come down off the clouds.

Howard Wilkinson and Keith Wright, with excellent support from the F.A.'s administrator in charge, Adrian Titcombe, had shown that football at this level could be organised and played with good spirit, pride and professionalism. Stafford Rangers and Northwich Victoria, the two host clubs, could not have been more helpful or efficient, and the sponsorship assistance from O.C.S. and Cold Shield during the tournament was greatly appreciated. Hopefully only good will come from this first-ever tournament of its kind, but it is now imperative that this new England side is kept together with regular international matches so that the whole of non-league football will continue to benefit.

SEMI-PROFESSIONAL INTERNATIONAL TOURNAMENT 1979

Semi-Final
Holland 3   Italy 0
England 5   Scotland 1 (at Stafford Rangers 31 May 1979)
England team: J. Arnold (Stafford R.), B. Thompson (Yeovil T.), J. Davison (Altrincham), D. Adamson (Boston U.), T. Peake (Nuneaton B.), A. Jennings (Enfield), E. O'Keefe (Mossley), B. Phillips (Nuneaton B.), L. Mutrie (Blyth Spartans), K. Houghton (Blyth Spartans), B. Whitbread (Runcorn). Subs: G. Simmonite (Boston U. – for Thompson), J. Watson (Wealdstone – for Houghton). Reserves: B. Parker (Yeovil T.), N. Ironton (Barking), R. Clayton (Kettering).
Goalscorers: Adamson 3 (2 pens.), Mutrie, Whitbread.

Final
England 1   Holland 0 (at Stafford Rangers 3 June 1979)
England team: J. Arnold (Stafford R.), B. Thompson (Yeovil T.), J. Davison (Altrincham), D. Adamson (Boston U.), T. Peake (Nuneaton B.), A. Jennings (Enfield), E. O'Keefe (Mossley), B. Phillips (Nuneaton B.), L. Mutrie (Blyth Spartans), J. Watson (Wealdstone), B. Whitbread (Runcorn). Sub: G. Simmonite (Boston U. – for Thompson). Reserves: B. Parker (Yeovil T.), K. Houghton (Blyth Spartans), R. Clayton (Kettering). S. Chapman (Stafford R.).
Goalscorer: O'Keefe.

O.C.S. INTER-LEAGUE CUP

As a non-league player, the choice of which club to play for must, for many, be made up by the player's geographical situation. However, for players who live in areas of the country where various non-league competitions overlap, then the choice can be interesting.

In the South, should a player join the ambitious and progressive Berger Isthmian League, with its fair play ideals and three points for a win system which encourages attacking play? Or should he play in the Southern League, where teams are often made up of ex-Football League players whose range of techniques and forceful style of play are always very professional.

In the North, the choice could be the Northern League, which has the glamorous and eye-catching Blyth Spartans and Spennymoor United as its standard-bearers, with teams that play with tremendous passion and zeal, or the Northern Premier League which, over recent seasons, has achieved an almost unbreakable stranglehold on the coveted F.A. Trophy, frequently disappointing the aspiring Isthmian and Southern League clubs with their resolute characters, and determination not to take risks or make mistakes.

For the managers, coaches, club officials, players and supporters, this subject has always been of great interest and, quite often, a bone of contention, to decide which league is the strongest. Until this year, the strength of the various leagues has always been judged by the measure of success derived by clubs in their respective F.A. Cup and F.A. Trophy performances. However, this year a new yardstick was introduced in the form of a competition backed by Office Cleaning Services Ltd to establish which league could produce a side capable of winning the first-ever O.C.S. Inter-League Cup. Only the four above-mentioned leagues were invited to compete this year owing to the poor weather and

57

extended programmes, but next year it is hoped that the competition will be extended to take in eight leagues, with the matches taking place throughout the season.

The draw was such that the two Northern leagues were paired, with the Isthmian and Southern also meeting in a semi-final. The first of these matches was played in appalling conditions at a windswept, rain-soaked Spennymoor. The Northern Premier League was managed by the highly-successful Bob Murphy of Mossley, while his counterpart for the Northern League was Stan Bradley, that well-seasoned campaigner from Spennymoor United. Both managers had problems to overcome with late withdrawals, but both sides coped more than adequately to provide a match of tremendous quality despite the terrible weather. The Northern League led through a Jackie Hather goal scored in the first half, but the Northern Premier League countered strongly, and eventually equalised late in the game through John Rogers who went on to score a spectacular winner in extra time.

The second match took place several hundred miles away at Maidstone and in completely different conditions. The Berger Isthmian League manager Brian Lee had, as always, prepared thoroughly, as had his counterpart Barry Watling. The game started with the Isthmians showing early dominance but there was nothing they could do to match the eager opportunism of Billy Kellock, who scored two goals in the first half when little or no chances appeared. The game was put beyond doubt early in the second half by Roy Clayton of Kettering and, although a late revival by the Isthmians saw O'Sullivan hitting the woodwork, it was the Southern League that deservedly qualified to play the Northern Premier League.

The final was played at Yeovil and was well supported despite the high temperatures. The game was extremely competitive and, after a very equal first half, the Southern League came into their own with repeated attacks set up by John Watson, Brendan Phillips and Brian Thompson. However, the Northern Premier League side was as resolute as ever and even when referee Clive Thomas awarded a penalty, Jim Arnold saved it at the first attempt, and then incredibly saved again, when the referee ordered it to be re-taken. However, the deadlock was finally broken when man-of-the-match, Brendan Phillips of Nuneaton, scored the all-important winner.

From this competition came the basis of the non-league squad, who would go on to play for England in the tournament with Holland, Scotland and Italy. The O.C.S. assistance and sponsorship succeeded in bringing together four of the major competitions outside the Football League and, in so doing, enabled the cream of non-league players once again to represent their country. Next season, with more leagues competing for the O.C.S. Cup, we shall see whether the Southern League can hold off the challenge of the new Alliance Premier League as well as the more established leagues. It should be an interesting competition, with more senior players staking their claim for English caps, and this can only be good for football at this level. *Jim Kelman*

O.C.S. INTER-LEAGUE CUP

Northern League (1) 1   Northern Premier League (0) 2 (*a.e.t.*)
at Spennymoor United, Monday 23 April 1979.
Northern League: Clarke, Butterfield, Swinburn, Dixon (Newton), Harmison, Hickman, McGinn (Waugh), Hindson, Hather, Mutrie, Reilly.
Northern Premier League: Fitton, Brown (Marshall), Thompson, Adamson, Smith, Davison, J. King, Rogers, O'Keefe, Skeate (Whitbread), Smith.

Southern League (2) 3   Berger Isthmian League (0) 0
at Maidstone United, Sunday 29 April 1979.
Southern League: Parker, Thompson, Edwards, Hill, Peake, Watson, Phillips, Kellock (Gardner), Tuohy (Coupland), Clayton, Jones. Reserves: Smelt, Merrick.
Berger Isthmian League: Moore, Barrett, Rains, Jennings, Elley, O'Sullivan, Ironton, Pritchard, Fox, Bond (Sharratt), Bishop (Kelly). Reserves: Maskell, Green.

Cup Final: Southern League (0) 1 (Phillips)   Northern Premier League (0) 0
at Huish, Yeovil, Somerset, Sunday 13 May 1979.
Southern League: Parker (Yeovil Town), Thompson (Yeovil Town), Edwards (Maidstone Utd), Merrick (Maidstone Utd), Peake (Nuneaton Boro), Watson (Wealdstone), Phillips (Nuneaton Boro), Iannone (Weymouth), Tuohy (Redditch), Henderson (Weymouth), Jones (Redditch).
Northern Premier League: Arnold (Stafford Rangers), Brown (Mossley), Simonite (Boston Utd), Knowles (Southport), O'Keefe (Mossley), Adamson (Boston Utd), Thompson (Boston Utd), King (Altrincham), Chapman (Stafford R.), Whitbread (Runcorn), Skeate (Mossley), Rogers (Altrincham), Davison (Altrincham).

59

PAST F.A. XI RESULTS

F.A. XI v CAMBRIDGE UNIVERSITY

Year	Date	Venue	Goals FA	CU
1965	Nov.	Eastbourne	4	0
1966	Nov.	Cambridge	5	1
1967	Nov.	Eastbourne	1	1
1968	Nov.	Cambridge	1	1
1969	Nov.	Eastbourne	3	0
1970	Nov.	Cambridge	7	0
1971	Nov.	Eastbourne	4	0
1972	Nov.	Cambridge	1	0
1973	Nov.	Eastbourne	3	0
1976	Nov.	Cambridge	1	0
1977	Nov.	Cambridge	4	0
1978	Nov.	Cambridge	6	1

F.A. XI v LONDON UNIVERSITY

Year	Date	Venue	Goals FA	LU
1965	Mar.	Motspur Pk.	6	2
1966	Mar.	Motspur Pk.	2	1
1967	Mar.	Hayes	3	1
1968	Mar.	Motspur Pk.	3	0
1969	Mar.	Motspur Pk.	3	0
1970	Mar.	Woking	9	0
1971	Mar.	Motspur Pk.	4	0
1973	Mar.	Motspur Pk.	4	1
1974	Mar.	Motspur Pk.	8	1
1976	Mar.	Kingston	4	1
1976	Dec.	Wealdstone	3	0
1977	Dec.	Imber Court	2	0
1978	Dec.	Harrow Boro	5	1

F.A. XI v AMATEUR FOOTBALL ALLIANCE

Year	Date	Venue	Goals FA	AFA
1965	Feb.	Wealdstone	2	2
1966	Feb.	Kingston	3	0
1967	Feb.	Bromley	1	2
1968	Feb.	Enfield	1	0
1969	Feb.	Dulwich Ground Unfit		
1970	Feb.	Clapton	2	2
1971	Feb.	Tooting	4	0
1973	Feb.	B. Stortford	3	1
1974	Feb.	Leytonstone	2	1

F.A. XI v ROYAL AIR FORCE

Year	Date	Venue	Goals FA	RAF
1969	Oct.	Halton	2	2
1970	Oct.	Halton	5	0
1971	Oct.	Halton	1	0
1972	Oct.	Uxbridge	2	1
1973	Oct.	Uxbridge	4	0
1976	Jan.	Wealdstone	2	1

F.A. XI v SOUTH WEST COUNTIES

Year	Date	Venue	Goals FA	SWC
1977	Oct.	Exeter	0	1
1978	Oct.	South'pton	1	0

F.A. XI v BRITISH COLLEGES SPORTS ASSOCIATION

Year	Date	Venue	Goals FA	BC
1972	Dec.	Chorley	2	1
1973	Dec.	Spennymoor	0	1
1976	Mar.	Cheltenham	0	1
1977	Feb.	Cheltenham	4	0
1978	Feb.	Cheltenham	0	1

F.A. XI v COMBINED SERVICES

Year	Date	Venue	Goals FA	CS
1977	Apr.	Aldershot	2	2
1978	Apr.	Aldershot	1	1
1979	Apr.	Aldershot	1	1

F.A. XI v NORTHERN LEAGUE

Year	Date	Venue	Goals FA	NL
1977	Mar.	Blyth	2	3
1978	Mar.	Consett	2	3
1979	Apr.	North Shields	0	2

Year	Date	Venue		
1976	Apr.	Dulwich	4	0
1977	Mar.	Leytonstone	2	2
1978	Mar.	Wealdstone	4	1
1979	Feb.	Imber Court	5	2

F.A. XI v OXFORD UNIVERSITY

Year	Date	Venue	Goals	
			FA	OU
1965	Nov.	Oxford	6	0
1966	Nov.	Eastbourne	3	0
1967	Nov.	Oxford	6	0
1968	Nov.	Eastbourne	5	0
1969	Nov.	Oxford	0	1
1970	Nov.	Eastbourne	1	0
1971	Nov.	Oxford	1	0
1972	Nov.	Eastbourne	5	0
1973	Nov.	Oxford	5	0
1976	Nov.	Oxford Utd	1	0
1977	Nov.	Oxford Utd	4	0
1978	Nov.	Oxford City	3	1

F.A. XI v UNIVERSITIES ATHLETIC UNION

Year	Date	Venue	Goals	
			FA	UAU
1965	Mar.	Coventry	1	3
1966	Mar.	Rugby	5	0
1967	Mar.	Sheffield	2	1
1968	Feb.	Nottingham	1	1
1969	Apr.	Sheffield	6	0
1970	Feb.	Morecambe	3	1
1971	Apr.	Durham	1	1
1971	Oct.	Aldershot	0	2
1973	Feb.	Newcastle	2	3
1974	Feb.	Nuneaton	2	2
1976	Feb.	York	2	2
1977	Mar.	York	2	2
1978	Mar.	Altrincham	2	1
1979	Mar.	Altrincham	1	1

F.A. REPRESENTATIVE MATCHES
1978-79

F.A. XI 1 (Ashton)   **South West Counties 0**
F.A. XI: D. Smith (Army); K. Elly (Enfield); T. Scales (Dagenham); K. Millet (Hillingdon Borough); A. Campbell (Hendon); D. Ingram (Hungerford Town); D. Dennis (Tooting & Mitcham); R. Townsend (Barnet); S. Meliedew (Hillingdon Borough); B. Salkeld (Leatherhead); J. Ashton (Hungerford Town). *Subs:* A. Young (Hungerford Town); M. Wright (Enfield); R. Wainwright (Hillingdon Borough).

F.A. XI 3 (Green 2, T. Evans)   **Oxford University 1**
F.A. XI: R. Wiltshire (Salisbury City); N. Ryan (Bath City); A. Glass (Oxford City); R. Legg (Trowbridge); A. Jefferies (Witney Town); K. Hallam (Salisbury City); A. Green (Andover); D. Evans (Banbury United); B. McCrae (Chipping Norton Town); P. Higgins (Bath City); T. Evans (Banbury United).

F.A. XI 6 (Pauley, Barnes 2, Wright 2, Tippett)   **Cambridge University 1**
F.A. XI: D. Blackwell (Barton Rovers); T. Oakley (St Neots Town); D. Bradford (Histon); A. Guild (St Neots Town); K. Davison (Potton United); B. Pauley (Histon); B. Roberts (Colchester United); J. Quilt (Somersham Town); J. Tippett (Soham Town Rangers); C. Barnes (Luton Labour Club); L. Glover (ex. Leicester City). *Subs:* K. Herridge (Cambridge City); G. Loveday (St Neots Town); E. Wright (Linton Grata).

F.A. XI 5 (L. Pritchard, Markham 3, Sharratt)   **London University 1**
F.A. XI: Wilson (Walthamstow Avenue); K. Waldron (Sutton United); C. Hutchins (Southall & EB); S. Hardwick (Wycombe Wanderers); T. Jennings (Enfield); L. Markham (Aylesbury United); P. Sharratt (Harrow Borough); L. Pritchard (Sutton United); K. Searle (Enfield); G. Swaby (Hendon); J. Worall (Walthamstow Avenue); R. Bennett (Harrow Borough); A. Cooling (Hampton); G. Huxley (Aylesbury United).

F.A. XI 5 (Lewis, Bayram 3, Gonzales)   **Football Alliance 2**
F.A. XI: D. Collyer (Sutton United); T. Maurice (Carshalton Athletic); K. Grose (Croydon); D. Cotterell (Woking); S. Rogers (Dulwich Hamlet); R. Gonzales (Croydon); S. Camp (Leatherhead); G. Frazer (Sutton United); T. Harris (Sutton United); M. Lewis (Dulwich Hamlet); O. Bayram (Dulwich Hamlet).

F.A. XI 1 (Garrett)   **Universities Athletic Union 1**
F.A. XI: Byram (Morecambe); Newton (Morecambe); Brooke (Altrincham); Jones (Northwich Victoria); Tobin (Altrincham); Mayman (Nantwich); Garrett (Chorley); Kennerley (Nantwich); Williams (Northwich Victoria); O'Connor (Northwich Victoria); Howard (Altrincham). *Subs:* Rogers (Altrincham); Ryder (Nantwich); Burton (Witton Albion); Bailey (Northwich Victoria); Goryl (Witton Albion).

63

F.A. XI 0   Northern League 0

F.A. XI: Broughton (Goole Town); Thompson (Boston Utd); Marshall (Scarborough); Simmonite (Boston Utd); Adamson (Boston Utd); Mitchinson (Gateshead); Donoghue (Scarborough); Sellers (Goole Town); Mutrie (Blyth Spartans); Fenoughty (Matlock Town); Gordon (Scarborough). *Subs:* Lukasic (Matlock Town); Meeham (Frickley Town); Topping (Gateshead); McLeod (Gateshead).

F.A. XI 1 (Kennedy)   Combined Services 1

F.A. XI: Nichols (Uxbridge); Wright (Enfield); Gates (Newport, I.O.W.); Torrance (The Army); Pittaway (Tooting & Mitcham); Dennis (Carshalton); Atkins (Wycombe Wanderers); Long (Wycombe Wanderers). *Subs:* McMahon (Hungerford Town); Bloxham (Stotfold); Gill (Devizes Town); Holland (Amersham Town); Connett (Dulwich Hamlet).

The fixture between the F.A. XI and British Colleges Sports Association was postponed twice and finally cancelled due to bad weather.

CLUB DIRECTORY

This section of the Annual proved so popular last year that more clubs have been included in this year's directory.

As the season was extended in many areas due to the bad winter weather, features concerning goalscorers and appearances have this year been listed separately in the latter part of the book. While most clubs responded quickly and efficiently to the circulars from the Football Association asking for club details, there was still a minority who did not submit up-to-date information, and in these cases there are obviously unfortunate omissions from the records featured. With club and league AGMs often being held after the time of going to press, it was impossible to record some of the changes of administration that have taken place.

However, it is hoped that the club directory is interesting and useful and suggestions for future additions are always welcomed.

KEY TO LEAGUES

Throughout the Annual, abbreviations for Leagues have been used, most of which are self-explanatory such as Kent, Town & Country, Yorkshire, Hellenic, etc. However, others have been abbreviated as follows: A.P.L. – Alliance Premier League; B.I.L. – Berger Isthmian League; Cheshire Co. – Cheshire County League; D. Northern – Drybroughs Northern League; Gl. Co. – Gloucestershire County League; K. Athenian – Kingsmead Athenian League; Lancs. Comb. – Lancashire Combination League; Leics. Sen. – Leicestershire Senior League; M. Comb. – Midland Combination League; Mid. Counties – Midland Counties League; Mid. L. – Midlands League; N.P.L. – Northern Premier League; S.L.M. – Southern League (Midland); S.L.S. – Southern League (South); Sussex Co. – Sussex County League; U. Counties – United Counties League; W. Midlands – West Midlands (Regional) League; P. Div – Premier Division.

ACCRINGTON STANLEY
(CHESHIRE CO. DIV 2)

Chairman: J. C. Prescott   Reformed: 1968
Secretary: J. S. Alty   Tel no: 061-330 2000
Team manager: David Baron
Previous league: (since re-formation) Lancs Combination
Colours: All red
Change colours: Sky blue shirts, black shorts, sky blue socks
Address of ground: Crown Ground, Whalley Road, Accrington, Lancs
                                  Record attendance: 1,200 (1978)
Ground capacity: 5,000   Seating capacity: 80
Covered accommodation: 300   Floodlights: No
Clubhouse details: None as yet
Best season in F.A. Cup: 1974-75, 4th Qual Rnd
Current players with Football League experience: I. Wilcox, D. Hargreaves
   (Blackburn Rovers); I. Warburton (Bury)
Major honours: Lancs Combination League champions 1973-74, 1977-78;
   Lancs Combination Cup winners 1971-72, 1972-73, 1973-74, 1976-77
Best season in F.A. Trophy: 1972-73 and 1978-79, 1st Rnd Proper
Club nickname: Stanley   Programme: 16 pages, 10p
Local newspapers: Accrington Observer, Lancashire Evening Telegraph

ADDLESTONE   (S.L.S.)

Chairman: B. Smith   Founded: 1885
Secretary: W. O'Farrell   Tel no: Weybridge 43408
Team manager: G. Goode
Previous leagues: Surrey Senior, Spartan, Athenian
Address and tel no of ground: Liberty Lane, Addlestone, Surrey
   (Weybridge 44054)
Ground capacity: 7,500   Seating capacity: 350
Covered accommodation: 2 sides   Floodlights: Yes
Clubhouse details: Open Monday to Saturday, bar, discos, steward: F.
   Higgs (Weybridge 44054)
Best season in F.A. Cup: 1975-76, 3rd Qual Rnd
Major honours: Surrey League champions 1960-61; Athenian League Div 2
   runners-up 1974-75; Spartan League runners-up 1966-67, 1969-70
Best seasons in F.A. Vase: 1974-75 and 1975-76, 6th Rnd
Club nickname: The Stones   Programme: 16 pages, 10p
Local newspaper: Surrey Herald

ALFRETON TOWN   (MID. COUNTIES)

Chairman: G. Brown   Founded: 1959
Secretary: T. McRoy   Tel no: Alfreton 4707
Team manager: S. Alton
Colours: Red shirts, white shorts, black socks
Change colours: All yellow

Address and tel no of ground: North Street, Alfreton, Derby
  (Alfreton 2819)   Record attendance: 5,072 (1960)
Ground capacity: 9,925   Seating capacity: 125
Covered accommodation: 1,500   Floodlights: Yes
Clubhouse details: Just outside ground, all social facilities
Best season in F.A. Cup: 1969-70
Major honours: Midland League champions; Midland League Cup win-
  ners; Derbyshire Senior Cup winners
Best season in F.A. Trophy: 1970-71, 1972-73 and 1973-74, 3rd Qual Rnd
Local newspapers: Derby Telegraph, Nottingham Evening Post, Derby-
  shire Times

ALMONDSBURY GREENWAY

(GL. CO.)

Chairman: G. Poole   Founded: Circa 1890
Secretary: K. Robbins   Tel no: Bristol 696970
Team manager: D. Rutter
Previous leagues: Bristol Suburban, Bristol Premier Combination
Colours: Royal blue shirts, white shorts, royal blue socks
Change colours: All white or yellow and green
Address and tel no of ground: The Field, Main Gloucester Road, Almonds-
  bury, Bristol (Almondsbury 612240)
Ground capacity: 2,000   Seating capacity: None
Covered accommodation: None   Floodlights: No
Clubhouse details: Bar, entertainment on Saturdays, catering facilities,
  darts, skittles, snooker, table tennis, open every evening from 7.30 p.m.
  and after football matches
Major honours: GFA Challenge Trophy winners 1978-79; Premier Com-
  bination champions 1969-70, 1970-71, 1971-72, 1972-73, 1973-74, 1974-
  75; Glos County League champions 1976-77, 1977-78, 1978-79
Best season in F.A. Vase: 1978-79, Final
Club nickname: The Almonds   Programme: 10 pages, 5p
Local newspapers: Bristol Evening Post, Western Daily Press, Northavon
  Gazette, Bristol Journal

ALTON TOWN   (K. ATHENIAN)

Chairman: E. Murray   Founded: 1947
Secretary: H. J. Scott   Tel no: Alton 83877
Team manager: G. Chapple
Previous league: Hampshire
Colours: White shirts, black shorts
Change colours: Blue shirts, white shorts
Address and tel no of ground: Anstey Park, Alton, Hants (Alton 82106)
Ground capacity: 2,800   Seating capacity: 300
Covered accommodation: 1,300   Floodlights: No
Best season in F.A. Cup: 1972-73, 1st Rnd Proper
Best season in F.A. Vase: 1978-79, 3rd Rnd
Local newspapers: Alton Gazette, Alton Herald

ALTRINCHAM (A.P.L.)

Chairman: N. White
Secretary: D. Baldwin

Founded: 1903
Tel no: 061-928 7121 (bus);
061-941 4506 (h)

Team manager: Tony Sanders
Previous leagues: Cheshire County, Northern Premier
Colours: Red and white striped shirts, black shorts, red socks
Change colours: Yellow shirts, blue shorts, yellow socks
Address and tel no of ground: Moss Lane, Altrincham, Cheshire, WA15 8AP
(061-928 1045/6905)   Record attendance: 35,530 (1975 – at
                                       Old Trafford)

Ground capacity: 10,000   Seating capacity: 1,200
Covered accommodation: 5,000   Floodlights: Yes
Clubhouse details: Run as nightclub only, not owned by club
Best seasons in F.A. Cup: 1965-66 v Wolves, 1974-75 v Everton and 1978-79
  v Spurs, 3rd Rnd Proper
League clubs defeated in F.A. Cup: Rochdale, Hartlepool, Scunthorpe
Current players with Football League experience: M. Bailey (Port Vale);
  I. Crossley (Coventry City); C. Darcy (Everton, Bury, Wigan Ath);
  B. Howard (Stockport); J. Johnson (Stockport); J. King (Everton,
  Shrewsbury); I. Morris (Stockport); J. Rogers (Port Vale)
Major honours: F.A. Trophy winners 1978-79; Northern Premier Chal-
  lenge Cup winners 1969-70; Cheshire League champions 1965-66, 1966-
  67; Cheshire League Challenge Cup winners 1932-33, 1963-64, 1950-51;
  Cheshire Senior Cup winners 1905-06, 1934-35, 1967-68
Best season in F.A. Trophy: 1978-79, Winners v Leatherhead
Club nickname: The Robins   Programme: 28 pages, 15p
Local newspapers: Altrincham Guardian, Sale & Altrincham Messenger,
  Manchester Evening News

ALVECHURCH (S.L.M.)

Chairman: Mr D. F. Pedley
Secretary: Mr B. Nevett

Founded: 1929
Tel no: Droitwich 71718

Team manager: Alan Grundy
Previous leagues: West Midland Premier, Midland Combination
Colours: Amber shirts, black shorts, amber socks
Change colours: All white
Address and tel no of ground: Lye Meadow, Alvechurch, Birmingham
(021-445 2929)   Record attendance: 12,500 (1964-65)
Ground capacity: 6,000   Seating capacity: 350
Covered accommodation: Yes   Floodlights: Yes
Clubhouse details: Bar, clubroom and lounge for members only
Best season in F.A. Cup: 1973-74
League clubs defeated in F.A. Cup: Exeter
Major honours: Worcs Senior Cup winners 4 times; West Midland League
  champions 4 times; Midland Combination League champions 4 times;
  F.A. Amateur Cup semi-finalists
Best season in F.A. Trophy: 1976-77, 3rd Qual Rnd
Club nickname: The Church   Programme: 6 pages, 10p
Local newspaper: Redditch Indicator

ANDOVER (S.L.S.)

Chairman: A. Baker   **Founded:** 1883
Secretary: K. J. Stevens
Team manager: Alan Green
Previous leagues: Hampshire, Western
Colours: Scarlet, black and white striped shirts, black shorts, black and scarlet socks
Change colours: Tangerine shirts, black shorts, tangerine socks
Address and tel no of ground: The Walled Meadow, London Road, Andover, Hants (Andover 3152)   **Record attendance:** 4,000 (1962)
Ground capacity: 7,000   **Seating capacity:** 400
Covered accommodation: 800   **Floodlights:** Yes
Clubhouse details: The Meadow Club open every day, entertainment, dinners, snacks, etc. (Andover 3152)
Best season in F.A. Cup: 1962-63, 1st Rnd Proper
Current players with Football League experience: J. Howarth (Aldershot); A. Green (Bournemouth and Mansfield)
Major honours: Hampshire League champions eight times; Hampshire Senior Cup winners four times; Western League runners-up twice
Best seasons in F.A. Trophy: 1969-70 and 1970-71, 3rd Qual Rnd
Club nickname: The Lions   **Programme:** 16 pages, 10p
Local newspaper: Andover Advertiser

A. P. LEAMINGTON (A.P.L.)

Chairman: I. Palmer   **Founded:** 1945
Secretary: W. C. Patrick   **Tel no:** Leamington Spa 27128
Team manager: Jim Knox
Previous leagues: Central Amateur, Birmingham Combination
Colours: Gold shirts, black shorts, gold and black socks
Change colours: All white with royal blue trim
Address and tel no of ground: 'The Windmill', Tachbrook Road, Leamington Spa, Warwicks (Leamington Spa 26039)
     Record attendance: 3,750 (1951)
Ground capacity: 6,000   **Seating capacity:** 440
Covered accommodation: 2,000   **Floodlights:** Yes
Clubhouse details: New social club, facilities for dances and club nights etc.
Best season in F.A. Cup: 1978-79
Current players with Football League experience: Three
Major honours: Southern League Cup winners 1973-74; Southern League Champions Cup winners 1973-74; Birmingham Senior Cup winners 5 times; West Midlands League champions 2 times; Midland League champions
Best seasons in F.A. Trophy: 1971-72, 1976-77 and 1977-78, 3rd Qual Rnd
Club nickname: The Brakes   **Programme:** 10p
Local newspapers: Leamington Spa Courier, Coventry Evening Telegraph

ARMITAGE (W. MIDLANDS)

Chairman: H. Bailey
Secretary: R. A. Hodson
Team manager: M. Hallam
Previous league: Staffs County South
Colours: All royal blue
Address and tel no of ground: Kings Bromley Road, Handsacre, Rugeley, Staffs (Armitage 491315)
Ground capacity: 2,500
Covered accommodation: 300
Clubhouse details: Open on Tuesdays, Thursdays, match days and training nights
Best season in F.A. Vase: 1978-79, 2nd Rnd
Club nickname: The Tage
Local newspapers: Rugeley Times, Express & Star

Reformed: 1946
Tel no: Armitage 490454

Change colours: Red and black
Record attendance: 620 (1974)
Seating capacity: 100
Floodlights: Yes

ARNOLD (MID COUNTIES)

Chairman: W. Parr
Secretary: M. Leivers
Team manager: J. Harrison
Previous league: Central Alliance
Colours: Yellow shirts, maroon shorts, yellow socks
Change colours: All blue
Address and tel no of ground: Gedling Round Ground, Arnold, Nottingham (Nottingham 263660)
Ground capacity: 1,850
Covered accommodation: 800
Clubhouse details: Open every night, steward: K. Whittaker
Programme: 12 pages, 5p
Local newspaper: Nottingham Evening Post

Founded: 1928
Tel no: Nottingham 265348

Seating capacity: 250
Floodlights: No

ASHFORD TOWN (S.L.S.)

Chairman: A. M. Batt
Secretary: A. G. Lancaster
Team manager: G. Burden
Previous league: Kent
Colours: Green shirts with white trim, green shorts with white trim, green and white socks
Change colours: All white
Address and tel no of ground: Essella Park, Essella Road, Ashford, Kent, TN24 8AN (Ashford 20528)
Ground capacity: 7,000
Covered accommodation: 2,000
Clubhouse details: Open on match days, licensed bar, snacks available
Best season in F.A. Cup: 1966–67, 2nd Rnd

Founded: 1930
Tel no: Ashford 21325

Record attendance: 6,250 (1961)
Seating capacity: 300
Floodlights: Yes

Major honours: Kent Senior Cup winners 1959, 1963
Best season in F.A. Trophy: 1972–73, Semi-final lost 1–0 to Scarborough
Programme: 4 pages, 5p
Local newspapers: Kentish Express, Tuesday Express

ASHINGTON (D. NORTHERN)

Chairman: E. Nichol
Secretary: R. A. Carr
Founded: 1901
Tel no: Cramlington 713399 (bus); Ashington 814768 (h)
Team manager: C. Irwin
Previous leagues: Northern, Alliance, Premier, North Eastern
Colours: Black and white striped shirts, black shorts, white socks
Change colours: All yellow
Address and tel no of ground: Portland Park, Ashington, Northumberland (Ashington 812240)
Ground capacity: 15,000
Seating capacity: 150
Covered accommodation: 2 stands
Floodlights: Yes
Clubhouse details: Open every night, bar, snacks, fortnightly disco, steward: J. Peary
Best season in F.A. Cup: 1926-27, 3rd Rnd
Best season in F.A. Trophy: 1975-76, 1st Rnd
Programme: 4 pages, 2p
Local newspapers: Ashington Post, Blyth News

ASHTON UNITED
(CHESHIRE CO. DIV 1)

Chairman: R. Donnelly
Secretary: D. Morris
Team manager: E. Hopkinson
Founded: 1878
Tel no: Bunbury 51788
Former name: Hurst F.C.
Previous leagues: Lancashire Comb., Midland
Colours: White shirts, red shorts
Change colours: Pale blue shirts
Address and tel no of ground: Hurst Cross, Ashton-under-Lyne, Lancs (061-330 1511)
Ground capacity: 10,000
Seating capacity: 380
Covered accommodation: Yes
Floodlights: Yes
Clubhouse details: Open seven days a week, steward: R. Forse
Best seasons in F.A. Cup: 1952-53 and 1955-56, 1st Rnd
Major honours: Manchester League champions 1911-12; Manchester Senior Cup winners 1885, 1978
Club nickname: United
Programme: 8 pages, 5p

ATHERSTONE TOWN (N.P.L.)

Chairman: B. E. Tunnicliffe
Secretary: B. J. Bannister
Founded: 1887
Tel no: Atherstone 4517
Colours: Red and white striped shirts, black shorts, red socks
Change colours: Yellow shirts, blue shorts, blue socks

Address and tel no of ground: Sheepy Road, Atherstone, Warwicks
(Atherstone 2377)
Ground capacity: 6,600   Seating capacity: 400
Covered accommodation: 600   Floodlights: Yes
Best seasons in F.A. Trophy: 1975-76 and 1977-78, 3rd Rnd Proper
Atherstone have resigned from the N.P.L.

AVELEY   (B.I.L. DIV 1)

Chairman: H. Foster   Founded: 1928
Secretary: K. W. Sutliff   Tel no: Rainham 55271
Team manager: L. Wilkinson
Previous leagues: Corinthian, Delphian
Colours: Royal blue and white   Change colours: All red
Address of ground: Mill Field, Mill Road, Aveley, Essex
                                       Record attendance: 4,800 (1972)
Ground capacity: 10,000   Seating capacity: 500
Covered accommodation: Yes   Floodlights: Yes
Clubhouse details: Keep fit, darts, bingo and dancing
Best seasons in F.A. Cup: 1970-71, 1st Rnd Proper
Major honours: London League champions 1954-55; Athenian League
champions 1970-71
Best seasons in F.A. Trophy: 1974-75, 3rd Qual Rnd
Club nickname: The Blues   Programme: 5p
Local newspaper: Thurrock Gazette

AYLESBURY UNITED   (S.L.S.)

Chairman: A. J. North   Founded: 1897
Secretary: K. Thornton   Tel no: Aylesbury 23521 (bus);
                                       81489 (h)
Team manager: L. S. Markham
Previous leagues: Spartan, Delphian, Athenian
Colours: Green shirts, white shorts, white socks
Change colours: All red
Address of ground: The Stadium, Turnfurlong Lane, Aylesbury,
Bucks (Aylesbury 24046)   Record attendance: 7,440 (1951-52)
Ground capacity: 7,500   Seating capacity: 500
Covered accommodation: Stand and terrace   Floodlights: Yes
Clubhouse details: Social club open daily, new extensions open 1979-80
Best season in F.A. Cup: 1951-52, lost to Watford 1st Rnd Proper
Current players with Football League experience: R. Lucas (Oxford Utd);
D. Jones (Oxford Utd); L. Markham (Watford)
Major honours: Berks and Bucks Senior Cup winners 1913-14; Spartan
League champions 1927-28; Delphian League champions 1953-54
Best season in F.A. Vase: 1975-76, 4th Rnd
Club nickname: The Ducks   Programme: 16 pages, 10p
Local newspapers: Bucks Herald, Bucks Advertiser

BANBURY UNITED (S.L.M.)

Chairman: R. Gilkes
Secretary: R. W. Alcock
Team manager: B. Stone
Founded: 1965
Tel no: Banbury 4970
Previous leagues: Birmingham Combination, West Midlands
Colours: Blue and white   Change colours: All red
Address and tel no of ground: The Stadium, off Station Road, Banbury, Oxon (Banbury 3354)   Record attendance: 7,000 (1947–48 as Banbury Spencer)
Ground capacity: 6,500   Seating capacity: 450
Covered accommodation: 2,500   Floodlights: Yes
Clubhouse details: Open for hire for all types of functions and regularly on match days
Best season in F.A. Cup: 1973–74, 1st Rnd Proper
Best seasons in F.A. Trophy: 1970-71 and 1973–74, 3rd Rnd
Programme: 8 pages, 10p   Local newspapers: Banbury Guardian, Oxford Mail

BANGOR CITY (A.P.L.)

Chairman: C. E. Roberts
Secretary: F. B. Jackson
Team manager: S. Storton
Founded: 1892
Tel no: Gaerwen 250
Previous leagues: Cheshire, Lancashire Combination, Northern Premier
Colours: Blue shirts, white shorts, blue socks
Change colours: Yellow shirts, white shorts, blue socks
Address and tel no of ground: Farrar Road, Bangor, Gwynedd (Bangor 53015)   Record attendance: 14,000 (1977-78
Ground capacity: 10,000   Seating capacity: 1,100
Covered accommodation: 3,000   Floodlights: Yes
Clubhouse details: Open every night and on match days, snacks, licensed, discos, club manager: Emlyn Hughes (Bangor 51889)
Best season in F.A. Cup: 1972-73, 2nd Rnd Proper
Major honours: N.P.L. Cup winners 1968-69; Welsh Cup winners three times
Best season in F.A. Trophy: 1972-73, Quarter-final
Programme: 16 pages, 15p
Local newspapers: North Wales Weekly News, North Wales Chronicle, Caernarfon Herald, Liverpool Daily Post

BANSTEAD ATHLETIC (K. ATHENIAN)

Chairman: E. C. Winser, M.B.E.
Secretary: G. A. Taylor
Team manager: A. Brazier
Founded: 1944
Tel no: 01-641 2957
Previous leagues: Surrey Senior, London Spartan
Colours: Amber and black   Change colours: Blue and white
Address and tel no of ground: Merland Rise, Tadworth, Surrey (Burgh Heath 50982)   Record attendance: 1,300 (1951)

73

Ground capacity: 4,000 Seating capacity: 150
Covered accommodation: Stand Floodlights: Yes
Clubhouse details: Two bars, boardroom and large dance hall
Best season in F.A. Cup: 1978-79
Current players with Football League experience: L. Prince (Crystal Palace)
Major honours: Surrey Senior League champions six times; Surrey Challenge Shield winners; Surrey Senior Cup winners twice
Best season in F.A. Vase: 1974-75, 3rd Rnd
Club nickname: The A's Programme: 4 pages, 5p
Local newspapers: Banstead Herald, Banstead Advertiser

BARKING (B.I.L. P. DIV)

Chairman: R. W. Herterich Founded: 1880
Secretary: R. J. Clark Tel no: 01-591 1471 (h);
01-476 6900 ext 95426 (bus)
Team manager: Edward McCluskey
Previous leagues: Athenian, South Essex, London
Colours: All blue Change colours: Yellow shirts,
white shorts, yellow socks
Address and tel no of ground: Mayesbrook Park, Lodge Avenue, Dagenham, Essex (01-595 6511)
Ground capacity: 3,900 Seating capacity: 210
Covered accommodation: 560 Floodlights: Yes
Clubhouse details: Dressing rooms with showers, members' bar, club bar, main hall with bar, car park for 250 cars
Best season in F.A. Cup: 1978-79, 2nd Rnd Proper
Current players with Football League experience: R. Arbour (Orient); G. Anderson (Northampton)
Major honours: Berger Isthmian League Prem Div champions 1978-79; London Senior Cup winners 1911-12, 1920-21, 1926-27, 1978-79; Essex Senior Cup winners 1895-96, 1919-20, 1945-46, 1962-63, 1969-70
Best season in F.A. Trophy: 1978-79, 1st Rnd Proper
Club nickname: The Blues Programme: 20 pages, 15p
Local newspapers: Barking Advertiser, Barking & Dagenham Post Stratford Express

---

BARNET (A.P.L.)

Chairman: D. Underwood Founded: 1888
Secretary: R. Andrews Tel no: 01-440 1978 (h)
Team manager: B. Meadows
Previous league: Athenian
Colours: Amber and black shirts, black shorts, amber socks
Change colours: White and red shirts, white shorts, white socks
Address and tel no of ground: Underhill, Barnet Lane, Barnet, Herts (01-449 4173)
Ground capacity: 11,000 Seating capacity: 880
Covered accommodation: 2,000 Floodlights: Yes

Clubhouse details: Open nightly, snacks and usual facilities
Best season in F.A. Cup: 3rd Rnd
Major honours: F.A. Trophy finalists 1972; F.A. Amateur Cup winners 1946, 1948, 1959; London Senior Cup winners 1938, 1941, 1947; Middlesex Senior Cup winners 1932-33; Athenian League champions seven times; Southern League Div 1 champions 1965-66, Div 1 S champions 1976-77
Programme: 10 pages, 10p
Local newspapers: Barnet Press, Hendon Times, Finchley Press

BARNSTAPLE TOWN (WESTERN)

Chairman: M. Page
Secretary: P. Dymond
Team manager: B. Perks
Previous leagues: North Devon Senior, Exeter & District
Colours: Red and white
Founded: 1895
Tel no: Barnstaple 73382

Change colours: Lemon and purple
Address and tel no of ground: Mill Road, Barnstaple, Devon (Barnstaple 3469)
Ground capacity: 4,000
Seating capacity: 500
Clubhouse details: Penalty Box social club open on Mondays, Tuesdays, Wednesdays Thursdays and Saturdays, canteen facilities available
Major honours: Western League champions 1952-53
Programme: 12 pages, 5p
Local newspaper: North Devon Journal Herald

BARROW (A.P.L.)

Chairman: Mr W. A. McCullough
Secretary: Mr G. Chetham
Team manager: Mr B. McManus
Previous leagues: Football League, Northern Premier
Colours: Blue shirts, white shorts, blue socks
Change colours: All red
Founded: 1901
Tel no: Barrow-in-Furness 23258

Address and tel no of ground: Holker Street, Barrow-in-Furness, Cumbria (Barrow-in-Furness 20346)
Ground capacity: 9,500
Covered accommodation: All sides
Record attendance: 15,000 (1953)
Seating capacity: 1,250
Floodlights: Yes
Clubhouse details: Modern social club opened 1972
Best season in F.A. Cup: 1953, 3rd Rnd v Wolves
League clubs defeated in F.A. Cup: Numerous when in Football League, none in non-league
Current players with Football League experience: A. Suddick; K. Thomas; B. McManus; M. Richmond
Major honours: Lancashire Cup winners
Best season in F.A. Trophy: 1972–73, 1973–74 and 1978–79, 2nd Rnd Proper
Programme: 20 pages, 15p
Local newspaper: Barrow News & Mail

75

BARRY TOWN (S.L.S.)

Chairman: John J. Bailey Founded: 1912
Secretary: Alan Whelan Tel no: Penarth 700472
Team manager: Emrys Evans
Previous league: Welsh
Colours: Green and white striped shirts, white shorts
Change colours: All white
Address and tel no of ground: Jenner Park, Barry, South Glam (Barry
  736909) Record attendance: 7,000 (1961)
Ground capacity: 10,000 Seating capacity: 300
Covered accommodation: 2,000 Floodlights: No
Clubhouse details: Two bars open every evening and Saturday and Sunday
  lunchtimes, refreshments, pool table, darts and discos
Best season in F.A. Cup: 1961, drew 1–1 with QPR 1st Rnd Proper
Current players with Football League experience: G. Young; J. Emanuel;
  P. Preece; D. Murray; P. Lewis; R. Jones
Major honours: Welsh Senior Cup winners 1955
Best seasons in F.A. Trophy: 1972–73 and 1978–79, 3rd Qual Rnd
Club nickname: The Linnets Programme: 28 pages, 15p
Local newspapers: Barry & District News, South Wales Echo

BARTON ROVERS (B.I.L. DIV 2)

Chairman: F. Osborne Founded: 1898
Secretary: P. Howarth Tel no: Luton 882022
Team manager: B. Reed
Previous leagues: Luton & District, South Midlands
Colours: All white with blue trim Change colours: All blue
Address and tel no of ground: Sharpenhoe Road, Barton, Beds
  (Luton 882607 – boardroom; 881075 – public)
  Record attendance: 1,900 (1977-78)
Ground capacity: 5,000 Seating capacity: 150
Covered accommodation: 1,000 Floodlights: Yes
Clubhouse details: Open evenings only except weekends when it opens at
  midday, snacks, entertainment at weekends
Best season in F.A. Vase: 1977-78, Final lost to Blue Star
Major honours: F.A. Vase finalists 1977-78; Beds. Senior Cup winners
  1971-72, 1973-74; South Midlands Prem Div champions 1970-71
  1971-72, 1972-73, 1974-75, 1975-76, 1976-77, 1977-78, 1978-79
  Programme: 16 pages, 10p
Local newspapers: Evening Post, Luton News

BASILDON UNITED (ESSEX SENIOR)

Chairman: R. Hill Reformed: 1963
Secretary: R. Cordey Tel no: Colchester 210505 (h)
Team manager: R. Hanley
Previous league: Greater London
Colours: Amber shirts, black shorts, black socks
Change colours: White shirts with green trim, green shorts, green socks

Address and tel no of ground: Gardiners Close (off Gardiners Lane South), Basildon, Essex (Basildon 20268) Record attendance: 4,000
Ground capacity: 3,600   Seating capacity: 350
Covered accommodation: 550   Floodlights: Yes
Clubhouse details: Capacity 150, new bar, club open every day at lunchtimes and in evenings except Wednesdays, hot food always available
Major honours: Essex Senior League champions 1976–77, 1977–78, 1978–79; Essex Senior (County) Trophy winners 1978–79; Essex Elizabethan Trophy winners 1977–78; Essex Senior League Cup and Reserve Cup winners 1977–78
Best season in F.A. Vase: 1975–76, 4th Rnd
Club nickname: The B's   Programme: 4 pages, 5p
Local newspapers: Basildon & Wickford Recorder, Southend Evening Echo, Basildon Radio (exclusive coverage of all midweek and Saturday matches)

BASINGSTOKE TOWN   (S.L.S.)

Chairman: Mr D. Ambrose   Founded: 1886
Secretary: Mr J. Hacker   Tel no: Basingstoke 64548
Team manager: Mr E. Lisle
Previous league: Hampshire
Colours: Yellow shirts with blue trim, blue shorts with yellow trim, yellow socks
Change colours: White shirts with navy blue trim, navy blue shorts with white trim, white socks
Address and tel no of ground: Camrose Ground, Western Way, Basingstoke, Hants (Basingstoke 64353) Record attendance: 5,000
Ground capacity: 6,000   Seating capacity: 820
Covered accommodation: 300   Floodlights: Yes
Clubhouse details: Open every night and at midday weekends, entertainment every weekend (Basingstoke 64353)
Best season in F.A. Cup: 1969–70, v Northampton Town
Major honours: Hampshire League Div 1 champions; Hampshire Senior Cup winners
Best season in F.A. Trophy: Never past 3rd Qual Rnd
Club nickname: Stoke   Programme: 18 pages, 10p
Local newspaper: Basingstoke Gazette

BATH CITY   (A.P.L.)

Chairman: Mr D. H. Counsell   Founded: 1889
Secretary: Mrs V. Burroughs   Tel no: Bath 23087
Team manager: Mr M. Burns
Previous leagues: None; joined Southern in 1921
Colours: White with black trim   Change colours: Red with white trim
Address and tel no of ground: Twerton Park, Bath (Bath 23087)
Record attendance: 18,020 (1960)
Ground capacity: 20,000   Seating capacity: 1,000
Covered accommodation: 8,000   Floodlights: Yes
Clubhouse details: President's Club (members only), three 'Sportsman' bars including facilities for cabaret, wedding receptions etc. for 250 people

Best seasons in F.A. Cup: 1959–60 and 1963–64, 3rd Rnd Proper
League clubs defeated in F.A. Cup: Crystal Palace, Millwall, Notts County, Newport, Exeter City, Southend
Current players with Football League experience: K. Book; R. Brown; R. Bourne; C. Tavener; P. Higgins; S. Crompton; F. McMahon
Major honours: Southern League champions 1959–60, 1977–78; Southern League Cup winners 1978–79; Somerset Premier Cup winners 8 times
Best seasons in F.A. Trophy: 1969–70, 1972–73, 1976–77 and 1978–79, 1st Rnd Proper
Club nickname: The City   Programme: 12 pages, 10p
Local newspaper: Bath & Wilts Evening Chronicle

BEDFORD TOWN (S.L.M.)

Chairman: A. Holley   Founded: 1908
Secretary: B. Hollis   Tel no: Oakley 2304
Team manager: T. Gould
Previous league: Northants Senior
Colours: White shirts, blue shorts, blue socks
Change colours: Blue shirts, white shorts, white socks
Address and tel no of ground: The Eyrie, Raleigh Street, Queens Park, Bedford (Bedford 59230)   Record attendance: 18,500
Ground capacity: 10,000   Seating capacity: 3,000
Covered accommodation: 2,500   Floodlights: Yes
Clubhouse details: Social club adjacent to ground with facilities for 200
Best season in F.A. Cup: 1964, 3rd Rnd Proper v Everton
League clubs defeated in F.A. Cup: Oxford Utd, Brighton, Norwich, Newcastle Utd
Current players with Football League experience: T. Gould (Northampton); B. Best (Northampton and Southend); K. Goodeve (Brighton and Watford)
Major honours: Southern League champions; Bedfordshire Professional Cup winners
Best season in F.A. Trophy: 1974–75, Semi-final v Scarborough
Club nickname: The Eagles   Programme: 12 pages, 15p
Local newspapers: Bedford County Press, Bedford Journal, Bedford Record

BEDWORTH UNITED (S.L.M.)

Chairman: Mr J. Davis   Founded 1968
Secretary: Keith Allen   Tel no: Nuneaton 69989 (h);
                                               384221 (bus)
Team manager: Len Harris
Previous leagues: West Midlands, Birmingham
Colours: Green and white stripes   Change colours: All yellow
Address and tel no of ground: The Oval, Miners Welfare Park, Bedworth, Warwicks (Bedworth 314302)
Ground capacity: 10,000   Seating capacity: 300
Covered accommodation: 1,500   Floodlights: Yes

Clubhouse details: Open every day and night, usual club entertainment and food
Best seasons in F.A. Cup: 1970–71 and 1973–74, 2nd Qual Rnd
Best season in F.A. Trophy: 1973–74, 1st Rnd Proper
Club nickname: The Greenbacks   Programme: 12 pages, 5p
Local newspapers: Nuneaton Evening Tribune, Coventry Telegraph, Bedworth Observer

BELPER TOWN   (MID COUNTIES)

Chairman: Mr A. Sims   Founded: 1951
Secretary: Mr N. Miller   Tel no: Belper 3573
Team manager: Phil Waller
Previous league: Central Alliance
Colours: Gold shirts, black shorts   Change colours: All white
Address and tel no of ground: Christ Church Meadow, Bridge Stree
    Belper, Derbys (Belper 5549)   Record attendance: 3,009 (1953)
Ground capacity: 3,000   Seating capacity: 200
Covered accommodation: 1,000   Floodlights: No
Clubhouse details: Social club on ground, licensed, discos on Tuesdays and Fridays
Best season in F.A. Cup: 1958–59, lost to Spalding Utd 4th Qual Rnd
Major honours: Derbys Senior Cup winners 1958–59, 1960–61, 1963–64
Best season in F.A. Trophy: 1973–74, 3rd Qual Rnd
Club nickname: The Nailers   Programme: 10 pages, free
Local newspapers: Belper News, Derby Evening Telegraph

BIDEFORD   (WESTERN)

Chairman: A. Loze   Found:ed: 1946
Secretary: A. Levick   Tel no Instow 860735 (h);
                                            Bideford 3233 (bus)
Team manager: Dudley Barry
Previous leagues: Southern, South Western
Colours: Red and white   Change colours: All blue
Address and tel no of ground: Sports Ground, Kingsley Road, Bideford,
    Devon (Bideford 4974)   Record attendance: 6,000 plus (1963)
Ground capacity: 6,500   Seating capacity: 300
Covered accommodation: 1,200   Floodlights: Yes
Clubhouse details: New clubhouse to open shortly, two bars, entertainment nightly, catering, etc.
Best seasons in F.A. Cup: 1963, 1971 and 1977, 1st Rnd Proper
Current players with Football League experience: J. Wingate; K. Etheridge; A. Hooker; G. Wake; B. O'Neil
Major honours: Western League champions 1970-71, 1971-72, runners-up 1977-78, 1978-79
Best season in F.A. Trophy: 1969-70, 1st Rnd Proper
Club nickname: The Robins   Programme: 20 pages, 10p
Local newspapers: Bideford Gazette, North Devon Journal & Herald

BILLERICAY TOWN (B.I.L. DIV 2)

Chairman: D. Hanks
Secretary: B. King
Team manager: Colin Searle
Previous leagues: Kingsmead Athenian, Essex Senior, Essex Olympian
Mid-Essex
Colours: Blue shirts with white trim, white shorts, blue socks
Change colours: Red shirts, white shorts, blue socks
Address and tel no of ground: New Lodge, Blunts Wall Road, Billericay,
Essex (Billericay 52188)
Ground capacity: 3,700
Covered accommodation: 600
Clubhouse details: Open nightly, discos, entertainment at weekends
Best season in F.A. Cup: 1977-78, 4th Qual Rnd
Major honours: F.A. Challenge Vase winners 1975-76, 1976-77, 1978-79;
Essex Senior Cup winners 1975-76; Essex Senior Trophy winners
1977-78; Rothmans Football Award winners 1977-78; Kingsmead
Athenian League Cup winners 1977-78; Philips Electrical Floodlights
Trophy winners 1976-77; Essex Floodlights Trophy winners 1977-78;
Essex Senior League Cup winners 1971-72, 1972-73, 1973-74, 1976-77,
runners-up 1974-75; Essex Senior League Challenge Cup winners
1972-73; J. T. Clark Memorial Trophy winners 1974-75, 1975-76, 1976-
77, 1977-78; Kingsmead Athenian League champions 1977-78, 1978-79;
Essex Senior League champions 1972-73, 1974-75, 1975-76, runners-up
1971-72, 1973-74
Best seasons in F.A. Vase: 1975-76, 1976-77 and 1978-79, Winners
Club nickname: The Town or The Blues   Programme: 16 pages, 10p
Local newspapers: Billericay Gazette, Billericay Recorder, Billericay Argus

Founded: 1890
Tel no: Chelmsford 60231 (h)

Record attendance: 3,641 (1977)

Seating capacity: 120
Floodlights: Yes

BILLINGHAM SYNTHONIA (D. NORTHERN)

Chairman: J. Dunlop
Secretary: P. E. Lax
Team manager: E. Nobbs
Previous league: Teesside
Colours: Green shirts, white shorts, green socks
Change colours: White shirts, black shorts, white socks
Address and tel no of ground: Central Avenue, Billingham, Cleveland
(Stockton 552358)
Ground capacity: 11,000
Covered accommodation: 3,000
Clubhouse details: Open every evening
Best seasons in F.A. Cup: 1948-49, 1949-50, 1951-52 and 1956-57, 1st Rnd
Current players with Football League experience: J. Cook (Stoke); D.
Hockerday (Blackpool)
Major honours: Northern League champions 1956-57; Northern League
Cup winners 1951-52; North Riding Senior Cup winners 1968-69
1972-73, 1978-79
Best season in F.A. Trophy: 1977-78, 2nd Qual Rnd
Club nickname: The Synners
Local newspaper: Middlesbrough Evening Gazette

Founded: 1923
Tel no: Stockton 555418

Seating capacity: 3,000
Floodlights: Yes

80

BILSTON   (W. MIDLANDS)

Chairman: K. Nicholls   Founded: 1895
Secretary: K. Cooper   Tel no: Bilston 43766
Team manager: A. Wakeman
Previous leagues: Birmingham Combination, Birmingham District, Walsall Senior
Colours: Tangerine shirts, white shorts, white socks
Change colours: All white
Address and tel no of ground: Queen Street, Bilston, West Midlands (Bilston 41498)
Ground capacity: 8,500   Seating capacity: 500
Covered accommodation: Yes   Floodlights: Yes
Clubhouse details Entertainment most nights, open 7 nights a week
Best season in F.A. Cup: 1961
Current players with Football League experience: G. O'Hara (Wolves); T. Wharton (Wolves)
Best seasons in F.A. Trophy: 1970-71 and 1974-75, 2nd Rnd Proper
Club nickname: The Steelmen   Programme: 8 pages, free
Local newspapers: Express & Star, Sandwell Evening Mail

BISHOP AUCKLAND   (D. NORTHERN)

Chairman: G. H. Metcalfe   Founded: 1886
Secretary: D. Liddle   Tel no: Bishop Auckland 5033
Team manager: Bobby Elwell
Colours: Light and dark blue shirts, dark blue shorts, blue socks
Change colours: Red shirts with white trim, white shorts, red and white socks
Address and tel no of ground: Kingsway Ground, Kingsway, Bishop Auckland, Co Durham (Bishop Auckland 603686)
     Record attendance: 16,319 (1952)
Ground capacity: 9,500   Seating capacity: 1,000
Covered accommodation: 1,200   Floodlights: Yes
Clubhouse details: Open every night, Saturday afternoons and Sunday lunchtimes, food available on match days, occasional evening entertainment
Best season in F.A. Cup: 1954-55, 4th Rnd Proper
League clubs defeated in F.A. Cup: Crystal Palace, Ipswich, Tranmere Rovers
Current players with Football League experience: A. Garrow (Newcastle United)
Major honours: F.A. Amateur Cup winners 1895-96, 1899-1900, 1913-14, 1920-21, 1922-23, 1934-35, 1938-39, 1954-55, 1955-56, 1956-57
Best season in F.A. Trophy: 1978-79, Quarter-final
Club nickname: The Bishops   Local newspaper: Northern Echo

81

BISHOP'S STORTFORD (B.I.L. DIV 1)

Chairman: E. A. Bentley
Secretary: V. C. Wallis
Team manager: R. Duke
Founded: 1874
Tel no: Bishop's Stortford 52531

Previous leagues: Athenian, Delphian, Spartan, Herts County
Colours: Blue and white striped shirts, blue shorts, blue socks
Change colours: All red
Address and tel no of ground: George Wilson Stadium, Rhodes Avenue, Bishop's Stortford, Herts (Bishop's Stortford 54140)

Record attendance: 6,000 (1972-73)
Ground capacity: 5,000
Seating capacity: Approx. 400
Covered accommodation: Approx 1,500
Floodlights: Yes
Clubhouse details: Licensed bar, refreshment bar, covered viewing lounge, open six days a week, available for hire
Best seasons in F.A. Cup: 1972-73 and 1975-76, 2nd Rnd
Current players with Football League experience: W. Carrick (Man Utd, Luton); T. Coakley (Motherwell, Arsenal, Morton); P. Ferry (Arsenal, Morton)
Major honours: F.A. Challenge Cup winners 1974; London Senior Cup winners 1974; Herts Senior Cup winners seven times; Herts Charity Cup winners three times; Athenian League champions 1969-70
Best season in F.A. Trophy: 1975-76, 2nd Rnd Proper
Club nickname: The Blues
Programme: 8 pages, 10p
Local newspapers: Herts & Essex Observer, Bishop's Stortford Gazette

BLAKENALL (W. MIDLANDS)

Chairman: A. Allport
Secretary: N. Harper
Team manager: Michael Harvey
Founded: 1946
Tel no: Bloxwich 77156

Previous leagues: Staffs County, Midland Combination
Colours: White shirts with blue trim, white shorts
Change colours: Claret and blue shirts
Address of ground: Somerfield Road, Bloxwich, Walsall, West Midlands
Ground capacity: 6–7,000
Seating capacity: None
Covered accommodation: 300
Floodlights: No
Clubhouse details: Social club open every evening
Major honours: Midland Combination League champions, Walsall Senior Cup winners four times
Best season in F.A. Vase: 1976–77, 5th Rnd
Local newspapers: Walsall Observer, Express & Star

BLUE STAR (WEARSIDE)

Chairman: W. Dryden
Secretary: F. S. Brown
Team manager: Peter Feenan
Founded: 1931
Tel no: Newcastle 28831

Previous leagues: Northern Combination, Tyneside Amateur

Colours: All royal blue   Change colours: All red
Address and tel no of ground: Woolsington Sports Ground, Newcastle -on-Tyne (Newcastle-on-Tyne 860425)
Ground capacity: 3,000   Seating capacity: None
Covered accommodation: 300   Floodlights: No
Clubhouse details: Small canteen, four dressing rooms, showers, sauna
Best season in F.A. Vase: 1977-78, Winners
Local newspapers: Sunday Sun, Newcastle Journal, Evening Chronicle

BLYTH SPARTANS   (D. NORTHERN)

Chairman: J. A. Turney   Founded: 1899
Secretary: G. Watson   Tel no: Blyth 2373
Team manager: J. Marks
Previous leagues: Northumberland, Northern Football Alliance, North Eastern, Midland, Northern Counties
Colours: Green and white striped shirts, black shorts, white socks
Change colours: Yellow shirts, green shorts, green socks
Address and tel no of ground: Croft Park, Plessey Road, Blyth, Northumberland (Blyth 4818 – clubhouse; 2373 – boardroom)
Record attendance: 42,000 (1978, at Newcastle Utd)
Ground capacity: 8,500   Seating capacity: 300
Covered accommodation: 2,500   Floodlights: Yes
Clubhouse details: Open every night and Saturday and Sunday lunchtimes, dancing, bingo and sandwiches at weekends
Best season in F.A. Cup: 1977-78, 5th Rnd Proper replay
League clubs defeated in F.A. Cup: Chesterfield, Stoke City, Crewe Alexandra, Stockport County, Hartlepool
Current players with Football League experience: D. Clarke (Newcastle Utd, Doncaster); R. Guthrie (Newcastle Utd, Sunderland); T. Johnson (Newcastle Utd, Southend, Brentford); L. Mutrie (Carlisle Utd)
Major honours: Northumberland Senior Cup winners 15 times; Amateur Cup semi-finalists 1972; Northern League champions 1973, 1975, 1976
Best season in F.A. Trophy: 1978-79, 2nd Rnd Proper replay
Club nickname: The Spartans   Programme: 16 pages, 5p
Local newspaper: News Post (Blyth edition)

BOGNOR REGIS TOWN   (S.L.S.)

Chairman: S. J. Rowlands   Founded: 1895
Secretary: A. I. McCutchion   Tel no: Bognor Regis 23917
Team manager: J. Pearce
Previous leagues: Sussex County, (West Sussex League up to 1921)
Colours: White shirts with green trim, green shorts, white socks
Change colours: All blue
Address and tel no of ground: Nyewood Lane, Bognor Regis, West Sussex (Bognor Regis 22325)   Record attendance: 3,200 (1948)
Ground capacity: 4,000   Seating capacity: 200
Covered accommodation: Yes   Floodlights: Yes
Clubhouse details: Members bar, various functions staged, bingo on Sundays, darts on Fridays, available for private hire

Best season in F.A. Cup: 1973
Major honours: Sussex County League champions 1948-49, 1954-55, 1955-56, 1971-72
Best season in F.A. Trophy: 1977-78, 3rd Rnd
Club nickname: The Rocks   Programme: 16 pages, 10p
Local newspapers: The Bognor Regis Observer, The Bognor Regis Post

BOOTLE (CHESHIRE CO. P. DIV)

Chairman: S. Heeney   Founded: 1953–54
Secretary: F. Doran   Tel no: 051–928 9495
Team manager: F. Doran
Previous leagues: Liverpool County Combination, Lancashire Combination
Colours: Royal blue with amber trim
Change colours: Amber with blue trim
Address of ground: 'Buck's Park', Northern Perimeter Road, Netherton, Merseyside
Ground capacity: 5,000   Seating capacity: None
Covered accommodation: Approx. 200
                                   Floodlights: No
Clubhouse details: Situated on ground, bar, snacks, 200 capacity
Best seasons in F.A. Trophy: 1976–77 and 1978–79, 2nd Qual Rnd
Club nickname: The Bucks
Local newspapers: Liverpool Daily Post & Echo, Bootle Times

BOREHAM WOOD (B.I.L. P. DIV)

Chairman: Mr W. F. O'Neill   Founded: 1948
Secretary/general manager: Mr C. Wilkinson   Tel no: 01–953 9883
Team manager: Michael Lennon
Previous leagues: Mid Herts, Patheneon, Spartan, Athenian
Colours: All white with red and black trim   Change colours: All red
Address and tel no of ground: Broughinge Road, Boreham Wood, Herts
(01–953 9883 – boardroom; 5097 – club)   Record attendance: 3,000
Ground capacity: 4,000   Seating capacity: 250
Covered accommodation: 1,500   Floodlights: Yes
Clubhouse details: Facilities for 250 people, bingo, discos, dancing, darts matches, club available for private hire
Best seasons in F.A. Cup: 1973–74, lost to Southend 1st Rnd, 1977–78, lost replay to Swindon 1st Rnd
Major honours: Herts Senior Cup winners; Athenian League champions; Isthmian League Div 2 champions
Best season in F.A. Trophy: 1978–79, 2nd Qual Rnd
Club nickname: The Wood   Programme: 8 pages, 10p
Local newspapers: Hendon Times, Barnet Press, Herts Advertiser, Evening Echo

BOSTON (MID. COUNTIES)

Chairman: W. M. Stanwell　　　　Founded: 1963
Secretary: Mrs D. Wilson　　　　Tel no: Boston 68312
Team manager: Bob Don-Duncan
Previous leagues: Lincolnshire, Central Alliance, Eastern Counties
Colours: Blue and white striped shirts, blue shorts, white socks
Change colours: Red shirts, red shorts, white socks
Address and tel no of ground: Tattershall Road, Boston, Lincs (Boston 65470)
Ground capacity: 8,000　　　　Record attendance: 4,000
Covered accommodation: 950　　Seating capacity: 450
　　　　　　　　　　　　　　　　Floodlights: No
Clubhouse details: Licensed bar, darts, music, dancing, etc.
Best season in F.A. Cup: 1976–77, lost to Barnsley 1st Rnd Proper
Current players with Football League experience: F. Taylor; P. Siothorne; M. Daley
Major honours: Lincolnshire League champions 1964–65; Central Alliance champions 1965–66; Midland League champions 1974–75
Best seasons in F.A. Trophy: 1972–73, 1973–74 and 1978–79, 3rd Qual Rnd.　　　　　　　　　　Programme: 10 pages, 10p
Local newspaper: Lincolnshire Standard

BOSTON UNITED (A.P.L.)

Chairman: Mr E. J. Malkinson　　Founded: 1935
Secretary: John Blackwell　　　　Tel no: Boston 64406 (bus); 65652 (h)
Team manager: Albert Phelan
Previous leagues: Midland, Southern, Central Alliance, United Counties, West Midland, Northern Premier
Colours: Amber shirts, black shorts, black socks
Change colours: Blue shirts, white shorts, blue and white socks
Address and tel no of ground: York Street, Boston, Lincs (Boston 65524/5)
Record attendance: 10,086 (1955)
Ground capacity: 9,000　　　　Seating capacity: 1,500
Covered accommodation: All round ground　Floodlights: Yes
Clubhouse details: Open every day except Tuesday, stewards Mr and Mrs Greenouch (tel no Boston 62967 – live entertainment)
Best seasons in F.A. Cup: 1955–56, won 6–1 Derby County 2nd Rnd Proper; 1973–74, lost 4–0 to Tottenham H. 3rd Rnd
League clubs defeated in F.A. Cup: Hartlepool, Southport
Current players with Football League experience: G. Stewart (Preston NE); A. Phelan (Chesterfield, Halifax); J. Moyes (Chesterfield); J. Cabia (Chesterfield); S. Towle (Notts Co); B. Brown (Sheffield W); R. Welch (Brighton, Chesterfield)
Major honours: Lincolnshire Senior Cup winners 1934–5–6, 1945–46, 1949–50, 1954–55, 1956–57, 1959–60, 1976–77; United Counties League champions and Cup winners 1965–66; West Midlands League champions 1966–7–8 and League Cup 1967–8; Non-League Champion of

85

Champions Cup winners 1972–73, 1977–78; Northern Premier League champions 1972–73, 1973–74, 1976–77, 1977–78; League Cup winners 1973–74, 1975–76; Challenge Shield winners 1973–74, 1974–75, 1976–77, 1977–78

Best seasons in F.A. Trophy: 1973–74 and 1978–79, 3rd Rnd
Club nickname: The Pilgrims   Programme: 10p
Local newspapers: Lincolnshire Standard, Lincolnshire Echo

BOURNE TOWN   (UTD. CO.)

Chairman: D. S. Bontoft   Founded: 1890
Secretary: D.W.F. Page   Tel no: Bourne 3358
Team manager: T. N. Bates
Previous leagues: Central Alliance, Midland, Lincolnshire
Colours: All red
Change colours: Yellow shirts, green shorts
Address and tel no of ground: Abbey Lawn, Abbey Road, Bourne, Lincs (Bourne 2292)
Ground capacity: 3,000   Seating capacity: 250
Covered accommodation: Yes   Floodlights: No
Clubhouse details: Open on match days, Thursday evenings for bingo and at other special times such as darts competitions
Best season in F.A. Cup: 1969-70, 4th Qual Rnd
Major honours: United Counties League champions 1968-69, 1969-70, 1971-72; United Counties League Cup winners 1969-70; Lincs Senior 'A' Cup winners 1971-72
Best seasons in F.A. Vase: 1974-75 and 1978-79, 3rd Rnd
Club nickname: The Wakes   Programme: 8 pages, 5p
Local newspapers: Stamford Mercury, Lincs Free Press

BRANDON UNITED (NORTHERN ALL.)

Chairman: K. Carr   Founded: 1971
Secretary: L. Burnip   Tel no: Meadowfield 780154
Team manager: J. Heavysides
Previous league: Durham & District
Colours: Red and white   Change colours: Blue and white
Address and tel no of ground: Brandon Welfare Ground, Brandon, Durham
Ground capacity: 6,000   Seating capacity: 500
Covered accommodation: 400   Floodlights: Yes
Clubhouse details: Open every night (Meadowfield 780330)
Major honours: Northern Alliance League champions 1977–78; Northern Alliance Cup winners 1977–78, finalists 1978–79
Local newspaper: Durham Advertiser

BRIDGEND TOWN   (S.L.M.)

Chairman: J. Eastment   Founded: 1954
Secretary: J. Williams   Tel no: Bridgend 55097
Team manager: Lyn Jones
Previous leagues: South Wales Amateur, Welsh

Colours: Sky blue shirts, navy blue shorts, sky blue socks
Change colours: All white
Address and tel no of ground: Coychurch Road, Bridgend, Mid Glam
(Bridgend 55097/63483)
Record attendance: 5,000 (1969)
Ground capacity: 5,000
Seating capacity: 200
Covered accommodation: Yes
Floodlights: Yes
Clubhouse details: Open daily, snacks, steward – M. Tanner (Bridgend
62974)
Best season in F.A. Cup: 1977-78, 3rd Qual Rnd
Current players with Football League experience: G. Bell; J. McInch; B.
Vassallo; G. Jones; E. Woods; C. Williams; S. Derrett
Major honours: South Wales Amateur League champions 1963-64, 1966-67
1968-69; Welsh League champions 1968-69, 1972-73
Best season in F.A. Trophy: 1977-78, 1st Rnd Proper
Local newspaper: Western Mail   Programme: 8 pages, 10p

BRIDGNORTH TOWN   (MID. COMB.)

Chairman: P. Fellows   Founded: 1949
Secretary: G. Thomas   Tel no: Bridgnorth 5178
Team manager: Ricky Wilde
Previous league: Kidderminster
Colours: Blue and white   Change colours: Red and white
Address and tel no of ground: Crown Meadow, Innage Lane, Bridgnorth,
Shropshire (Bridgnorth 2747)   Record attendance: 1,100 (1976)
Ground capacity: 2,000   Seating capacity: None
Covered accommodation: 300   Floodlights: No
Clubhouse details: Open every night and Saturday and Sunday lunchtimes
Best season in Welsh F.A. Cup: 1976-77, 4th Rnd
Major honours: Shropshire County Challenge Cup winners 1970-71,
1972-73, 1976-77, 1978-79; Midland Combination League Cup winners
1978-79
Best season in F.A. Vase: 1975-76, 5th Rnd
Club nickname: The Town   Programme: 4 pages, free
Local newspapers: Bridgnorth Journal, Shropshire Star

BRIDGWATER TOWN   (WESTERN)

Chairman: D. Combes   Founded: 1948
Secretary: G. Marson   Tel no: North Petherton 662129
Team manager: C. Porter
Previous league: Somerset Senior
Colours: All red and white
Change colours: White shirts, black shorts
Address and tel no of ground: Castlefields, Bristol Road, Bridgwater,
Somerset (Bridgwater 3642)   Record attendance: 5,000
Ground capacity: 5,000   Seating capacity: 250
Covered accommodation: 1,000   Floodlights: Yes
Clubhouse details: Robins Club (on ground), capacity 250, no cooked
meals

Best season in F.A. Cup: 1st Rnd, v Oxford Utd, Reading, Crystal Palace, Luton
Current players with Football League experience: C. Porter; P. Charles; T. Kirk
Major honours: Western League champions, Somerset Premier Cup winners
Best seasons in F.A. Trophy: 1969-70 and 1972-73, 3rd Rnd Proper
Club nickname: The Robins   Programme: 5p
Local newspaper: Bridgwater Mercury

BRIDLINGTON TOWN   (YORKSHIRE)

Chairman: K. Robson   Founded: 1935
Secretary: I. Bristow   Tel no: Bridlington 76625
Team manager: G. Quinn
Colours: Yellow shirts with blue trim, blue shorts, yellow socks
Change colours: White shirts
Address and tel no of ground: Queensgate Football Ground, Queensgate, Bridlington, N. Humberside (Bridlington 74797)
Ground capacity: 3,757   Seating capacity: 300
Covered accommodation: 800   Floodlights: No
Best season in F.A. Cup: 1960–61
Major honours: Yorkshire League Cup winners
                                       Programme: 10p
Local newspapers: Hull Daily Mail, Bridlington Free Press

BRIDLINGTON TRINITY
(MID. COUNTIES)

Chairman: H. F. Catt   Founded: 1935
Secretary: H. F. Catt   Tel no: Bridlington 73974
Team manager: J. Thompson
Previous leagues: East Riding Amateur, Yorkshire
Colours: Green shirts, white shorts, white socks
Change colours: Maroon shirts, white shorts, white socks
Address and tel no of ground: Queensgate, Bridlington, N. Humberside (Bridlington 74797)
Ground capacity: 3,575   Seating capacity: 300
Covered accommodation: 800   Floodlights: No
Clubhouse details: Club in Blenheim Road, Bridlington, N. Humberside
Best season in F.A. Cup: 1970-71
Major honours: Yorkshire League Div 2 champions; Yorkshire League Div 1 champions three times; Yorkshire League Cup winners twice; ERCFA Cup winners five times
Best season in F.A. Trophy: 1969-70 and 1973-74, 1st Rnd Proper
Club nickname: The Emerald Greens Programme: 8 pages, free
Local newspapers: Hull Daily Mail, Bridlington Free Press

BRIDPORT (WESTERN)

Chairman: N. Frampton
Secretary: E. Aylott
Team manager: R. Hanford
Previous league: Dorset Combination
Colours: Black and red stripes
Change colours: White with black and red trim
Address and tel no of ground: St Mary's Field, South Street, Bridport, Dorset (Bridport 23834)
Ground capacity: 2,500   Seating capacity: 150
Covered accommodation: 400   Floodlights: No
Clubhouse details: Clubhouse (The Beehive) on ground, weekend dancing, bar snacks, licensed for 250
Best season in F.A. Cup: 4th Qual Rnd
Major honours: Dorset Senior Cup winners 1971, 1976; Western League Cup winners 1970-71, 1972-73, 1977-78
Club nickname: The Bees   Programme: 6 pages, 10p

Founded: 1887
Tel no: Burton Bradstock 224

BRIERLEY HILL (WEST MIDLANDS)

Chairman: D. S. Lawley
Secretary: A. R. Billingham
Team manager: R. Whitehouse
Previous leagues: Birmingham League founder members, league name later changed to West Midlands
Colours: White shirts, black shorts, black socks Change colours: All red
Address of ground: The Dell Stadium, Bryce Road, Pensnett, Brierley Hill, West Midlands   Record attendance: 8,000 (1962)
Ground capacity: 5,000   Seating capacity: 200
Covered accommodation: 200   Floodlights: No
Clubhouse details: New clubhouse open 1979-80
Best season in F.A. Cup: 1962, beaten by Shrewsbury Town 2nd Rnd
Current players with Football League experience: M. Fudge (WBA and Exeter)
Major honours: Birmingham League champions 1951, 1952; Birmingham Senior Cup winners; Worcestershire Senior Cup winners; West Midlands Premier League Cup winners 1978-79
Best season in F.A. Vase: Never past 1st Rnd
Club nickname: The Lions   Programme: 8 pages, 5p
Local newspaper: Express & Star

Founded: 1888
Tel no: Brierley Hill 70634

BRIGG TOWN (MID COUNTIES)

Chairman: H. Williams
Secretary: F. Major
Team manager: J. Lakin
Previous league: Lincs
Colours: Black and white stripes

Founded: 1864
Tel no: Brigg 52553

Change colours: All blue or blue and white
Address and tel no of ground: Hawthorn Avenue, Brigg, S. Humberside
  (Brigg 52767)
Ground capacity: 5,000   Seating capacity: 700
Covered accommodation: Stand and 2 enclosures   Floodlights: No
Clubhouse details: Open seven nights a week and at lunchtimes on Saturday
  and Sunday, hot and cold snacks, steward: K. Parker (Scunthorpe 2759)
Major honours: Midland Counties League champions 1977-78; Lincoln-
  shire League champions eight times; Lincolnshire Senior Cup winners
  1976, 1977, 1978
Programme: 4 pages, 5p

BROMLEY   (B.I.L. DIV 1)

Chairman: G. T. Ransom   Founded: 1892
Secretary: J. M. Cooper   Tel no: 01-464 3005
Team manager: J. W. Biddle
Colours: White shirts, black shorts, black socks
Change colours: Red shirts, black shorts, white socks
Address and tel no of ground: Hayes Lane, Bromley, Kent (01-460 5291)
                                   Record attendance: 10,000
Ground capacity: 15,000   Seating capacity: 2,000
Covered accommodation: 3,000   Floodlights: Yes
Clubhouse details: Open on match days and for functions
Best season in F.A. Cup: 1976-77
Major honours: F.A. Amateur Cup winners 3 times; London Senior Cup
  winners 3 times; Kent Senior Cup winners 2 times; Athenian League
  champions 3 times; Isthmian League champions 4 times
Best season in F.A. Trophy: Never past 2nd Qual Rnd
Local newspapers: Bromley Times, Bromley Advertiser

BROMSGROVE ROVERS   (S.L.M.)

Chairman: C. W. Poole   Founded: 1885
Secretary: S. A. Cross   Tel no: 021-445 3809 (h);
                                   Bromsgrove 73028 (bus)
Team manager: R. Martin
Previous leagues: West Midlands (R), Birmingham Combination
Colours: Green and white   Change colours: All white
Address and tel no of ground: Victoria Ground, Birmingham Road (A38),
  Bromsgrove, Worcs (Bromsgrove 73028)
                                   Record attendance: 7,563 (1957-58)
Ground capacity: 7,000   Seating capacity: 350
Covered accommodation: 1,350   Floodlights: Yes
Clubhouse details: Licensed club, open from Monday to Saturday
Best season in F.A. Cup: 1st Rnd Proper four times
Major honours: Birmingham Combination League champions 1946-47;
  Birmingham Senior Cup winners 1946-47; Birmingham League cham-
  pions 1959-60; Worcs Senior Cup winners 1946-47, 1947-48, 1959-60;
  Southern League Cup winners 1973-74
Best season in F.A. Trophy: 1975-76, 4th Rnd
Club nickname: The Greens   Programme: 12 pages, 10p
Local newspaper: Bromsgrove Messenger

BURNHAM (K. ATHENIAN)

Chairman: Jack Adaway **Founded:** 1878
Secretary: Michael Boxall **Tel no:** Maidenhead 31518
Team manager: Malcolm Higton
Previous leagues: South Bucks & East Berks, Great Western Suburban, Windsor Slough & District, Great Western Combination, Wycombe Combination, Reading Combination, Hellenic
Colours: Blue and white quartered shirts, black shorts
Change colours: All red
Address and tel no of ground: Wymers Wood Road, Burnham, Slough, Berks, SL1 8JG (Burnham 2697/2467)
Ground capacity: 2,000 **Seating capacity:** 200
Covered accommodation: Stands **Floodlights:** No
Clubhouse details: Open every lunchtime and evening, regular live entertainment, lunches and bar snacks, full-time steward
Best season in F.A. Cup: 1975–76, 2nd Qual Rnd
Current players with Football League experience: M. James (Reading); M. Jones (Fulham, Orient, Charlton Ath); B. Gould (Peterborough Utd)
Major honours: Hellenic League Prem Div champions 1975–76; Hellenic League Cup winners 1975–76
Best season in F.A. Vase: 1977–78, 6th Rnd
Programme: 20 pages, 5p
Local newspapers: Slough Observer, Windsor Slough & Eton Express, Evening Mail, Bucks Free Press, Maidenhead Advertiser

BURSCOUGH (CHESHIRE CO. DIV 1)

Chairman: F. Parr **Founded:** 1946
Secretary: G. T. Clarke **Tel no:** Burscough 880159
Team manager: George Rooney
Previous leagues: Liverpool County Combination, Lancashire Combination
Colours: Green shirts, white shorts, white socks
Change colours: All red
Address and tel no of ground: Victoria Park, Mart Lane, Burscough, Lancs (Burscough 893237) **Record attendance:** 3,500 (1951)
Ground capacity: 5,000 **Seating capacity:** 500
Covered accommodation: Stand, back of goal covered **Floodlights:** Yes
Clubhouse details: 'Linnets' social club, variety entertainment at weekends, bingo on Mondays, under-18 disco on Fridays
Best seasons in F.A. Cup: 1959–60, lost to Crewe Alexandra 5–1 1st Rnd Proper; 1977–1978, lost to Blyth Spartans 1–0 1st Rnd Proper
Major honours: Cheshire League Cup winners 1974–75; Lancashire Junior Cup winners 1947–48, 1949–50, 1966–67
Best seasons in F.A. Trophy: 1970–71, 1973–74 and 1974–75, 2nd Rnd Proper
Club nickname: The Linnets **Programme:** 8 pages, 5p
Local newspaper: Ormskirk Advertiser

BURTON ALBION (S.L.M.)

Chairman: C. B. Robinson Founded: 1950
Secretary: David M. Mellor Tel no: Burton 812116
Team manager: Ian Storey-Moore
Previous league: Birmingham Senior
Colours: Amber shirts, black shorts, black socks
Change colours: All white
Address and tel no of ground: Eton Park, Burton-on-Trent, Staffs (Burton-on-Trent 65938) Record attendance: 5,100 (1975)
Ground capacity: 8,000 - 10,000 Seating capacity: 300
Covered accommodation: Behind one goal and three-quarters of one side
Floodlights: Yes
Clubhouse details: Open every night and lunchtimes on match days, bar, discos, snacks, steward Mr P. Harding
Best season in F.A. Cup: 1956, lost to Charlton 5th Rnd
Current players with Football League experience: I. Storey-Moore; J. McCann; K. Blair; P. Annable
Major honours: Southern League Cup winners 1964; Birmingham Senior Cup winners 1954; Staffs Senior Cup winners 1956
Best season in F.A. Trophy: 1975, Semi-final
Club nickname: The Brewers Programme: 10p
Local newspapers: Burton Daily Mail, Derby Evening Telegraph

BURY TOWN (TOWN & COUNTRY)

Chairman: R. Mingay Founded: 1875
Secretary: E. F. Barbrooke Tel no: Bury St Edmunds 4115
Team manager: P. Smith
Previous leagues: Norfolk & Suffolk, Metropolitan, Southern
Colours: Blue shirts with white trim, white shorts
Change colours: Orange shirts, blue shorts
Address and tel no of ground: Ram Meadow, Cotton Lane, Bury St Edmunds, Suffolk (Bury St Edmunds 4721)
  Record attendance: 3,500 (1968)
Ground capacity: 5,000 Seating capacity: 200
Covered accommodation: Being built Floodlights: Yes
Best season in F.A. Cup: 1969-70
Major honours: Suffolk Premier Cup winners 1958-59, 1959-60, 1960-61 1961-62, 1963-64, 1964-65, 1965-66, 1970-71, 1977-78
Club nickname: The Blues Programme: 4 pages, 5p
Local newspapers: East Anglian, Bury Free Press

BUXTON (N.P.L.)

Chairman: S. Wheatcroft Founded: 1877
Secretary: R. A. Malpass Tel no: Buxton 3443
Team manager: C. Whitaker
Previous leagues: Combination, Manchester, Cheshire County
Colours: White shirts, blue shorts, white socks

Change colours: Amber shirts, blue or white shorts, amber socks
Address and tel no of ground: The Silverlands, Buxton, Derbyshire
  (Buxton 4733)   Record attendance: 5,000 plus (1962-63)
Ground capacity: 6,500   Seating capacity: 654
Covered accommodation: 2,500   Floodlights: Yes
Clubhouse details: Open most nights and Sunday lunchtimes, no food,
  bingo two nights per week, darts, dominoes (Buxton 3197)
Best seasons in F.A. Cup: 1951, 3rd Rnd Proper v Doncaster Rovers; 1958,
  2nd Rnd v Accrington Stanley; 1962, 1st Rnd v Barrow
League clubs defeated in F.A. Cup: Aldershot
Current players with Football League experience: K. Deakin (Brighton);
  D. Herbert (Chesterfield); G. Collier (Scunthorpe, York); W. Boslem
  (Rochdale); J. Hardman (Preston); G. Hull (Sheffield Wednesday,
  Barnsley)
Major honours: Manchester League champions 1931-32, 1961-62; Cheshire
  League champions 1972-73; Gilgryst Cup winners 1925, 1926, 1961;
  D.S. Cup winners 1938, 1945, 1956, 1959; Cheshire League Cup winners
  1956, 1957, 1958; Division Cup winners 1924-25, 1928-29, 1929-30,
  1931-32, 1932-33, 1935-36, 1953-54, 1959-60, 1962-63
Best seasons in F.A. Trophy: 1970-71 v Hillingdon Borough and 1971-72 v
  Telford, Quarter-finals
Club nickname: The Bucks   Programme: 4 pages, 10p
Local newspapers: Buxton Advertiser, Manchester Pink, Sheffield Green

---

CAMBERLEY TOWN   (B.I.L. DIV 1)

Chairman: P. G. Marsh   Founded: 1896
Secretary: J. A. Bartlett   Tel no: Camberley 35420 (h)
Team manager: P. Finn
Previous leagues: Surrey Senior, Spartan, Athenian
Colours: White shirts, white shorts, blue socks
Change colours: All red
Address and tel no of ground: Krooner Park, Camberley, Surrey
  (Camberley 65392/61203)
Ground capacity: 5,500   Seating capacity: 250
Covered accommodation: 250   Floodlights: Yes
Clubhouse details: New building, good facilities
Best season in F.A. Cup: 2nd Qual Rnd
Major honours: Berger Isthmian League Div 2 runners-up 1978-79
Club nickname: The Town   Programme: 8 pages, 5p
Local newspaper: Camberley News

CAMBRIDGE CITY   (S.L.M.)

Chairman: Mr D. G. Few   Founded: 1908
Secretary: Mr Pete Woolston   Tel no: Cambridge 57973 (club);
                                      Teversham 2558 (h)
Team manager: Mr Bill Leivers
Previous leagues: Southern Amateur, Athenian
Colours: White shirts, black shorts, red, white and black socks

93

Change colours: Red shirts, white shorts, red socks
Address and tel no of ground: City Ground, Milton Road, Cambridge, CB4 1UY (Cambridge 57973)   Record attendance: 11,574 (1963)
Ground capacity: 16,000   Seating capacity: 1,000
Covered accommodation: 8,000   Floodlights: Yes
Clubhouse details: Open every night, discos, dances, darts, stag nights, etc.
Best season in F.A. Cup: 1965, 1st Rnd Proper
Current players with Football League experience: D. Lyon; D. Simmons; D. Lill
Major honours: Cambridgeshire Professional Cup winners; Southern League Cup winners; East Anglian Cup winners; Cambridgeshire Invitation Cup winners; Southern League champions; Eastern Professional Floodlight League champions
Best seasons in F.A. Trophy: 1971–72 and 1977–78, 1st Rnd Proper
Club nickname: The City Devils   Programme: 16 pages, 10p
Local newspaper: Cambridge Evening News

CANTERBURY CITY   (S.L.S.)

Chairman: F. Wood   Founded: 1946
Secretary: V. H. Heslop   Tel no: Canterbury 68555 (h)
Team manager: Mike Buscall
Previous leagues: Kent, Metropolitan
Colours: Green shirts, white shorts, green socks
Change colours: All blue
Address and tel no of ground: Kingsmead Stadium, Kingsmead Road, Canterbury, Kent (Canterbury 64732)
Record attendance: 3,001 (1964-65)
Ground capacity: 10,000   Seating capacity: 600
Covered accommodation: 1,500   Floodlights: Yes
Clubhouse details: Open on match days
Best seasons in F.A. Cup: 1968-69, 1st Rnd Proper
Major honours: Kent League Div 1 Cup winners 1949-50; Kent League Div 2 Cup winners 1948-49; Kent Senior Cup winners 1953-54; Kent Intermediate Cup winners 1973-74; Kent Messenger Trophy winners 1974-75
Best season in F.A. Trophy: 1974-75, 2nd Rnd Proper
Club nickname: The City   Programme: 12 pages, 10p
Local newspapers: Kent Herald, Kentish Gazette

CARSHALTON ATHLETIC
(B.I.L. P. DIV)

Chairman: W. Stephenson   Founded: 1905
Secretary: C. R. Steward   Tel no: 01-640 5898
Team manager: P. Amato
Previous leagues: London, Corinthian, Suburban, Athenian, Surrey Senior
Colours: Maroon shirts, white shorts
Change colours: All white with maroon trimmings

94

Address and tel no of ground: War Memorial Sports Ground, Colston Avenue, Carshalton, Surrey (01-642 6858 – boardroom; 8425 clubhouse)

Record attendance: 8,000 (1949-50)

Ground capacity: 8,000   **Seating capacity:** 100

Covered accommodation: 5,000   **Floodlights:** Yes

Clubhouse details: Bands at weekends, bingo on Mondays, four men's and two ladies' darts teams

Best season in F.A. Cup: 1960, 1st Rnd Proper

Current players with Football League experience: M. Kelly (Charlton and Millwall); C. Allen (Birmingham)

Major honours: Amateur Cup winners twice; Surrey Senior Cup finalists; Surrey Senior Shield winners

Best season in F.A. Trophy: Never past 2nd Qual Rnd

Club nickname: The Robins   **Programme:** 16 pages, 10p

Local newspapers: Carshalton Times, Carshalton Advertiser

CHALFONT ST PETER (K. ATHENIAN)

Chairman: R. A. Clark   **Founded:** 1926

Secretary: P. D. Putman   **Tel no:** Chalfont St Giles 3664

Team manager: Keith Molton

Previous leagues: Great Western, London, Spartan, London Spartan, Athenian

Colours: Green shirts, white shorts, red socks

Change colours: Red shirts, black shorts, green socks

Address and tel no of ground: The Playing Fields, Amersham Road, Chalfont St Peter, Bucks (Gerrards Cross 85797)

Ground capacity: 4,000   **Seating capacity:** 220

Covered accommodation: Stand   **Floodlights:** Yes

Clubhouse details: Open every evening, match day afternoons and Sunday lunchtimes from 12.00 p.m. to 2 p.m., two bars, dance hall

Best season in F.A. Cup: 1978-79, 2nd Qual Rnd

Major honours: London Spartan League Div 2 champions 1975-76; Berks & Bucks Senior Cup finalists 1977-78; Athenian League Cup winners 1976-77; Berks & Bucks Benevolent Cup winners 1964-65

Best seasons in F.A. Vase: 1975-76, 1976-77 and 1977-78, 3rd Rnd

Club nickname: The Saints   **Programme:** 16 pages, 10p

Local newspapers: Bucks Advertiser, Bucks Examiner, Bucks Free Press

CHATHAM TOWN   (KENT)

Chairman: G. D. Swayland   **Founded:** 1882

Secretary: A. E. Cook   **Tel no:** Medway 35314

Team managers: A. Hughes and J. Whiteley   **Previous name:** Medway

Previous leagues: Southern, South Eastern, Aetolian, Metropolitan

Colours: Red with gold trim   **Change colours:** All white

Address and tel no of ground: Maidstone Road Sports Ground, Chatham, Kent (Medway 43678)

Ground capacity: 6,000   **Seating capacity:** 750

Covered accommodation: 850   **Floodlights:** Yes

Clubhouse details: Open Tuesday, Thursday and Saturday and as required, fully licensed, hot snacks

Best season in F.A. Cup: 1888–89, quarter-final

Current players with Football League experience: R. Harrison (Gillingham)
Major honours: Kent League champions 1972, 1974, 1977; Kent Cup winners; Kent County Medal winners; Kent Senior Cup winners; Kent Victory Cup winners; Kent League champions; Aetolian League champions; Aetolian Cup winners
Best season in F.A. Trophy: 1973–74, 3rd Qual Rnd
Club nickname: The Chats   Programme: 16 pages, 10p
Local newspapers: Chatham News & Standard, Kent Evening Post, Kent Messenger

CHELMSFORD CITY (S.L.S.)

Chairman: C. Seymour   Founded: 1938
Secretary: V. A. W. Keeble   Tel no: Earls Colne 2978
Team manager: John Newman
Previous league: Southern .
Colours: White shirts with claret trim, white shorts, white socks
Change colours: All blue
Address and tel no of ground: The Stadium, New Writtle Street, Chelmsford, Essex (Chelmsford 353052)   Record attendance: 16,807 (1949)
Ground capacity: 16,500   Seating capacity: 1,500
Covered accommodation: 12,500   Floodlights: Yes
Clubhouse details: Social club on ground, open match days, most evenings and Sunday lunchtimes, membership 25p per year
Best season in F.A. Cup: 1938–39, lost to Birmingham City 4th Rnd
League clubs defeated in F.A. Cup: Darlington, Southampton, Oxford Utd
Current players with Football League experience: F. Peterson (Millwall) P. Beal (Spurs, Brighton); S. Bright (Colchester)
Major honours: Southern League champions 1945-46, 1967-68, 1971-72; Southern League Cup winners 1945-46, 1959-60; Essex Pro Cup winners 1957-58, 1969-70, 1973-74, 1974-75; Non-League Champions Challenge Cup winners 1971-72
Best season in F.A. Trophy: 1969-70, Semi-final lost to Telford Utd
Club nickname: The City   Programme: 16 pages, 15p
Local newspapers: Essex Chronicle, Essex Weekly News

CHELTENHAM TOWN (S.L.M.)

Chairman: H. F. W. Bishop   Founded: 1892
Secretary: Reg Woodward   Tel no: Cheltenham 602261 (h); 56328 (bus); 53397 (club)
Team manager: Terry Paine, MBE
Previous league: Birmingham Combination
Colours: All red with white trimmings   Change colours: All blue
Address and tel no of ground: Whaddon Road, Cheltenham, Gloucestershire (Cheltenham 53397/21974)   Record attendance: 8,326 (1956)
Ground capacity: 13,000   Seating capacity: 2,000
Covered accommodation: 8,000   Floodlights: Yes
Clubhouse details: Steward: Les Trinder, two bars, function room (Robins' Nest) to hire, entertainment most Saturday nights

Best season in F.A. Cup: 1933–34, v Carlisle
Current players with Football League experience: J. Miles (Newport);
R. Dean (Aldershot and Reading); D. Dangerfield (Swindon and
Charlton); D. Brown (Chelsea, Swindon, Northampton and Aldershot)
Major honours: Gloucestershire Senior Cup (North) winners 23 times;
Southern League Cup winners 1956–57; Southern League runners-up
1955–56
Best season in F.A. Trophy: 1978–79, 3rd Rnd Proper
Club nickname: The Robins   Programme: 16 pages, 10p
Local newspaper: Gloucestershire Echo

CHESHAM UNITED   (B.I.L. DIV 1)

Chairman: D. W. Flitney   Founded: 1917
Secretary: G. M. Povey   Tel no: Chesham 76372
Team manager: M. Hall
Previous leagues: Spartan, Corinthian, Athenian
Colours: Claret and blue shirts, white shorts, yellow socks
Change colours: White shirts, white shorts, red socks
Address and tel no of ground: Sports Ground, Amersham Road, Chesham,
Bucks (Chesham 2456)   Record attendance: 4,500 (1968)
Ground capacity: 4,500   Seating capacity: 426
Covered accommodation: Both sides   Floodlights: Yes
Clubhouse details: Open most nights, bar, regular dances, also available for
private hire
Best seasons in F.A. Cup: 1966-67, 1st Rnd v Enfield, 1968-69 1st Rnd v
Colchester Utd and 1976-77 1st Rnd v Brentford
Current players with Football League experience: J. Watt (Watford)
Major honours: Berks and Bucks Senior Cup winners nine times; Spartan
League champions 1922, 1923, 1925, 1933; Amateur Cup finalists 1968
Best season in F.A. Trophy: 1976-77, 2nd Qual Rnd
Club nickname: United   Programme: 12 pages, 10p
Local newspaper: Bucks Examiner

CHESHUNT   (B.I.L. DIV 2)

Chairman: J. L. Rea   Founded: 1946
Secretary: R. H. Carter   Tel no: 01-802 5860
Team manager: G. Sedgley
Previous leagues: London, London Premier, Delphian, Aetolian, Spartan,
Athenian
Colours: Yellow with blue trim
Change colours: Blue with yellow trim or all red
Address and tel no of ground: The Stadium, Theobalds Lane, Cheshunt,
Herts (Waltham Cross 26752)   Record attendance: 8,000 (1950)
Ground capacity: 4,000   Seating capacity: 300
Covered accommodation: 400   Floodlights: Yes
Clubhouse details: Open every night, two bars, discos, pool, cabaret, snacks

Best seasons in F.A. Cup: 1958-59, 1966-67, 1970-71 and 1977-78, 4th Qual Rnd

Major honours: London League champions 1947, 1948, 1949, 1950; Spartan League champions 1962-63; Athenian League Div 1 champions 1967-68; Athenian League champions Prem Div 1975-76; Athenian Challenge Cup winners 1974, 1975, 1976; Spartan Challenge Cup winners 1963-64; Mithras Cup winners 1970-71; London Charity Cup winners 1973-74; East Anglian Cup winners 1974-75

Best season in F.A. Vase: 1978-79, 5th Rnd

Programme: 16 pages, 10p

Local newspapers: Cheshunt & Waltham Telegraph, Lea Valley Mercury

---

CHIPPING NORTON TOWN
(M. COMB.)

Chairman: J. Sale   Founded: 1893
Secretary: D. Mason   Tel no: Chipping Norton 3246
Team manager: B. Robinson
Previous leagues: Oxfordshire Senior, Hellenic
Colours: Black and white striped shirts, black shorts, black socks
Change colours: All blue
Address and tel no of ground: Hailey Road Ground, Chipping Norton, Oxon (Chipping Norton 2562)   Record attendance: 2,000
Ground capacity: 2,000   Seating capacity: None
Covered accommodation: Two stands Floodlights: No
Clubhouse details: Open every night, entertainment two nights a week
Current players with Football League experience: M. Way (Oxford United)
Major honours: Midland Combination League champions 1977-78
Best season in F.A. Vase: 1974-75, 4th Rnd
Club nickname: The Magpies   Programme: 10 pages, 5p
Local newspapers: Oxford Mail and Times

CHORLEY
(CHESHIRE CO. P. DIV)

Chairman: J. Tolson   Founded: 1875
Secretary: J. R. Warburton   Tel no: Chorley 77362
Team manager: A. N. Spence
Previous leagues: Lancashire Combination, Northern Premier
Colours: Black and white striped shirts, black shorts, white socks
Change colours: All blue or all white
Address and tel no of ground: Victory Park, Duke Street, Chorley, Lancs PR7 3DU (Chorley 3406)
Ground capacity: 13,000   Seating capacity: 830
Covered accommodation: Grandstand and behind goals   Floodlights: Yes
Clubhouse details: Large concert room, games room, lounge, snacks
Best season in F.A. Cup: 1978-79, 1st Rnd Proper
Best season in F.A. Trophy: 1976-77, Quarter-final,
Club nickname: The Magpies   Programme: 8 pages 10p
Local newspapers: Chorley Guardian, Lancs Evening Post

CINDERFORD TOWN (M. COMB.)

Chairman: H. Morgan   Founded: 1920
Secretary: M. M. Bradley   Tel no: Cinderford 24018
Team manager: Len Hill
Previous leagues: Western, Warwickshire Combination, West Midlands, Gloucestershire County
Colours: All royal blue
Change colours: White shirts, black shorts
Address and tel no of ground: Causeway Ground, Hilldene, Cinderford. Glos (Cinderford 22039)
Ground capacity: 3,000   Seating capacity: 400
Covered accommodation: 900   Floodlights: No
Clubhouse details: Open seven nights a week, live groups, disco, skittles, bar snacks, steward: C. Hale (Cinderford 22039)
Best season in F.A. Cup: 3rd Qual Rnd
Programme: 12 pages, 5p

CLACTON TOWN (TOWN & COUNTRY)

Chairman: F. G. Darling   Founded: 1892
Secretary: S. R. L. Stean   Tel no: Clacton-on-Sea 22039
Team manager: C. I. Henson
Previous leagues: Eastern Counties, Essex & Suffolk Border, Essex Senior, Southern
Colours: Light blue shirts, royal blue shorts, light blue socks
Change colours: All red
Address and tel no of ground: Clacton Stadium, Old Road, Clacton-on-Sea, Essex (Clacton-on-Sea 32590)   Record attendance: 7,000 (1945)
Ground capacity: 2,500   Seating capacity: 750
Covered accommodation: None   Floodlights: No
Clubhouse details: Supporters' social club and bar, Vice-President club and bar
Best season in F.A. Cup: 1953-54 and 1960-61, 1st Rnd Proper
Current players with Football League experience: A. Dennis (Colchester Utd)
Major honours: Southern League Div 1 champions 1959-60; Eastern Counties League runners-up 1936-37, 1953-54, 1964-65, 1974-75; Southern League Cup winners 1973-74, finalists 1968-69; Essex Professional Cup finalists 1953-54, 1969-70; East Anglian Cup winners 1953-54, 1954-55, finalists 1955-56
Best seasons in F.A. Trophy: Never past 1st Qual Rnd
Club nickname: The Seasiders   Programme: 4 pages, 5p
Local newspapers: East Anglian Daily Times, East Essex Gazette, Evening Gazette

CLAPTON (B.I.L. DIV 1)

Chairman: A. Williams, M.B.E.
Secretary: M. McShea
Team manager: Bernie Dixson
Previous league: Southern
Colours: Red and white striped shirts, black shorts
Change colours: All white
Address and tel no of ground: Old Spotted Dog Ground, Upton Lane, Forest Gate, London, E.7 (01-472 1655)

Founded: 1878
Tel no: 01-472 3844 (bus)

Record attendance: 12,000 (1898-99)
Ground capacity: 5,500   Seating capacity: 378
Covered accommodation: Two stands Floodlights: Yes
Clubhouse details: Open Monday, Tuesday, Wednesday and Thursday evenings, Saturday afternoons and evenings and Sunday lunchtimes, steward – Eddie O'Donoghue
Best season in F.A. Cup: 1957-58, 1st Rnd Proper
Major honours: F.A. Amateur Cup winners 1906-07, 1908-09, 1914-15, 1923-24, 1924-25; London Senior Cup winners 1889-90, 1908-09, 1910-11; Essex Senior Cup winners 1890-91, 1914-15, 1925-26, 1954-55; Isthmian League champions 1910-11, 1922-23
Club nickname: The Tons   Programme: 6 pages, 5p
Local newspapers: Newham Recorder, Stratford Express

CLEVEDON TOWN (WESTERN)

Chairman: L. G. Stacey
Secretary: J. W. MacColl

Founded: 1880
Tel no: Clevedon 874826 (h); Bristol 668141 (bus)

Team manager: D. R. Robbins
Previous leagues: Bristol & District, Bristol & Suburban, Somerset Senior, Bristol Charity, Bristol Premier Combination
Colours: Royal blue shirts, white shorts, blue socks
Change colours: White shirts, navy blue shorts, white socks
Address and tel no of ground: Teignmouth Road, Clevedon, Avon (Clevedon 871636)   Record attendance: 10,000 (1947)
Ground capacity: 2,500   Covered accommodation: One side and small area behind one goal
Floodlights: No
Clubhouse details: Skittle alley, social club, new clubhouse planned late 1979
Current players with Football League experience: R. Mabbutt (Bristol Rovers, Newport County)
Major honours: Somerset Senior Cup winners 1902, 1905, 1929, 1977; Somerset Senior League champions 1936-37; Bristol Charity League champions 1937-38
Best season in F.A. Trophy: Never past 1st Qual Rnd
Club nickname: Formerly The Seasiders   Programme: Free
Local newspapers: South Avon Mercury, Western Daily Press, Bristol Evening Post

CONSETT (D. NORTHERN)

Chairman: Ernest Swinburn
Secretary: Alan Shearer
Team manager: J. B. Suddes
Founded: Early 1900s
Tel no: Lanchester 520895

Previous leagues: Northern Combination, Midland, North Eastern,
Northern Counties, Wearside
Colours: All tangerine with black trim
Change colours: Blue shirts, white shorts, blue socks
Address and tel no of ground: Belle Vue Park, Consett, Co Durham
(Consett 503788)
Record attendance: 7,500 (1947–48)
Ground capacity: 10,000 plus
Seating capacity: 500
Covered accommodation: 2,000
Floodlights: Yes
Clubhouse details: Open Tuesday evenings and home matches
Best season in F.A. Cup: 1958–59, 1st Rnd Proper v Doncaster Rovers
Current players with Football League experience: A. Foggon (Newcastle,
Cardiff, Man Utd, Middlesbro); G. Hindson (Newcastle, Luton Town);
C. Symm (Sheff Wed, Sunderland)
Major honours: North Eastern League champions 1939–40; Northern
Counties League champions 1961–62; Northern League runners-up
1976–77; Durham County Challenge Cup winners 1945–46, 1947–48,
1958–59, 1960–61, 1968–69
Best season in F.A. Trophy: 1978–79, 2nd Rnd Proper
Club nickname: The Steelmen
Programme: 12 pages, 5p
Local newspapers: Consett Chronicle, Consett Guardian

CORBY TOWN (S.L.M.)

Chairman: J. G. Kane
Secretary: M. McIlwain
Team manager: M. McIlwain
Founded: 1948
Tel no: Corby 4650

Previous leagues: United Counties, Midland
Colours: White shirts, black shorts
Change colours: Claret and blue shirts, sky blue shorts
Address and tel no of ground: P.O. Box 7, Occupation Road, Corby, North-
hants (Corby 3619)
Record Attendance: 11,500 (1954)
Ground capacity: 14,000
Seating capacity: 600
Covered accommodation: 10,000
Floodlights: Yes
Clubhouse details: Open seven days a week, usual club facilities, steward:
A. McNair (Corby 3619)
Best season in F.A. Cup: 1st Rnd Proper five times
Major honours: United Counties League champions 1950-51, 1951-52;
Northants Senior Cup winners 1951, 1963, 1976
Best season in F.A. Trophy: 1975-76, 2nd Rnd Proper
Club nickname: The Steelmen
Programme: 16 pages, 15p
Local newspaper: Kettering Evening Telegraph

CORINTHIAN CASUALS (B.I.L. DIV 2)

Chairman: T. R. Liddle   Founded: 1939
Secretary: N. F. Epps   Tel no: Brighton 736882
Team secretary: J. A. Cracknell
Previous leagues: Isthmian (The Casuals), Southern (Cornithians), pre-amalgamation
Colours: White shirts, navy blue shorts, white socks
Change colours: Chocolate and pink shirts, chocolate shorts, chocolate and pink socks
Address and tel no of ground: Sandy Lane, Mitcham, Surrey (01-648 3248)
Ground capacity: 8,000-10,000   Seating capacity: 1,900
Covered accommodation: 2,000   Floodlights: Yes
Clubhouse details: Situated under the stand, facilities for approx. 100
Best season in F.A. Cup: 1965-66, 1st Rnd Proper
Current players with Football League experience: K. East; S. Hamer; S. Pitt
Best season in F.A. Trophy: 1978-79, 2nd Qual Rnd
Programme: 8 pages, 10p
Local newspaper: South London Press

CRAWLEY TOWN (S.L.S.)

Chairman: B. H. Finer   Founded: 1946
Secretary: S. H. Markham   Tel no: Crawley 22371
Previous leagues: Sussex County, Metropolitan
Colours: All red
Change colours: White shirts, black shorts, blue socks
Address and tel no of ground: Town Mead, Ifield Avenue, West Green, Crawley, Sussex (Crawley 21800)   Record attendance: 3,052 (1969)
Ground capacity: 5,000   Seating capacity: 250
Covered accommodation: 1,500   Floodlights: Yes
Clubhouse details: Private membership
Best seasons in F.A. Cup: 1970-71 and 1971-72, 1st Rnd Proper
Best season in F.A. Trophy: Never past 2nd Qual Rnd
Programme: 6 pages, 5p
Local newspapers: Crawley Observer, Crawley Advertiser

CROCKENHILL (KENT)

Chairman: A. Buck   Founded: 1946
Secretary: C. J. A. Nicholls   Tel no: Swanley 62719
Previous leagues: Kent Amateur, Aetolian, Greater London
Colours: Red and white striped shirts, black shorts, red and black socks
Change colours: Blue and yellow
Address and tel no of ground: 'Wested', Eynsford Road, Crockenhill, Swanley, Kent (Swanley 62097)   Record attendance: 800 (1948)
Ground capacity: 2,000   Seating capacity: 200
Covered accommodation: 400   Floodlights: No
Clubhouse details: Licensed bar seating 100 persons
Best season in F.A. Vase: 1974-75, 4th Rnd
Club nickname: The Crocks   Programme: 4 pages
Local newspapers: Kentish Times, Kent Messenger

CROOK TOWN (D. NORTHERN)

Chairman: W. Collingwood
Secretary: R. W. Singleton
Team manager: B. Newton
Previous league: North Eastern
Colours: Amber and black
Founded: 1889
Tel no: Crook 2175

Change colours: All white

Address and tel no of ground: Milfield Ground, Crook, Co Durham (Crook 2959)
Ground capacity: 9,000
Covered accommodation: 1,500
Seating capacity: 1,000
Floodlights: Yes
Clubhouse details: Open every night, entertainment, steward: Mrs A. Nicholson (Crook 2959)
Best season in F.A. Cup: 1931-32, 3rd Rnd
Major honours: F.A. Amateur Cup winners 1901, 1954, 1957, 1962,1964; Northen League champions five times; Durham County Cup winners 1927, 1932, 1955, 1960
Best season in F.A. Trophy: 1976-77, 3rd Rnd
Programme: 6-8 pages, 5p
Local newspaper: Northern Echo

CROYDON (B.I.L. P. DIV)

Chairman: J. H. Milsted
Secretary: R. Guest
Team manager: T. Shepherd
Previous leagues: Surrey Senior, Spartan, Athenian
Colours: Light and dark blue
Founded: 1953
Tel no: 01-656 9230

Change colours: All red

Address and tel no of ground: Croydon Sports Arena, Albert Road, South Norwood, London, S.E.25 (01-654 5524)
Record attendance: 1,450 (1976)
Ground capacity: 15,000
Covered accommodation: 500
Seating capacity: 500
Floodlights: Yes
Clubhouse details: Open every night and Sunday lunchtimes, entertainment on Saturdays and Sundays, bingo and functions mid-week, steward: F. Sterling (01-654 8555)
Best season in F.A. Cup: 1975-76, 4th Qual Rnd
Current players with Football League experience: P. Bonetti (Chelsea); A. Jackson (Chelsea)
Major honours: Isthmian League Div 2 runners-up 1975-76; Athenian League Div 1 runners-up 1971-72; Athenian League Div 2 champions 1965-66, runners-up 1970-71; Spartan League champions 1963-64
Best season in F.A. Trophy: 1978-79, 3rd Qual Rnd
Club nickname: The Blues
Programme: 12 pages, 10p
Local newspaper: Croydon Advertiser

CURZON ASHTON
(CHESHIRE CO. DIV 1)

President: Maurice Rubin
Secretary: Harry Twamley
Team manager: Bill Chell
Previous league: Manchester
Colours: Blue and white

Founded: 1963
Tel no: 061-330 3028

Change colours: White and blue
Address and tel no of ground: National Park, Burlington Street, Ashton-under-Lyne, Lancs (061-308 3906) Record attendance: 1,100 (1978)
Ground capacity: 4,320
Seating capacity: 120
Covered accommodation: Two stands Floodlights: No
Clubhouse details: Open for club social functions, meetings, match days, etc.
Best season in F.A. Cup: 1978-79
Major honours: Manchester League Intermediate Cup winners 3 times
Best season in F.A. Vase: 1977-78, 4th Rnd
Programme: 4 pages, 5p
Local newspaper: Ashton-under-Lyne Reporter

DAGENHAM
(B.I.L. P. DIV)

Chairman: V. Sparrow
Secretary: E. J. Collier

Founded: 1949
Tel no: Stanford-le-Hope 3830
(h); 01-637 5781 (bus)

Team manager: Eddie Presland
Previous leagues: Metropolitan, Delphian, Corinthian, Athenian, Isthmian
Colours: All red
Change colours: All white or blue shirts, black shorts, blue socks
Address and tel no of ground: Victoria Road Ground, Dagenham, Essex (01-592 1549 - club; 01-592 7194 - offices; 01-593 3864 - promotions)
Record attendance: 7,100 (1968)
Ground capacity: 8,000
Seating capacity: 507
Covered accommodation: 2,500
Floodlights: Yes
Clubhouse details: Four bars, socials, cabaret shows, bingo, light meals on Saturdays before matches, Athenian and Isthmian Rooms available for private hire
Best season in F.A. Cup: 1967-68, lost to Reading 2nd Rnd Replay
Current players with Football League experience: T. Scales (Brentford); D. Bond (Watford, Charlton and Tottenham); Tommy Horan (West Ham)
Major honours: Essex Senior Cup winners 1962, 1968, 1971, 1978, finalists 1956, 1973, 1975; London Senior Cup winners 1968, finalists 1965, 1969; F.A. Amateur Cup finalists 1970, 1971; F.A. Challenge Trophy finalists 1977; Isthmian League Prem Div runners-up 1978; Isthmian League Div 2 champions 1974
Best season in F.A. Trophy: 1976-77, Final
Club nickname: The Daggers
Programme: 16 pages, 10p
Local newspapers: Barking Advertiser, Dagenham Post

DARTFORD (S.L.S.)

Chairman: E. Boyle Cussen
Secretary: J. Vigar
Team manager: Graham Carr
Previous league: Kent
Colours: White shirts, black shorts, black socks
Change colours: Red shirts, white shorts, red socks
Address and tel no of ground: Watling Street, Stone, Dartford, Kent, DA2
6EN (Dartford 24200/76486/73639

Founded: 1921
Tel no: Dartford 22839

Record attendance: 11,004 (1951-52)
Ground capacity: 9,750
Seating capacity: 750
Covered accommodation: 750 plus
Floodlights: Yes
Clubhouse details: Open match days and Monday, Tuesday, Thursday and
Saturday evenings
Best season in F.A. Cup: 1935-36, 2nd Rnd
League clubs defeated in F.A. Cup: Swindon, Bristol Rovers, Bristol City,
Bournemouth, Leyton Orient, Darlington, Port Vale, Exeter City, Aldershot, Cardiff, Derby County
Current players with Football League experience: A. Horsfield (Newcastle,
Charlton, Watford); A. Burns (Plymouth); A. Burman (Charlton,
QPR); W. O. Sullivan (Charlton); R. Tumbridge (Charlton)
Major honours: F.A. Trophy finalists 1973-74; Southern League champions 1930-31, 1931-32, 1973-74; Kent Senior Cup winners 1930-31,
1931-32, 1932-33, 1934-35, 1946-47, 1969-70, 1972-73
Best season in F.A. Trophy: 1973-74, Finalists
Club nickname: The Darts
Programme: 24 pages, 15p
Local newspapers: Kentish Times, Gravesend & Dartford Reporter, Kent
(Gravesend and Dartford) Evening Post

DARWEN (CHESHIRE CO. DIV. 1)

Chairman: Mr R. Eccles
Secretary: Mr A. W. Durkin
Team manager: J. D. Birkett
Previous leagues: Football League Divisions 1 and 2, Lancs Combination
Colours: All sky blue
Change colours: All maroon
Address and tel no of ground: Anchor Ground, Anchor Road, Darwen,
Lancs (Darwen 75627)
Ground capacity: 9,000
Founded: 1875
Tel no: Darwen 772029

Record attendance: 9,000 (pre-1914)
Seating capacity: None
Covered accommodation: Two sides Floodlights: No
Clubhouse details: No clubhouse, but canteen with light refreshments
open on match days
Major honours: Lancashire Junior Cup winners 1932; Lancashire Combination champions 1931, 1933, 1973, 1975; Lancashire Combination
Cup winners 1975
Best season in F.A. Trophy: 1969-70, 3rd Qual Rnd
Club nickname: The Anchormen
Programme: 8 pages, 5p
Local newspaper: Darwen Advertiser & News

DAWLISH (WESTERN)

Chairman: R. J. Richards
Secretary: G. R. Turner
Team manager: P. Amos
Previous leagues: Western, Devon & Exeter
Colours: All green and white   Change colours: All royal blue
Address of ground: Playing Fields, Exeter Road, Dawlish, Devon
Founded: 1889
Tel no: Dawlish 862438

Record attendance: 1,200
Ground capacity: 2,000   Seating capacity: 200
Covered accommodation: None   Floodlights: No
Clubhouse details: None as yet
Current players with Football League experience: D. Harrison (Leicester, Torquay, Colchester)
Major honours: Devon Premier Cup winners twice, Devon Senior Cup winners twice
Best season in F.A. Trophy: 1977   Programme: 12 pages, 5p
Local newspapers: Dawlish Gazette, Exeter Express & Echo

DENABY UNITED (YORKSHIRE)

Chairman: K. Homer
Secretary: A. Jones
Team manager: J. Thompson
Previous league: Midland
Colours: Red shirts, white shorts
Change colours: Yellow shirts, black shorts
Address of ground: Tickhill Square, Denaby Main, Doncaster, South Yorkshire
Founded: 1902
Tel no: Rotherham 866316

Record attendance: 5,600
Ground capacity: 6,000   Seating capacity: 750
Covered accommodation: Two stands Floodlights: No
Clubhouse details: No clubhouse, but miners' welfare next to ground
Best season in F.A. Cup: 1958, 1st Rnd Proper
Major honours: Yorkshire League Cup winners; Sheffield Senior Cup winners
Best season in F.A. Vase: 3rd Rnd
Local newspapers: South Yorkshire Times, Doncaster Evening Post

DORCHESTER TOWN (S.L.S.)

Chairman: E. H. Ford
Secretary: A. E. Miller
Team manager: David Best
Previous league: Western
Colours: Black and white striped shirts, black shorts
Change colours: All red
Address and tel no of ground: The Avenue Ground, Dorchester, Dorset (Dorchester 2451)
Founded: 1880
Tel no: Dorchester 4843

Record attendance: 4,300 (1954-55)
Ground capacity: 6,000   Seating capacity: 300
Covered accommodation: 2,000   Floodlights: Yes

Clubhouse details: Magpie social club and Vice Presidents club within the ground, open every evening with a varying programme of events
Best seasons in F.A. Cup: 1954-55 and 1957-58, 2nd Rnd
Current players with Football League experience: D. Best (Bournemouth, Oldham, Ipswich, Portsmouth); H. Steele (Exeter City); W. Forman (Bristol Rovers)
Major honours: Western League champions 1954-55; Southern League Div 1 South runners-up 1977-78
Best season in F.A. Trophy: 1971-72, 3rd Rnd Proper
Club nickname: The Magpies   Programme: 16 pages, 10p
Local newspapers: Dorset Evening Echo, Western Gazette, Western Daily Press

DORKING TOWN   (K. ATHENIAN)

Chairman: T. Connors   Founded: 1977
Secretary: R. Young   Tel no: Dorking 882284 ext 50 (h);
Team manager: Stan Fry   ext 26 (bus)
Previous leagues: Suburban, Surrey Senior, Athenian
Colours: Green and white shirts, white shorts
Change colours: White shirts, red shorts
Address of ground: Meadowbank, Mill Lane, Dorking, Surrey
                                        Record attendance: 700
Ground capacity: 5,000   Seating capacity: 250
Covered accommodation: 600   Floodlights: Yes
Clubhouse details: Fully licensed, open on match days
Club nickname: The Chicks
Local newspapers: Dorking Advertiser, Surrey Advertiser

DOVER   (S.L.S.)

Chairman: J. Shearn   Founded: 1891
Secretary: J. Taylor   Tel no: Dover 202623
Team manager: A. Bentley
Previous league: Kent
Colours: White shirts, black shorts, red socks
Change colours: Yellow shirts, blue shorts, yellow socks
Address and tel no of ground: Crable Athletic Ground, Lewisham Road, Dover, Kent (Kearnsey 2306)   Record attendance: 6,900 (1955-56)
Ground capacity: 6,000   Seating capacity: 1,500
Covered accommodation: Three sides Floodlights: Yes
Clubhouse details: Social club with bars open each match day and on Thursday, Friday and Saturday evenings, cabaret on Sundays, light refreshments
Best season in F.A. Cup: 1975-76
League clubs defeated in F.A. Cup: Peterborough, Southend Utd
Current players with Football League experience: J. Horsfall (Halifax, Southend); A. Keeley (Gillingham); P. Hilton (Brighton, Blackburn); K. Rogers (Gillingham); A. Knight (Luton)
Major honours: Southern League Div 1 South champions 1978-79; Kent Senior Cup winners 1952, 1960, 1962, 1967, 1968, 1971, 1972
Best season in F.A. Trophy: 1970-71, 3rd Rnd Proper
Club nickname: The Lilywhites   Programme: 16 pages, 5p
Local newspaper: Dover Express

DROYLSDEN   (CHESHIRE CO. DIV 1)

Chairman: S. Orchant   **Founded:** 1866
Secretary: J. R. Gould   **Tel no:** 061-793 3174 (bus)
Team manager: A. Tivey
Previous leagues: Lancashire Combination, Manchester
Colours: All red   **Change colours:** All blue
Address of ground: Butchers Arms, Market Street, Droylsden, Manchester
         Record attendance: 4,250 (1976)
Ground capacity: 5,000   **Seating capacity:** 250
Covered accommodation: Stand and terracing
         Floodlights: Yes
Clubhouse details: Normal evening licensing hours, open during matches,
    bingo Wednesdays, Fridays, Saturdays and Sundays, entertainment
    Saturdays and Sundays
Best season in F.A. Cup: 1978-79
League clubs defeated in F.A. Cup: Rochdale
Current players with Football League experience: B. Wilson (Stockport
    County); A. Sweeney (Oldham); A. Jackson (Oldham)
Major honours: Manchester Senior Cup winners, Manchester Shield
    winners, Manchester Junior Cup winners, Cheshire League Cup winners
Best seasons in F.A. Trophy: 1973-74 and 1976-77, 3rd Qual Rnd
Club nickname: The Bloods   **Programme:** 8 pages, 5p
Local newspapers: Droylsden Reporter, Manchester Evening News

DUDLEY TOWN   (W. MID. R.)

Chairman: S. Bradley   **Founded:** 1893
Secretary: N. Jeynes   **Tel no:** Stourbridge 5741 (h)
Team manager: J. Edwards
Previous league: Birmingham Combination
Colours: Red shirts, white shorts, black and red socks
Change colours: All yellow
Address of ground: The Sports Centre, Birmingham Road, Dudley,
    West Midlands
Ground capacity: 3,000   **Seating capacity:** 1,200
Covered accommodation: 1,500   **Floodlights:** No
Clubhouse details: Open from Monday to Saturday, licensed bar, refresh-
    ment bar, steward: B. Bourne (Sedeley 72822 – home)
Best season in F.A. Cup: 1976, 1st Rnd Proper
Major honours: Worcestershire Combination League champions 1929–30,
    1931–32
Club nickname: The Robins   **Programme:** 8 pages, 5p

DULWICH HAMLET   (B.I.L.P. DIV)

Chairman: S. Gray   **Founded:** 1893
Secretary: N. Robinson   **Tel no:** 01–639 5726
Team manager: Alan Smith
Previous leagues: Camberwell, Southern Suburban, Dulwich

Colours: Pink and blue shirts, blue shorts, blue socks
Change colours: All yellow
Address and tel no of ground: Champion Hill Ground, Dog Kennel Hill, Dulwich, London, S.E.22 (01–274 5187)
Record attendance: 20,500 (1933)

Ground capacity: 20,000	Seating capacity: 2,000
Covered accommodation: 7,000	Floodlights: Yes

Clubhouse details: Two bars open on match days
Best seasons in F.A. Cup: 8 times to 1st Rnd Proper
Current players with Football League experience: A. Hart (Charlton Ath, Millwall)
Major honours: Isthmian League Prem Div champions 1919–20, 1925–26, 1932–33, 1948–49, Div 1 champions 1977–78; F. A. Amateur Cup winners 1919–20, 1931–32, 1933–34, 1936–37; London Senior Cup winners 1924–25, 1938–39, 1949–50; Surrey Senior Cup winners 1904–05, 1905–06, 1908–09, 1909–10, 1922–23, 1924–25, 1927–28, 1933–34, 1936–37, 1946–47, 1949–50, 1957–58, 1958–59, 1973–74, 1974–75
Best season in F.A. Trophy: 1975–76, 1st Rnd Proper
Club nickname: The Hamlet   Programme: 20 pages, 10p
Local newspapers: South London Press, South East London Mercury, West Norwood & Dulwich News

DUNSTABLE   (S.L.M.)

Chairman: Mr W. Kitt	Founded: 1895
Secretary: Mr Harold Stew	Tel no: Dunstable 63755

Team manager: Mr Brendan McNally
Previous leagues: Metropolitan, United Counties, Hellenic
Colours: Royal blue   Change colours: All white
Address and tel no of ground: Creasey Park, Brewers Hill Road, Dunstable, Beds (Dunstable 606691 – boardroom; 63800 – club)
Record attendance: 6,000 (1974)

Ground capacity: 10,000	Seating capacity: 500
Covered accommodation: 500	Floodlights: Yes

Clubhouse details: Large clubroom and bar, small room and bar, restaurant, full catering facilities
Best season in F.A. Cup: 1956, 1st Rnd Proper
Current players with Football League experience: D. Martin (Northampton)
Best seasons in F.A. Trophy: 1971–72 and 1975–76, 3rd Qual Rnd
Club nickname: The Blues   Programme: 6 pages, 10p
Local newspapers: Dunstable Gazette, Evening Post & Echo

DURHAM CITY   (D. NORTHERN)

Chairman: D. W. Asbery	Founded: 1949
Secretary: A. Young	Tel no: Durham 730727

Team manager: J. Raynor
Previous league: Wearside
Colours: Gold shirts, blue shorts, gold socks
Change colours: Blue shirts, black shorts, blue socks

Address and tel no of ground: Ferens Park, The Sands, Durham, DH1 1JY
  (Durham 3929) Record attendance: 7,000 (1956)
Ground capacity: 6,300 Seating capacity: 300
Covered accommodation: Stand Floodlights: Yes
Clubhouse details: Open every night
Best season in F.A. Cup: 1955–56, 2nd Rnd v Tranmere Rovers
Major honours: Durham Benevolent Bowl winners 1955–56; Northern
  League runners-up 1970–71; Durham Challenge Cup runners-up 1971–
  72, 1973–74
Best season in F.A. Trophy: 1977–78, 2nd Qual Rnd
Club nickname: The Citizens Programme: 8 pages, 5p
Local newspapers: Northern Echo, Durham Advertiser

EASTBOURNE UNITED (B.I.L. DIV 2)

Chairman: J. R. Stephens Founded: 1894
Secretary: D. Sissons Tel no: Eastbourne 30634
Team manager: Gerry Boon
Previous leagues: Eastbourne, Sussex County, Metropolitan, Spartan,
  Athenian
Colours: White shirts, black shorts, black socks
Change colours: Red shirts, white shorts, white socks
Address and tel no of ground: The Oval, Channel View Road, Eastbourne,
  Sussex (Eastbourne 26989) Record attendance: 1,500 (1979)
Ground capacity: 7,500 Seating capacity: 500
Covered accommodation: 2,500 Floodlights: Yes
Clubhouse details: Open five nights a week, club bar manager P. Colthrup
Best season in F.A. Cup: 1978–79
Best season in F.A. Vase: 1978–79, 6th Rnd
Club nickname: The U's Programme: 24 pages, 10p
Local newspaper: Eastbourne Gazette & Herald

EASTWOOD HANLEY
(CHESHIRE CO. DIV 2)

Chairman: A. J. Howle Founded: 1946
Secretary: C. R. Plant Tel no: Stoke-on-Trent 273275
Team manager: J. Wallace
Previous leagues: West Midlands Premier, Manchester
Colours: White shirts, blue shorts
Change colours: All blue or blue shirts, white shorts
Address and tel no of ground: Trentmill Road, Hanley, Stoke-on-Trent,
  Staffs (Stoke-on-Trent 29174)
Ground capacity: 12,500 Seating capacity: 300
Covered accommodation: 500 Floodlights: No
Clubhouse details: Open on Saturdays from 1 p.m. to 11 p.m., Sunday
  lunchtimes and every weekday from 3.30 p.m. to 10.30 p.m., excluding
  Wednesday, snacks available on match days
Programme: 6 pages, 5p

EASTWOOD TOWN (MID. COUNTIES)

Chairman: J. E. Sanby
Secretary: P. Farrell
Team manager: Bill Jeffrey
Founded: 1953
Tel no: Langley Mill 5500
Previous leagues: Notts Alliance, Central Alliance, East Midlands Premier
Colours: Black and white striped shirts, black shorts, black socks
Change colours: All yellow
Address and tel no of ground: Coronation Park, Eastwood, Notts
(Langley Mill 5823)
Ground capacity: 6,500
Covered accommodation: 1,000
Record attendance: 2,500 (1967-68)
Seating capacity: 100
Floodlights: No
Clubhouse details: Two bars, meals available, stewards – Mr and Mrs Jack Watson
Best season in F.A. Cup: 1975-76, 3rd Qual Rnd
Current players with Football League experience: M. Wright (Chesterfield); C. Egan (Derby County)
Major honours: Notts Senior Cup winners 1975-76, 1977-78, 1978-79; Midland League champions 1975-76; Midland League Cup winners 1977-78
Best season in F.A. Trophy: 1978-79, 1st Rnd Proper
Local newspapers: Eastwood & Kimberley Advertiser, Nottingham Evening Post

EDGWARE (K. ATHENIAN)

Chairman: E. Walker
Secretary: R. Lowe
Team manager: D. N. Finn
Founded: 1939
Tel no: 01–952 8790
Previous leagues: Delphian, Nemean
Colours: White with green and black trim
Change colours: Amber with black trim
Address and tel no of ground: White Lion Ground, High Street, Edgware, Middlesex (01–952 6799)
Ground capacity: 10,000
Covered accommodation: 1,200
Record attendance: 8,500 (1948)
Seating capacity: 250
Floodlights: Yes
Clubhouse details: Open seven days a week including lunchtimes, cabaret twice weekly, snacks, available for private hire
Best season in F.A. Cup: 1978–79, 4th QualRnd
Major honours: Middlesex Senior Cup runners-up twice
Best season in F.A. Vase: 1976–77, 3rd Rnd
Club nickname: The Wares
Programme: 4 pages, 5p
Local newspaper: Edgware & Mill Hill Times

EGHAM TOWN (B.I.L. DIV 2)

Chairman: A. L. Doye
Secretary: A. L. Doye
Team manager: G. Cooper
Founded: 1963
Tel no: Staines 55591
Previous leagues: Middlesex, Surrey Senior, Spartan, Athenian
Colours: Blue and gold
Change colours: All white

111

Address and tel no of ground: Tempest Road, Egham, Surrey (Egham 5226
Ground capacity: 5,000　　　　　Seating capacity: 250
Covered accommodation: Yes　　　Floodlights: Yes
Clubhouse details: Lounge bar, clubhouse capacity approx 120
Major honours: Spartan League champions 1971–72; Athenian League
champions 1974–75
Best seasons in F.A. Vase: 1975–76 and 1977–78, 3rd Rnd
Programme: 5p　　　　　　　　　Local newspapers: Staines & Egham
　　　　　　　　　　　　　　　　News, Evening Mail

EMLEY (YORKSHIRE)

Chairman: A. F. Hardy　　　　　　Founded: 1903
Secretary: G. Adamson　　　　　　Tel no: Kirkburton 2720
Team manager: Michael Pamment
Previous league: Huddersfield
Colours: White shirts with maroon and blue trim, blue shorts, blue socks
Change colours: Red shirts, white shorts, blue socks
Address and tel no of ground: Emley Welfare Sports Ground, Emley, Hud-
dersfield, West Yorkshire (Flockton 848398)
　　　　　　　　　　　　　　　　Record attendance: 5,134 (1969)
Ground capacity: 5,000　　　　　Seating capacity: None
Covered accommodation: 1,000　　Floodlights: No
Clubhouse details: Open seven nights a week, dancing, concerts, snacks
Best season in F.A. Cup: 3rd Qual Rnd
Current players with Football League experience: M. Pamment (Bradford
City)
Major honours: Sheffield Senior Cup winners 1975–76; Yorkshire League
Cup winners 1969–70; Yorkshire League champions 1975–76, 1977–78
Best seasons in F.A. Trophy: 1975–76 and 1977–78, 3rd Qual Rnd
Local newspaper: Huddersfield Examiner　Programme: 4 pages, 5p

ENDERBY TOWN (S.L.M.)

Chairman: Mr Arthur Capers　　　Founded: 1900
Secretary: Mr Garry Glover　　　　Tel no: Sutton Elms 282539
Team manager: Mr Thomas Elliott
Previous leagues: Leicestershire Senior, East Midland Regional
Colours: All red　　　　　　　　　Change colours: White shirts, black
　　　　　　　　　　　　　　　　shorts, black socks
Address and tel no of ground: George Street Ground, Coleridge Drive,
Enderby, Leics (Leicester 863154)　Record attendance: 6,000 (1979)
Ground capacity: 9,750　　　　　Seating capacity: 750
Covered accommodation: 2,250　　Floodlights: Yes
Clubhouse details: Open every night except Sundays, light refreshments
Best season in F.A. Cup: 1977–78, 1st Rnd Proper
Current players with Football League experience: N. Matthams; C. Balder-
stone
Major honours: Leics Senior League champions; Leics Senior Cup win-
ners; East Midland Regional League champions
Best season in F.A. Trophy: 1978–79, 3rd Rnd Proper
Club nickname: The Town　　　　Programme: 8 pages, 5p
Local newspaper: Leicester Mercury

ENFIELD (B.I.L. P. DIV)

Chairman: T. Unwin
Secretary: A. Diment
Team manager: T. Hardy
Founded: 1900
Tel no: 01–366 0441
Previous leagues: North Middlesex, Athenian
Colours: White shirts, blue shorts, white socks
Change colours: All yellow
Address and tel no of ground: Enfield Stadium, Southbury Road, Enfield, Middx (01–363 2858/5734)
Ground capacity: 8,000
Covered accommodation: 1,500
Seating capacity: 750
Floodlights: Yes
Clubhouse details: Open every night, 'Starlight' nightclub open lunchtimes and usually Friday, Saturday and Sunday night
Best season in F.A. Cup: 1977–78, 3rd Rnd Proper
League clubs defeated in F.A. Cup: 1977–78, v Wimbledon 1st Rnd; 1977–78 v Northampton
Major honours: Anglo-Italian Amateur Cup winners 1970; F.A. Amateur Cup winners 1967, 1970, finalists 1964, 1972; Athenian League champions 1962, 1963; Isthmian League champions 1968, 1969, 1970, 1976, 1977, 1978
Best season in F.A. Trophy: 1975–76, Semi-final
Programme: 12 pages, 10p
Local newspapers: Enfield Gazette, Weekly Herald

EPPING TOWN (B.I.L. DIV 2)

Chairman: I. W. Harper
Secretary: G. Auger
Team manager: Tom Fearey
Founded: 1888
Tel no: 01–527 7470
Previous leagues: Spartan, Parthenon, London, Greater London, Metropolitan, Metropolitan London, Athenian
Colours: White shirts with red and black hoops, black shorts
Change colours: Blue shirts, white shorts
Address and tel no of ground: Stonards Hill, Fairfield Road, Epping, Essex (Epping 74992)
Record attendance: 1,800 (1973)
Ground capacity: 3,750
Covered accommodation: 600
Seating capacity: 250
Floodlights: Yes
Clubhouse details: Open every night except Sundays, available for private hire, darts, cards, pool, etc.
Best season in F.A. Cup: 1973–74, last Qual Rnd
Current players with Football League experience: D. Keefe (Southend Utd, Torquay Utd)
Major honours: London League champions 1963–64; Greater London League champions 1966–67; Metropolitan League champions 1970–71; Metropolitan London League champions 1971–72, 1973–74; Athenian League Div 2 champions 1975–76; Spartan League Cup winners 1953–54; Metropolitan London Cup winners 1971–72
Best season in F.A. Vase: 1976–77, 5th Rnd
Programme: 12 pages, 10p
Local newspapers: West Essex Gazette & Independent

EPSOM AND EWELL (B.I.L. DIV 1)

Chairman: Mr I. Grant
Secretary: Mr S. A. Bailey
Founded: 1917
Tel no: 01–739 4105
Team manager: Pat O'Connell
Previous leagues: Surrey Senior, Corinthian, Athenian
Colours: All royal blue
Change colours: All yellow
Address and tel no of ground: West Street, Ewell, Surrey (01–393 7077)
Ground capacity: 4,750
Seating capacity: 250
Covered accommodation: 250
Floodlights: Yes
Clubhouse details: Open Saturdays only, drinks only, snack bar during games
Best season in F.A. Cup: 1933–34, lost to Clapton Orient 1st Rnd Proper
Major honours: F. A. Vase finalists 1974–75; Isthmian League Div 2 champions 1977–78; Surrey Senior League champions 1974–75
Best season in F.A. Vase: 1974–75, lost to Hoddesdon in final
Club nickname: The EEs
Programme: 16 pages, 10p
Local newspaper: Sutton & Cheam Advertiser

ERITH & BELVEDERE (K. ATHENIAN)

Chairman: J. Rolfe
Secretary: R. Culpitt
Founded: 1922
Team manager: P. Peters
Previous leagues: Kent, London, South East Comb, Corinthian
Colours: Blue and white
Change colours: Green and white
Address and tel no of ground: Park View, Lower Road, Belvedere, Kent (Erith 33975)
Ground capacity: 5,000
Seating capacity: 800
Covered accommodation: 500
Floodlights: Yes
Clubhouse details: Open on training nights, music, approx. 110 capacity, available for hire Friday and Saturday evenings, steward: Mrs P. Tozer (Erith 30229)
Major honours: Kent Senior Cup winners 1942; London Senior Cup winners 1945; Athenian League Div 1 runners-up 1970–71
Programme: 4 pages, 5p

EVENWOOD TOWN (D. NORTHERN)

Chairman: A. F. Monk
Secretary: A. B. Harland
Founded: 1931
Tel no: Aycliffe 316430
Team manager: T. Monkhouse
Colours: All blue with white trim
Change colours: All yellow
Address of ground: Welfare Ground, Evenwood, Bishop Auckland, Co Durham
Record attendance: 2,500 (1969-70)
Ground capacity: 3,000
Seating capacity: 250
Covered accommodation: 250
Floodlights: No
Best season in F.A. Cup: 1936, 1st Rnd Proper
Major honours: Northern League champions 1948-49, 1969-70, 1970-71; Durham County Cup winners 1969-70
Best season in F.A. Trophy: 1976-77, 2nd Qual Rnd
Programme: 8 pages, 5p
Local newspapers: Northern Echo, Auckland Chronicle

FALMOUTH TOWN   (WESTERN)

Chairman: D. R. C. Brown   Founded: 1946
Secretary: T. T. Pendleton   Tel no: Falmouth 312540
Team manager: Keith Manley
Previous league: South Western
Colours: Amber and black shirts, black shorts, black socks
Change colours: Red and black striped shirts, black shorts, black socks
Address and tel no of ground: Bickland Park, Bickland Vale, Falmouth,
   Cornwall (Penryn 73427)   Record attendance: 8,000 (1962)
Ground capacity: 12,000   Seating capacity: 400
Covered accommodation: 5,000   Floodlights: Yes
Clubhouse details: Open every night, at present situated in Arwenack
   Avenue, Falmouth, but new club on ground imminent
Best seasons in F.A. Cup: 1962–63, 1967–68 and 1969–70, 1st Rnd Proper
Current players with Football League experience: K. Manley (Plymouth
   Argyle); M. Rich (Plymouth Argyle); B. Helley (Torquay Utd)
Major honours: Western League champions between 1974–75 and 1977–
   78; South Western League champions 1961–62, 1965–66, 1967–68,
   1970–71, 1971–72, 1972–73, 1973–74
Best season in F.A. Trophy: 1977–78, 2nd Rnd Proper
Programme: 8 pages, 5p
Local newspaper: Falmouth Packet

FAREHAM TOWN   (S.L.S.)

Secretary: K. F. Atkins   Tel no: Gosport 83049
                    Founded: 1947
Colours: Red shirts, black shorts, red socks
Change colours: Blue shirts, blue shorts, white socks
Address and tel no of ground: Cams Alders, Highfield Avenue, Fareham,
   Hants (Fareham 231151)
Ground capacity: 5,500   Seating capacity: 500
Covered accommodation: 500   Floodlights: Yes
Best season in F.A. Cup Trophy: 1975-76, 2nd Qual Rnd

FARNBOROUGH TOWN   (B.I.L. DIV 1)

Chairman: J. J. Roberts   Founded: 1967
Secretary: K. L. Davis   Tel no: Farnborough 47548
Team manager: E. A. Pearce
Previous leagues: Athenian, London Spartan, Spartan, Surrey Senior
Colours: Yellow shirts, blue shorts, yellow socks
Change colours: Red and white shirts, white shorts, red socks
Address and tel no of ground: The J. J. Roberts Ground, Cherrywood Road,
   Farnborough, Hants (Farnborough 45553)
Record attendance: 3,000 (1975-76 and 1976-77)
Ground capacity: 4,000   Seating capacity: 320
Covered accommodation: Yes   Floodlights: Yes

Clubhouse details: Open seven nights a week
Best season in F.A. Cup: 1976-77, 3rd Qual Rnd
Current players with Football League experience: J. Harley (Aldershot and Reading); J. McHale (Reading)
Major honours: Isthmian League Div 2 champions 1978-79; Athenian League Div 2 champions 1976-77; Spartan League champions 1972-73, 1973-74, 1974-75; London Spartan League champions 1975-76; Spartan League Challenge Cup winners 1974-75; London Spartan League Challenge Cup winners 1975-76; Hampshire Senior Challenge Cup winners 1974-75
Best seasons in F.A. Vase: 1975-76 and 1976-77, Semi-final
Local newspaper: Farnborough News Programme: 40 pages, 10p

FAVERSHAM TOWN (KENT)

Chairman: B. D. Harris
Secretary: K. F. Hammond
Team manager: A. Jones
Previous leagues: London Metropolitan, Athenian
Colours: All white
Address and tel no of ground: Salters Lane, Faversham, Kent (Faversham 2738)
Ground capacity: 6,000
Covered accommodation: 3,000

Founded: 1946
Tel no: Faversham 5612

Change colours: Yellow and blue

Record attendance: 1,100 (1978)
Seating capacity: 400
Floodlights: Yes

Clubhouse details: Open on match days and nights, training nights and for numerous social functions
Current players with Football League experience: D. Hoosden (Gillingham); A. Jones (Fulham)
Major honours: Kent Amateur Cup winners 1956-57, 1958-59, 1971-72, 1972-73, 1973-74; Kent Senior Trophy winners 1976-77, 1977-78; Kent League champions 1969-70, 1970-71, 1977-78; Kent League Cup winners 1970-71
Best season in F.A. Vase: Never past 2nd Rnd
Club nickname: The Lillywhites or The Town Programme: 8 pages, 10p
Local newspapers: Faversham News, Faversham Times, Medway Evening Post

FELTHAM (B.I.L. DIV 2)

Chairman: H. T. Brown
Secretary: J. E. Pauling

Founded: 1946
Tel no: 01-898 0515 (h);
Uxbridge 30111 (bus)

Team manager: B. Laing
Previous leagues: Surrey Senior, Spartan, Athenian
Colours: Blue and white hooped shirts, blue shorts, blue socks
Change colours: All red
Address and tel no of ground: Feltham Arena, Shakespeare Avenue, Feltham, Middx (01-890 6119 – ground; 6241 – club)
Record attendance: 1,938 (1972-73)

Ground capacity: 15,000   Seating capacity: 1,500
Covered accommodation: 3,500   Floodlights: Yes
Clubhouse details: Two bars, dance floor for 120 people, open nightly,
    regular live entertainment
Best season in F.A. Cup: 1977-78, 3rd Qual Rnd
Best season in F.A. Vase: 1975-76, 3rd Rnd
Club nickname: The Blues   Programme: 12 pages, 10p
Local newspaper: Middlesex Chronicle

FERRYHILL ATHLETIC (D. NORTHERN)

Chairman: D. Higgins   Founded: 1921
Secretary: F. W. Briggs   Tel no: Ferryhill 53175
Team manager: Kenny Banks
Previous league: Palatine
Colours: Amber shirts, black shorts, amber socks
Change colours: White shirts, black shorts, white socks
Address and tel no of ground: Darlington Road, Ferryhill, Co Durham
    (Ferryhill 51937)
Ground capacity: 5,800   Seating capacity: 770
Covered accommodation: 770   Floodlights: Yes
Clubhouse details: Open every evening and Saturday and Sunday lunch-
    times, stewards: Mr and Mrs J. Mavin
Best season in F.A. Cup: 1953-54, 2nd Rnd Proper
Current players with Football League experience: K. Ross (Grimsby)
Major honours: Northern League champions 1937-38, 1947-48, 1957-58;
    Durham Challenge Cup winners 1923-24, 1970-71; Durham Benevo-
    lent Bowl winners 1953-54, 1956-57, 1961-62
Best season in F.A. Trophy: Never past 1st Qual Rnd
Club nickname: The Lactics   Programme: 10p
Local newspaper: Auckland Chronicle

FINCHLEY   (B.I.L. DIV 1)

Chairman: W. R. Hunt   Founded: 1874
Secretary: A. S. Layson   Tel no: 01-449 4707
Team manager: Alan Davies
Previous leagues: Athenian, London, Premier Midweek
Colours: Blue and white striped shirts, blue shorts, white socks
Change colours: All tangerine
Address and tel no of ground: Summers Lane, High Road, Finchley
    London, N.12 (01-445 1400)   Record attendance: 7,983 (1955)
Ground capacity: 6,200   Seating capacity: 650
Covered accommodation: 850   Floodlights: Yes
Clubhouse details: Spacious hall, two bars, well-equipped kitchen
Best season in F.A. Cup: 1952-53, 2nd Rnd
League clubs defeated in F.A. Cup: Crystal Palace
Major honours: Finchley Cup winners 1898-99, 1899-1900, 1900-01; North
    Middx League champions 1899-90, 1900-01; Baron von Reifferstein
    Trophy winners 1904-05; Daily Chronicle Shield winners 1925-26;

Middx Senior Cup winners 1928-29, 1943-44, 1951-52, finalists 1952-53, 1963-64; London Senior Cup winners 1932-33, 1951-52, 1952-53, finalists 1957-58; London League Challenge Cup winners 1934-35, 1938-39; Middx Charity Cup winners 1942-43, 1950-51, 1957-58, 1964-65; Athenian League Challenge Cup winners 1946-47; Athenian League champions 1953-54, runners-up 1956-57, 1963-64, 1965-66; London Charity Cup winners 1964-65
Best season in F.A. Trophy: Never past 2nd Qual Rnd
Programme: 5p
Local newspapers: Barnet Press, Finchley Times, Hendon Times

FLEETWOOD T. (CHESHIRE CO. DIV 1)

Chairman: R. W. Read | Founded: 1977
Secretary: K. J. Byrne | Tel no: Fleetwood 71986
Team manager: Alan Tinsley
Previous leagues: Blackpool & Fylde Comb, Blackpool & Flyde Sunday Alliance
Colours: Red and white shirts, white shorts, red socks
Change colours: Yellow and green shirts, green shorts, yellow socks
Address and tel no of ground: Highbury Stadium, Highbury Avenue, Fleetwood, Lancashire (Fleetwood 6443) Record attendance: 1,237 (1978)
Ground capacity: 8,000 | Seating capacity: 400
Covered accommodation: 1,400 | Floodlights: Yes
Clubhouse details: Highbury soccer and social club, open for drinks and entertainment each night (Fleetwood 2676)
Best season in F.A. Cup: 1977-78, 3rd Qual Rnd
Current players with Football League experience: A. Tinsley; C. Gisbourne
Best season in F.A. Vase: 1977-78, 2nd Rnd
Club nickname: The Fishermen | Programme: 12 pages, 10p
Local newspapers: West Lancs Evening Gazette, Fleetwood Chronicle

FOLKESTONE & SHEPWAY (S.L.S.)

Chairman: D. J. Setterfield | Founded: 1884
Secretary: R. H. Speake | Tel no: Medway 668260
Team manager: To be appointed
Previous league: Kent
Colours: Black and amber shirts, black shorts
Change colours: Red and white shirts, blue shorts
Address and tel no of ground: Cheriton Road, Folkestone, Kent (Folkestone 51374) Record attendance: 1965-66
Ground capacity: 7,300 | Seating capacity: 900
Covered accommodation: 3,900 | Floodlights: Yes
Clubhouse details: Open seven nights a week, darts, pool, discos and live entertainment
Best seasons in F.A. Cup: 1932-33 and 1965-66, 3rd Rnd
League clubs defeated in F.A. Cup: Gillingham
Current players with Football League experience: M. Goodburn; A. Wilks
Major honours: Kent Senior Cup winners
Best seasons in F.A. Trophy: 1971-72 and 1976-77, 3rd Qual Rnd
Club nickname: The Town | Programme: 12 pages, free
Local newspaper: Folkestone & Hythe & District Herald and Gazette

FORMBY (CHESHIRE CO. DIV 1)

Chairman: T. Hitchen
Secretary: B. Hewitt
Team manager: B. Griffiths
Previous leagues: Liverpool County Comb, Lancs Comb
Colours: Gold and blue   Change colours: Pale blue
Address and tel no of ground: Brows Lane, Formby, Merseyside (Formby 72603)
Ground capacity: 4,000   Seating capacity: None
Covered accommodation: Yes   Floodlights: No
Clubhouse details: Open every night except Monday, steward: Mrs Yates (Formby 72603)
Best season in F.A. Cup: 1973–74, 1st Rnd

Founded: 1919
Tel no: Formby 72971

FRIAR LANE OLD BOYS (LEICS. SEN.)

Chairman: I. Bircham
Secretary: T. Scriggins
Team manager: D. White
Previous league: Leicester Mutual
Colours: Black and white stripes   Change colours: All white
Address and tel no of ground: Knighton Lane East, Leicester (Leicester 833629)
Ground capacity: 6,000   Seating capacity: None
Covered accommodation: 500   Floodlights: None
Clubhouse details: Open every night except Sunday, disco, food, steward: K. Jewitt (Leicester 833629)
Programme: 2 pages, 5p

Founded: 1961
Tel no: Leicester 881300

FRICKLEY ATHLETIC (N.P.L.)

Chairman: W. Sykes, MBE
Secretary: R. L. Bates
Team manager: G. Sleight
Previous leagues: Yorkshire, Cheshire County, Midland
Colours: Blue and white striped shirts, white shorts, white socks
Change colours: Yellow shirts, blue shorts, yellow socks
Address and tel no of ground: Westfield Lane, South Elmsall, Pontefract, West Yorks (Pontefract 44575)   Record attendance: 6,700 (1971-72)
Ground capacity: 10,000   Seating capacity: 900
Covered accommodation: 4,000   Floodlights: Yes
Clubhouse details: New social club outside ground
Best seasons in F.A. Cup: 1957-58, 1963-64, 1971-72 and 1973-74
Current players with Football League experience: B. Gill; R. Belfitt; G. Sleight
Best season in F.A. Trophy: 1978-79
Club nickname: The Blues   Programme: 10p
Local newspaper: South Yorkshire Times

Founded: 1910
Tel no: Pontefract 44575

FROME TOWN (WESTERN)

Chairman: Mr E. G. Berry   Founded: 1904
Secretary: Mr P. M. Bishop   Tel no: Frome 61794
Team manager: Mr R. Boyd
Colours: All red with white trim   Change colours: All blue
Address and tel no of ground: Badgers Hill, Frome, Somerset (Frome 4087)
Ground capacity: 7,750   Seating capacity: 250
Covered accommodation: 500   Floodlights: No
Clubhouse details: Modern clubhouse, entertainment every Saturday and Sunday
Current players with Football League experience: B. Drysdale (Bristol City)
Major honours: Somerset Premier Cup winners 1967–68; Somerset Senior Cup winners 1933, 1934, 1951; Western League champions 1978–79
Club nickname: The Robins   Programme: 10p
Local newspapers: Western Daily Press, Evening Post, Bath Evening Chronicle, Somerset Standard

GAINSBOROUGH TRINITY (N.P.L.)

Chairman: J. M. Davis   Founded: 1973
Secretary: K. Marsden   Tel no: Gainsborough 2577
Team manager: Roy Ellam
Previous leagues: Football League, Midland Counties
Colours: Royal blue shirts, white shorts, blue socks
Change colours: Yellow shirts, black shorts, yellow socks
Address of ground: The Northolme, Gainsborough, Lincs
Ground capacity: 12,000   Seating capacity: 400
Covered accommodation: 6,000   Floodlights: Yes
Clubhouse details: Open seven days a week, entertainment, food on certain nights, steward: D. Rawson (Gainsborough 3688)
Best seasons in F.A. Cup: 1959–60 and 1966–67
Major honours: Northern Premier Cup finalists 1972; Lincolnshire Senior Cup winners 1958, 1959, 1964, 1971
Best season in F.A. Trophy: 1975–76, 2nd Rnd
Club nickname: The Blues   Programme: 8 pages, 10p
Local newspapers: Gainsborough News, Lincolnshire Echo

GATESHEAD (N.P.L.)

Chairman: J. W. Gibson   Founded: 1977
Secretary: J. L. Battla   Tel no: Low Fell 878782
Team manager: R. Wilkie
Colours: All white   Change colours: All red
Address and tel no of ground: International Stadium, Park Road, Gateshead, Tyne and Wear (Gateshead 783883)
Record attendance: 3,000 (1977)
Ground capacity: 13,000   Seating capacity: 200
Covered accommodation: 200   Floodlights: Yes

Clubhouse details: Negotiations proceeding for building club
Best season in F.A. Cup: 1978-79, 4th Qual Rnd
Current players with Football League experience: S. Holbrook (Darlington);
  F. McIver (Sunderland, Sheffield Wed); R. McLeod (Hartlepool); B.
  Stonehouse (Middlesbrough)
Best season in F.A. Trophy: 1978-79, 3rd Qual Rnd
Programme: 20-24 pages, 10p
Local newspapers: Northern Echo, Evening Chronicle, Newcastle Journal,
  Gateshead Post

GLASTONBURY   (WESTERN)

Chairman: G. V. Jestico   **Founded:** 1890
Secretary: L. J. C. Heal   **Tel no:** Glastonbury 32037
Team manager: D. Noake
Previous league: Bristol & District
Colours: Tangerine shirts, black shorts, tangerine socks
Change colours: All white
Address of ground: Abbey Park, Magdalene Street, Glastonbury, Somerset
                                        Record attendance: 3,892 (1951)
Ground capacity: 4,000   **Seating capacity:** 450
Covered accommodation: 300   **Floodlights:** No
Clubhouse details: No club, but provision made on new ground to be
  occupied in 1980
Best season in F.A. Cup: 1951-52, v Exeter City 1st Rnd Proper
Current players with Football League experience: K. Wookey (Cardiff City
  and Welsh under-23s); M. D. Nias (Luton Town, Bristol City)
Major honours: Western League champions 1948-49, 1950-51, 1960-70,
  runners-up 1947-48, 1951-52; Western League Challenge Cup winners
  1965 to 1970
Best season in F.A. Trophy: 1969-70, 1st Rnd Proper
Programme: 8 pages, 5p

GLOSSOP   (CHESHIRE CO. DIV 2)

Chairman: A. Lockett   **Founded:** 1886
Secretary: B. A. Price   **Tel no:** Glossop 4082
Team manager: D. Partridge
Previous leagues: Manchester, Lancashire Combination, Football League
Colours: All white with black trim   **Change colours:** All red
Address and tel no of ground: Surrey Street, Glossop, Derbys
  (Glossop 5469)
Ground capacity: 5,000   **Seating capacity:** None
Covered accommodation: 1,000   **Floodlights:** No
Best season in F.A. Cup: 1908-09, Quarter-final
Major honours: Football League Div 2 runners-up 1909-10
Best season in F.A. Vase: 1974-75, 3rd Rnd
Club nickname: The Hillmen   **Programme:** 16 pages, 5p
Local newspaper: Glossop Chronicle

GLOUCESTER CITY   (S.L.S.)

Chairman: Mr R. F. Etheridge   Founded: 1889
Secretary: D. H. Gettings   Tel no: Gloucester 31080
Team manager: Bob Morsell
Previous league: Midland Combination
Colours: Red and black shirts, black shorts, black socks
Change colours: Yellow shirts, blue shorts, blue socks
Address and tel no of ground: The Stadium, Horton Road, Gloucester
    (Gloucester 23883)   Record attendance: 8,500 (1964–65)
Ground capacity: 10,000   Seating capacity: 450
Covered accommodation: 4,000   Floodlights: No
Clubhouse details: Main hall holds 400, small hall 100, four bars open
    every evening
Best season in F.A. Cup: 1950–51
Current players with Football League experience: G. Bell (Cardiff City and
    Wales)
Major honours: Southern League Cup winners 1956
Best season in F.A. Trophy: 1970–71, 1st Rnd Proper
Club nickname: The City   Programme: 12 pages, 15p
Local newspaper: Gloucester Citizen

GOOLE TOWN   (N.P.L.)

Chairman: E. Lawton   Founded: 1900
Secretary: H. Harrison   Tel no: Goole 4172
Team manager: A. Turner
Previous leagues: Yorkshire, Midland
Colours: Blue and white shirts, blue shorts, red socks
Change colours: Red shirts, white shorts, red socks
Address and tel no of ground: Goole Victoria Pleasure Ground, Goole,
    N. Humberside (Goole 2794)
Ground capacity: 8,000   Seating capacity: 200
Covered accommodation: Two sides   Floodlights: Yes
Best season in F.A. Cup: 1977, 2nd Rnd Proper
League clubs defeated in F.A. Cup: Workington
Current players with Football League experience: M. Thompson
Major honours: W. R. County finalists during the past four years; W. R.
    County Cup winners 1976, 1977, 1978, finalists 1979
Best season in F.A. Trophy: 1974-75, 4th Rnd Proper
Programme: 8 pages, 10p
Local newspapers: Goole Times, Hull Daily Mail

GORLESTON   (TOWN & COUNTRY)

Chairman: Mr J. Jones   Founded: 1908
Secretary: E. W. H. Proudfoot   Tel no: Lowestoft 730952
Team manager: Mal Lucas
Previous leagues: Eastern Counties, Magnet, Norfolk & Suffolk
Colours: All green   Change colours: All yellow

Address and tel no of ground: Gorleston Recreation Ground, Church Lane, Gorleston-on-Sea, Great Yarmouth, Norfolk (Gt Yarmouth 62870)
Record attendance: 10,000 (1953)
Ground capacity: 4,000   **Seating capacity:** 300
Covered accommodation: 2,250   **Floodlights:** Yes
Clubhouse details: Fully licensed, colour television, pools table, darts, hot snacks
Best season in F.A. Cup: 1951–52, 1st Rnd Proper
Major honours: Eastern Counties League champions 1952–53, 1972–73; Norfolk Senior Cup winners 12 times
Best season in F.A. Trophy: 1976–77, 1st Qual Rnd
Club nickname: The Greens   **Programme:** 14 pages, 10p
Local newspaper: Yarmouth Mercury

GOSPORT BOROUGH   (S.L.S.)

Chairman: P. Wall   **Founded:** 1944
Secretary: W. J. Adams   **Tel no:** Gosport 81604
Team managers: A. J. Brickwood and P. Edgar
Previous league: Hampshire
Colours: Blue shirts, yellow shorts, blue socks
Change colours: All white
Address and tel no of ground: Privett Park, Privett Road, Gosport, Hants
(Gosport 83986)   **Record attendance:** 4,000 (1950-51)
Ground capacity: 5,000   **Seating capacity:** 600
Covered accommodation: 100   **Floodlights:** Yes
Clubhouse details: Bar, facilities available to club members and visitors on match days, separate boardroom/committee room for special guests
Best season in F.A. Cup: 1975-76, 3rd Qual Rnd
Major honours: Hampshire League Div 1 champions 1945-46, 1976-77, 1977-78; South Western Counties Pratten Cup winners 1977-78, semi-finalists 1976-77
Best season in F.A. Vase: 1976-77, Quarter-final v Barton Rovers
Club nickname: The Borough   **Programme:** 8 pages, 5p
Local newspapers: Portsmouth Evening News, Gosport Standard

GRANTHAM   (N.P.L.)

Chairman: P. Rawlinson   **Founded:** 1876
Secretary: J. F. Toon   **Tel no:** Grantham 68577
Team manager: Robert Norris
Previous leagues: Central Comb, Midland, Central Alliance.
Colours: All yellow
Change colours: All blue, all red or all white
Address and tel no of ground: London Road, Grantham, Lincs
(Grantham 2011)   **Record attendance:** 6,578 (1974)
Ground capacity: 7,000   **Seating capacity:** 1,000
Covered accommodation: 4,500   **Floodlights:** Yes
Clubhouse details: Open all week, live entertainment, discos, annual quizzes, darts, cribbage, food (Grantham 5349)
Best season in F.A. Cup: 1973-74, 3rd Rnd
League clubs defeated in F.A. Cup: Stockport, Rochdale

Current players with Football League experience: C. Chamberlain (Derby Co); S. Hodson (Peterborough); G. Taylor (Lincoln City); K. Collins (Notts Forest); D. Hailwood (Mansfield); R. Norris (Notts Forest); R. Cooke (Mansfield); D. Benskin (Notts Co)
Major honours: Lincs County Cup winners 1972-73; Lincs Senior Cup winners 1884, 1885, 1936, 1937, 1953, 1954, 1960, 1961, 1962; Midland Counties League champions 1963-64, 1970-71, 1971-72; Midland Counties Cup winners 1968-69, 1970-71; Southern League Div 1 N champions 1972-73, 1977-78; Southern Premier League runners-up 1973-74; Southern League Merit Cup winners 1972-73
Best season in F.A. Trophy: 1971-72, Quarter-final
Club nickname: The Gingerbreads   **Programme:** 26 pages, 10p
Local newspapers: Grantham Journal, Notts Evening Post, Lincolnshire Echo

GRAVESEND & NORTHFLEET (A.P.L.)

Chairman: R. J. Easterby   **Founded:** 1946
Team manager: T. Sitford   **Tel no:** Gravesend 3796
Secretary: c/o club
Previous league: Southern
Colours: Red shirts, white shorts, red socks
Change colours: White shirts, black shorts, black socks
Address and tel no of ground: Stonebridge Road, Northfleet, Kent (Gravesend 3796)   **Record attendance:** 12,032 (1963)
Ground capacity: 10,000   **Seating capacity:** 1,366
Covered accommodation: Three sides   **Floodlights:** Yes
Clubhouse details: Open match days, Thursday evenings and Sunday lunchtimes
Best season in F.A. Cup: 1962-63, 4th Rnd
League clubs defeated in F.A. Cup: Exeter, Carlisle
Current players with Football League experience: G. Jacks (Gillingham); S. Brown (Millwall); A. Woon (Brentford)
Major honours: Southern League Cup winners 1957-58, 1977-78; Southern League Div 1 South champions 1974-75; Southern League Championship Cup winners 1977-78; Kent Senior Cup winners 1948-49, 1952-53; Kent Floodlight Cup winners 1969-70
Best seasons in F.A. Trophy: 1969-70 and 1977-78, 2nd Rnd Proper
Club nickname: The Fleet   **Programme:** 16 pages
Local newspapers: Gravesend Reporter, Gravesend Evening Post

GRAYS ATHLETIC   (K. ATHENIAN)

Chairman: F. W. Wakeling   **Founded:** 1890
Secretary: P. W. Plom   **Tel no:** Grays Thurrock 5461
Team managers: J. Saxton and F. Saxton
Previous league: Essex Senior
Colours: Royal blue shirts with red and white trim, red socks
Change colours: All white
Address and tel no of ground: The Recreation Ground, Grays, Essex (Grays Thurrock 73424)

124

Ground capacity: 12,000   Seating capacity: 250
Covered accommodation: 4,000   Floodlights: Yes
Clubhouse details: Open normal licensing hours except Sundays, discos, family evenings, junior discos on Wednesdays
Major honours: Essex Senior Cup winners 1914-15, 1920-21, 1922-23, 1944-45, 1956-57; Corinthian League champions 1945-46
Club nickname: The Blues   Programme: 8 pages, 10p

GREAT YARMOUTH TOWN
(TOWN & COUNTRY)

Chairman: G. Faulder   Founded: 1897
Secretary: J. H. Pegg   Tel no: Great Yarmouth 2652
Team manager: Bill Punton
Previous leagues: Eastern Counties, Anglian Combination
Colours: Amber and black shirts, black shorts, amber socks
Change colours: Dark blue shirts, white shorts, red socks
Address and tel no of ground: Wellesley Road, Great Yarmouth, Norfolk (Great Yarmouth 2936)   Record attendance: 5,000 (1950s)
Ground capacity: Approx 5,000   Seating capacity: 600
Covered accommodation: 2,100   Floodlights: No
Clubhouse details: In process of construction
Best season in F.A. Cup: 1956-57, 1st Rnd Proper
Major honours: Eastern Counties League champions 1968-69, runners-up 1977-78, 1978-79; Norfolk Senior Cup winners 1978-79
Club nickname: The Bloaters   Programme: 4 pages, 4p
Local newspapers: Great Yarmouth Mercury, Eastern Evening News

GUISELEY
     (YORKSHIRE)

Chairman: N. Threapleton   Founded: 1909
Secretary: W. Chatwin   Tel no: Bradford 594757
Team manager: M. Beck
Previous leagues: Leeds, Wharfedale, West Riding County Amateur, West Yorkshire
Colours: Yellow shirts, blue shorts   Change colours: All blue
Address and tel no of ground: Nethermoor Park, Otley Road, Guiseley-near Leeds (Guiseley 72872)   Record attendance: 2,500 (1932)
Ground capacity: 5,000   Seating capacity: 400
Covered accommodation: Yes   Floodlights: No
Clubhouse details: Fully licensed social club open every night
Current players with Football League experience: I. Cooper (Bradford City); P. Barlow (Bradford City, Lincoln United); S. Harmey (Bradford City)
Major honours: West Riding County Cup winners
Best season in F.A. Vase: 1976-77, 3rd Rnd
Programme: Free
Local newspapers: Wharfedale Observer, Yorkshire Post, Bradford Telegraph & Argus

HALESOWEN TOWN (W. MIDLANDS)

Chairman: L. Wood
Secretary: H. Rudge
Team manager: P. Page
Founded: 1873
Tel no: 021-550 1456

Previous leagues: Birmingham Combination, Worcs Combination
Colours: Blue shirts, white shorts, blue socks
Change colours: Red and white striped shirts, red shorts, red socks
Address and tel no of ground: Grove Recreation Ground, Stourbridge Road, Halesowen, W. Midlands (021-550 2179)

Ground capacity: 6,000
Covered accommodation: 1,850
Record attendance: 4,500 (1955)
Seating capacity: 350
Floodlights: No

Clubhouse details: Social club open every night and on match days, occasional concert evenings, bingo, etc.
Best season in F.A. Cup: 1955-56, 1st Rnd Proper
Major honours: Birmingham League champions 1946-47; Worcestershire Senior Cup winners 1951-52, 1961-62
Best season in F.A. Vase: 1977-78, 4th Rnd
Club nickname: The Yeltz
Programme: 4 pages, 5p
Local newspapers: County Express, Sports Argus, Birmingham Mail, Express & Star

HAMPTON (B.I.L. DIV 1)

Chairman: E. Brion
Secretary: B. W. Francis
Team manager: T. Murphy
Founded: 1920
Tel no: 01-560 8506

Previous leagues: Surrey Senior, Spartan, Athenian
Colours: White shirts, black shorts
Change colours: Red and white shirts, red shorts
Address and tel no of ground: 'Beveree', Station Road, Hampton, Middlesex (01-979 2456)

Ground capacity: 3,800
Covered accommodation: 2,000
Seating capacity: 350
Floodlights: Yes

Clubhouse details: Open six nights a week and Sunday lunchtimes during the season, snack bar on match days, entertainment, fortnightly bingo
Best season in F.A. Cup: 1977-78, 4th Qual Rnd
Major honours: Spartan League champions 1964-65, 1965-66, 1966-67 1969-70
Best season in F.A. Trophy: 1976-77, 2nd Qual Rnd
Programme: 16 pages, 6p
Local newspapers: Surrey Comet, Middlesex Chronicle, Richmond-Twickenham Times

HAREFIELD UNITED (K. ATHENIAN)

Chairman: L. Wiggins
Secretary: G. South
Team manager: S. Bowden
Founded: 1868
Tel no: Harefield 3568

Previous leagues: Middlesex, Spartan
Colours: All green with yellow trim
Change colours: Red and white stripes
Address and tel no of ground: Preston Park, Breakspear Road North, Harefield, Middx (Harefield 3474)
Ground capacity: 4,000   Seating capacity: 250
Covered accommodation: Yes   Floodlights: Yes
Clubhouse details: Social functions, bingo, discos, etc.
Club nickname: The Hares   Programme: 16 pages, 5p
Local newspapers: Evening Echo, Hillingdon Mirror, Middlesex Advertiser

HARINGEY BOROUGH (K. ATHENIAN)

Chairman: W. Jackson   Founded: 1907
Secretary: J. T. Gates   Tel no: Waltham Cross 64400
Team manager: G. Makeling
Previous leagues: London, Middlesex, Athenian, Isthmian, Herts & Middlesex, Delphian
Colours: Amber and black   Change colours: Green and white
Address and tel no of ground: White Hart Lane, Wood Green, London, N. 17 (01-888 4586)
Ground capacity: 2,300   Seating capacity: 220
Covered accommodation: 220   Floodlights: Yes
Clubhouse details: Open Tuesdays, Wednesdays, Thursdays and Saturdays, food available
Major honours: Athenian League Div 2 runners-up 1969-70
Programme: 10 pages, 10p

HARLOW TOWN (B.I.L. P. DIV)

Chairman: D. G. Norris   Founded: 1879
Secretary: J. L. McCree   Tel no: Harlow 28453
Team manager: I. Wolstenholme
Previous leagues: Spartan, London, Delphian, Athenian
Colours: All scarlet
Change colours: Amber shirts, blue shorts, amber socks
Address and tel no of ground: Harlow Sport Centre, Hammarskjold Road, Harlow, Essex (Harlow 419872)   Record attendance: 12,000 (1971)
Ground capacity: 15,000   Seating capacity: 450
Covered accommodation: 450   Floodlights: Yes
Clubhouse details: Large licensed bar, darts, complex pool tables
Best season in F.A. Cup: 1979
Current players with Football League experience: A. Gough (Fulham)
Major honours: London League Challenge Cup winners 1959-60; Athenian League Div 2 champions 1971-72; Berger Isthmian League Div 1 champions 1978-79; Essex Senior Cup winners 1979
Best season in F.A. Trophy: 1978-79, 1st Rnd Proper
Club nickname: The Owls   Programme: 12 pages, 15p
Local newspapers: Harlow Gazette & Guardian, Harlow Observer

HARROGATE TOWN (YORKSHIRE)

Chairman: L. E. Watson
Secretary: C. Hartley   Tel no: Harrogate 884493
Team manager: A. Smith
Previous leagues: Midland, West Yorkshire, Harrogate & District
Colours: Amber and black   Change colours: Royal blue
Address of ground: Wetherby Road, Harrogate, North Yorks
Ground capacity: 5,000   Seating capacity: 150
Covered accommodation: One stand   Floodlights: No
Clubhouse details: Situated on ground, open most nights, available for private hire, licensed bar, darts, hot snacks and drinks on match days
Best season in F.A. Cup: 1963-64, 2nd Qual Rnd
Best season in F.A. Trophy: 1974-75, 1st Qual Rnd
Best season in F.A. Vase: 1974-75, 3rd Rnd
Programme: 4 pages, 2p
Local newspapers: Harrogate Herald, Harrogate Advertiser

HARROW BOROUGH (B.I.L. P. DIV)

Chairman: R. C. Churchill   Founded: 1933
Secretary: B. Rogers   Tel no: 01-422 8606
Team manager: Mike Tomkys
Previous leagues: Harrow & District, Spartan, Delphian, Athenian
Colours: All red   Change colours: All yellow or all blue
Address and tel no of ground: Earlsmead Stadium, Carlyon Avenue, South Harrow, Middx, HA2 8SS (01-422 5221 – manager; 5989 – foyer)
Ground capacity: 4,000   Seating capacity: 250
Covered accommodation: Two sides   Floodlights: Yes
Clubhouse details: Open seven days a week, three bars, ballroom, restaurant, games room, meeting room, varied entertainments, venue for major sporting occasions
Best season in F.A. Cup: 1960–61, last Qual Rnd
Current players with Football League experience: R. Bennett (Southend and Scunthorpe); G. Lidster (Darlington)
Major honours: Berger Isthmian League Div 1 runners up 1978–79
Best seasons in F.A. Trophy: 1977–78 and 1978–79, 1st Rnd Proper
Club nickname: The Boro'   Programme: 12 pages, 10p
Local newspaper: Harrow Observer

HARWICH & PARKESTON
(B.I.L. DIV 1)

Chairman: D. A. Jordan   Founded: 1877
Secretary: A. C. Lowe   Tel no: Harwich 4605
Team manager: Tony Armstrong
Previous leagues: Eastern Counties, Essex & Suffolk, Athenian
Colours: Black and white striped shirts, black shorts, red socks

Change colours: Yellow shirts, blue shorts, yellow socks
Address and tel no of ground: Main Road, Dovercourt, Essex
    (Harwich 3649)
Ground capacity: 4,000　　　　　Seating capacity: 886
Covered accommodation: Yes　　Floodlights: Yes
Clubhouse details: Social club with clubroom for 150, varied social activities arranged
Major honours: F.A. Amateur Cup finalists 1952-53
Best season in F.A. Trophy: 1975-76, 3rd Rnd Proper
Club nickname: The Shrimpers　　Programme: 10 pages, 10p
Local newspaper: Harwich & Manningtree Standard

HASTINGS UNITED　　　　　　(S.L.S.)

Chairman: Mr D. E. Wratten　　　Founded: 1948
Secretary: Mr R. A. Cosens　　　Tel no: Hastings 427867
Team manager: Peter Sillett
Colours: Claret and blue　　　　Change colours: Maroon and white
Address and tel no of ground: Hastings Stadium, Elphinstone Road,
    Hastings, East Sussex (Hastings 437187)
Record attendance: 12,760
Ground capacity: 10,000　　　　Seating capacity: 1,750
Covered accommodation: 3,500　Floodlights: Yes
Clubhouse details: Members' club open Tuesday, Thursday and Saturday
    evenings and on match days
Best season in F.A. Cup: 1954-55, 3rd Rnd Proper
League clubs defeated in F.A. Cup: Norwich City
Current players with Football League experience: S. Gill (West Ham);
    M. Westburgh (Everton); F. Fraser (Brighton); N. Howell (Bristol
    City); G. Thomas (Crystal Palace)
Major honours: Sussex Senior Cup runners-up 1975-76; Southern League
    Div 1 runners-up 1976-77
Best seasons in F.A. Trophy: 1970-71, 1971-72 and 1975-76, 2nd Rnd
    Proper
Club nickname: The U's　　　　Programme: 12 pages, 10p
Local newspapers: Hastings News, Hastings & St Leonards Observer,
    Evening Argus

HAVERHILL ROVERS
(TOWN & COUNTRY)

Chairman: R. C. Jay　　　　　　Founded: Approx. 1890
Secretary: M. J. Nunn　　　　　Tel no: Haverhill 5596
Team manager: R. Staples
Previous league: Essex & Suffolk Border
Colours: All red　　　　　　　Change colours: All blue
Address and tel no of ground: Hamlet Croft, Haverhill, Suffolk
    (Haverhill 2137)　　　　　　Record attendance: 1,300 (1979)

Ground capacity: Approx. 2,000   Seating capacity: 200
Covered accommodation: Yes   Floodlights: No
Clubhouse details: Clubhouse open on Saturdays, Tuesdays and Thursdays, darts every other week, dances every fortnight
Best season in F.A. Cup: Never past 2nd Qual Rnd
Major honours: Town and County League champions 1978-79; Eastern Counties League KO Cup winners 1965-66
Best season in F.A. Vase: 1978-79, 1st Rnd
Club nickname: The Rovers   Programme: News sheet, free
Local newspapers: Haverhill Echo, Cambridge Evening News

HAYES   (B.I.L. P. DIV)

Chairman: E. G. May   Founded: 1930
Secretary: C. A. Sage   Tel no: 01-573 0908
Team manager: Martin Hackett
Previous leagues: Great Western Suburban, Spartan, Athenian
Colours: All gold   Change colours: All red
Address and tel no of ground: Church Road, Hayes, Middx
    (01-573 4598 – ground; 0933 – clubhouse)
    Record attendance: 16,000 (1952)
Ground capacity: 10,000   Seating capacity: 450
Covered accommodation: 2,000   Floodlights: Yes
Clubhouse details: Open every evening and Saturday and Sunday lunchtimes, snacks, dance hall, bar and kitchen facilities, large car park, fulltime steward
Best season in F.A. Cup: 1972-73, 2nd Rnd Proper
League clubs defeated in F.A. Cup: Bristol Rovers
Current players with Football League experience: V. Akers (Cambridge Utd, Watford); L. Craker (Watford); M. McGovern (Q.P.R.); P. Morrissey (Coventry C, Aldershot, Watford)
Major honours: Amateur Cup finalists 1930-31; Middlesex Senior Cup winners seven times; London Senior Cup winners 1930-31
Best season in F.A. Trophy: 1978-79, Quarter-final
Programme: 12 pages, 10p
Local newspapers: Hayes Gazette, Hayes News, Hillingdon Mirror, Evening Mail

HEANOR TOWN   (MID. COUNTIES)

Chairman: Mr H. Baker   Founded: 1883
Secretary: Mr K. Costello   Tel no: Langley Mill 67228
Team manager: Mr J. McCulloch
Previous leagues: Central Alliance, West Midlands Regional
Colours: White shirts, red shorts, red socks
Change colours: Yellow shirts, blue shorts, yellow socks
Address and tel no of ground: The Town Ground, Mayfield Avenue, Heanor, Derbys (Langley Mill 3742)
Record attendance: 6,511 (1959)
Ground capacity: 4,000   Seating capacity: Nil

Clubhouse details: Hope to complete new clubhouse during closed season
Best seasons in F.A. Cup: 1959 and 1963, 1st Rnd Proper
Major honours: Central Alliance League champions 1955–56, 1956–57,
  runners-up 1959–60; D.F.A. Senior Cup winners 1965–66, 1966–67,
  1967–68, 1968–69, runners-up 1953–54, 1958–59
Best season in F.A. Trophy: 1970–71, 1971–72 and 1974–75, 2nd Qual Rnd
Club nickname: The Lions   Programme: 8 pages, 5p
Local newspapers: Ripley & Heanor News, Derby Evening Telegraph

---

HEDNESFORD TOWN   (W. MID. R.)

Chairman: Post vacant   Founded: 1880
Secretary: Mr H. F. Holden   Tel no: Hednesford 2346
Team manager: Mr M. V. Owen
Previous leagues: Birmingham Combination, Midland
Colours: White shirts, black shorts, black and white socks
Change colours: Blue and white shirts, white shorts, blue and white socks
Address and tel no of ground: Cross Keys Ground, Hill Street, Hednesford,
  Staffs (Hednesford 2870)
Ground capacity: 9,000   Seating capacity: 180
Covered accommodation: One stand, two covered enclosures
Floodlights: Yes
Clubhouse details: Licensed club open match days
Best season in F.A. Cup: 1977–78 and 1978–79, 4th Qual Rnd
Major honours: West Midland League champions 1977–78; Birmingham
  Senior Cup winners 1936; Staffs Senior Cup winners 1970, 1974
Best season in F.A. Trophy: 1977–78, 2nd Rnd Proper
Club nickname: The Pitmen   Programme: 4 pages, 10p
Local newspapers: Cannock Advertiser, Express & Star

HEMEL HEMPSTEAD   (B.I.L. DIV2)

Chairman: D. Budd   Founded: 1885
Secretary: W. J. McGrae   Tel no: Hemel Hempstead 51503
Team manager: T. Woodrow
Previous leagues: Athenian, Delphian
Colours: Tangerine and black
Change colours: Red and black
Address and tel no of ground: Vauxhall Road, Adeyfield, Hemel Hemp-
  stead, Herts (Hemel Hempstead 42081 – clubhouse; 59777 – boardroom
  match days)   Record attendance: 3,000 (1960)
Ground capacity: 3,500   Seating capacity: 200
Covered accommodation: 300   Floodlights: Yes
Clubhouse details: Large bar and entertainment room with small saloon
  bar and boardroom, open seven days a week, music and dancing at
  weekends
Major honours: Herts Senior Cup finalists
Best seasons in F.A. Vase: 1975–76 and 1976–77, 3rd Rnd
Club nickname: Hemel   Programme: 6 pages, 5p
Local newspapers: Hemel Hempstead Gazette, Evening Echo

131

HENDON (B. I. L. P. DIV)

Chairman: Post vacant   Founded: 1908
Presidents: M. Hyams and R. Butlin
Secretary: E. C. Abrey   Tel no: 01–458 3163
Team manager: Rod Haider
Previous league: Athenian
Colours: Green shirts, white shorts, green socks
Change colours: White shirts, green shorts, white socks
Address and tel no of ground: Claremont Road, Cricklewood, London,
NW2 1AE (01–455 9185)   Record attendance: 8,000 (1952–53)
Ground capacity: 8,000   Seating capacity: 500
Covered accommodation: 5,500   Floodlights: Yes
Clubhouse details: Two bars open during normal licensing hours and match
days, refreshments, bingo on Wednesdays, Fridays and Sundays
Best season in F.A. Cup: 1972–73, drew at Newcastle in 3rd Rnd Proper
(lost replay at Watford)
League clubs defeated in F.A. Cup: Reading, 1975–76 1st Rnd Proper
Major honours: European Amateur champions 1972–73; Amateur Cup
winners 1959–60, 1964–65, 1971–72, runners-up 1954–55, 1965–66;
Isthmian League champions 1964–65, 1972–73; Isthmian League Cup
winners 1976–77; Athenian League champions three times; Middlesex
Senior Cup winners nine times; London Senior Cup winners twice
Best seasons in F.A. Trophy: 1976–77 and 1977–78, 3rd Rnd Proper
Club nickname: The Greens or The Dons
Programme: 12 pages, 10p
Local newspapers: Hendon Times, Hampstead & Highgate Express

HERTFORD TOWN (B.I.L. DIV 1)

Chairman: J. Garrett   Founded: 1907
Secretary: J. B. Gillan   Tel no: Hertford 52835
Team manager: T. Barnett
Previous leagues: Spartan, Delphian, Athenian, Eastern Counties
Colours: Blue shirts, white shorts
Change colours: Red shirts, white shorts
Address and tel no of ground: Hertingfordbury Park, West Street, Hertford
(Hertford 53716)
Ground capacity: 7,000   Seating capacity: 300
Covered accommodation: 1,500   Floodlights: Yes
Clubhouse details: Open each evening for a variety of social functions, run
by bar committee (Hertford 53716)
Best seasons in F.A. Cup: 1972-73 and 1977-78, 3rd Qual Rnd
Major honours: Herts Senior Cup winners 1967
Best season in F.A. Trophy: 1976–77
Local newspaper: Hertfordshire Mercury

HIGHGATE UNITED (M. COMB.)

Chairman: N. Smith
Secretary: A. Walker
Founded: 1948
Tel no: 021-430 5763
Team manager: F. O'Hare
Previous leagues: South Birmingham, West Midland Alliance, Worcester Combination
Colours: All red with white trim **Change colours:** All white with red trim
Address and tel no of ground: The Coppice, Tythe Barn Lane, Shirley, Solihull, West Midlands (021-744 4194)
Record attendance: 4,000 (1967)
Ground capacity: 5,000 **Seating capacity:** 350
Covered accommodation: 1,250 **Floodlights:** No
Clubhouse details: Saturday dances, Monday, Tuesday and Friday dominoes, darts, pool, food on Saturdays and match days only
Players with Football League experience: K. Lenard to Aston Villa; G. Scot to Stoke City
Major honours: Amateur Cup semi-finalists 1972-73, quarter-finalists 1967-68, 1971-72; Birmingham Senior Cup finalists 1971-72, winners 1973-74
Best season in F.A. Trophy: 1974-75, 3rd Rnd Proper
Club nickname: The Gate **Programme:** 24 pages, 10p
Local newspaper: Solihull News

HILLINGDON BOROUGH (S.L.S.)

Chairman: H. T. Brown
Secretary: S. R. Palmer
Founded: 1872
Tel no: Uxbridge 54679
Team manager: A. Batsford **Previous name:** Yiewsley Town
Previous leagues: Great Western Suburban, Spartan, Delphian, Corinthian
Colours: All sky blue **Change colours:** All red
Address and tel no of ground: The Leas Stadium, Falling Lane, Yiewsley, West Drayton, Middx (West Drayton 45292/42948)
Record attendance: 9,033 (1969)
Ground capacity: 15,000 **Seating capacity:** 800
Covered accommodation: 5,000 **Floodlights:** Yes
Clubhouse details: Full facilities available from Thursday to Sunday
Best season in F.A. Cup: 1969-70, beat Sutton United (replay) in 3rd Rnd Proper
League clubs defeated in F.A. Cup: Torquay Utd, Luton Town
Current players with Football League experience: T. Ryan; G. Phillips; I. Osborne; S. Melledew; A. Davies; E. Reeve; K. Millett; R. Wainwright; G. Williams; S. Adams; G. Smith
Major honours: F. A. Challenge Trophy runners-up 1970-71; Southern League 1st Div runners-up 1965-66, 1974-75; Southern League Prem Div runners-up 1968-69; Southern League Cup runners-up 1972-73
Best season in F.A. Trophy: 1970-71, lost in final
Club nickname: The Blues or The Boro'
Programme: 16-20 pages, 10p
Local newspapers: Uxbridge Gazette, Hillingdon Mirror

HINCKLEY ATHLETIC (W. MIDLANDS)

Chairman: D. W. Loakes   Founded: 1879
Secretary: J. Colver   Tel no: Hinckley 30263
Team manager: D. Callow
Previous leagues: Birmingham Combination, Southern
Colours: Red shirts, white shorts, white socks
Change colours: All white
Address and tel no of ground: Middlefield Sports Ground, Middlefield Lane, Hinckley, Leics (Hinckley 34137 – club; 613553 – ground)
Ground capacity: 6,000   Seating capacity: 340
Covered accommodation: 1,000   Floodlights: Yes
Clubhouse details: New club with bar, lounge and concert room
Best season in F.A. Cup: 1963
Best seasons in F.A. Vase: 1976, 1977, 1978 and 1979, 4th Rnd
Club nickname: The Robins   Programme: 4 pages, free
Local newspapers: Hinckley Times, Leicester Mercury, Nuneaton Tribune

HITCHIN TOWN (B.I.L. P. DIV)

Chairman: C. Quinn   Founded: 1865
Secretary: K. C. Wayling   Tel no: Hitchin 50692 (eve);
    2622 (day)
Team manager: Ray Freeman
Previous leagues: Athenian, Spartan
Colours: Yellow shirts with blue trim, yellow shorts
Change colours: All white
Address and tel no of ground: 'Topfield', Fishponds Road, Hitchin, Herts (Hitchin 59237/4483)   Record attendance: 1955-56
Ground capacity: 6,000   Seating capacity: 600
Covered accommodation: Two sides   Floodlights: Yes
Clubhouse details: Lounge, kitchen, VIP room, two bars, open every night
Best season in F.A. Cup: 1976, 2nd Rnd Proper
Current players with Football League experience: W. Baldry (Cambridge Utd)
Major honours: London Senior Cup winners 1970; Amateur Cup semi-finalists 1961-63; Herts Senior Cup winners 18 times; Isthmian League runners-up 1969
Best season in F.A. Trophy: 1976-77, 3rd Rnd
Club nickname: The Canaries   Programme: 20 pages, 10p
Local newspapers: Hitchin Gazette, Hitchin Comet

HODDESDON TOWN (K. ATHENIAN)

Chairman: E. E. Elliott   Founded: 1879
Secretary: D. Planton   Tel no: Hoddesdon 68886 (h);
    67272 ext 303 (bus)
Team manager: B. Moye
Previous leagues: East Herts, Herts County, Spartan, London Spartan

134

Colours: White shirts, black shorts, black, red and white socks
Change colours: All gold
Address and tel no of ground: Lowfield, Parkview, Hoddesdon, Herts
(Hertford 63133)
Ground capacity: 3,000   Seating capacity: 150
Covered accommodation: Yes   Floodlights: Yes
Major honours: F.A. Vase winners 1975; Spartan League champions
1970-71
Programme: 4 pages, 5p

HORDEN C.W.   (D. NORTHERN)

Chairman: J. Hickman   Founded: 1908
Secretary: R. Robinson   Tel no: 867093
Team manager: T. Kirkbride
Previous leagues: North Eastern, Midlands, Wearside
Colours: Red and white shirts, white shorts, red socks
Change colours: All white
Address of ground: Welfare Park, Horden, Peterlee, Co Durham
                                Record attendance: 8,000 (1937)
Ground capacity: 7,000   Seating capacity: 300
Covered accommodation: Grandstand Floodlights: Yes
Clubhouse details: Plans in operation for new clubhouse
Best season in F.A. Cup: 1947
Current players with Football League experience: J. Hather; R. Huntingdon;
P. Walker; D. Johnston; C. Cain
Major honours: Durham Challenge Cup winners twice, runners-up twice;
Wearside League champions
Best seasons in F.A. Trophy: 1970-71 and 1972-73, 1st Rnd Proper
Local newspapers: Hartlepool Mail, Northern Echo

HORNCHURCH   (B.I.L. DIV 2)

Chairman: J. Bradshaw   Founded: 1923
Secretary: D. W. Gooday   Tel no: Hornchurch 52676
Team manager: B. Kelly
Previous leagues: Athenian, Spartan, Corinthian, Delphian
Colours: White shirts with red trim, red shorts, red socks
Change colours: Blue shirts, black shorts
Address and tel no of ground: The Stadium, Bridge Avenue, Upminster,
Essex (Upminster 20080)
Ground capacity: 6,000   Seating capacity: 350
Covered accommodation: Yes   Floodlights: Yes
Clubhouse details: Open each evening, bar facilities, light snacks, disco at
weekends
Best season in F.A. Cup: 1958
Current players with Football League experience: P. Armstrong (Arsenal)
Best season in F.A. Vase: 1974-75, 5th Rnd
Club nickname: The Urchins   Programme: 12 pages, 10p
Local newspapers: The Post, Romford Recorder, Romford Observer

HORSHAM (B.I.L. DIV 1)

Chairman: F. King   **Founded:** 1885
Secretary: K. C. Taylor   **Tel no:** Horsham 65929
Team manager: John Laker
Previous leagues: Sussex County, Metropolitan, Athenian
Colours: Amber and green   **Change colours:** All blue
Address and tel no of ground: Queen Street, Horsham, West Sussex
(Horsham 2310)   **Record attendance:** 6,000 (1966)
Ground capacity: 4,250   **Seating capacity:** 500
Covered accommodation: Stand   **Floodlights:** Yes
Clubhouse details: Open match days and functions only
Best seasons in F.A. Cup: 1947-48 and 1966-67, 1st Rnd Proper
Major honours: Athenian League Div 1 champions 1972-73, Div 2 champions 1969-70
Best season in F.A. Trophy: 1976-77, 1st Rnd Proper
Club nickname: The Hornets   **Programme:** 8 pages, 6p
Local newspaper: West Sussex County Times

HORWICH R.M.I. (CHESHIRE CO. DIV 1)

Chairman: C. J. Healey   **Founded:** 1896
Secretary: W. M. Seddon   **Tel no:** Bolton 693946
Team manager: A. Kirkman
Previous leagues: Lancashire Combination, West Lancashire
Colours: Blue and white striped shirts, white shorts, blue socks
Change colours: All red
Address and tel no of ground: Grundy Hill, Victoria Road, Horwich, Bolton,
Lancs (Horwich 693946)
Ground capacity: 6,000   **Seating capacity:** 450
Covered accommodation: Two sides and one end
Floodlights: No
Clubhouse details: Social club
Best season in F.A. Cup: 1978–79, 4th Qual Rnd
Current players with Football League experience: J. Pearson (Man Utd); P. Burrows (Man City)
Best season in F.A. Trophy: 1978–79, 1st Rnd Proper
Club nickname: The Railwaymen   **Programme:** 10p
Local newspapers: Horwich Journal, Bolton Evening News

HOUNSLOW (S.L.S.)

Chairman: R. R. Simmons   **Founded:** 1884
Secretary: V. W. Bull   **Tel no:** 01-751 0884
Team manager: Phil Duggan
Previous leagues: Middlesex, Great Western Suburban, Spartan, Corinthian, Athenian
Colours: Red with black stripes   **Change colours:** All white

Address and tel no of ground: Denbigh Road, Hounslow, Middx
 (01-570 4983)
Ground capacity: 6,000　　　　　Seating capacity: 400
Covered accommodation: 2,500　　Floodlights: Yes
Clubhouse details: Open Tuesday, Thursday, Friday and Saturday evenings
 and Sunday lunchtimes
Best season in F.A. Cup: 1962-63, 1st Rnd
Current players with Football League experience: J. Auguste (Blackpool);
 M. Doherty (Southampton)
Best season in F.A. Trophy: Never past Prelim Rnd
Club nickname: The Town　　　　Programme: 8 pages, 10p
Local newspapers: Middlesex Chronicle, Evening Mail

HUNGERFORD TOWN　　(B.I.L. DIV 2)

Chairman: R. Tarry　　　　　　Founded: 1886
Secretary: A. K. Williams　　　Tel no: Hungerford 3207 (bus)
Team manager: James Kelman
Previous leagues: Newbury & District, Swindon District, Hellenic
Colours: White shirts with red trim, black or white shorts
Change colours: All red
Address and tel no of ground: Town Ground, Hungerford, Berks
 (Hungerford 2939)　　　　　　Record attendance: 1,541
Ground capacity: 5,000　　　　　Seating capacity: 200
Covered accommodation: 700　　Floodlights: Yes
Clubhouse details: Open every evening and on match day afternoons at
 4 p.m., entertainments every weekend, two bars, dance hall, food and
 refreshments
Best season in F.A. Cup: 1978-79, 2nd Qual Rnd replay
Current players with Football League experience: J. Ashton (Reading)
Major honours: Berks and Bucks Senior Cup finalists 1975-76, 1976-77,
 1978-79; Hellenic League Cup winners 1977-78
Best season in F.A. Vase: 1977-78, Semi-final replay
Club nickname: The Crusaders　　Programme: 12 pages, 20p
Local newspapers: Newbury Weekly News, Reading Evening Post, Swin-
 don Advertiser

HYDE UNITED　　(CHESHIRE CO. DIV 1)

Chairman: J. Cooper　　　　　　Founded: 1919
Secretary: D. Goodwin　　　　　Tel no: 061-368 6689
Team manager: L. Sutton
Previous leagues: Northern Premier, Manchester
Colours: Red and white striped shirts, black shorts
Change colours: Green and yellow striped shirts, green shorts
Address and tel no of ground: Ewen Fields, Miles Street, Hyde, Cheshire
 (061-368 1031)　　　　　　　Record attendance: 9,500 (1952)
Ground capacity: 7,500　　　　　Seating capacity: 650
Covered accommodation: All four sides Floodlights: Yes
Clubhouse details: Open most nights, full facilities, seats 180, stewards:
 Jim and Claire Rowbotham

Best season in F.A. Cup: 1954, lost to Workington 1st Rnd Proper
Major honours: Cheshire Senior Cup winners 1945–46, 1962–63, 1969–70;
    Cheshire League champions 1954–55, 1955–56
Best season in F.A. Trophy: 1975–76, 2nd Rnd Proper
Club nickname: The Tigers   Programme: 16 pages, 10p
Local newspapers: North Cheshire Herald, Hyde Reporter

HYTHE TOWN   (KENT)

Chairman: J. E. Robb   Founded: 1922
Secretary: A. J. Maycock   Tel no: Hythe 68346
Team manager: R. H. Davis
Previous league: Kent Amateur
Colours: White shirts, blue shorts
Change colours: Blue shirts, white shorts
Address of ground: Reachfield Stadium, Fort Road, Hythe, Kent
        Record attendance: 400 (1977)
Ground capacity: 2,000   Floodlights: No
Covered accommodation: Yes
Clubhouse details: Bar, social and dance facilities for 200 people
Current players with Football League experience: G. Towse (Crystal Palace,
    Brentford)
Major honours: Ken tLeague runners-up 1978–79
Best season in F.A. Vase: 1977–78, 1st Rnd
Club nickname: The Town   Programme: 8 pages, 10p
Local newspapers: Kentish Express, Folkestone Herald

ILFORD*   (B.I.L. DIV 1)

Chairman: L. G. Reeve   Founded: 1881
Secretary: D. J. York   Tel no: 01-590 8545
Previous leagues: Southern, London, South Essex
Colours: Blue and white hooped shirts
Change colours: Yellow and blue
Major honours: F.A. Amateur Cup winners 1928-29, 1929-30
Best season in F.A. Trophy: 1974-75, 3rd Rnd
Club nickname: The Fords   Programme: 12 pages, 10p
Local newspapers: Ilford Recorder, Ilford Post
* To amalgamate with Leytonstone F.C. in 1979-80 season to form Ilford
& Leytonstone F.C.

IRTHLINGBOROUGH DIAMONDS
(U. COUNTIES)

Chairman: A. C. Jones
Secretary: G. W. Slawson   Tel no: Wellingborough 650672
Team manager: A. Sabey
Previous leagues: Rushden & District Youth, Rushden & District, Ketter-
ing & District Amateur

Colours: Red shirts, blue shorts, red socks
Change colours: All blue
Address and tel no of ground: Nene Park, Irthlingborough, Wellingborough, Northants (Wellingborough 650672)

Record attendance: 2,412 (1978)

Ground capacity: 3,000   Seating capacity: 250
Covered accommodation: One side only   Floodlights: Yes
Clubhouse details: "Olde-worlde" style clubhouse, open each even in at 8 p.m., after Saturday games at 4 p.m. and at Sunday lunchtimes 12 – 1.30 p.m.
Best season in F.A. Cup: 1978-79, 4th Qual Rnd
Current players with Football League experience: S. Ferris (Chesterfield); B. Myton (Middlesbrough)
Major honours: United Counties League Prem Div champions 1970-71, 1976-77
Best season in F.A. Vase: 1977-78, 6th Rnd
Club nickname: The Diamonds   Programme: 8 pages, free
Local newspaper: Northamptonshire Evening Telegraph

KEMPSTON ROVERS
(UTD COUNTIES)

Chairman: D. J. Jack   Founded: 1884
Secretary: M. T. Parker   Tel no: Bedford 51913
Team manager: M. Bartlett
Previous leagues: Bedford & District, Biggleswade & District
Colours: Red and white striped shirts, white shorts, red socks
Change colours: Green shirts, black shorts, green socks
Address and tel no of ground: Hill Grounds Road, Kempston, Bedford (Bedford 852346)
Ground capacity: Approx. 1,500   Seating capacity: 30-40
Covered accommodation: Approx. 90 Floodlights: No
Clubhouse details: Main clubroom with bar (200 capacity), lounge bar (40 capacity)
Best season in F.A. Cup: 1977-78
Major honours: United Counties League champions 1973-74; Bedfordshire Senior Cup winners 1976-77
Best season in F.A. Vase: 1974-75, 5th Rnd
Local newspapers: Bedfordshire Times, Bedford Record

KETTERING TOWN   (A.P.L.)

Chairman: T. G. Bradley   Founded: 1875
Secretary: M. Marston   Tel no: Kettering 2760 (bus); 722855 (h)
Team manager: M. Jones
Previous leagues: Midland, Northamptonshire, Birmingham, Southern
Colours: Red shirts, white shorts
Change colours: White shirts, white shorts, red socks
Address and tel no of ground: Rockingham Road, Kettering, Northants (Kettering 2760)

Record attendance: 11,526 (1947-48)

Ground capacity: 12,000   Seating capacity: 2,290
Covered accommodation: 6,000   Floodlights: Yes
Best seasons in F.A. Cup: 1968-69 and 1976-77, 3rd Rnd
League clubs defeated in F.A. Cup: Oxford, Swansea, Millwall, Swindon
Current players with Football League experience: F. Lane; J. Lee; R.
    Dixey; W. Kellock; R. Clayton; G. Felton; L. Hughes
Major honours: Southern League champions 1927-28, 1956-57, 1972-73;
    Southern League Cup winners 1974-7; F.A. Trophy runners-up 1978-79
Best season in F.A. Trophy: 1978-79, Finalists
Club nickname: The Poppies   Programme: 12 pages, 15p
Local newspapers: Northamptonshire Evening Telegraph, Northampton
    Chronicle & Echo

KIDDERMINSTER HARRIERS (S.L.M.)

Chairman: Michael Savery   Founded: 1886
Secretary: Ray Mercer   Tel no: Kidderminster 61824 (h);
                                                  66111 (bus)
Team manager: John Chambers
Previous leagues: Birmingham, Birmingham Combination, Worcs Com-
    bination
Colours: Red shirts, white shorts   Change colours: All white
Address and tel no of ground: Aggborough Sports Ground, Hoo Road,
    Kidderminster, Worcs (Kidderminster 3931)
                                      Record attendance: 9,155 (1948)
Ground capacity: 8,000   Seating capacity: 1,500
Covered accommodation: 2,000   Floodlights: Yes
Clubhouse details: Open seven days a week, adjoins football club, all star
    cabaret, ballroom dancing, disco, bingo, etc.
Best season in F.A. Cup: 1935, 2nd Rnd
Current players with Football League experience: D. Seddon (Rochdale);
    J. Chambers (Aston Villa, Southend); J. Griffiths (Aston Villa, Stock-
    port County); I. Smith (Birmingham City)
Major honours: Worcestershire Senior Cup winners 13 times; Birmingham
    Senior Cup winners seven times; Border Counties League champions;
    Border Counties Cup winners; West Midlands League champions three
    times
Best season in F.A. Trophy: 1970-71, 3rd Rnd
Club nickname: The Harriers   Programme: 16 pages, 10p
Local newspapers: Kidderminster Times, Kidderminster Shuttle, Worcester
    Evening News, Worcester Express & Star, Worcester Evening Mail

KING'S LYNN (S.L.M.)

Chairman: J. Portfleet   Founded: 1879
Secretary: C. S. Hardy   Tel no: King's Lynn 3567
Team manager: B. Bridges
Previous leagues: Midland, Eastern Counties
Colours: Blue shirts, white shorts, white socks
Change colours: All yellow

140

Address and tel no of ground: The Walks Stadium, King's Lynn, Norfolk
(King's Lynn 3567)
Ground capacity: 18,000
Covered accommodation: 8,000
Best season in F.A. Cup: 1961-62, v Everton 3rd Rnd
League clubs defeated in F.A. Cup: Coventry City, Aldershot
Best season in F.A. Trophy: 1978-79, 2nd Rnd Proper
Club nickname: The Linnets
Local newspapers: Lynn News & Advertiser, Eastern Daily Press

Record attendance: 13,000
Seating capacity: 1,800
Floodlights: Yes

Programme: 10 pages, 10p

KINGSTONIAN (B.I.L. DIV 1)

Chairman: F. R. Jones
Secretary: Mrs M. W. Rowat
Team manager: Ken Ballard
Previous leagues: Kingston & District, Athenian
Colours: Light blue shirts, dark blue shorts
Change colours: Yellow shirts, blue shorts
Address and tel no of ground: Richmond Road, Kingston-upon-Thames,
Surrey (01-546 4116)
Ground capacity: 6,500
Covered accommodation: 2,500
Clubhouse details: Open every night, dances, dinners, meetings, socials,
steward: L. Rowat (01-546 4116 – ground)
Major honours: London Senior Cup winners 1963, 1964, 1965; F.A.
Amateur Cup winners 1933, finalists 1960; Isthmian League champions
1934, 1937; Surrey Senior Cup winners on 10 occasions
Best season in F.A. Trophy: 1977-78, 3rd Qual Rnd
Club nickname: The K's
Local newspapers: Surrey Comet, Kingston Borough News

Founded: 1885
Tel no: 01-546 4116 (bus)

Seating capacity: 1,200
Floodlights: Yes

Programme: 12 pages, 10p

KIRKBY TOWN (CHESHIRE CO. DIV 2)

Chairman: E. Kelly
Secretary: J. Smith
Team manager: Jack Prytherch
Previous leagues: Liverpool, Lancs Comb
Colours: Yellow and blue shirts, blue shorts, yellow socks
Change colours: Black and white shirts, black shorts, black socks
Address and tel no of ground: Simonswood Lane, Kirkby, Liverpool
(051-546 2159/4760)
Ground capacity: 10,000
Covered accommodation: 1,000
Clubhouse details: Open every afternoon and evening, meals available
during weekday afternoons, licensed bar, weekend concerts
Current players with Football League experience: F. Darcy Everton)
Best season in F.A. Trophy: 1969-70, 2nd Rnd Proper
Local newspapers: Liverpool Echo, Kirkby Reporter

Founded: 1962
Tel no: 051-546 0138

Seating capacity: 500
Floodlights: Yes

LANCASTER CITY (N.P.L.)

Chairman: W. Aspinall
Secretary: T. B. Eastwood
Team manager: S. Gallagher
Previous league: Lancashire Combination
Colours: All blue
Change colours: Yellow shirts, blue shorts, yellow socks
Address and tel no of ground: Giant Axe Field, West Road, Lancaster (Lancaster 65349)
Ground capacity: 6,000
Covered accommodation: 1,000
Founded: 1905
Tel no: Lancaster 65089

Record attendance: 7,509 (1936)
Seating capacity: 500
Floodlights: Yes
Clubhouse details: Open every night, cabaret on Sundays, bingo on Mondays and Wednesdays
Best seasons in F.A. Cup: 1973-74 and 1974-75, 4th Qual Rnd
League clubs defeated in F.A. Cup: Barrow, Stockport County
Current players with Football League experience: K. Dyson (Newcastle Utd, Blackpool)
Major honours: Lancashire Junior Cup winners 1927-28, 1928-29, 1930-31, 1933-34, 1951-52, 1974-75
Best seasons in F.A. Trophy: 1974-75 and 1975-76, 3rd Rnd Proper
Club nickname: The Dollies   Programme: 12 pages, 10p
Local newspapers: Morecambe Visitor, Lancaster Guardian

LEATHERHEAD (B.I.L. P. DIV)

Chairman: J. W. Hewlett
Secretary: J. J. O'Malley
Team manager: W. R. Miller
Previous leagues: Surrey Senior, Metropolitan, Delphian, Corinthian, Athenian
Colours: Green and white
Change colours: Red and black stripes
Address and tel no of ground: Guildford Road, Leatherhead, Surrey (Leatherhead 72634)
Ground capacity: 7,500
Covered accommodation: 2,000
Founded: 1946
Tel no: Ashtead 75789

Record attendance: 3,500 (1974)
Seating capacity: 452
Floodlights: Yes
Clubhouse details: Two club rooms available for hire, bingo, discos, youth social club
Best season in F.A. Cup: 1974-75, 4th Rnd
League clubs defeated in F.A. Cup: Colchester United, Northampton Town, Brighton & Hove, Cambridge United
Current players with Football League experience: S. Camp (Fulham, Peterborough); C. Kelly (Millwall); J. Swannell (Stockport Co, Crystal Palace)
Major honours: Surrey Senior League champions eight times, Surrey Senior Cup winners 1969
Best season in F.A. Trophy: 1977-78, Final
Club nickname: The Tanners   Programme: 20 pages, 10p
Local newspaper: Leatherhead Advertiser

LEEK TOWN (CHESHIRE CO. DIV 1)

Chairman: F. C. Ball
Secretary: P. Cope
Team manager: K. Hancock
Previous leagues: Staffs County, Manchester
Colours: Blue shirts, white shorts, white socks
Change colours: All white
Address and tel no of ground: Hamil Park, Macclesfield Road, Leek, Staffordshire (Leek 383374/385712)
Ground capacity: 5,000
Covered accommodation: 2,000
Clubhouse details: Licensed club, open match days and special events
Best season in F.A. Cup: 1975-76, 4th Qual Rnd
Major honours: Cheshire League champions 1974-75; Challenge Shield winners 1974-75
Best season in F.A. Trophy: 1973, 1st Rnd Proper
Club nickname: The Blues
Local newspapers: Staffs Evening Sentinel, Leek Post & Times

Founded: 1946
Tel no: Leek 373011

Record attendance: 3,500 (1973)
Seating capacity: 150
Floodlights: Yes

Programme: 8 pages, 10p

LETCHWORTH GARDEN CITY
(B.I.L. DIV 2)

Chairman: J. Mason
Secretary: A. Arnold
Team manager: G. Todd
Previous leagues: Herts County, Delphian, Spartan, Athenian
Colours: Royal blue and white
Address and tel no of ground: Baldock Road, Letchworth, Herts (Letchworth 4691)
Ground capacity: 3,500
Covered accommodation: Main stand Floodlights: Yes
Clubhouse details: Licensed, 250 capacity, bar open from 7.30 to 10.30 p.m. (Sunday to Thursday), 7.30 to 11 p.m. (Friday and Saturday) and 12 to 2.00 p.m. Sunday lunchtimes
Best season in F.A. Cup: 1977-78, last Qual Rnd replay
Major honours: Herts Senior Cup winners 1913, 1936, 1952; Athenian League champions 1974; Herts County League champions 1912; Spartan League champions 1930, 1936; Delphian League champions 1958
Best season in F.A. Vase: 1978-79, 2nd Rnd
Club nickname: The Bluebirds
Local newspapers: Letchworth Citizen Gazette, Letchworth Comet

Founded: 1906
Tel no: Ware 67089

Change colours: All red

Seating capacity: 266

Programme: 7p

LEWES (B.I.L. DIV 2)

Chairman: W. D. Carr
Secretary: P. B. Hiscox
Team manager: R. Smith
Previous leagues: Athenian, Sussex County, Mid-Sussex
Colours: Red shirts, black shorts, black socks
Change colours: White and black

Founded: 1885
Tel no: Brighton 557867

Address and tel no of ground: The Dripping Pan, Lewes, East Sussex
(Lewes 2100)   Record attendance: 5,500
Ground capacity: 10,000   Seating capacity: 400
Covered accomodation: 400   Floodlights: Yes
Clubhouse details: Bar and club room
Best season in F.A. Cup: 1976-77, 4th Qual Rnd
Major honours: Sussex Senior Cup winners; Athenian League Div 1 and 2
champions; Athenian League Cup winners
Best season in F.A. Vase: 1972-73
Club nickname: The Rooks   Programme: 10p
Local newspapers: Evening Argus, Sussex Express & County Herald

LEYTONSTONE*   (B.I.L. DIV 1)

Chairman: D. J. Andrews   Founded: 1886
Secretary: W. A. J. Ferguson   Tel no: 01-539 8114
Team manager: J. Still
Previous league: South Essex
Colours: Red shirts, black shorts, black socks
Change colours: White shirts, black shorts, black socks
Address and tel no of ground: Granleigh Road, Leytonstone, London, E.11
(01-539 6117)   Record attendance: 9,740 (1949)
Ground capacity: 8,000   Seating capacity: 500
Covered accomodation: 1,500   Floodlights: Yes
Clubhouse details: Open daily, full facilities, steward: F. Wilkes (01-556
7270)
Best season in F.A. Cup: 1948-49, 2nd Rnd Proper
League clubs defeated in F.A. Cup: Watford
Current players with Football League experience: D. J. Danson (West Ham,
Bournemouth)
Major honours: European Cup Winners Cup 1968; F.A. Amateur Cup
winners 1946-47, 1947-48, 1967-68; Essex Senior Cup winners 1904-05,
1913-14, 1947-48, 1948-49, 1964-65, 1965-66, 1966-67; London Senior
Cup winners 1919-20, 1947-48, 1965-66; Isthmian League champions
1937-38, 1938-39, 1946-47, 1947-48, 1949-50, 1950-51, 1951-52, 1965-
66
Best seasons in F.A. Trophy: 1974-75 and 1976-77, 2nd Qual Rnd
Club nickname: The Stones   Programme: 12 pages, 10p
Local newspaper: Walthamstow Guardian and Independent
*To amalgamate with Ilford F.C. to become Ilford and Leytonstone F.C.
this season

LEYTON-WINGATE   (K. ATHENIAN)

Chairman: G. Gross   Founded: 1868
Secretary: J. C. Sorrell   Tel no: 01-524 2884 (h);
                                     01-989 3980 (bus)
Team manager: S. Underwood
Colours: Blue shirts, white shorts, blue socks
Change colours: White shirts, blue shorts, white socks

144

Address and tel no of ground: Wingate-Leyton Stadium, 282 Lea Bridge
Road, Leyton, London, E10 7ID (01–539 5405)
Ground capacity: 1,000   Seating capacity: 100
Covered accommodation: 150   Floodlights: Yes
Clubhouse details: Open each night, darts, pool
Best season in F.A. Cup: 1978–79, 3rd Qual Rnd
Major honours: Athenian League champions 1977–78, runners-up 1978–79
Best season in F.A. Vase: 1978–79, 5th Rnd
                                Programme: 8 pages, 10p
Local newspaper: Waltham Forest Guardian

LISKEARD ATHLETIC
(SOUTH WESTERN)

Chairman: R. J. Peake   Founded: 1888
Secretary: W. R. Collins   Tel no: Liskeard 42421
Team manager: B. Hodge
Previous league: East Cornwall Premier
Colours: Blue shirts and shorts with white trim
Change colours: White shirts, blue shorts
Address and tel no of ground: Lux Park, Liskeard, Cornwall
   (Liskeard 42665)   Record attendance: 1,500 (1972)
Ground capacity: 3,500   Seating capacity: 200
Covered accommodation: 700   Floodlights: Yes
Clubhouse details: Open every day, fully licensed, dancing on Saturdays
   food on match days, steward: B. Lorenz
Best season in F.A. Cup: 1978–79, 3rd Qual Rnd
Current players with Football League experience: R. Davis (Plymouth
   Argyle, Southampton); B. Murphy (Torquay United)
Major honours: South Western League champions 1976-77, 1978-79;
   South Western League Cup winners 1976-77, 1978-79
Club nickname: The Blues   Programme: 20 pages, 5p
Local newspaper: Cornish Times

LONG EATON UNITED
(MID COUNTIES)

Chairman: Mr C. Connell   Founded: 1957
Secretary: Mr G. W. Whitehead   Tel no: Draycott 2849
Team manager: Mr D. Berresford
Previous league: Central Alliance
Colours: Royal blue or blue and white striped shirts, blue shorts, blue socks
Change colours: All yellow
Address and tel no of ground: Grange Park, Long Eaton, Nottingham
   (Long Eaton 5700)
Ground capacity: 3,000   Seating capacity: None
Covered accommodation: Partial   Floodlights: No
Clubhouse details: Plans for clubhouse in 1979-80 season

Current players with Football League experience: J. Inger; R. Limb; S. Holder; J. Mee
Major honours: Derbyshire Senior Cup winners 1960-61, 1975-76
Best season in F.A. Trophy: 1976-77, 3rd Qual Rnd
Club nickname: The Blues   Programme: 8 pages, 5p
Local newspapers: Long Eaton Advertiser, Nottingham Evening Post, Derby Evening Telegraph

LOUTH UNITED   (MID. COUNTIES)

Chairman: W. Allinson   Founded: 1947
Secretary: P. Smith   Tel no: Grimsby 79356
Team manager: R. Gooch
Previous league: Lincolnshire
Colours: White shirts with blue trim, blue shorts, blue socks
Change colours: All red
Address and tel no of ground: Park Avenue, Louth, Lincs (Louth 3253)   Record attendance: 2,000 (1977)
Ground capacity: 2,800   Seating capacity: 100
Covered accomodation: Stand   Floodlights: Yes
Clubhouse details: Improved facilities available shortly
Best season in F.A. Cup: 1978-79
Current players with Football League experience: A. Marley; W. Howells
Major honours: Lincolnshire F.A. Senior 'A' Cup winners 1977-78
Best seasons in F.A. Trophy: 1971-72 and 1974-75, 3rd Qual Rnd
Local newspapers: Louth Standard, Grimsby Evening Telegraph

LOWESTOFT TOWN
(TOWN & COUNTRY)

Chairman: R. Butcher   Founded: 1890
Secretary: M. J. Reeve   Tel no: Lowestoft 84335
Team manager: M. Antcliffe
Previous leagues: Norfolk & Suffolk, Eastern Counties
Colours: Blue shirts, white shorts   Change colours: All white
Address and tel no of ground: Crown Meadow, Love Road, Lowestoft, Suffolk (Lowestoft 3818)
Ground capacity: 5,000   Seating capacity: 500
Covered accommodation: Stand and lean-to
          Floodlights: Yes
Clubhouse details: Open daily, full facilities, social club secretary: Mrs P. Read (Lowestoft 67210)
Best season in F.A. Cup: 1977-78, 1st Rnd Proper
Major honours: East Anglian Cup winners; Suffolk Premier Cup winners; Eastern Counties League champions and Cup winners; Town and Country League champions
Best season in F.A. Trophy: 1971-72, 2nd Rnd Proper
Club nickname: The Blues   Programme: 10 pages, 6p
Local newspaper: Lowestoft Journal

146

LYE TOWN   (W. MIDLANDS)

Chairman: G. Ball   Founded: 1931
Secretary: G. F. Yates   Tel no: Brierley Hill 77188
Team manager: R. Evans
Colours: All blue   Change colours: All red
Address of ground: Lye Sports Ground, Stourbridge Road, Lye, Stour-
bridge, Worcs
Ground capacity: 4,500   Seating capacity: 150
Covered accommodation: Yes   Floodlights: Yes
Clubhouse details: Dressing rooms, social club
Major honours: Worcestershire Combination League champions 1935-36
Best season in F.A. Trophy: 1975-76, 3rd Qual Rnd
Programme: 6 pages, 5p
Local newspapers: Birmingham Mail, Express & Star

MACCLESFIELD TOWN   (N.P.L.)

Chairman: A. Brocklehurst   Founded: 1875
Secretary: A. Cash
Team manager: P. Staley
Previous league: Cheshire
Colours: All royal blue   Change colours: All yellow
Address and tel no of ground: Moss Rose Ground, London Road, Maccles-
field, Cheshire (Macclesfield 24324)
Ground capacity: 10,000   Seating capacity: 585
Covered accommodation: Stand and terrace
     Floodlights: Yes
Clubhouse details: Social club on ground under main stand
Best season in F.A. Cup: 1968–69, 3rd Rnd
League clubs defeated in F.A. Cup: Stockport County
Major honours: Northern Premier League champions 1968–69, 1969–70
Best season in F.A. Trophy: 1969–70, Winners
Club nickname: The Silkmen   Programme: 8 pages, 10p
Local newspapers: Macclesfield Express, Macclesfield Advertiser

MAIDENHEAD UNITED   (B.I.L. DIV 1)

Chairman: C. L. West   Founded: 1869
Secretary: C. H. Harwood   Tel no: Bracknell 25139
Team manager: G. Anthony
Previous leagues: Athenian, Corinthian, Spartan
Colours: White shirts, black shorts, white and black socks
Change colours: Amber shirts, black shorts, amber socks
Address and tel no of ground: York Road, Maidenhead, Berks
(Maidenhead 24739)
Ground capacity: 9,400   Seating capacity: 400
Covered accommodation: 400   Floodlights: Yes
Clubhouse details: Open five nights a week, dances, discos
Best season in F.A. Cup: 1872-73, Semi-final

Major honours: Berks & Bucks Senior Cup winners 1961, 1963, 1966, 1970
Best season in F.A. Trophy: 3rd Qual Rnd
Club nickname: United   Programme: 16 pages, 10p
Local newspapers: Maidenhead Advertiser, Evening Mail, Evening Post

MAIDSTONE   (A.P.L.)

Chairman: J. C. Thompson   Founded: 1897
Secretary: J. Leeds   Tel no: Maidstone 62276
Team manager: B. J. Watling
Previous leagues: Kent, Thames & Medway Combination, Corinthian,
    Athenian, Isthmian, Southern
Colours: Amber shirts, black shorts, black socks
Change colours: All white
Address and tel no of ground: The Stadium, London Road, Maidstone,
    Kent (Maidstone 54403/57275/55812)
                                  Record attendance: 10,500 (1979)
Ground capacity: 15,000   Seating capacity: 1,000
Covered accommodation: 3,500   Floodlights: Yes
Clubhouse details: Open every night, greyhound racing and various enter-
    tainments, fully licensed, catering available
Best season in F.A. Cup: 1978-79, 3rd Rnd Proper
League clubs defeated in F.A. Cup: Exeter City
Current players with Football League experience: D. Guy; W. Edwards;
    K. Hill; N. Merrick; G. Aitken; P. Silvester; D. Wiltshire
Major honours: Southern League Div 1 South champions 1972-73; Kent
    Senior Cup winners 1966, 1976, 1979
Best season in F.A. Trophy: 3rd Rnd Proper v Kettering
Club nickname: The Stones   Programme: 24 pages, 15p
Local newspapers: Kent Messenger, Maidstone Gazette, Kent Evening
    Post

MANGOTSFIELD UNITED   (WESTERN)

Chairman: C. Packer   Founded: 1950
Secretary: B. P. Tilling   Tel no: Bitton 3009
Team manager: D. Hillard
Previous leagues: Bristol & District, Bristol Premier
Colours: White with sky blue and claret trim
Change colours: Red and black
Address and tel no of ground: Cossham Street, Mangotsfield, Bristol
    (Bristol 560119)
Ground capacity: 3,000   Seating capacity: None
Covered accommodation: 500   Floodlights: Yes
Clubhouse details: Open every night and Saturday and Sunday lunchtimes,
    pool, darts, discos, entertainment on occasional Saturdays, steward: R.
    Williams (Bristol 560019)
Programme: 12 pages, 5p

MARCH TOWN UNITED
(TOWN & COUNTRY)

Chairman: C. R. W. Woodcock   Founded: 1908
Secretary: P. J. H. Frost   Tel no: Peterborough 203391
Team manager: David Eldred
Previous leagues: Peterborough & District, United Counties
Colours: Yellow shirts, blue shorts, yellow socks
Change colours: All red
Address and tel no of ground: G.E.R. Sports Ground, Robingoodfellows Lane, March, Cambs (March 3073) Record attendance: 5,858 (1951)
Ground capacity: 5,000   Seating capacity: 800
Covered accommodation: 400   Floodlights: Yes
Clubhouse details: Bar open every evening and on match days, darts and dominoes teams
Best seasons in F.A. Cup: 1955-56 and 1978-79, 1st Rnd Proper
League clubs defeated in F.A. Cup: Brentford, Swindon Town
Major honours: United Counties League champions 1953-54; East Anglian Cup winners 1953-54; Cambridgeshire Football Association Invitation Cup winners 1954-55
Best season in F.A. Vase: 1975-76, 3rd Rnd
Club nickname: The Hares   Programme: 4 pages, 5p
Local newspapers: Cambridgeshire Times, Fenland Advertiser, Peterborough Evening Telegraph

MARGATE
(S.L.S.)

Chairman: R. Crittenden   Founded: 1929
Secretary: J. Kemp   Tel no: Thanet 41003 (h);
    01-283 3100 (bus)
Team manager: D. Hunt
Previous league: Kent
Colours: White shirts, blue shorts, blue and white socks
Change colours: All yellow or yellow shirts, blue shorts, blue socks
Address and tel no of ground: Hartsdown Park, Margate, Kent (Thanet 21769)
Ground capacity: 8,500   Seating capacity: 650
Covered accommodation: 2,650   Floodlights: Yes
Clubhouse details: Blue and White Club open on match days and by arrangement, snacks available
Best seasons in F.A. Cup: 1936 and 1972-73, 3rd Rnd
Major honours: Southern League Div 1 S champions 1977-78
Best season in F.A. Trophy: 1975, 2nd Rnd
Programme: 6 pages, 10p
Local newspapers: Isle of Thanet Gazette, Thanet Times, East Kent Times

MARINE
(CHESHIRE CO. DIV 1)

Chairman: P. T. Culshaw   Founded: 1894
Secretary: E. D. Graham   Tel no: 051-924 5717
Team manager: R. Howard

Previous leagues: I. Zingari, Liverpool County Combination, Lancashire
Combination
Colours: White shirts, black shorts, white socks
Change colours: Yellow shirts, blue shorts, yellow socks
Address and tel no of ground: Rossett Park, College Road, Crosby, Mersey-
side, L23 (051-924 4046)
Ground capacity: 4,000   Seating capacity: 400
Covered accommodation: One side and shelter
                                                 Floodlights: Yes
Clubhouse details: Full facilities available
Best season in F.A. Cup: 1975-76, 2nd Rnd Proper
League clubs defeated in F.A. Cup: Barnsley
Current players with Football League experience: J. Smith (Carlisle, Ever-
ton); D. McClatchley (Barrow, Liverpool); R. Pritchard (Tranmere
Rovers)
Major honours: Cheshire League champions 1973-74, 1975-76, 1977-78;
F.A. Amateur Cup finalists 1931-32
Best season in F.A. Trophy: 1978-79, 2nd Rnd
Club nickname: The Marines or The Lilywhites
                                          Programme: 20 pages, 10p
Local newspapers: Liverpool Echo, Crosby Herald

MARLOW   (K. ATHENIAN)

Chairman: K. T. Budd   Founded: 1870
Secretary: P. C. Burdell   Tel no: Marlow 3722
Team manager: P. Jarratt
Previous leagues: Southern, Spartan
Colours: Royal blue and white trim Change colours: Old gold
Address and tel no of ground: Alfred Davis Memorial Ground, Oak Tree
Road, Marlow, Bucks (Marlow 3970)
Ground capacity: 8,000   Seating capacity: 300
Covered accommodation: 300   Floodlights: Yes
Clubhouse details: Open most evenings and Sunday lunchtimes
Best season in F.A. Cup: 1881-82, Semi-final
Best season in F.A. Vase: 1974-75, 5th Rnd
Club nickname: The Blues   Programme: 2 pages, 5p
Local newspapers: Bucks Free Press, Evening Mail

MATLOCK TOWN   (N.P.L.)

Chairman: C. Britland   Founded: 1900
Secretary: K. F. Brown   Tel no: Matlock 4231
Team manager: T. Fenoughty
Previous leagues: Midland, Central Alliance
Colours: Royal blue shirts, white shorts, royal blue socks
Change colours: Yellow shirts, blue shorts, yellow socks
Address and tel no of ground: Causeway Lane, Matlock, Derbyshire
(Matlock 55362/3866)   Record attendance: 5,123 (1975)
Ground capacity: 7,500   Seating capacity: 200

Covered accommodation: 1,200   Floodlights: Yes
Clubhouse details: Gladiators social club situated on ground
Best season in F.A. Cup: 1976–77, 3rd Rnd Proper
Current players with Football League experience: T. Fenoughty (Sheffield Utd, Chesterfield); K. Stott (Crewe, Chesterfield); C. Smith (Bury)
Major honours: F.A. Trophy winners 1974–75; Northern Premier Cup winners 1977–78; Derbyshire Senior Cup winners; Northern Premier Shield winners 1974–75, 1976–77, 1977–78, 1978–79
Best season in F.A. Trophy: 1974–75, Winners
Club nickname: The Gladiators   Programme: 8 pages, 5p
Local newspapers: Matlock Mercury, Derbyshire Times

MERTHYR TYDFIL   (S.L.M.)

Chairman: D. Owen   Founded: 1945
Secretary: K. Tucker   Tel no: Merthyr Tydfil 3884
Team manager: D. Evans
Previous league: Welsh
Colours: White shirts, black shorts   Change colours: Amber and black
Address and tel no of ground: Pendarren Park, Merthyr Tydfil, Mid Glam (Merthyr Tydfil 71395)
Ground capacity: 6,000   Seating capacity: 300
Covered accommodation: 3,000   Floodlights: Yes
Clubhouse details: Full social club activities, open every night, steward: D. Miles (Merthyr Tydfil 71395)
Best season in F.A. Cup: 1973-74, 2nd Rnd
Major honours: Welsh Cup winners 1949, 1951; Southern League champions 1947-48, 1949-50, 1951-52, 1953-54; Southern League Cup winners 1948, 1951
Best season in F.A. Trophy: 1977-78, Quarter-final
Programme: 6 pages, 5p
Local newspaper: Merthyr Express

METROPOLITAN POLICE (B.I.L. DIV 1)

Chairman: J. S. Wilson, O.B.E.   Founded: 1919
Secretary: D. J. F. Alldridge, M.B.E. Tel no: Burgh Heath 50527
Team manager: V. Rouse
Previous leagues: Spartan, Herts & Middlesex Comb, South Eastern Comb, Metropolitan, Southern
Colours: All blue   Change colours: All red or all yellow
Address and tel no of ground: Police Sports Ground, Imber Court, Thames Ditton, East Molesey, Surrey (01-398 1267)
    Record attendance: 4,500 (1934)
Ground capacity: 4,000   Seating capacity: 600
Covered accommodation: 800   Floodlights: Yes
Clubhouse details: Lounge, cafeteria, sportsman bar, billiard room, dining room, ballroom, kitchen and bar facilities
Best season in F.A. Cup: 1934
Current players with Football League experience: G. Stride (Bournemouth); C. Mackleworth (West Ham, Leicester)

Major honours: Spartan League champions 1929, 1930, 1937, 1939, 1946,
1947, 1954, 1955; Middlesex Senior Cup winners 1928; Surrey Senior
Cup winners 1933; London Senior Cup winners 1933; Herts & Middlesex
Comb League champions 1940; Surrey Charity Shield winners 1939
Best season in F.A. Trophy: 1974-75, 3rd Qual Rnd
Club nickname: The Blues   Programme: 12 pages, free
Local newspaper: Surrey Comet

MEXBOROUGH TOWN ATHLETIC
(MID COUNTIES)

Chairman: P. Ryall   Founded: 1962
Secretary: D. Cope   Tel no: Mexborough 582675
Team manager: Harold Sapey
Previous league: Yorkshire
Colours: Blue and white striped shirts, blue shorts, red socks
Change colours: Yellow shirts, blue shorts, blue socks
Address and tel no of ground: Hampden Road, Mexborough, South York-
shire (Mexborough 586479)   Record attendance 2,000 (1973)
Ground capacity: 5,000   Seating capacity: 250
Covered accommodation: Stand   Floodlights: No
Clubhouse details: Mexborough Athletic Club
Best season in F.A. Cup: 1976-77, lost to Macclesfield Prelim Rnd
Current players with Football League experience: S. Kulic (Rotherham);
D. Downing (Middlesborough); K. Eades (Rotherham)
Major honours: Yorkshire League champions; Yorkshire Cup winners;
Sheffield Senior Cup winners
Best season in F.A. Trophy: 1973, 3rd Rnd Proper
Club nickname: The Boro'   Programme: 8 pages, 5p
Local newspaper: South Yorkshire Times

MIDDLEWICH ATHLETIC
(CHESHIRE CO. DIV 2)

Chairman: D. Millington   Reformed: 1952
Secretary: S. D. Larkin   Tel no: Middlewich 3589
Team manager: Dave Nixon
Previous league: Mid-Cheshire
Colours: White shirts with black trim, black shorts, black socks
Change colours: All red
Address and tel no of ground: Seddon Street, Middlewich, Cheshire
(Middlewich 2003)   Record attendance: 2,500 (1955-56)
Ground capacity: 5,000   Seating capacity: None
Covered accommodation: 300   Floodlights: No
Clubhouse details: Open every night, Saturday and Sunday lunchtimes
and match day afternoons, varied entertainment
Major honours: Mid-Cheshire League champions five times
Best season in F.A. Vase: 1974-75, 5th Rnd
Club nickname: The Witch   Programme: 12 pages, 10p
Local newspapers: Middlewich Chronicle, Middlewich Guardian

MILTON KEYNES CITY (S.L.M.)

Chairman: E. Sherry   Founded: 1946 as Bletchley Town
present name since 1974

Secretary: E. Bartlett   Tel no: Milton Keynes 77004
Team manager: R. Bailey
Previous leagues: North Bucks, South Midlands, Spartan, Hellenic, United Counties, Metropolitan
Colours: Tangerine shirts, black shorts, blue socks
Change colours: White shirts, blue shorts, blue socks
Address and tel no of ground: City Ground, Manor Fields, Bletchley, Milton Keynes, Bucks (Milton Keynes 75256)

Record attendance: 1,997 (1967)

Ground capacity: 4,000   Seating capacity: 150
Covered accommodation: 2,000   Floodlights: Yes
Clubhouse details: Open daily, licensed bar and hall, club and private functions, snacks
Best seasons in F.A. Cup: 1964-65 and 1965-66, 4th Qual Rnd
Best season in F.A. Trophy: 1973-74, 2nd Rnd Proper
Club nickname: The Gladiators   Programme: 2 pages, 5p
Local newspapers: Milton Keynes Gazette, Milton Keynes Express

MINEHEAD (S.L.M.)

Chairman: A. T. Copp   Founded: 1889
Secretary: D. A. Hawker   Tel no: Minehead 2474
Team manager: W. Brown
Previous leagues: Western, Somerset Senior
Colours: All blue   Change colours: All yellow
Address and tel no of ground: The Recreation Ground, Alexandra Road, Minehead, Somerset (Minehead 4989 – club; 5573 – office)

Record attendance: 3,161 (1977)

Ground capacity: 4,500   Seating capacity: 500
Covered accommodation: 650   Floodlights: Yes
Clubhouse details: Open daily, full facilities available
Best seasons in F.A. Cup: 1976–77, lost to Portsmouth 1-2 2nd Rnd; 1977–78 lost to Exeter City 0-3 2nd Rnd
League clubs defeated in F.A. Cup: Swansea City
Current players with Football League experience: W. Brown (Torquay Utd); R. Walker, J. Macey, A. White, R. Guscott, B. Preece (all Newport County)
Major honours: Somerset Premier Cup winners 1960–61, 1976–77; Southern League Div 1 South champions 1975–76; Southern League Prem Div runners-up 1976–77; Southern League Merit Cup winners 1975–76
Best seasons in F.A. Trophy: 1973–74, 1976–77 and 1978–79, 2nd Rnd Proper
Club nickname: The Sky Blues   Programme: 12p
Local newspapers: West Somerset Free Press, Somerset County Gazette

MOLESEY (B.I.L. DIV 2)

Chairman: J. Jones
Founded: 1953
Secretary: R. Rudley
Tel no: 01-979 8300
Team manager: J. Sullivan
Previous leagues: Surrey Intermediate, Surrey Senior, Spartan, Athenian
Colours: All white with red striped sleeves
Change colours: All red
Address of ground: Walton Road, West Molesey, Surrey
Ground capacity: 2,000
Seating capacity: 400
Covered accommodation: Yes
Floodlights: Yes
Clubhouse details: Open every night, two bars, Saturday and Sunday disco,
   live artists on occasional Saturdays, bar nights, table tennis club, darts
   eight-ball pool, bingo, steward: R. Rudley (01-979 3734 – club)
Best season in F.A. Cup: 1975-76, 3rd Qual Rnd
Major honours: Surrey Senior League champions 1957-58
Best seasons in F.A. Vase: 1974-75 and 1975-76, 5th Rnd
Programme: 8-10 pages, 10p
Local newspapers: Surrey Comet, Molesey News

MOOR GREEN (MID. COMB.)

Chairman: J. A. Davis
Founded: 1901
Secretary: J. S. Notley
Tel no: 021-704 3616 (h)
Colours: Light and dark blue shirts, blue shorts, yellow socks
Change colours: All white
Address and tel no of ground: The Moorlands, Sherwood Road, Hall
   Green, Birmingham, B28 OEX (021-777 2757)
Ground capacity: 5,000
Seating capacity: 300
Covered accommodation: 1,000
Floodlights: No
Clubhouse details: Open six nights (not Monday), dances, cabaret, bar, etc.
Major honours: A.F.A. Challenge Cup winners 1938-39; Birmingham
   Senior Cup winners 1957-58; Birmingham & District A.F.A. Senior
   Challenge Cup winners 1926-27, 1935-36; Central Amateur League
   champions 1936-39
Best season in F.A. Trophy: 1974-75, 1st Qual Rnd
Club nickname: The Moors
Local newspaper: Solihull News

MORECAMBE (N.P.L.)

Chairman: J. H. Dixon
Founded: 1920
Secretary: K. D. Ormrod
Tel no: Morecambe 415324
Team manager: M. Hoggarth
Previous league: Lancashire Combination
Colours: All red
Change colours: White shirts, blue shorts
Address and tel no of ground: Christie Park, Lancaster Road. Morecambe,
   Lancs, LA4 5TJ (Morecambe 411797)
Record attendance: 12,000 (1962)
Ground capacity: 9,000
Seating capacity: 1,500
Covered accommodation: Behind each goal and in front of main stand
Floodlights: Yes

Clubhouse details: Open every night, entertainment, bingo and cabaret Mondays, Wednesdays, Fridays, Saturdays and Sundays, secretary: Mrs P. Dickinson (Morecambe 418178)
Best season in F.A. Cup: 1962, 3rd Rnd
League clubs defeated in F.A. Cup: Chester, York City, Lincoln City, Stockport County
Current players with Football League experience: K. Newton (Burnley, Blackburn, Everton, England); M. Darling (Blackburn, Stockport Co); D. Helliwell (Blackburn, Workington)
Best season in F.A. Trophy: 1973-74, Winners
Club nickname: The Shrimps   Programme: 6 pages, 5p
Local newspapers: Morecambe Visitor, Morecambe Guardian

MORETON TOWN   (GL. CO.)

Chairman: C. F. Miles   Founded: Pre-1920
Secretary: P. A. Gardner   Tel no: Moreton-in-Marsh 51079
Team manager: C. Shepherd
Colours: White shirts, blue shorts, blue socks
Change colours: All blue
Address of ground: London Road, Moreton-in-Marsh, Gloucestershire
Ground capacity: 1,000 plus   Seating capacity: 100 plus
Covered accommodation: Yes   Floodlights: Yes
Clubhouse details: Club room, bar, dancing facilities
Major honours: Biggart Cup winners 1969-70, 1973-74, 1975-76; Hellenic League champions 1973-74; Gloucestershire County Cup winners
Best season in F.A. Vase: 1976-77, 3rd Rnd
Club nickname: The Lilywhites   Programme: None
Local newspaper: Evesham Journal

MOSSLEY   (N.P.L.)

Chairman: I. S. Morecroft   Founded: 1909
Secretary: A. Hardy   Tel no: Mossley 2369 (bus);
Team manager: B. Murphy   061-620 5584 (h)
Previous leagues: Ashton, South East Lancs, Lancs Comb, Cheshire
Colours: White shirts, white shorts, red socks
Change colours: Yellow shirts, blue shorts, blue socks
Address and tel no of ground: Seel Park, Market Street, Mossley, Ashton-under-Lyne, Lancs (Mossley 2369) Record attendance: 4,493 (1969-70)
Ground capacity: 8,000   Seating capacity: 300
Covered accommodation: 2,000   Floodlights: Yes
Clubhouse details: Open every evening from 7.30 p.m., Saturday and Sunday lunchtime from 12 noon
Best season in F.A. Cup: 1949-50, 2nd Rnd
Current players with Football League experience: L. Skeete (Rochdale); B. Grundy (Bury); J. Fitton (Oldham Ath); J. O'Connor (Bury); A. Brown (Bradford)
Major honours: N.P.L. champions 1978-79; N.P.L. Cup winners 1978-79, runners-up 1975-76; Cheshire League runners-up 1919-20, 1969-70; Cheshire League Cup winners 1920-21, 1960-61
Best season in F.A. Trophy: 1969-70, Quarter-final
Club nickname: The Lilywhites   Programme: 16 pages, 10p
Local newspaper: Mossley & Saddleworth Reporter

NANTWICH TOWN
(CHESHIRE CO. DIV 1)

Chairman: G. E. Lockyer
Secretary: J. Lindop
Team manager: C. Hutchinson
Previous leagues: Mid-Cheshire, Manchester
Colours: Green shirts, white shorts Change colours: Red shirts, white shorts
Address and tel no of ground: Jackson Avenue, Nantwich, Cheshire (Nantwich 64098)
Ground capacity: 2,500
Covered accommodation: 750
Current players with Football League experience: P. Mayman (Crew Alex)
Major honours: Cheshire Cup winners 1976
Best season in F.A. Trophy: 1973–74, 1st Rnd Proper
Club nickname: The Dabbers
Local newspapers: Evening Sentinel, Manchester Evening News

Founded: 1884
Tel no: Nantwich 626458

Seating capacity: 250
Floodlights: No

NETHERFIELD
(N.P.L.)

Chairman: N. Sharpe
Secretary: G. Edmondson
Team manager: K. Kirby
Previous leagues: Westmorland, North Lancs, Lancs Combination
Colours: Black and white striped shirts, black shorts, red socks
Change colours: All amber
Address and tel no of ground: Parkside Road, Kendal, Cumbria (Kendal 22278)
Ground capacity: 6,000
Covered accommodation: 1,500
Clubhouse details: Seating for 280, two bars, owned by supporters club
Best season in F.A. Cup: 1962, 2nd Rnd v Barnsley
Current players with Football League experience: E. Banks (Workington); K. Galley (Southport)
Major honours: Lancs Comb champions twice, Lancs Comb Cup winners 3 times
Best season in F.A. Trophy: 1970-71 and 1977-78, 3rd Qual Rnd
Programme: 4 pages, 3p
Local newspapers: Westmorland Gazette, Lancashire Evening Post

Founded: 1920
Tel no: Kendal 20230

Record attendance: 3,700 (1957)
Seating capacity: 300
Floodlights: Yes

NEW BRIGHTON (CHESHIRE CO. DIV 1)

Chairman: L. C. Ainscough
Secretary: A. E. Foulds
Team manager: J. Butler
Previous leagues: Football League Div 3 (North), Lancashire Combination
Colours: Tangerine shirts, black shorts, black socks
Change colours: All sky blue

Founded: 1921
Tel no: 051-638 5282

156

Address and tel no of ground: Carr Lane, Hoylake, Merseyside
  (051-632 2452/2703)   Record attendance: 13,500 (1957)
Ground capacity: 2,000
Covered accommodation: Yes   Floodlights: No
Clubhouse details: Open every night until 10.30 p.m., disco Fridays and
  Sundays, variety Saturdays, darts Wednesdays and Thursdays
Best season in F.A. Cup: 1956–57
League clubs defeated in F.A. Cup: Stockport, Derby County, Torquay
  United
Major honours: Liverpool Senior Cup winners 1957, 1960, 1963
Best season in F. A. Trophy: 1971, 3rd Qual Rnd
Club nickname: The Rakers   Programme: 4 pages, 3p
Local newspapers: Hoylake Advertiser, Liverpool Echo

NEWBURY TOWN   (HELLENIC)

Chairman: R. F. Todd   Founded: 1887
Team manager: D. Tune
Previous leagues: Great Western Suburban, Hampshire, Reading & Dis-
  trict, Metropolitan
Colours: Old gold and black   Change colours: White and black
Address and tel no of ground: Faraday Road, Newbury, Berks
  (Newbury 40048)
Ground capacity: 2,000   Seating capacity: None
Covered accommodation: 400   Floodlights: No
Clubhouse details: Open Tuesdays, Thursdays, Saturdays and Sundays,
  refreshments, on Thursdays bingo, entertainment at weekends
Major honours: Berks & Bucks Senior Cup winners 1891; Hellenic League
  champions 1978-79; Hellenic Cup winners 1959-60, 1968-69
Best season in F.A. Vase: 3rd Rnd
Club nickname: The Town   Programme: 8 pages, 5p
Local newspaper: Newbury Weekly News

NEW MILLS   (CHESHIRE CO. DIV 1)

Chairman: J. Bowker   Founded: 1912
Secretary: R. M. Walker   Tel no: 061-427 3454
Team manager: B. Taylor
Previous league: Manchester
Colours: Amber and black   Change colours: Blue and white
Address and tel no of ground: Church Lane, New Mills, Derbys
  (New Mills 42180)   Record attendance: 3,000 (1970s)
Ground capacity: 3,000   Seating capacity: 300
Covered accommodation: Approx. 500 Floodlights: No
Clubhouse details: Open on match days and training nights, fully licensed
Current players with Football League experience: M. Stevens (Stockport
  County)
Major honours: Derbyshire Senior Cup winners and runners-up; Gilchrist
  Cup winners and runners-up
Club nickname: The Millers   Programme: 6 pages, 10p
Local newspaper: High Peak Reporter

NEWPORT (IOW) (HAMPSHIRE)

Chairman: R. Dew   Founded: 1888
Secretary: R. Curling   Tel no: Newport 524951
Team manager: D. Edwards
Colours: Yellow with blue trim, blue shorts, yellow socks
Change colours: White shirts, white shorts, blue socks
Address and tel no of ground: Church Litten, Newport, Isle of Wight
(Newport 525027)   Record attendance: 6,000 (1976)
Ground capacity: 6,000   Seating capacity: 500
Covered accommodation: 1,000   Floodlights: Yes
Clubhouse details: Under stand, facilities for about 70 persons, £35,000
extension is now being built
Best seasons in F.A. Cup: 1945 and 1952
League clubs defeated in F.A. Cup: Orient, Swindon
Major honours: IOW Gold Cup winners 20 times, including nine consecutive years from 1971 to 1979; Hants Floodlight Cup winners 1977, 1978; Russell Cotes Cup winners 1978, 1979
Best seasons in F.A. Vase: 1976-77, 1977-78 and 1978-79, 2nd Rnd
                                      Programme: 6 pages, 5p
Local newspapers: County Press, Evening News, Weekly Post, Echo

NORTH FERRIBY UNITED (YORKSHIRE)

Chairman: L. N. Wilson   Founded: 1935
Secretary: A. R. Sutton   Tel no: Hull 632018
Team manager: D. King
Previous league: East Riding Amateur
Colours: Green and white hooped shirts, white shorts, white socks
Change colours: White shirts, green shorts, white socks
Address of ground: Church Road, North Ferriby, North Humberside
                                      Record attendance: 650 (1970)
Ground capacity: 3,000   Seating capacity: None
Covered accommodation: 300   Floodlights: No
Clubhouse details: Clubhouse being built
Best season in F.A. Vase: 1976-77, 3rd Rnd
Local newspaper: Hull Daily Mail   Programme: 4 pages, 10p

NORTH SHIELDS (D. NORTHERN)

Chairman: L. Murphy   Founded: 1898
Secretary: C. Munro   Tel no: North Shields 76759
Team manager: G. Allen
Previous leagues: Northern Alliance, North Eastern, Midland Counties, Northern Counties
Colours: All red   Change colours: All light blue
Address and tel no of ground: Appleby Park, Hawkey's Lane, North
Shields, Tyne and Wear (North Shields 70513)
                                      Record attendance: 12,500 (1956)

158

Ground capacity: 8,500   Seating capacity: 800
Covered accommodation: 4,500   Floodlights: Yes
Clubhouse details: Open all week, full facilities available
Best seasons in F.A. Cup: 1955–56, 1961–62 and 1969–70, 1st Rnd
Current players with Football League experience: R. Young (Hull City, Hartlepool); M. Moore (Sunderland, Tranmere, Hartlepool, Workington)
Major honours: F. A. Amateur Cup winners 1968–69; Northumberland Senior Cup winners 1975-76, finalists 1977-78, 1978–79
Best seasons in F.A. Trophy: 1974–75 and 1975–76, 3rd Qual Rnd
Club nickname: The Robins   Programme: 16 pages, 10p
Local newspaper: Shields Weekly News

NORTHWICH VICTORIA   (N.P.L.)

Chairman: D. Nuttall   Founded: 1873
Secretary: J. R. Rowe
Team manager: R. Williams
Previous leagues: Football League, Manchester, Cheshire, N.P.L.
Colours: Green and white   Change colours: Claret and blue
Address and tel no of ground: Drill Field, Northwich, Cheshire (Northwich 41450 – office, 3120 – club)   Record attendance: 10,000 (1976-77)
Ground capacity: 9,990   Seating capacity: 600
Covered accommodation: Behind each goal and two sides
                    Floodlights: Yes
Clubhouse details: Open every night and most lunchtimes, entertainmen and food available
Best season in F. A. Cup: 1976–77, 4th Rnd Proper v Oldham
League clubs defeated in F.A. Cup: Rochdale, Peterborough, Watford
Current players with Football League experience: J. Collier (Stockport); L. Wain (Crewe, Southport); K. Eccleshare (Bury); D. Ryan (Man Utd, Southport); T. Bailey (Port Vale); R. Williams (Port Vale); P. Jones (Blackpool); M. Brennan (Man City)
Major honours: Cheshire Senior Cup winners 14 times; N.P.L. Cup winners 1972–73; N.P.L. runners-up 1976–77
Best season in F.A. Trophy: Never past 2nd Rnd Proper
Club nickname: The Vics   Programme: 28 pages, 10p
Local newspapers: Northwich Guardian, Northwich Chronicle, Manchester Evening News

NUNEATON BOROUGH   (A.P.L.)

Chairman: N. Kelly   Founded: 1937
Secretary: Dr J. Evans, B.A., Ph.D   Tel no: Nuneaton 68416
Team manager: R. Barry
Previous leagues: Central Amateur, Birmingham Combination, Birmingham
Colours: Blue and white striped shirts, blue shorts, blue socks
Change colours: Yellow shirts, green shorts, yellow socks

159

Address and tel no of ground: Manor Park, Beaumont Road, Nuneaton, Warwicks (Nuneaton 385738)   Record attendance: 22,114 (1967)
Ground capacity: 22,000   Seating capacity: 450
Covered accommodation: 5,000   Floodlights: Yes
Clubhouse details: Open match days, each evening and Sunday lunchtime (Nuneaton 383152)
Best seasons in F.A Cup: 1949-50, and 1966-67, 3rd Rnd
League clubs defeated in F.A. Cup: Watford, Swansea Town, Oxford Utd
Current players with Football League experience: R. Cross (Port Vale); M. Shotton (Leicester City); B. Phillips (Leicester City); G. Livsey; P. Cooper
Major honours: Birmingham League champions 1954-55, 1955-56; Southern League Cup finalists 1962-63; County Senior Cup winners 4 times; Southern League Prem Div runners-up 1966-67, 1974-75
Best season in F.A Trophy: 1976-77, Quarter-final replay
Club nickname: The Boro'   Programme: 20 pages, 10p
Local newspapers: Nuneaton Evening Tribune, Coventry Evening Telegraph

OSWESTRY TOWN   (N.P.L.)

Chairman: A. Jones   Founded: 1876
Secretary: R. Morris   Tel no: Oswestry 62225
Team manager: Freddie Hill
Previous leagues: Birmingham & District, Cheshire County, Southern
Colours: All blue
Change colours: All red
Address and tel no of ground: Victoria Road, Oswestry, Salop (Oswestry 3800 – office; 2608 – social club)
Ground capacity: 5,500   Seating capacity: 500
Covered accommodation: Yes   Floodlights: Yes
Clubhouse details: Open every day, lounge, concert room, food, steward: Mr Trow (Oswestry 2608)
Current players with Football League experience: F. Hill (Manchester City, Bolton, England); A. Gregory (Shrewsbury)
Major Honours: Shropshire Senior Cup winners; Welsh Cup winners
Best season in F.A. Cup: 1974, 1st Rnd
Programme: 12 pages, 10p
Local newspapers: Border Counties Advertiser, Shropshire Star

OXFORD CITY   (B.I.L. P.DIV)

Chairman: To be appointed   Founded: 1882
Secretary: J. Shepperd   Tel no: Wheatley 2181
Team manager: G. Denial
Colours: Blue and white hooped shirts, white shorts, blue socks
Change colours: All white or all blue
Address and tel no of ground: White House Ground, Abingdon Road, Oxford (Oxford 48391)   Record attendance: 9,500 (1946)
Ground capacity: 9,000   Seating capacity: 1,300
Covered accommodation: 500   Floodlights: Yes

The England Semi-professional International squad: *Back row, left to right:* Dr Taybor, **Keith Wright** (assistant manager), Gordon Simmonite, Les Mutrie, Trevor Peake, Brian Parker, Howard Wilkinson (manager), Keith Houghton, Jim Arnold, Nick Ironton, John Watson, Adrian Titcombe (F.A.), Alan Smith (physiotherapist, Blackpool). *Front row, left to right:* Roy Clayton, Jeff Lee, Stuart Chapman, Eamonn O'Keefe, David Adamson, Tony Jennings (captain), Brian Thompson, John Davison, Barry Whitbread, Brendan Phillips.   *Roger Price.*

Doug Young of Billericay Town scoring the first goal of his hat-trick at Wembley. Chris Tudor of Almondsbury Greenway, one of the *F.A. Non-league Football Annual*'s Personalities of the Season, is on the left.   *Billericay Evening Echo.*

Altrincham's goalkeeper, Peter Eales, with defenders rallying round in support during the Northern Premier League team's exciting Third Round Cup Tie against Tottenham Hotspur at White Hart Lane.

Press Association.

Stafford Rangers, keeping up the Northern Premier League's tremendous F.A. Trophy record, seen here in jubilant mood after their 2–0 defeat of Kettering Town at Wembley.

Bob Thomas

Brian Thompson (Yeovil Town), captain of the Southern League side, receives the O.C.S. Cup from the sponsors' chairman, Mr George Goodliffe. Man of the Match, Brendan Phillips, is on the left, and a third member of England's semi-professional squad, John Watson, is in the centre.

Clubhouse details: Supporters club open every evening, refreshments available at certain events, darts, bingo, cribbage and dancing on Saturday nights
Best season in F.A. Cup: 1970-71, 2nd Rnd Proper v Swansea City
Major honours: F.A. Amateur Cup winners 1906, runners-up 1903 to 1913; Oxon Senior Cup winners 25 times; Isthmian League Div 1 runners-up 1977-78
Best season in F.A. Trophy: 1978-79, 3rd Qual Rnd
Club nickname: The City   Programme: 8 pages, 10p
Local newspapers: Oxford Mail, Oxford Times

PAULTON ROVERS   (WESTERN)

Chairman: R. MacDonald   Founded: 1881
Secretary: K. Simmons   Tel no: Midsomer Norton 418030
Team manager: Clive Herron
Previous leagues: Somerset Senior, Wiltshire Premier
Colours: White and maroon shirts, maroon shorts, sky blue socks
Change colours: Maroon, red or blue shirts, white shorts, white socks
Address and tel no of ground: Athletic Field, Winterfield Road, Paulton, Bristol (Midsomer Norton 412907)
Ground capacity: 5,000   Seating capacity: None
Covered accommodation: Approx. 300 Floodlights: No
Clubhouse details: Dance hall with 450 capacity, skittle alley, bar, lounge
Major honours: Somerset Senior Cup winners more times than anyone else; Somerset League champions four times
Best seasons in F.A. Trophy: 1976-77 and 1977-78, 2nd Qual Rnd
Club nickname: The Rovers   Programme: 8 pages, 5p
Local newspapers: Bath Chronicle, Bristol Evening Post

PEACEHAVEN & TELESCOMBE
(SUSSEX CO.)

Chairman: J. Edwards   Founded: 1923
Secretary: P. Andrews   Tel no: Peacehaven 5666
Team manager: Peter Andrews
Previous leagues: Brighton, Lewes
Colours: White shirts, black shorts, black socks
Change colours: All blue
Address and tel no of ground: Sports Ground, Piddinghoe Avenue, Peacehaven, Newhaven, East Sussex (Peacehaven 4729)
Record attendance: 1977
Ground capacity: 800   Seating capacity: None
Covered accommodation: Approx. 300 Floodlights: No
Clubhouse details: Capacity 200, large bar
Best season in F.A. Cup: 1977-78
Major honours: Sussex County League Div 2 runners-up, Div 1 champions and runners-up; R.U.R. Cup winners
Club nickname: The Tye or The Haven   Programme: 3p
Local newspapers: Evening Argus, Brighton Gazette, Sussex Express, County Herald

161

PENRITH (D. NORTHERN)

Chairman: S. V. Goodman
Secretary: W. Brogden
Team manager: M. Cleasby
Previous league: Carlisle & District
Colours: Blue shirts, white shorts, blue and white socks
Change colours: Red shirts, white shorts, red socks
Address and tel no of ground: Southend Road Ground, Penrith, Cumbria
(Penrith 3212)
Founded: 1894
Tel no: Penrith 2551

Record attendance: 4,000 (1961)
Ground capacity: 4,000
Covered accommodation: 1,000
Clubhouse details: Situated on ground, staffed by voluntary labour
Best season in F.A. Cup: 1964-65, 3rd Qual Rnd
Current players with Football League experience: D. Marshall; K. Wallace
Major honours: Northern League runners-up 1961-62
Best season in F.A. Trophy: Never past 2nd Qual Rnd
Club nickname: The Cumbrians Programme: 3 pages, 5p
Seating capacity: 250
Floodlights: Yes
Local newspapers: Cumberland & Westmorland Herald, Cumberland News

POOLE TOWN (S.L.S.)

Chairman: J. Weatherley
Secretary: P. S. Hough
Team manager: R. Bazeley
Previous league: Western
Colours: Yellow shirts, blue shorts, yellow socks
Change colours: Blue shirts, white shorts, white socks
Address and tel no of ground: The Stadium, Wimborne Road, Poole, Dorset
(Poole 4747)
Founded: 1880
Tel no: Parkstone 746244

Record attendance: 11,155 (1962-63)
Ground capacity: 8,500
Covered accommodation: 750
Clubhouse details: Open every evening and lunchtime
Best season in F.A. Cup: Beat Newport County (year not known)
League clubs defeated in F.A. Cup: Newport County
Current players with Football League experience: J. O'Rourke
Major honours: Western Counties Floodlight Cup winners 1969-70; Mark Frowde Cup winners 1978-79
Best seasons in F.A. Trophy: 1969-70, 1970-71 and 1974-75, 1st Rnd Proper
Club nickname: The Dolphins Programme: 6/8 pages, 10p
Seating capacity: 1,500
Floodlights: Yes
Local newspapers: Evening Echo, Poole & East Dorset Herald

PRESCOT TOWN (CHESHIRE CO. DIV 2)

Chairman: G. Stokes
Secretary: W. Marsh
Team manager: D. Smith
Previous leagues: Lancashire Combination, Cheshire County
Colours: Amber and black Change colours: All red
Address and tel no of ground: Hope Street, Prescot, Merseyside
(051-426 6819)
Founded: 1928
Tel no: 051-430 0194

Record attendance: 13,000

Ground capacity: 10,000   Seating capacity: 2,000
Covered accommodation: Two stands Floodlights: No
Clubhouse details: Two licensed bars
Best season in F.A. Cup: 1957, 1st Rnd Proper
Major honours: Liverpool Senior Cup winners four times; Liverpool
  Challenge Cup winners six times; Lancashire Combination Division 1
  champions once and Division 2 once, runners-up five times; Lythgor
  Mem. Cup winners; George Mahon Cup winners; Lord Haverface Cup
  winners
Best season in F.A. Vase: 1977-78
Club nickname: The Tigers   Programme: 10p
Local newspapers: Liverpool Echo, Prescot & Huyton Reporter

PRESTWICH HEYS (CHES. CO DIV 2)

Chairman: B. Sternberg   Founded: 1938
Secretary: D. Todd   Tel no: 061-798 0744
Team manager: R. Freeman
Previous leagues: Prestwich & Whitefield, Bury Amateur, S.E. Lancs,
  Manchester, Lancs Combination
Colours: Red shirts, white shorts with red trim
Change colours: Blue shirts, white shorts
Address and tel no of ground: Grimshaws, Heys Road, Prestwich, Lancs
  (061-773 8888)   Record attendance: 4,000 plus
Ground capacity: 4,000   Seating capacity: 500
Covered accommodation: 400   Floodlights: No
Clubhouse details: Facilities for 40 members, bar
Best season in F.A. Cup: 1978-79, 2nd Qual Rnd
Current players with Football League experience: P. Cuddy (Rochdale);
  E. Makin (Wigan); P. Critchley (Wigan Ath, Oldham Ath); J. Thomp-
  son (Bury); J. Murty (Rochdale)
Major honours: F.A. Amateur Cup quarter-finalists 1969-70; Watson
  Trophy winners 1970-71; Challenge Cup winners; League Cup winners;
  Lancs Combination champions; S.E. Lancs League champions 1959-60,
  1960-61, 1963-64; Manchester Amateur Cup winners 1971-72
Best season in F.A. Trophy: 1974-75, 2nd Qual Rnd
Club nickname: Heys   Programme: 5p
Local newspapers: Bolton Evening News, Bury Times, Prestwich & White-
  field Guide, Manchester Evening News

PWLLHELI   (WELSH L. N)

Chairman: P. Davies
Secretary: D. Hughes   Tel no: Pwllheli 3369
Team manager: J. Dunn
Colours: White shirts, black shorts, black socks
Change colours: Blue shirts, white shorts, blue socks
Address of ground: Recreation Ground, Cardiff Road, Pwllheli, Gwynedd
Ground capacity: 3,000   Seating capacity: 200
Covered accommodation: One stand and shelter
                                   Floodlights: No
Best season in F.A. Trophy: 1973-74, 1st Rnd Proper
Local newspapers: Caernarvon & Denbigh Herald, Cambrian News,
  Liverpool Daily Post

RADCLIFFE BOROUGH
(CHESHIRE CO. DIV 1)

Chairman: J. Pimlott
Secretary: J. Higham
Founded: 1949
Tel no: 061-724 8344
Team manager: G. Jones
Previous leagues: South East Lancashire, Manchester, Lancashire Combination, Cheshire
Colours: Blue shirts, white shorts, white socks
Change colours: All amber
Address and tel no of ground: Stainton Park, Pilkington Road, Radcliffe, Lancs (061-723 2407)
Record attendance: 1,000
Ground capacity: 4,000
Covered accommodation: Yes
Floodlights: No
Clubhouse details: Membership of 400, cabaret nights, bingo, games room, pool, darts, dominoes
Best season in F.A. Cup: 1974-75, 2nd Qual Rnd
Current players with Football League experience: G. Jones; J. Dowthwaite; J. McGlynn
Major honours: Lancashire Combination Cup winners; Cheshire Counties League runners-up
Best season in F.A. Trophy: 1972-73, 1st Rnd Proper
Club nickname: The Borough
Programme: 5p
Local newspapers: Manchester Evening News, Bolton News, Radcliffe Times

RAINHAM TOWN
(B.I.L. DIV 2)

Chairman: G. Burrell
Secretary: T. M. King
Founded: 1945
Tel no: Rainham 57596
Team manager: P. Delea
Previous leagues: Delphian, Metropolitan London, Athenian
Colours: All red
Change colours: Blue and black
Address and tel no of ground: Deri Park, Wennington Road, Rainham, Essex (Rainham 53280/54868/54778)
Record attendance: 176 (1978)
Ground capacity: 4,600
Seating capacity: 600
Covered accommodation: 1,500
Floodlights: Yes
Clubhouse details: Open seven days and nights, food and snacks available
Best season in F.A. Cup: 1974-75, 2nd Qual Rnd
Best season in F.A. Vase: 1977-78, 5th Rnd
Club nickname: The Reds
Programme: 4 pages, 5p
Local newspapers: Hornchurch Express, Havering Post, Romford Observer, Romford Recorder

RAMSGATE
(KENT)

Chairman: J. A. March
Secretary: J. Hutchinson
Founded: 1946
Tel no: Thanet 33046
Team manager: R. Harrop
Previous league: Southern
Colours: Red shirts, white shorts, red socks

Change colours: Blue and white
Address and tel no of ground: Southwood Football Ground, Prices Avenue, Ramsgate, Kent (Thanet 51636)   Record attendance: 5,081 (1967-68)
Ground capacity: 7,000   Seating capacity: 1,000
Covered accommodation: 6,000   Floodlights: Yes
Clubhouse details: Open every night, steward Tony King
Best season in F.A. Cup: 1955-56, 1st Rnd Proper v Watford
Major honours: Kent League champions 1949-50, 1955-56, 1956-57; Kent Senior Cup winners 1963-64; Southern League Cup finalists 1967-68; Southern League Div 1 South runners-up 1971-72
Best seasons in F.A. Trophy: 1969-70 and 1975-76, 3rd Qual Rnd
Club nickname: The Rams   Programme: 8 pages

REDDITCH UNITED   (A.P.L.)

Chairman: W. A. Lawrenson   Reformed: 1948
Secretary: M. A. Langfield   Tel no: Redditch 26603
Team manager: S. Bradley
Previous leagues: Birmingham Combination, West Midlands, Southern
Colours: All red with white trim, black socks
Change colours: All white
Address and tel no of ground: Valley Stadium, Bromsgrove Road, Redditch, Worcs (Redditch 64519)   Record attendance: 5,250
Ground capacity: 10,000   Seating capacity: 600
Covered accommodation: 3,500   Floodlights: Yes
Clubhouse details: Open match days and Monday evenings, available for private functions
Best season in F.A. Cup: 1971-72, 1st Rnd Proper
Current players with Football League experience: R. Edwards (Port Vale)
Major honours: Southern League Div 1 champions 1975-76; Birmingham Combination champions 1913-14, 1932-33, 1952-53, 1954-55; Worcestershire Senior Cup winners 1894, 1931, 1975, 1976; Camp Kin Cup holders since 1971-72
Best season in F.A. Trophy: 1978-79, 1st Rnd Proper
Club nickname: The Reds   Programme: 4 pages, 5p/8 pages, 10p
Local newspapers: Redditch Indicator, Redditch Advertiser, Birmingham Post & Mail

RHYL (CHESHIRE CO. DIV 1)

Chairman: D. Rhodes   Founded: 1928
Secretary/general manager: J. B. Williams Tel no: Rhyl 50566
Team manager: A. McDermott
Previous leagues: Birmingham Combination, Welsh National
Colours: All white   Change colours: Blue shirts, white
      shorts, white socks
Address and tel no of ground: Belle Vue, Grange Road, Rhyl, Clwyd,
      N. Wales (Rhyl 50346)   Record attendance: 12,000 (1951–52)
Ground capacity: 6,000   Seating capacity: 500
Covered accommodation: Grandstand   Floodlights: Yes
Clubhouse details: Dancing, television, disco, pool, darts, etc., late nights
      Thursday, Friday and Saturday
Best season in F.A. Cup: 1956–57, 4th Rnd Proper
League clubs defeated in F.A. Cup: Stoke City, Halifax Town, Notts
      County, Barnsley, Hartlepool, Wigan Athletic
Current players with Football League experience: N. Whitehead (Brentford,
      Chester, Rochdale), R. Aindow; (Southport)
Major honours: Welsh Cup winners twice; Cheshire League champions
      three times; Cheshire League Cup winners three times
Best seasons in F.A. Trophy: 1970–71, 1971–72 and 1975–76, 3rd Qual Rnd
Club nickname: The Lilywhites   Programme: 10p
Local newspapers: Rhyl Journal, Liverpool Daily Post, Liverpool Echo,
      Manchester Evening News

RUISLIP MANOR (K. ATHENIAN)

Chairman: C. Gregory   Founded: 1938
Secretary: K. Thornton   Tel no: Ruislip 38658
Team manager: J. Gadston
Previous leagues: Spartan, London, Middlesex Senior
Colours: White shirts, black shorts, black and red socks
Change colours: All yellow
Address and tel no of ground: Grosvenor Vale, Ruislip, Middx
      (Ruislip 37487)   Record attendance: 2,000
Ground capacity: 2,000   Seating capacity: 280
Covered accommodation: Two stands   Floodlights: No
Clubhouse details: Open every evening and lunchtime, entertainment
Current players with Football League experience: J. Gadston; A. Hawley
Major honours: Middlesex Senior Cup semi-finalists five times
Best season in F.A. Vase: 1977-78, 3rd Rnd
Club nickname: The Manor   Programme: 12 pages, 10p
Local newspapers: Ruislip-Northwood Gazette, Hillingdon Mirror,
      Weekly Post

RUNCORN (N.P.L.)

Chairman: A. A. Littler
Secretary: G. Carter
Team manager: A. King
Founded: 1918
Tel no: Runcorn 66730
Previous league: Cheshire County
Colours: Green and yellow striped shirts, green shorts, yellow socks
Change colours: Blue and white quartered shirts, blue shorts, white socks
Address and tel no of ground: Canal Street, Runcorn, Cheshire
(Runcorn 72237)
Record attendance: 10,111 (1939)
Ground capacity: 7,000
Seating capacity: 400
Covered accommodation: Yes
Floodlights: Yes
Clubhouse details: Social club adjacent to ground, open seven nights a
week and on match days, available for private hire
Best season in F.A. Cup: 1939
League clubs defeated in F.A. Cup: Southport, Notts County
Current players with Football League experience: A. King; D. Rylands;
P. Wilson; J. Kenyon
Major honours: Cheshire League champions 1936-37, 1938-39, 1962-63;
Cheshire Senior Cup winners 1924-25, 1935-36, 1961-62, 1964-65, 1967-
68, 1973-74, 1974-75; Northern Premier League champions 1975-76;
Northern Premier League Cup winners 1974-75
Best seasons in F.A. Trophy: 1975-76, 1977-78 and 1978-79, Semi-final
Club nickname: The Linnets
Programme: 20 pages, 10p
Local newspapers: Runcorn Weekly News, Runcorn Guardian, Liverpool
Echo, Manchester Evening News

SAFFRON WALDEN TOWN (TOWN & COUNTRY)

Chairman: M. Haddock
Secretary: P. M. Daw
Team manager: B. Grant
Founded: 1872
Tel no: Saffron Walden 21281
Previous leagues: Essex Senior, Herts County, Spartan, Essex & Suffolk
Border, North Essex
Colours: Red shirts with black trim, black shorts, black socks
Change colours: Sky blue shirts, black shorts, sky blue socks
Address and tel no of ground: Catons Lane, Saffron Walden, Essex
(Saffron Walden 22789)
Record attendance: 6,000 (1926)
Ground capacity: 3,500
Seating capacity: 350
Covered accommodation: 3 grandstands
Floodlights: Yes
Clubhouse details: Open on match days, training evenings and Saturday
evenings
Best season in F.A. Cup: 1946-47, Prelim Rnd
Major honours: Essex Senior League champions 1973-74; Spartan League
Div 2 champions 1937-38
Best season in F.A. Vase: 1977-78, 2nd Rnd
Club nickname: The Bloods
Programme: 8 pages, 5p
Local newspapers: Saffron Walden Weekly News, Herts & Essex Observer

ST ALBANS CITY (B.I.L. DIV 1)

Chairman: J. Howard
Secretary: R. T. Mann
Team manager: R. Murphy
Previous leagues: Spartan, Athenian
Colours: Yellow and blue
Address and tel no of ground: Clarence Park, St Albans, Herts
(St Albans 64296)
Ground capacity: 8,000
Covered accommodation: 300
Clubhouse details: Open on match days
Best season in F.A. Cup: 1968, 3rd Rnd Proper
Major honours: Isthmian League champions 1923-24, 1926-27; 1927-28; Athenian League champions 1920-21, 1921-22; Spartan League champions 1911-12; London Senior Cup winners 1971; Herts Senior Cup winners 12 times
Best season in F.A. Trophy: 1975-76, 3rd Qual Rnd
Club nickname: The Saints
Local newspaper: Herts Advertiser

Founded: 1908
Tel no: St Albans 50886

Change colours: Blue and yellow

Seating capacity: 1,000
Floodlights: Yes

Programme: 6 pages, 4p

ST HELENS TOWN (CHESHIRE CO.DIV1)

Chairman: J. Jones
Secretary: B. Burrows
Team manager: A. Wellens
Previous leagues: Lancashire Combination, Liverpool Combination
Colours: Blue shirts, white shorts, blue socks
Change colours: Yellow shirts, blue shorts, yellow socks
Address and tel no of ground: Houghton Road, Sutton, St Helens, Merseyside (St Helens 817225 – club, office – 817225)
Ground capacity: 7,000
Covered accommodation: Yes
Clubhouse details: Large clubhouse seating 800 people, luxury lounge bar, sports room
Best season in F.A. Trophy: Never past 3rd Qual Rnd
Club nickname: The Town
Local newspapers: St Helens Reporter, St Helens Star

Founded: 1945
Tel no: St Helens 811856

Seating capacity: 500
Floodlights: No

ST NEOTS TOWN (UTD COUNTIES)

Chairman: R. G. Crampton
Secretary: J. S. Walker
Team manager: Terry Reedman
Previous leagues: Eastern Counties, Metropolitan
Colours: Sky blue, navy blue and white
Change colours: Red and white, or white with green trim
Address and tel no of ground: Shortsands, Cambridge Street, St Neots, Cambs (Huntingdon 72457)

Founded: 1879
Tel no: Huntingdon 77295

Record attendance: 2,000 (1966)

Ground capacity: 2,000   Seating capacity: 270
Covered accommodation: Two sides   Floodlights: No
Clubhouse details: Plans for new clubhouse under consideration
Best season in F.A. Cup: 1966-67, 1st Rnd Proper
Current players with Football League experience: A. Guild (Cambridge United, Luton Town)
Major honours: Hunts Senior Cup winners 30 times between 1888 and 1978; Metropolitan League champions 1949-50; United Counties League champions 1956-57, 1967-68; Hinchinbrooke Cup winners 1970-71, 1973-74
Best season in F.A. Vase: 1978-79, 3rd Rnd
Club nickname: The Saints   Programme: 8 pages, free
Local newspapers: Cambridge News, Hunts Post, St Neots Advertiser, Trader

---

SALISBURY (S.L.S.)

Chairman: L. G. Whitmarsh   Founded: 1947
Secretary: D. F. Sharp   Tel no: Salisbury 27248
Previous league: Western
Colours: White shirts, black shorts
Change colours: Red shirts, white shorts
Address and tel no of ground: Victoria Park, Castle Road, Salisbury, Wilts (Salisbury 6689)
Ground capacity: 8,000   Seating capacity: 300
Covered accommodation: 1,000   Floodlights: Yes
Clubhouse details: Open every night and Saturday and Sunday lunchtimes, lounge bar, dance room, bingo, live entertainment most weekends, steward: Mrs G. Blake (Salisbury 27699)
Best season in F.A. Cup: 1959-60, 2nd Rnd
Major honours: Western League champions 1957-58, 1960-61; Hampshire League champions 1954-55; Hampshire Senior Cup winners 1962, 1964
Best season in F.A. Trophy: 3rd Qual Rnd
Programme: 8 pages, 5p
Local newspapers: Salisbury Times & Journal, Southern Daily Echo

---

SALTASH UNITED (WESTERN P. DIV)

Chairman: E. G. Lewis   Founded: 1946
Secretary: A. White   Tel no: Saltash 3669 (h);
     Plymouth 21312 ext 5171 (bus)
Team manager: D. Lean
Previous leagues: East Cornwall Premier, South Western
Colours: Red and white striped shirts, black shorts, black socks
Change colours: Blue shirts, white shorts, blue socks
Address and tel no of ground: Kimberley Stadium, Callington Road, Saltash, Cornwall (Saltash 5746)
Ground capacity: 4,000   Seating capacity: 200
Covered accommodation: 200   Floodlights: No
Clubhouse details: Open every night, lunchtimes, and weekends, dancing, disco, bingo, etc.
Current players with Football League experience: D. Lean (Plymouth

Argyle); D. Rickard (Plymouth Argyle)
Major honours: South Western Football League champions 1953-54, 1975-76; Western League Div 1 champions 1976-77
Club nickname: The Ashes   **Programme:** 10 pages, 10p
Local newspapers: Western Morning News, Western Evening Herald, Sunday Independent

SCARBOROUGH   (N.P.L.)

Chairman: D. Robinson
Secretary: Mrs M. Crawford   **Tel no:** Scarborough 65655
Team manager: C. Appleton
Previous leagues: Northern Counties, Midland, Northern
Colours: All red   **Change colours:** All white
Address and tel no of ground: The Athletic Ground, Seamer Road, Scarborough, North Yorkshire (Scarborough 75094)
               Record attendance: 11,124 (1938)
Ground capacity: 10,000   **Seating capacity:** 800
Covered accommodation: 3,000   **Floodlights:** Yes
Clubhouse details: Fully licensed bar, concert room, dance floor
Best seasons in F.A. Cup: 1938, 1976 and 1978, 3rd Rnd Proper
League clubs defeated in F.A. Cup: Brighton, Preston North End, Crewe Alexandra, Rochdale, Oldham
Current players with Football League experience: J. Woodall; C. Simpkin; K. McKechnie; R. Smith; D. Smith
Major honours: F.A. Challenge Trophy winners 1973, 1976, runners-up 1975; N.P.L. Cup winners 1977; Midland League champions 1929–30; N.P.L. runners-up 1972-73; North Riding Senior Cup winners 1909, 1929, 1939, 1949, 1956, 1959, 1961, 1962, 1969, 1973, 1974
Best seasons in F.A. Trophy: 1973, 1976 and 1977, Winners
Club nickname: The Boro'   **Programme:** 12 pages, 10p
Local newspaper: Scarborough Evening News

SHEFFIELD   (YORKSHIRE)

Chairman/president: D. Scaife   **Founded:** 1857
Secretary: J. Gisborne   **Tel no:** Sheffield 350620
Team managers: C. Stanley and R. Ford
Previous leagues: Sheffield & Hallamshire County, Football Association – County Senior
Colours: All red
Change colours: Blue shirts, black shorts
Address and tel no of ground: Abbeydale Park, Dore, Sheffield 17 (Sheffield 362040)   **Record attendance:** 1,100 (1977)
Ground capacity: 2,000   **Seating capacity:** None
Covered accommodation: 150   **Floodlights:** No
Clubhouse details: Bar and catering facilities
Major honours: Yorkshire League Div 2 champions 1976-77; Yorkshire League Cup winners 1978
Best season in F.A. Vase: 1977, Final
Local newspapers: Sheffield Star, Telegraph Green

SHEPPEY UNITED (KENT)

Chairman: P. Sharrock   Founded: 1889
Secretary: G. E. Carpenter   Tel no: Sheerness 2013
Team manager: J. Adams
Previous leagues: Southern Metropolitan, Aetolian, London, Thames & Medway
Colours: Red and white striped shirts, black shorts, red socks
Change colours: All light blue
Address and tel no of ground: Botany Road, St George's Avenue, Sheerness, Kent (Sheerness 5299)   Record attendance: 4,500 (1898-99)
Ground capacity: 5,000   Seating capacity: 400
Covered accommodation: 2,000   Floodlights: Yes
Clubhouse details: Open match days, licensed bar, music, light refreshments, private parties, steward: W. Jacobs (Sheerness 2375)
Best season in F.A. Cup: 1920, lost to Thornecroft 4th Qual Rnd
Major honours: Kent League champions; Kent Amateur Cup winners; Thames & Medway Kent Floodlight Trophy winners
Best season in F.A. Trophy: 1969-70, 3rd Qual Rnd
Club nickname: The Islanders   Programme: 6 pages, 10p
Local newspaper: Sheerness Times & Guardian

SHEPSHED CHARTERHOUSE (LEICS. SEN.)

Chairman: M. F. Clayton   Founded: 1975
Secretary: G. T. Spencer   Tel no: Shepshed 2086
Team manager: T. Ashton
Colours: White shirts, black shorts, red socks
Change colours: Red shirts, white shorts, white socks
Address and tel no of ground: Dovecots, Loughborough Road, Shepshed Leics (Shepshed 2684)   Record attendance: 2,600
Ground capacity: 4,000   Seating capacity: Nil
Covered accommodation: 400   Floodlights: No
Clubhouse details: Open to members and vice-presidents
Current players with Football League experience: M. Hollis; L. Glover; W. Wilcox
Major honours: Senior Cup winners 1977-78, runners-up 1977-78; Senior League Div 2 champions; Senior League Div 1 champions
Best season in F.A. Vase: 1978-79, Semi-final
Club nickname: Charterhouse   Programme: 8 pages, 10p
Local newspapers: Loughborough Echo, Loughborough News

SHEPTON MALLET TOWN (WESTERN)

Chairman: F. Gooding   Founded: 1933
Secretary: K. J. Hurrell   Tel no: Shepton Mallet 2653
Team manager: K. J. Wrintmore
Previous league: Somerset Senior

Colours: Yellow shirts, royal blue shorts, royal blue socks
Change colours: All sky blue
Address of ground: Playing Fields, West Shepton, Shepton Mallet, Somerset
Ground capacity: 2,500   Seating capacity: 500
Covered accommodation: 500   Floodlights: No
Clubhouse details: Open every night, bingo, shows, discos, skittle alley food, part-time steward: R. Neal (Shepton Mallet 3897)
Major honours: Somerset Senior Cup winners 1950, 1965
Programme: 8 pages, 8p

SHILDON (D. NORTHERN)

Chairman: J. I. Littlefair   Founded: 1892
Secretary: J. M. Armitage   Tel no: Aycliffe 316322
Team manager: B. Roughley
Previous league: North Eastern
Colours: All red
Change colours: All sky blue or all white
Address of ground: Dean Street, Shildon, Co Durham
    Record attendance: 14,000
Ground capacity: 4,000   Seating capacity: 500
Covered accommodation: Grandstand   Floodlights: No
Clubhouse details: None as yet, plans in hand
Best seasons in F.A. Cup: 1936-37 and 1927-28, 2nd Rnd Proper
League clubs defeated in F.A. Cup: York
Current players with Football League experience: C. Smith (Leeds Utd)
Major honours: Northern League champions 1934, 1935, 1936, 1937, 1940; Northern League Cup winners 1934, 1935, 1938, 1939, 1940, 1953; Durham Challenge Cup winners 1908, 1921, 1972
Best season in F.A. Trophy: 1974-75, 3rd Qual Rnd
Club nickname: The Railwaymen   Programme: 12 pages, 5p
Local newspapers: Northern Echo, Evening Despatch, Evening Gazette

SITTINGBOURNE (KENT)

Chairman: A. F. Stedman   Founded: 1881
Secretary: L. Davies
Team manager: P. Laraman
Previous leagues: South Eastern, Metropolitan Southern
Colours: Red and black striped shirts, black shorts, black and red socks
Change colours: White shirts with red and black trim, red or white shorts
Address of ground: Bull Ground, Rear High Street, Sittingbourne, Kent
    Record attendance: 5,728 (1957-58)
Ground capacity: 8,750   Seating capacity: 500
Covered accommodation: 3-5,000   Floodlights: Yes
Clubhouse details: Situated on the ground, bar, main hall seating 120, capacity of 180 for dancing
Best season in F.A. Cup: 1961-62
Major honours: Kent Senior Cup winners 1901-02, 1928-29, 1929-30, 1957-58; Kent League Div 1 champions 1902-03, 1957-58, 1958-59;

Kent League Div 1 Cup winners 1902-03, 1925-26, 1957-58, 1958-59, 1973-74, Div 2 Cup winners 1954-55; Kent Senior Shield winners 1926-27, 1927-28, 1953-54; Thames and Medway Cup winners 1955-56, 1958-59; Kent League champions 1975-76
Best season in F.A. Trophy: 1970-71, 2nd Qual Rnd
Club nickname: The Brickies   Programme: 4 pages, 5p
Local newspapers: East Kent Gazette, Sittingbourne Times, Evening Post

SKEGNESS TOWN   (MID. COUNTIES)

Chairman: J. Boulton
Secretary: M. W. Bocock   Tel no: Skegness 5374
Team manager: A. Woodward
Previous leagues: Lincolnshire, Central Alliance
Colours: All white with red trim   Change colours: All red
Address and tel no of ground: Burch Road, Skegness, Lincs (Skegness 4385)
                              Record attendance: 4,000 (1977)
Ground capacity: 6,000   Seating capacity: 200
Covered accommodation: Two stands
                                   Floodlights: No
Clubhouse details: Seating for 150 open throughout the year
Best season in F.A. Cup: 1951-52, 1st Rnd Proper
Current players with Football League experience: G. Peden (Lincoln); A. Woodward (Grimsby); K. Brown (Grimsby)
Best season in F.A. Vase: 1978-79, last 32
Club nickname: The Lilywhites   Programme: 4 pages, 5p
Local newspaper: Skegness Standard

SKELMERSDALE UNITED
(CHESHIRE CO. DIV 2)

Chairman: S. West
Secretary: R. L. Ford   Founded: 1882
                                   Tel no: Skelmersdale 21187 (h);
                                           24234 ext 32 (bus)
Team manager: D. A. G. Coutts
Previous leagues: Lancashire Combination, Northern Premier
Colours: Blue shirts, white shorts, blue socks
Change colour: All yellow
Address of ground: White Moss Park, White Moss Road, Skelmersdale, Lancs
Ground capacity: 10,000   Seating capacity: 350
Covered accommodation: 500 plus   Floodlights: Yes
Best season in F.A. Cup: 1967-68 and 1971-72, 1st Rnd
Major honours: Amateur Cup finalists 1966-67; F.A. Amateur Cup winners 1970-71
Best season in F.A. Trophy: 1972-73, 2nd Proper
Club nickname: The Skemmers
Local newspapers: Skelmersdale Advertiser, Skelmersdale Report, Liverpool Echo

173

SLOUGH TOWN (B.I.L. P. DIV)

Chairman: C. W. Grieg
Secretary: R. N. Lee
Team manager: J. Arpino
Previous leagues: Spartan, Herts & Middlesex, Corinthian, Athenian
Colours: Amber shirts, blue shorts, blue socks
Change colours: All red
Address and tel no of ground: Wexham Park Stadium, Wexham Road, Slough, Berks (Slough 23358/9) Record attendance: 8,000 (1953)
Ground capacity: 8,000 Seating capacity: 395
Covered accommodation: Approx 300

Floodlights: Yes
Clubhouse details: Open daily, full facilities, available for hire
Best season in F.A. Cup: 1970-71, 2nd Rnd Proper
Current players with Football League experience: R. Teale; I. Cooke; A. Cane; P. Feely; B. Friend
Major honours: Berks and Bucks Senior Cup winners; Corinthian League champions; Athenian League champions; Champions Amateur Cup finalists 1973, semi-finalists 1967
Best season in F.A. Trophy: 1976-77, Semi-final
Club nickname: The Rebels Programme: 12 pages, 10p
Local newspapers: Slough Observer, Evening Mail, Slough Express

SOUTHALL & EALING BOROUGH (B.I.L. DIV 2)

Chairman: K. Pike
Secretary: A. Bevis
Team manager: G. Taylor
Previous leagues: Great Western Suburban, Athenian
Colours: All white Change colours: All red
Address and tel no of ground: Western Road, Southall, Middx (01-574 1084) Record attendance: 19,094 (1935-36)
Ground capacity: 10,000 Seating capacity: 130
Covered accommodation: 500 Floodlights: Yes
Clubhouse details: Open every evening, darts on Tuesdays and Thursdays
Best season in F.A. Cup: 1935-36, 3rd Rnd Proper
League clubs defeated in F.A. Cup: Swindon
Major honours: Middlesex Senior Cup winners 1907-08, 1910-11, 1912-13, 1922-23, 1924-25, 1926-27, 1936-37, 1944-45, 1953-54, 1954-55
Best season in F.A. Trophy: Never past 2nd Qual Rnd
Club nickname: The Hall Programme: 8 pages, 10p
Local newspaper: Ealing Gazette

SOUTH BANK (D. NORTHERN)

Chairman: F. C. Nash
Secretary: R. J. Kidd
Team coaches: F. Storr and D. Mason
Colours: Red and white striped shirts, black shorts, red and white socks
Change colours: All white with red trim
Address and tel no of ground: Normanby Road Ground, Normanby Road, South Bank, Cleveland (Eston Grange 3193)
Founded: 1868
Tel no: Middlesbrough 243412

Record attendance: 10,000 (pre-War)
Ground capacity: 8,000 Seating capacity: 400
Covered accommodation: Grandstand and terrace Floodlights: Yes
Clubhouse details: Open seven afternoons and nights a week, Thursday and Sunday concerts, Saturday disco and dancing, snacks and wedding parties
Current players with Football League experience: M. Gormley; T. Harrison; J. Graggs
Major honours: F. A. Amateur Cup winners 1913, finalists 1910, 1922; Northern League champions 1908, 1920, 1922; North Riding Senior Cup winners 1898, 1908, 1910, 1911, 1924, 1932, 1936
Best season in F.A. Trophy: 1974-75, 2nd Rnd Proper
Club nickname: The Bankers Programme: 6 pages, 5p
Local newspaper: Evening Gazette

SOUTH LIVERPOOL (N.P.L.)

Chairman: E. Ogden
Secretary: S. Evison
Team manager: R. Perkins
Previous leagues: Cheshire County, Lancashire Combination
Colours: White shirts, black shorts, red socks
Change colours: All sky blue
Address and tel no of ground: Holly Park, Woolton Road, Garston, Liverpool, 19 (051-427 7372 – match days only)
Founded: Re-formed 1934
Tel no: 051-256 8024

Record attendance: 13,000
Ground capacity: 15,000 Seating capacity: 500
Covered accommodation: 5,000 Floodlights: Yes
Clubhouse details: Open afternoons from 1.30 – 5.00 p.m., nightly from 7.00 – 10.30 p.m., fully licensed (051-427 4645)
Best season in F.A. Cup: 1964-65, 2nd Rnd Proper
Major honours: Liverpool Senior Cup winners 1953-54, 1967-68, 1969-70
Best season in F.A. Trophy: 1974-75, 2nd Rnd Proper
Club nickname: The South Programme: 12 pages, 10p
Local newspapers: Liverpool Daily Post & Echo, Liverpool Weekly News

SOUTHPORT (N.P.L.)

Chairman: W. S. Giller
Secretary: G. I. Brown
Team manager: H. McNally
Founded: 1881
Tel no: 051-489 2585

175

Previous league: Football League
Colours: Yellow with blue trim
Change colours: Blue with white trim
Address and tel no of ground: Haig Avenue, Southport, Merseyside
   (Southport 33422)   Record attendance: 20,000 (1968)
Ground capacity: 20,000   Seating capacity: 3,000
Covered accommodation: Three sides Floodlights: Yes
Clubhouse details: Directors' lounge, ladies' lounge, V.I.P. lounge, sup-
   porters' club on ground
Best season in F.A. Cup: 1930-31, 6th Rnd
Current players with Football League experience: C. Kisby; P. Birchall
Major honours: Promotion to Football League Div 3 1966-67
Best season in F.A. Trophy: 1978-79, 1st Rnd Proper
Club nickname: The Sandgrounders Programme: 10p
Local newspapers: Liverpool Daily Post & Echo, Southport Visitor

SPALDING UNITED   (UTD. CO.)

Chairman: R. Mason   Founded: 1922
Secretary: C. A. Feakes   Tel no: Spalding 67190
Team manager: F. Fox
Previous leagues: Eastern Counties, Central Alliance, United Counties,
   Midland
Colours: Blue shirts, white shorts, blue socks
Change colours: Red shirts, white shorts, red socks
Address and tel no of ground: Sir Halley Stewart Field, Winfret Avenue,
   Spalding, Lincs (Spalding 4957)   Record attendance: 6,972 (1952)
Ground capacity: 7,000   Seating capacity: 350
Covered accommodation: 2,500   Floodlights: No
Clubhouse details: Open match days, Tuesday and Thursday evenings
Best season in F.A. Cup: 1964-65, 1st Rnd v Newport County
Major honours: United Counties League champions 1954-55, 1974-75
Best season in F.A. Trophy: Never past 2nd Qual Rnd
Club nickname: The Tulips   Programme: 12 pages, 5p
Local newspapers: Lincolnshire Free Press, Spalding Guardian

SPENNYMOOR UNITED
(D. NORTHERN)

Chairman: J. Smith   Founded: 1901
Secretary: J. Hindmarch   Tel no: Spennymoor 815168
Team manager: S. Bradley
Previous leagues: North Eastern, Midland Counties
Colours: Black and white striped shirts, black shorts, white socks with
   black trim
Change colours: All red or all white
Address and tel no of ground: 'Brewery Field', Durham Road, Spennymoor,
   Co Durham (Spennymoor 814100)
Ground capacity: 8,500   Seating capacity: 320
Covered accommodation: 1,500   Floodlights: Yes

Clubhouse details: Open nightly, refreshments for matches provided by
supporters club on ground
Best seasons in F.A. Cup: 1937, 1975, 1978
League clubs defeated in F.A. Cup: Southport
Major honours: Northern League champions 1967-68, 1971-72, 1973-74,
1976-77, 1977-78, 1978-79, runners-up 1974-75; Northern League
Challenge Cup winners 1965-66, 1967-68; Durham County Challenge
Cup winners 1930, 1945, 1946, 1953, 1963, 1968, 1973, 1974, 1975,
1976, 1978, 1979 (joint holders of record with Sunderland for most
consecutive wins); Vaux Floodlit League champions 1974; Durham
Benevolent Bowl winners 1927, 1930, 1932, 1948, 1959, 1962; North
Eastern League champions 1909-10, 1944, 1945-46, 1956-57, runners-
up 1936-37
Best season in F.A. Trophy: 1977-78, Semi-final
Club nickname: The Moors   Programme: 4 pages, 10p
Local newspapers: Northern Echo, Newcastle Journal

STAFFORD RANGERS   (A.P.L.)

Chairman: E. D. Weetman   Founded: 1876
Secretary: R. F. Pepper   Tel no: Stafford 53135 (home);
                                          42839 (bus)
Team manager: R. Chapman
Previous leagues: Birmingham, Birmingham Combination, Cheshire
Colours: White shirts with black trim, black shorts
Change colours: Red shirts, white shorts
Address and tel no of ground: Marston Road, Stafford
  (Stafford 42750)   Record attendance: 8,523 (1975)
Ground capacity: 9,500   Seating capacity: 426
Covered accommodation: 3,000   Floodlights: Yes
Clubhouse details: Open daily, bar, snacks, Saturday night entertainment
  (Stafford 52284)
Best season in F.A. Cup: 1973-74, lost 1–2 to Peterborough 4th Rnd
League clubs defeated in F.A. Cup: Halifax, Stockport, Rotherham
Current players with Football League experience: A. Wood; B. Seddon;
  S. Chapman; M. Cullerton; K. Kennerley; B. Thomson
Major honours: F.A. Trophy winners 1972; Northern Premier League
champions 1972; Staffs Senior Cup winners 1972
Best season in F.A. Trophy: 1971-72, Winners v Barnet
Club nickname: The Boro'   Programme: 16 pages, 15p
Local newspapers: Stafford Newsletter, Express & Star, Evening Sentinel

STAINES TOWN   (B.I.L.P. DIV)

Chairman: C. Lane   Founded: 1892
Secretary: C. L. Bateson   Tel no: 01-751 1053
Team manager: R. Williams
Previous leagues: Hellenic, Spartan, Athenian
Colours: Old gold shirts, blue shorts, old gold socks
Change colours: All sky blue

Address and tel no of ground: Wheatsheaf Lane, Staines, Middx
(Staines 55988)   Record attendance: 3,325 (1975)
Ground capacity: 5,000   Seating capacity: 300
Covered accommodation: Two sides and behind one goal
                                   Floodlights: Yes
Clubhouse details: Open every evening, large hall and main bar, food
mainly sandwiches, snacks, etc.
Best season in F.A. Cup: 3rd Qual Rnd (year not known)
Current players with Football League experience: B. Greenhaigh (Aston
Villa, Cambridge Utd, Chesterfield)
Major honours: Spartan League runners-up 1970-71; Athenian League
Div 2 champions 1971-72; Athenian League Div 1 runners-up 1972-73;
Rothmans Isthmian League Div 2 champions 1974-75; Barassi Cup
winners 1975-76; London Senior Cup runners-up 1976-77; Middlesex
Senior Cup winners 1974-75, 1975-76, 1976-77
Best season in F.A. Trophy: 1976-77, 2nd Rnd Proper
Club nickname: The Swans   Programme: 12 pages, 10p
Local newspapers: Evening Mail, Middlesex Chronicle, Staines & Egham
News

STALYBRIDGE CELTIC
(CHESHIRE CO. DIV 1)

Chairman: L. McDonald   Founded: 1909
Secretary: J. Dillon   Tel no: 061-698 2593
Team manager: P. Wragg
Previous leagues: Football League, Central, Southern, Lancashire Com-
bination
Colours: All royal blue   Change colours: All white or all red
Address and tel no of ground: Bower Fold, Mottram Road, Stalybridge,
Cheshire (061-338 2828)   Record attendance: 9,753 (1953)
Ground capacity: 7,550   Seating capacity: 550
Covered accommodation: 7,000   Floodlights: Yes
Clubhouse details: Bower Club
Best season in F.A. Cup: 1923, 1st Rnd Proper
League clubs defeated in F.A. Cup: West Bromwich Albion
Current players with Football League experience: M. Higgins (Blackburn,
Workington)
Major honours: Manchester Senior Cup runners-up 1923; Lancashire
Comb League champions 1911-12; 4th Central League champions
1912-13
Best season in F.A. Trophy: 1973-74, 2nd Rnd Proper
Club nickname: Celtic   Programme: 8 pages, 10p
Local newspaper: Stalybridge Reporter

STAMFORD   (UTD. COUNTIES)

Chairman: A. L. Twiddy   Founded: 1895
Secretary: D. J. Barnett   Tel no: Stamford 3842
Team manager: Ray Medwell
Previous leagues: Northants Senior, Central Alliance, Midland
Colours: All red

Change colours: Yellow with blue trim
Address and tel no of ground: Wothorpe Road, Stamford, Lincs
  (Stamford 3079)
Ground capacity: 3,000   Seating capacity: 250
Covered accommodation: Yes   Floodlights: No
Major honours: F.A. Vase finalists 1976; United Counties League cham-
  pions 1911-12, 1975-76, 1977-78
Programme: None

STONEHOUSE (GLOUCS. CO.)

Chairman: B. Gabb   Founded: 1976
Secretary: F. V. Wilks   Tel no: Stonehouse 3708
Team manager: Joe Matthews
Previous league: Gloucestershire Northern Senior
Colours: Black and white striped shirts, black shorts, red socks
Change colours: All green or all red
Address and tel no of ground: Magpies Ground, Oldends Lane, Stone-
  house, Gloucs (Stonehouse 3168)
Ground capacity: 4,000   Seating capacity: 250
Covered accommodation: Approx. 300 Floodlights: No
Clubhouse details: Magpies Social Club
Best season in F.A. Vase: 1975-76, 2nd Rnd
Club nickname: The Magpies
Local newspapers: Stroud & District News & Journal, Gloucestershire
  Citizen

STOURBRIDGE (S.L.M.)

Chairman: W. Poulton   Founded: 1876
Secretary: R. Barlow   Tel no: Stourbridge 5474
Team manager: Terry Wharton
Previous leagues: West Midlands Regional, Birmingham
Colours: Red and white shirts, white shorts, red and white socks
Change colours: White shirts, black shorts, white socks
Address and tel no of ground: War Memorial Athletic Ground, High Street,
  Amblecote, Stourbridge, West Midlands (Stourbridge 4040)
Ground capacity: 7,000   Seating capacity: 475
Covered accommodation: Yes   Floodlights: Yes
Clubhouse details: Open every night, club room, lounge, live entertain-
  ment on Saturdays, bingo three nights a week, steward: L. Tibbetts
  (Stourbridge 4040)
Best season in F.A. Cup: 4th Qual Rnd
Major honours: Southern League Div 1 champions 1973-74; Birmingham
  League champions; Birmingham Senior Cup winners 1950, 1959, 1968
Best season in F.A. Trophy: Quarter-final
Programme: 8 pages, 10p
Local newspapers: Stourbridge County Express, Wolverhampton Express
  & Star, Birmingham Evening Mail

SUDBURY TOWN (TOWN & COUNTRY)

Chairman: H. D. J. Yallop
Secretary: H. D. J. Yallop
Team manager: C. Harper
Previous league: Essex & Suffolk Border
Founded: 1898
Tel no: Sudbury 72585
Colours: Amber shirts with blue trim, blue shorts, amber and blue socks
Change colours: All sky blue
Address and tel no of ground: Priory Stadium, Friars Street, Sudbury, Suffolk (Sudbury 72795)　**Record attendance:** 3,500 (1963-64)
Ground capacity: 3,000　**Seating capacity:** 300
Covered accommodation: 750 standing　**Floodlights:** No
Clubhouse details: Licensed bar, small dance hall for 150 people
Best season in F.A. Cup: 1974-75, 4th Qual Rnd
Current players with Football League experience: C. Harper
Major honours: Suffolk Premier Cup winners 1972-73, 1973-74, 1975-76; Suffolk Premier League champions 1973-74, 1974-75, 1975-76; Town and Country Cup winners 1974-75, 1975-76, 1976-77
Best season in F.A. Trophy: 1974-75, 3rd Qual Rnd
Club nickname: The 'Boro'　**Programme:** 6 pages
Local newspaper: Suffolk Free Press

SUTTON COLDFIELD TOWN
(M. COMB.)

Chairman: M. Flint
Secretary: G. Humpherson
Team manager: Rhys Davies
Founded: 1879
Tel no: Tamworth 66260
Previous leagues: Walsall Senior, Staffs County, Birmingham, West Midlands
Colours: Royal blue shirts, white shorts
Change colours: All white
Address and tel no of ground: Central Ground, Coles Lane, Sutton Coldfield, West Midlands, B72 1NL (021-354 2997)
Ground capacity: 4,450　**Seating capacity:** 250
Covered accommodation: 200　**Floodlights:** No
Clubhouse details: Open every night, dancing, bingo, cabaret, etc., stewards: R. Timmings and A. Aston
Major honours: Midland Combination League champions 1977-78
Programme: 4 pages, 2p

SUTTON TOWN (MID COUNTIES)

Chairman: C. Straw
Secretary: D. Skermer
Team manager: B. Curry
Founded: 1886
Tel no: Mansfield 752798
Previous leagues: Notts & District Senior, Notts & Derby, Central Alliance, Midland, Midland Combination, Derbyshire Senior, Central Combination, Central Alliance

Colours: Royal blue shirts with white trim, white shorts, white socks
Change colours: All white
Address and tel no of ground: Lowmoor Road, Kirkby-in-Ashfield, nr Sutton-in-Ashfield, Notts (Mansfield 752181)
Record attendance: 761 (1978)
Ground capacity: 8,000   Floodlights: No
Covered accommodation: One end and one side
Clubhouse details: None at the moment due to moving ground
Best season in F.A. Cup: 1933–34
League clubs defeated in F.A. Cup: Rochdale
Current players with Football League experience: P. Lyons (Mansfield Town); B. Grozier (Mansfield Town)
Major honours: Notts Senior Cup winners 17 times; Central Alliance League champions 1950–51; Derbyshire Senior League champions 1931–2–3; Notts & District Senior League champions 1905–6–7
Best seasons in F.A. Trophy: 1969–70, 1977–78 and 1978–79, 3rd Qual Rnd
Club nickname: The Snipes   Programme: 16 pages, 5p
Local newspapers: Notts Free Press, Chronicle Advertiser, Evening Post

SUTTON UNITED   (B.I.L. P. DIV)

Chairman: P. D. Molloy   Founded: 1898
Secretary: R. B. Carr   Tel no: Burgh Heath 58103
Team manager: K. Williams
Previous league: Athenian
Colours: Chocolate and amber   Change colours: All white
Address and tel no of ground: Boro Sports Ground, Gander Green Lane, Sutton, Surrey (01-644 4440/5437)   Record attendance: 15,000 (1970)
Ground capacity: 15,000   Seating capacity: 1,800
Covered accommodation: Main stand   Floodlights: Yes
Clubhouse details: Large clubhouse with full facilities, two bars
Best season in F.A. Cup: 1969-70, 4th Rnd
Major honours: Amateur Cup finalists 1962-63, 1968-69; Anglo Italian Semi-Pro Tournament winners 1979; London Senior Cup/Surrey Cup winners 1945-46, 1964-65, 1967-68, 1969-70; Isthmian League champions 1966-67; Athenian League champions 1927-28, 1945-46, 1957-58
Best season in F.A. Trophy: Never past 1st Rnd Proper
                                   Programme: 20 pages, 10p
Local newspapers: Sutton & Cheam Herald, Sutton & Cheam Advertiser

TAMWORTH   (S.L.M.)

Chairman: M. J. Tongue   Founded: 1933
Secretary: R. A. Challens   Tel no: Tamworth 52743
Team manager: D. Robinson
Previous leagues: Birmingham, West Midlands
Colours: Red shirts, white shorts, red socks
Change colours: White shirts, blue shorts, white socks
Address of ground: Lamb Ground, Kettlebrook Road, Tamworth, Staffs
Ground capacity: 5,000   Seating capacity: 500

Covered accommodation: 250   Floodlights: Yes
Best season in F.A. Cup: 1969-70, 2nd Rnd
League clubs defeated in F.A. Cup: Torquay United
Current players with Football League experience: N. Attney; B. Barnes;
D. Robinson
Major honours: West Midlands League champions
Best season in F.A. Trophy: 1970-71, 4th Rnd
Programme: 12 pages, 10p
Local newspapers: Tamworth Herald, Tamworth Trader

TAUNTON TOWN   (S.L.M.)

Chairman: To be appointed   Founded: 1947
Secretary: G. K. Nelson   Tel no: Taunton 71167 (h):
                               Bridgewater 58496 (bus)
Previous league: Western
Colours: Claret and sky blue shirts, white shorts, sky blue socks
Change colours: White shirts, white shorts, sky blue socks
Address and tel no of ground: Wordsworth Drive, Taunton, Somerset
(Taunton 89608)   Record attendance: 2,800 (1956)
Ground capacity: 4,000   Seating capacity: 120
Covered accommodation: Terraces   Floodlights: Yes
Clubhouse details: Social club incorporating two bars, separate hall for
functions
Best seasons in F.A. Cup: 1958-59, 1970-71 and 1978-79, 4th Qual Rnd
Current players with Football League experience: D. Burnside (WBA,
Southampton, Crystal Palace, Wolves, Plymouth); B. McAuley (Ply-
mouth)
Major honours: Somerset Senior League champions 1952-53, runners-up
1951-52, 1953-54; Western League champions 1968-69, runners-up
1972-73, 1973-74, 1974-75, 1975-76
Best seasons in F.A. Trophy: 1969-70, 1972-73, 1973-74 and 1978-79, 1st
Rnd Proper
Club nickname: The Peacocks   Programme: 16 pages, 10p
Local newspaper: Somerset County Gazette

TELFORD UNITED   (A.P.L.)

Chairman: G. E. Smith   Founded: 1877
Secretary: W. J. Fletcher   Tel no: Telford 44831
Team manager: To be appointed
Previous leagues: Birmingham & District, Cheshire County, Southern
Colours: All white   Change colours: All red
Address and tel no of ground: The Bucks Head Ground, Watling Street,
Wellington, Telford, Salop (Telford 3838)
                               Record attendance: 12,000
Ground capacity: 15,000   Seating capacity: 1,500
Covered accommodation: 3,000   Floodlights: Yes
Clubhouse details: Open every night, weekend entertainment, snacks
available (Telford 55662)
Best seasons in F.A. Cup: 1970-71 and 1972-73, 2nd Rnd

Current players with Football League experience: P. Weir (Wolves); B. Clarke (Exeter, WBA); M. Buttress (Aston Villa, Gillingham); K. Moore (Shrewsbury); M. Williams (Newport County)
Major honours: F.A. Trophy winners 1971; Southern League Cup winners 1971
Best season in F.A. Trophy: 1971, Winners
Club nickname: The Lilywhites   Programme: 16 pages, 10p
Local newspapers: Shropshire Star, Telford Journal

THAME UNITED   (HELLENIC)

Chairman: N. McRae   Founded: 1883
Secretary: P. Newitt   Tel no: Thame 3494
Team manager: R. Eele
Previous league: Oxfordshire Senior
Colours: Red shirts with white and blue striped sleeves, white shorts
Change colours: All yellow
Address and tel no of ground: Windmill Road, Thame, Oxon (Thame 3494)
Ground capacity: 5,000   Seating capacity: 250
Covered accommodation: Stand   Floodlights: No
Clubhouse details: Large clubhouse with separate members' bar, seating capacity for 200, own catering staff
Current players with Football League experience: P. Buck
Major honours: Oxfordshire Senior Cup winners; Hellenic Cup winners; Hellenic League champions
Best season in F.A. Vase: 1975-76, 2nd Rnd
Programme: Free   Local newspaper: Thame Gazette

TILBURY   (B.I.L. P. DIV)

Chairman: G. A. Paisley   Founded: 1900
Secretary: G. G. Paisley   Tel no: Tilbury 77616 (h);
                                           01-626 6719 (bus)
Team manager: P. Carey
Previous leagues: Corinthian, London, Delphian, Athenian
Colours: White shirts, black shorts, black socks
Change colours: Red shirts, black shorts, white socks
Address and tel no of ground: St Chad's Road, Tilbury, Essex
   (Tilbury 3373/3093)   Record attendance: 5,500 (1949)
Ground capacity: 7,200   Seating capacity: 200
Covered accommodation: 2,200   Floodlights: Yes
Clubhouse details: Two separate clubhouses each running social functions, darts, friendly club, dancing, snacks
Best season in F.A. Cup: 1977-78, 3rd Rnd
Current players with Football League experience: D. Barnett (Southend)
Major honours: Essex Senior Cup winners four times; Essex Professional Cup winners once; London League champions four times; Athenian League Div 1 and Div 2 champions; Isthmian League Div 1 champions
Best season in F.A. Trophy: 1978-79, 3rd Qual Rnd
Club nickname: The Dockers   Programme: 12 pages, 10p
Local newspapers: Thurrock Gazette, Thurrock Times & Guardian

TIVERTON TOWN (WESTERN)

Chairman: D. W. Long   Founded: 1920
Secretary: A. Disney   Tel no: Tiverton 3829
Team manager: M. Howe
Previous league: Devon & Exeter
Colours: Amber shirts with black trim, black shorts, amber and black socks
Change colours: Royal blue shirts, white shorts, royal blue socks
Address and tel no of ground: 'Ladymead', Bolham Road, Tiverton, Devon
(Tiverton 56716)
Ground capacity: 3,000 approx   Seating capacity: 200
                                     Floodlights: No
Clubhouse details: Pool table, skittle alley, regular discos, parties, licensed
bar, open in evenings
Current players with Football League experience: J. Mitten (Leicester City,
Exeter City)
Major honours: Devon and Exeter Premier League champions 1926-7-8,
1933-34, 1964-5-6; Devon Premier Cup winners 1955-56, 1965-66
Best season in F. A. Vase: 1977-78, 4th Rnd
Club nickname: Tivvy
Local newspapers: Tiverton News, Tiverton Gazette, Express & Echo

TIVIDALE (W. MIDLANDS)

Chairman: D. McDonald   Founded: 1954
Secretary: E. Jones   Tel no: Dudley 58261
Team manager: W. Bowen
Previous leagues: Handsworth & District, Warwicks & West Midlands
Alliance
Colours: Amber shirts, amber shorts, blue socks
Change colours: All white
Address and tel no of ground: 'The Beeches', Packwood Road, Tividale,
Warley, West Midlands (Dudley 54868/211743)
                                     Record attendance: 2,300 (1977)
Ground capacity: 3,000   Seating capacity: 200
Covered accommodation: 1,500   Floodlights: Yes
Clubhouse details: Open from Sunday to Thursday (8 p.m. to 10.30 p.m.),
Friday to Saturday (8 p.m. to 11 p.m.), Sunday (12 noon to 2 p.m.),
Saturday (12 noon to 2.30 p.m.)
Best season in F.A. Cup: 1977-78, 3rd Qual Rnd
Current players with Football League experience: D. Isherwood
Major honours: West Midlands League P Div Cup winners; West Midlands
Div 1 Cup winners 1974-75; West Midlands League Div 1 champions
1974-75
Best season in F.A. Vase: 1976-77, 4th Rnd
Club nickname: The Dale   Programme: 5p
Local newspapers: Express & Star, County Express, Sandwell Mail

TONBRIDGE (S.L.S.)

Chairman: W. Wheeler
Secretary: Mrs P. Westguard
Team manager: E. Morgan
Colours: All blue

Reformed: 1976
Tel no: Tonbridge 358492

Change colours: All yellow
Address and tel no of ground: Office – 16a Vale Road, Tonbridge, Kent
(Tonbridge 352417); Ground – Angel Ground, Vale Road, Tonbridge,
Kent (Tonbridge 350250)
Record attendance: 8,236 (1951)
Ground capacity: 10,000
Seating capacity: 400
Covered accommodation: Two stands Floodlights: Yes
Clubhouse details: Bar and tea bar open on match days only
Best seasons in F.A. Cup: 1951-52, 1952-53, 1967-68 and 1972-73, 1st Rnd
Current players with Football League experience: D. Light (Crystal Palace,
Colchester); M. Griffiths (Crystal Palace); A. Payne (Peterborough)
Major honours: Kent Senior Cup winners 1964-65, 1974-75; Southern
League Cup finalists 1954-55, 1956-57; Southern League Div 1 South
runners-up 1972-73
Best seasons in F.A. Trophy: 1970-71 and 1971-72, 1st Rnd Proper
Club nickname: The Angels   Programme: 8 pages, 10p
Local newspapers: Tonbridge Advertiser, Kent & Sussex Courier, Kent
Messenger

TON PENTRE (WELSH)

Chairman: J. Orrells
Secretary: P. Willoughby
Team manager: Gwyn Lloyd
Colours: All red

Founded: 1935
Tel no: Tonypandy 438281

Change colours: All sky blue
Address and tel no of ground: Ynys Park, Ton Pentre, Rhondda, Mid
Glam (Tonypandy 432813)
Record attendance: 5,000 (1969)
Ground capacity: 6,000
Seating capacity: 700
Covered accommodation: Three stands Floodlights: Yes
Clubhouse details: Situated adjacent to ground, tel no as ground
Best season in F.A. Cup: 1969-70, 4th Qual Rnd
Current players with Football League experience: K. Evans (Swansea);
J. Coombes (Bristol R); N. Foulkes (WBA); S. Vaughan (C Palace)
Major honours: Welsh League Prem Div champions 1957-58, 1960-61,
1973-74; Welsh Amateur Cup winners 1951-52; South Wales Senior
Cup winners 1947-48, 1960-61, 1961-62, 1963-64
Best season in F.A. Trophy: 1970-71, 3rd Qual Rnd
Club nickname: The Bulldogs   Programme: 10p
Local newspaper: Rhondda Leader

TOOTING & MITCHAM UNITED (B.I.L.P. DIV)

Chairman: H. L. Walters
Secretary: L. W. Hellard
Team manager: J. Payne
Previous league: Athenian

Founded: 1932
Tel no: 01-764 2821

185

Colours: Black and white striped shirts, black shorts
Change colours: Light and dark blue
Address and tel no of ground: Sandy Lane, Mitcham, Surrey (01-648 3248)
Ground capacity: 8,000-10,000   Record attendance: 42,000 (1959)
Covered accommodation: 2,000   Seating capacity: 1,900
Clubhouse details: Situated under the stand, facilities for approx. 100   Floodlights: Yes
Best season in F.A. Cup: 1976, 4th Rnd v Bradford City
League clubs defeated in F.A. Cup: Brighton & Hove, Bournemouth, Boscombe, Northampton Town, Swindon
Current players with Football League experience: J. Dunn; P. Sommerill; S. Grubb; F. Cowley; G. Sproul
Major honours: Surrey Senior Cup winners 1976, 1977, 1978; Isthmian League champions 1958, 1960; London Senior Cup winners 1943, 1949, 1959, 1960
Best season in F.A. Trophy: 1975-76, 4th Rnd Proper
Club nickname: The Tooting Terrors   Programme: 10p
Local newspapers: Mitcham News, South London Press, Mitcham Guardian

TOW LAW TOWN   (D. NORTHERN)

Chairman: H. Hodgson   Founded: 1890
Secretary: B. D. Fairbairn   Tel no: Darlington 50743
Team manager: Billy Bell
Colours: Black and white striped shirts, black shorts, black and white socks   Change colours: All red
Address and tel no of ground: Ironworks Road, Tow Law, Bishop Auckland, Co Durham (Tow Law 325)   Record attendance: 5,000 (1968)
Ground capacity: 8,000   Seating capacity: 700
Covered accommodation: 1,000   Floodlights: No
Clubhouse details: Small bar and lounge area
Best season in F.A. Cup: 1967-68
League clubs defeated in F.A. Cup: Mansfield, Shrewsbury
Current players with Football League experience: R. Ellison (Newcastle Sunderland)
Major honours: Northern League Cup winners 1973-74; Rothmans National Cup winners 1976-77
Best season in F.A. Trophy: 1977-78, 1st Rnd Proper
Club nickname: The Lawyers   Local newspaper: Northern Echo

TRING TOWN   (B.I.L. DIV 2)

Chairman: G. A. Smith   Founded: 1905
Secretary: D. A. Smith   Tel no: High Wycombe 33568
Team manager: J. Delaney
Previous leagues: Athenian, Spartan, Great Western
Colours: Red shirts, white shorts, red socks
Change colours: All sky blue
Address and tel no of ground: Pendley Sports Centre, Cow Lane, Tring, Herts (Tring 3075)   Record attendance: 2,500

Ground capacity: 3,000   Seating capacity: 200
Covered accommodation: 200   Floodlights: Yes
Clubhouse details: Capacity 200, bars, entertainment, open every night membership of 1,000, refreshments and meals available, steward: R, Waterton (Tring 3979)
Current players with Football League experience: J. Delaney; G. Mabb; B. Walsh
Major honours: Herts Senior Cup runners-up 1978–79; Athenian League runners-up 1977–78; Spartan League winners
Best season in F.A. Vase: 1976–77, 5th Rnd
Programme: Free
Local newspapers: Bucks Herald, Berkhamsted Gazette, Sports Echo

TROWBRIDGE TOWN   (S.L.S.)

Chairman: J. Oram, M.B.E.   Founded: 1888
Secretary: B. L. Coleman   Tel no: Trowbridge 5725
Team manager: T. Senter
Previous league: Western
Colours: White shirts, blue shorts, white socks
Change colours: All red
Address and tel no of ground: Frome Road, Trowbridge, Wilts (Trowbridge 65086)   Record attendance: 9,009
Ground capacity: 6,000   Seating capacity: 600
Covered accommodation: 1,600   Floodlights: Yes
Clubhouse details: Open on Tuesdays from 6 to 10.30 p.m., Wednesdays from 6 to 10.30 p.m., Saturdays from 12.00 to 2.30 p.m. and 5.30 to 11.00 p.m.
Best season in F.A. Cup: 1948-49
Major honours: Western League champions 1947-48, 1948-49
Best season in F.A. Trophy: 1970-71, 1st Rnd Proper
Programme: 12 pages, 10p
Local newspapers: Wiltshire Times, Western Daily Press

TUNBRIDGE WELLS   (KENT)

Chairman: J. F. Oakley   Founded: 1967
Secretary: P. C. Wager   Tel no: Tunbridge Wells 24182
Team manager: M. Cloude
Colours: Red and white shirts, white shorts, red socks
Change colours: All blue
Address of ground: Culverden Stadium, Culverden Down, Tunbridge Wells, Kent
Ground capacity: 5,000   Seating capacity: 400
Covered accommodation: 600   Floodlights: No
Clubhouse details: Refreshments, snacks, bar, open match days
Best season in F.A. Cup: 3rd Qual Rnd
Current players with Football League experience: D. Huddart (Gillingham)
Major honours: Kent League Cup winners 1974–75, 1977–78
Best seasons in F.A. Vase: 1974–75, 1975–76 and 1978–79, 4th Rnd
Club nickname: The Wells   Programme: 4 pages, 5p
Local newspaper: Kent & Sussex Courier

UXBRIDGE (K. ATHENIAN)

Chairman: T. H. Barnard
Secretary: D. L. Tucker
Team manager: R. Clack
Founded: 1871
Tel no: 01-876 3063 (h)
Previous leagues: Corinthian, Great Western, Southern
Colours: Red shirts, white shorts, red socks
Change colours: All white
Address and tel no of ground: 'Honeycroft', Horton Road, West Drayton Middlesex, UB7 8XH (West Drayton 43557)
Ground capacity: 5,000
Covered accommodation: 150
Seating capacity: 150
Floodlights: No
Clubhouse details: Large clubhouse and bar with dance hall, open every evening except Monday
Best season in F.A. Cup: 1873-74, 2nd Rnd
Major honours: F.A. Amateur Cup runners-up 1897-98; Corinthian League champions 1959-60
Best season in F.A. Vase: 1978-79, 3rd Rnd
Club nickname: The Reds
Programme: 10 pages, free
Local newspapers: Middlesex Advertiser & Gazette, Hillingdon Mirror

VS RUGBY (W. MIDLANDS)

Chairman: M. J. Vousden
Secretary: K. Coughlan
Team manager: Syd Hall
Founded: 1955
Tel no: Rugby 814746
Previous leagues: Rugby & District, Coventry & North Warwickshire, United Counties
Colours: White shirts with red trim, black shorts
Change colours: Green and black striped shirts, black shorts
Address and tel no of ground: Butlin Road, Rugby, Warwicks, CV21 3ST (Rugby 3692)
Covered accommodation: 200
Floodlights: No
Seating capacity: 200
Clubhouse details: Clubhouse open every night, Saturday and Sunday lunchtimes and after matches, two men's and three ladies' darts teams, pool, dominoes
Best seasons in F.A. Cup: 1977-78 and 1978-79, 1st Qual Rnd
Current players with Football League experience: I. Goodwin (Brighton, Coventry City)
Major honours: United Counties League Div 3 Cup winners
Best seasons in F.A. Vase: 1974-75 and 1975-76, 2nd Rnd
Programme: 4 pages, 5p
Local newspapers: Rugby Advertiser, Coventry Evening Telegraph

WALTHAMSTOW AVENUE
(B.I.L.P. DIV)

Chairman: W. F. Palmer
Secretary: N. R. J. Moss
Team manager: T. Matthews
Founded: 1900
Tel no: 01-531 0468
Previous leagues: Athenian, Spartan
Colours: Light and dark blue hooped shirts, royal blue shorts, light blue socks
Change colours: All white
Address and tel no of ground: Green Pond Road, Higham Hill Road, Walthamstow, London E.17 (01-527 1130/2795)
Record attendance: 12,500 (1939)
Ground capacity: 10,000
Seating capacity: 980
Covered accommodation: Three sides Floodlights: Yes
Clubhouse details: Club hall and lounge, two bars
Best season in F.A. Cup: 1952-53, 4th Rnd Proper
Major honours: F.A. Amateur Cup winners 1951-52, 1960-61; London Senior Cup winners eight times; Essex Senior Cup winners 11 times; Isthmian League champions 1945-46, 1952-53, 1954-55
Best season in F.A. Trophy: 1977-78, 3rd Rnd
Club nickname: The A's
Programme: 8 pages, 10p
Local newspapers: Waltham Forest Guardian, Waltham Forest Echo

WALTON & HERSHAM (B.I.L. DIV 1)

Chairman: To be appointed
Secretary: G. Pouncey
Team manager: G. Talbot
Founded: 1896
Tel no: Weybridge 53946
Previous leagues: Corinthian, Athenian
Colours: All red with white trim
Change colours: All white with red trim
Address of ground: Stompond Lane Sports Ground, Hersham Road, Walton-on-Thames, Surrey
Ground capacity: 6,000
Seating capacity: 420
Covered accommodation: 2,500
Floodlights: Yes
Clubhouse details: Open six nights a week, licensed bar, refreshment bar, open on match days, pool table, bingo, darts, discos
Best seasons in F.A. Cup: 1972–73 and 1973–74, 2nd Rnd
Best season in F.A. Trophy: 1974–75, 3rd Qual Rnd
Club nickname: The Swans
Programme: 18 pages, 15p
Local newspapers Surrey Herald

WARE (B.I.L. DIV 1)

Chairman: M. Allington
Secretary: C. T. Hudson
Team manager: T. Godleman
Founded: 1892
Tel no: Hertford 51862
Previous leagues: Herts County, Spartan, Delphian, Athenian

189

Colours: Blue and white striped shirts, blue shorts
Change colours: Amber and black shirts, black shorts
Address and tel no of ground: Buryfield, Park Road, Ware, Herts
(Ware 3247)   Record attendance: 2,500 (1974)
Ground capacity: 4,000-5,000   Seating capacity: 250
Covered accommodation: 400-500   Floodlights: Yes
Clubhouse details: Fully licensed, socials, dances, bingo, open Tuesdays,
  Thursdays, Fridays, Saturdays and Sundays
Best season in F. A. Cup: 1968-69, lost to Luton Town 1-6 1st Rnd Proper
Major honours: Herts Senior Cup winners 1899, 1904, 1907, 1922, 1954;
  Herts County League champions 1908-09, 1921-22; Spartan League
  champions 1926-27, 1951-52, 1952-53
Best seasons in F.A. Trophy: 1977-78 and 1978-79, 1st Qual Rnd
Club nickname: The Blues   Programme: 8 pages, 5p
Local newspaper: Hertfordshire Mercury

WARRINGTON TOWN (CHESHIRE CO.)

Chairman: To be appointed   Founded: 1949
Secretary: J. H. Drinkwater   Tel no: Warrington 642116
Team manager: S. Farmer
Previous league: Mid-Cheshire
Colours: All red   Change colours: Amber and black
Address and tel no of ground: Loushers Lane, Latchford, Warrington,
  Cheshire (Warrington 31932)   Record attendance: 3,000 (1957)
Ground capacity: 3,000   Seating capacity: None
Covered accommodation: 300   Floodlights: No
Clubhouse details: Capacity 200, top entertainments
Best season in F.A. Vase: 1977-78, 4th Rnd
Programme: 10p
Local newspaper: Warrington Guardian

WATERLOOVILLE   (S.L.S.)

Chairman: P. Faulkner   Founded: 1910
Secretary: T. Manns   Tel no: Waterlooville 4455 (bus);
Team manager: A. Avery   4888 (h)
Previous leagues: Hampshire County, Portsmouth Premier
Colours: White shirts, blue shorts, blue socks
Change colours: All yellow
Address and tel no of ground: Jubilee Park, Aston Road, Waterlooville,
  Hants (Waterlooville 4215)   Record attendance: 4,500
Ground capacity: 5,000   Seating capacity: 600
Covered accommodation: 1,000   Floodlights: Yes
Clubhouse details: Five bars, disco room, cabaret room, function room,
  plans for seven squash courts, gymnasium
Best seasons in F.A. Cup: 1968-69 and 1976-77, 1st Rnd Proper
Current players with Football League experience: M. Mellows; M. Seymour
Major honours: Southern League Div 1 South champions 1971-72;
  County Cup winners 1970, 1973; Victory Cup winners 1960, 1970
Best season in F.A. Trophy: 1976-77, 2nd Rnd Proper
Club nickname: The Ville   Programme: 12 pages, 10p
Local newspaper: Portsmouth News

190

WEALDSTONE (A.P.L.)

Chairman: To be appointed
Secretary: K. E. Wiltshire
Team manager: A. Fogarty
Previous leagues: Spartan, Athenian, Isthmian, Southern
Colours: Royal blue with white facings
Change colours: Yellow with royal blue facings
Address and tel no of ground: Lower Mead Stadium, Station Road, Harrow,
    Middx, HA1 2TU (01-427 2840 – club; 4064 – office)
Founded: 1900
Tel no: 01-204 5252 (home)
Record attendance: 13,540 (1952)
Ground capacity: 10,000
Seating capacity: 800
Covered accommodation: 6,000
Floodlights: Yes
Clubhouse details: Two bars, dance hall for 250 people, complete catering
    facilities for 150
Best season in F.A. Cup: 1977-78, 3rd Rnd Proper
League clubs defeated in F.A. Cup: Reading, Hereford Utd
Current players with Football League experience: I. Cranstone; J. McVeigh;
    N. Johnson; G. Duck; J. Watson; A. Fursdon; B. Moss
Major honours: F.A. Amateur Cup winners 1966; London Senior Cup
    (joint holders) 1961; Middx Senior Cup winners 11 times
Best season in F.A. Trophy: 1969, Quarter-final v South Shields
Club nickname: The Royal Stones   Programme: 8 pages, 12p
Local newspapers: Harrow Observer, Harrow Independen

WELLINGBOROUGH TOWN (S.L.M.)

Chairman: C. McCormick
Secretary: M. Walden
Team manager: B. Knight
Previous leagues: West Midland, Metropolitan, United Counties
Colours: White and blue   Change colours: All red
Address and tel no of ground: London Road, Wellingborough, Northants
    (Wellingborough 223536)
Founded: 1867
Tel no: Wellingborough 79561
Ground capacity: 5,000   Seating capacity: 300
Floodlights: Yes
Clubhouse details: Open every night, snacks available on match days
Best season in F.A. Cup: 1966–67
Current players with Football League experience: B. Knight
Major honours: Metropolitan League champions 1969–70
Best season in F.A. Trophy: 1971–72, 1st Rnd Proper
Club nickname: The Doughboys   Programme: 4 pages, free
Local newspaper: Northants Evening Telegraph

WELTON ROVERS (WESTERN)

Chairman: A. M. White
Secretary: A. A. Salvidge
Team manager: J. Llewellin
Previous league: Somerset Senior
Colours: Royal blue with white flash
Founded: 1887
Tel no: Midsomer Norton 413330

Change colours: Red shirts, black shorts, red socks
Address and tel no of ground: 'West Clewes', North Road, Midsomer
  Norton, nr Bath, Avon (Midsomer Norton 412097)
Record attendance: 2,000 (1965)
Ground capacity: 3,000
Seating capacity: 350
Covered accommodation: 350
Floodlights: No
Clubhouse details: Large clubhouse, dance floor, skittle alley, snacks and
  hot food on match days, open every night
Best season in F.A. Cup: 1967
Major honours: Western League champions three times
Best season in F.A. Trophy: 1973-74, 1st Rnd Proper
Local newspaper: Somerset Guardian

WEMBLEY (B.I.L. DIV 1)

Chairman: D. K. Long
Secretary: E. G. Stringer
Tel no: 01-205 1485 (h)
Previous league: Athenian
Colours: All red
Change colours: Sky blue shirts, black shorts
Ground capacity: 1,500
Seating capacity: 200
Covered accommodation: 700
Floodlights: Yes
Clubhouse details: Open nightly, large bar, usual club functions
Best season in F.A. Cup: 1976-77, 4th Qual Rnd
Best season in F.A. Trophy: 1977-78, 1st Rnd Proper
Programme: 12 pages, 5p
Local newspaper: Wembley & Harrow Observer

WEST AUCKLAND (D. NORTHERN)

Chairman: G. Laskey
Secretary: N. Ayton
Manager: R. Tookey
Founded: 1907
Tel no: Bishop Auckland 4375 (h)
Colours: White shirts with amber trim, white shorts, white socks
Change colours: Red shirts, white shorts, red socks
Address of ground: Darlington Road, West Auckland, Bishop Auckland,
  Co Durham
Ground capacity: 6,000
Seating capacity: 200
Covered accommodation: 200
Floodlights: Yes
Clubhouse details: Light refreshments available on match days
Best seasons in F.A. Cup: 1st Rnd Proper twice
Major honours: F.A. Amateur Cup finalists; Northern League champions
  1959-60, 1960-61; Durham County Cup winners 1965
Best season in F.A. Trophy: 1976-77, 1st Rnd Proper

WESTON-SUPER-MARE (WESTERN)

Chairman: S. Gillard
Secretary: B. T. White
Team manager: D. Stone
Colours: All royal blue
Founded: 1948
Tel no: Weston-super-Mare 25554
Change colours: Red and black

Address and tel no of ground: Langford Road, Weston-super-Mare, Avon
(Weston-super-Mare 21618)   Record attendance: 2,100 (1961)
Ground capacity: 3,000
Covered accommodation: 400   Floodlights: No
Clubhouse details: Open every night and Saturday and Sunday lunchtimes,
skittles, darts, pool, bingo, etc.
Best season in F.A. Cup: 1961
Current players with Football League experience: D. Stone (Bristol Rovers);
G. Duxsworth (Bristol Rovers); T. Woodhead (Swindon)
Major honours: Western League runners-up 1976-77; Western League Cup
winners 1976-77
Best season in F.A. Trophy: 1977-78, 3rd Qual Rnd
Club nickname: The Seasiders   Programme: 12 pages, 10p
Local newspapers: Western Daily Press, Evening Post, Western Mercury

WEYMOUTH   (A.P.L.)

Chairman: W. Bowering   Founded: 1890
Secretary: A. Mitchell   Tel no: Weymouth 785558
Team manager: S. Morgan
Previous leagues: Dorset Combination, Western
Colours: Terra cotta shirts, pale blue shorts, pale blue socks
Change colours: Yellow and blue shirts, yellow shorts, yellow socks
Address and tel no of ground: Recreation Ground, Weymouth, Dorset
(Weymouth 785558)   Record attendance: 12,512 (1948)
Ground capacity: 9,975   Seating capacity: 550
Covered accommodation: 6,500   Floodlights: Yes
Clubhouse details: Terra Cotta Club open nightly to 2 a.m. during summer
season, meals, dancing nightly during summer season, weekends winter
Best season in F.A. Cup: 1961-62, Quarter-final v Preston N.E.
League clubs defeated in F.A. Cup: Aldershot, Bournemouth, Bristol
Rovers, Cambridge Utd, Colchester Utd, Coventry City, Gillingham,
Leyton Orient, Man Utd, Merthyr Tydfil, Newport County, Northamp-
ton, Peterborough Utd, Preston N.E., Reading, Shrewsbury, South-
ampton, Southend Utd, Swansea, Torquay Utd
Current players with Football League experience: S. Dyer; S. Morgan; N.
Townsend; S. Chalk; P. Hawkins; A. Leitch; T. Henderson; J. McCaf-
ferty
Major honours: Southern Premier League champions 1964-65, 1965-66;
Southern League Cup winners 1973, runners-up 1963-4-5, 1971-1978
Best seasons in F.A. Trophy: 1973-74 and 1976-77, Quarter-final
Club nickname: The Terras   Programme: 15p
Local newspaper: Dorset Evening Echo

WHICKHAM   (WEARSIDE)

Chairman: B. Wright   Founded: 1944
Secretary: T. Wood   Tel no: Whickham 882518
Team manager: C. Richardson
Previous league: Northern Combination
Colours: Black and white striped shirts, black shorts, white socks
Change colours: All blue

Address and tel no of ground: Glebe Ground, Whagg's Lane, Whickham,
Newcastle-on-Tyne, NE16 4TB (Whickham 883054)

Record attendance: 2,128 (1979)

Ground capacity: 4,000
Covered accommodation: None
Clubhouse details: Fully licensed, lounge, bar
Major honours: Wearside League champions 1977–78
Best season in F.A. Vase: 1978–79, Semi-final
Programme: Special matches only
Local newspapers: Newcastle Journal, Blaydon Courier

Seating capacity: None
Floodlights: No

WHITBY TOWN (D. NORTHERN)

Chairman: D. Dunwell
Secretary: H. K. Graham
Team manager: S. Smelt
Colours: All blue

Founded: 1896
Tel no: Whitby 3713

Change colours: All white

Address and tel no of ground: Turnbull Ground, Upgang Lane, Whitby,
North Yorks (Whitby 3193)

Ground capacity: 4,000
Covered accommodation: 200
Clubhouse details: Open 7 p.m. to 10 p.m. every night
Best season in F.A. Cup: 1969-70, lost 2–0 to York City 1st Rnd
Current players with Football League experience: D. Burluraux; M. Bloor;
T. Jones; E. Kyle; D. Chapman
Major honours: North Riding Senior Cup winners, Northern League Cup
winners, Rothmans Knock-out Overseas Cup winners
Best season in F.A. Trophy: 1977-78, 2nd Rnd Proper
Club nickname: The Seasiders   Programme: 14 pages, 5p
Local newspaper: Whitby Gazette

Record attendance: 4,000 (1965-66)
Seating capacity: 200
Floodlights: No

WHITLEY BAY (D. NORTHERN)

Chairman: Capt C. E. Fuller, M.B.E.
Secretary: T. Moody
Team manager: M. Clifford
Colours: White shirts, blue shorts, white socks with blue hoops
Change colours: All yellow

Founded: 1958
Tel no: Whitley Bay 520087

Address and tel no of ground: Hillheads Park, Whitley Bay, Tyne and
Wear (Whitley Bay 526823)

Ground capacity: 9,000
Covered accommodation: Yes
Clubhouse details: Seahorse Club, capacity 200
Major honours: Northern League champions 1964–65, 1965–66, runners-
up 1959–60, 1966–67, 1968–69, 1969–70; Northern League Cup winners
1964–65, 1970–71, runners-up 1967–68; Northumberland Senior Cup
winners 1952–53, 1960–61, 1963–64, 1964–65, 1967–68, 1968–69, 1969–
70, 1970–71, 1972–73, runners-up 1953–54, 1954–55, 1965–66, 1976–77
Best season in F.A. Trophy: Never past 1st Qual Rnd
Club nickname: The Bay   Programme: 1 page, free
Local newspaper: Whitley Bay Guardian

Record attendance: 7,301 (1965)
Seating capacity: 350
Floodlights: Yes

WILLENHALL TOWN (W. MID R.)

Chairman: J. Williams
Secretary: T. Turpin

Founded: Reformed 1953
Tel no: 021-526 4122 (bus);
Bloxwich 75541 (h)

Team manager: B. Stobart
Previous leagues: Wolverhampton & District Amateur, Staffordshire County League (South)
Colours: All red
Change colours: White shirts, blue shorts
Address and tel no of ground: Noose Lane, Willenhall, West Midlands (Willenhall 65132)   Record attendance: 2,000
Ground capacity: 5,000   Seating capacity: 350
Covered accommodation: 550   Floodlights: No
Clubhouse details: Open every evening, Saturday and Sunday lunchtimes, cosy atmosphere, bar snacks available
Best season in F.A. Cup: 1978-79, 3rd Qual Rnd
Current players with Football League experience: K. Gough; B. Beresford
Best season in F.A. Vase: 1978-79, 6th Rnd
Club nickname: The Reds   Programme: 4 pages, 5p
Local newspaper: Wolverhampton Express & Star

WILLESDEN (B.I.L. DIV 2)

Chairman: M. Power
Secretary: Miss H. Baldwin
Team manager: M. Power

Founded: 1946
Tel no: 01-205 9967

Previous leagues: Middlesex Senior, Spartan, Delphian, Parthenon, Greater London, Metropolitan London, Athenian
Colours: All red
Change colours: Blue and white shirts, black shorts, blue socks
Address and tel no of ground: Willesden Stadium, Donnington Road, London N. W. 10 (01-459 7565/7416)
Ground capacity: 10,750   Seating capacity: 750
Covered accommodation: 750   Floodlights: Yes
Clubhouse details: Open every night and Saturday and Sunday daytimes, music, steward: Mrs O'Sullivan
Best season in F.A. Cup: 1977-78, 2nd Qual Rnd
Best season in F.A. Vase: 1977-78, 1st Rnd Proper
Programme: 16 pages, 10p
Local newspapers: Willesden & Barnet Chronicle. Wembley News & Observer

WILLINGTON (D. NORTHERN)

Chairman: D. H. Warner
Secretary: H. W. Edwards
Team manager: Peter Mulcaster
Colours: Blue and white

Founded: 1911
Tel no: Willington 6311

Change colours: Yellow and green

Address and tel no of ground: Hall Lane, Willington, Co Durham
  (Willington 6221)
Ground capacity: 7,000   Seating capacity: 350
Covered accommodation: 350   Floodlights: Yes
Clubhouse details: Open daily from 7.30 to 10.30 p.m. and on match days
  from 2 to 3 p.m. and 4.30 to 5.30 p.m. (members and visitors only)
Best season in F.A. Cup: 1973
Major honours: F.A. Amateur Cup winners
Best season in F.A. Trophy: 1976-77, 3rd Rnd Proper
Local newspaper: Northern Echo

WINDSOR & ETON   (K. ATHENIAN)

Chairman: A. Cornwall   Founded: 1902
Secretary: . KR. Drummie   Tel no: Windsor 66952
Team manager: B. Caterer
Previous leagues: South Bucks & East Berks, Great Western Suburban,
  Athenian, Spartan, Great Western Comb, Corinthian, Metropolitan,
  Delphian
Colours: Red and green   Change colours: All gold
Address and tel no of ground: Stag Meadow, St Leonard's Road, Windsor,
  Berks (Windsor 60656)
Ground capacity: 5,000   Seating capacity: 350
Covered accommodation: 400   Floodlights: Yes
Clubhouse details: Open every evening (except Sundays), Saturday after-
  noons during season and Sunday lunchtimes, food available
Best season in F.A. Cup: 1925-26
Major honours: Berks & Bucks Senior Cup winners 12 times
Best season in F.A. Vase: 1978-79, 4th Rnd
Club nickname: The Royalists   Programme: 12 pages, 10p
Local newspaper: Windsor & Eton Express

WINSFORD UNITED
(CHESHIRE CO. DIV 1)

Chairman: C. Noden   Founded: 1883
Secretary: P. Warburton   Tel no: Winsford 54295
Team manager: John Williams
Colours: Blue shirts with white trim, white shorts, white socks
Change colours: Yellow shirts with black trim, yellow shorts, yellow socks
Address and tel no of ground: Barton Stadium, Winsford, Cheshire
  (Winsford 2054)
Ground capacity: 8,000   Seating capacity: 300
Covered accommodation: 2,500   Floodlights: Yes
Clubhouse details: Open every night, entertainments, snacks, steward: Mrs
  N. Collas (Winsford 3021)
Best season in F.A. Cup: 1975
Current players with Football League experience: K. Bebbington (Stoke
  City, Oldham Ath); M. Laski (Liverpool); P. Maguire (Birmingham
  City)

Major honours: Cheshire League Challenge Cup winners
Best season in F.A. Trophy: 1977-78, Quarter-final
Programme: 16 pages, 10p
Local newspapers: Winsford Guardian, Winsford Chronicle

WINTERTON RANGERS (YORKSHIRE)

Chairman: B. K. Shore   Founded: 1933-34
Secretary: B. K. Shore   Tel no: Scunthorpe 732975
Team manager: John Beresford
Previous leagues: Scunthorpe & District, Lincolnshire
Colours: White shirts with red trim, navy blue shorts, red socks
Change colours: Green and black striped shirts, white shorts, green socks
Address and tel no of ground: West Street, Winterton, Scunthorpe, South
   Humberside (Scunthorpe 732628)   Record attendance: 2,700 (1978)
Ground capacity: 5,000   Seating capacity: 165
Covered accommodation: 165   Floodlights: Yes
Clubhouse details: Open every night except Sunday, dance hall, lounge,
   two licensed bars, bingo on Tuesdays and Fridays, Saturday evening
   discos
Best season in F.A. Cup: 1976-77, 4th Qual Rnd
Current players with Football League experience: P. Walker (Cambridge
   United)
Major honours: Yorkshire League champions 1971-72, 1976-77, 1978-79,
   runners-up 1977-78; Philips Floodlighting winners 1978
Best season in F.A. Vase: 1976-77, 6th Rnd
Club nickname: The Rangers   Programme: 12 pages, free
Local newspapers: Scunthorpe Evening Telegraph, Scunthorpe Star,
   Lincolnshire Times

WISBECH TOWN (TOWN & COUNTRY)

Chairman: D. Bates   Founded: 1920
Secretary: A. S. 'Sonny' Roseberry   Tel no: Wisbech 3527
Team manager: D. McCallum (player-manager)
Previous leagues: Midland, Southern, Eastern Counties
Colours: All red   Change colours: All blue
Address and tel no of ground: Fenland Park, Lerowe Road, Wisbech, Cambs
   (Wisbech 4176 – ground; 3434 – club)
Floodlights: Yes   Record attendance: 8,044 (1957)
Clubhouse details: Bar, lounge room for dancing, etc.
Best season in F.A. Cup: 1957-58, 2nd Rnd v Reading
League clubs defeated in F.A. Cup: Colchester, Newport
Current players with Football League experience: J. Duncliffe (Peter-
   borough); D. Clarke (Notts County)
Major honours: United Counties League champions; Eastern Counties
   League Cup winners; United Counties League Cup winners; Midland
   League runners-up; Southern League 1st Div champions
Best season in F.A. Trophy: Never past 2nd Qual Rnd
Club nickname: The Fenmen   Programme: None
Local newspapers: Wisbech Standard, Fenland Advertiser, Eastern Daily
   Press

WITNEY TOWN (S.L.S.)

Chairman: A. N. Oakey
Secretary: C. F. J. Miles
Player/coach: John Shuker
Previous leagues: Reading & District, Oxfordshire Senior, Hellenic
Colours: Yellow shirts with blue trim, royal blue shorts
Change colours: All white
Address and tel no of ground: Marriots Close, Welsh Way, Witney, Oxon (Witney 2549/5930)

Founded: 1885
Tel no: Witney 3592

Ground capacity: 3,500
Covered accommodation: 1,500
Seating capacity: 150
Floodlights: Yes
Clubhouse details: Open every evening, three bars including clubroom, lounge and function bar, entertainment several nights a week, basket meals and snacks, steward: J. Drinkwater (Witney 2549)
Best season in F.A. Cup: 1971-72, 1st Rnd Proper
Major honours: Southern League Div 1 N champions 1977-78; Hellenic League champions eight times; Oxfordshire Senior Cup winners six times
Best season in F.A. Trophy: 1974-75, 1st Rnd Proper
Programme: 24 pages, 5p
Local newspapers: Witney Gazette, Oxford Mail

WITTON ALBION (N.P.L.)

Chairman: T. Stelfox
Secretary: D. Leather
Team manager: Brian Booth
Previous leagues: Lancashire Combination, Cheshire County
Colours: Red and white striped shirts, black shorts, red socks
Change colours: All white with red trim
Address and tel no of ground: The Central Ground, Albion Way, off Witton Street, Northwich, Cheshire (Northwich 3008)

Founded: 1890
Tel no: Northwich 76488

Record attendance: 1948
Ground capacity: 9,500
Covered accommodation: 2,000
Seating capacity: 690
Floodlights: Yes
Clubhouse details: Situated on the ground, open every night and at Sunday lunchtimes, available for private hire (Northwich 3493)
Best season in F.A. Cup: 1951-52, 2nd Rnd Proper
Current players with Football League experience: A. McNeill (Oldham Ath, Stockport County); A. Keyes (Stockport County); G. Felix (Chester)
Major honours: Cheshire Counties League Cup winners 1975-76, runners-up 1978-79; Cheshire Senior Cup winners 1977-78; N. W. Floodlit League champions 1976-77, 1977-78; Cheshire Counties League runners-up 1978-79
Best seasons in F.A. Trophy: 1972-73 and 1978-79, 3rd Rnd Proper
Club nickname: The Albion
Programme: 14 pages, 10p
Local newspapers: Northwich Guardian, Northwich Chronicle

WOKING (B.I.L. P. DIV)

Chairman: R. C. Hicks   Founded: 1889
Secretary: T. J. Smith   Tel no: Airshaw 46358
Team manager: S. Callaghan
Colours: Red shirts, white shorts, red socks
Change colours: White shirts, blue shorts, blue socks
Address of ground: Kingfield Sports Ground, Woking, Surrey
Ground capacity: 6,000   Seating capacity: 1,200
Covered accommodation: Yes   Floodlights: Yes
Clubhouse details: Members' bar and separate hall for functions
Best season in F.A. Cup: 1978–79, 2nd Rnd
Current players with Football League experience: F. Parsons; A. Morton;
     J. Love
Major honours: F.A. Amateur Cup winners, 1958; Surrey Senior Cup
     winners 1913, 1927, 1956, 1957, 1972: Isthmian League runners-up
     1956–57
Best seasons in F.A. Trophy: 1977–78 and 1978–79, 1st Rnd Proper
Club nickname: The Cardinals   Programme: 15p
Local newspapers: Woking News & Mail, Woking Herald

WOKINGHAM TOWN (B.I.L. DIV 1)

Chairman: G. P. Gale   Founded: 1875
Secretary: M. Dixon   Tel no: Reading 26453
Team manager: R. A. B. Merryweather
Previous leagues: Delphian, Corinthian, Metropolitan, Athenian
Colours: Amber shirts with black trim, black shorts, amber socks with
     black trim
Change colours: White shirts with black and gold trim, black shorts,
     amber socks
Address and tel no of ground: Town Ground, Finchampstead Road,
     Wokingham, Berks (Wokingham 780253)
Ground capacity: 4,500   Seating capacity: 250
Covered accommodation: 1,000   Floodlights: Yes
Clubhouse details: Open daily, business lunches available daily, function
     hall, catering for weddings, exhibitions, dances, dart competitions,
     licensed, whippet racing and skateboard park within club's ground
Best seasons in F.A. Cup: 1976–77 and 1978–79, 3rd Qual Rnd
Current players with Football League experience: G. Cox (Brentford);
     T. Bell (Reading, Aldershot); M. Dixon (Reading, Aldershot); J.
     Richardson (Brentford, Fulham)
Best season in F.A. Trophy: 1974–75, 2nd Qual Rnd
Club nickname: The Town   Programme: 16 pages, 10p
Local newspapers: Reading Evening Post, Wokingham Times, Woking-
     ham & Bracknell News

WORCESTER CITY (A.P.L.)

Chairman: G. W. Goode

Secretary: D. G. Fulbrook

Team manager: N. Clark

Previous league: Birmingham (now West Midlands)

Colours: Blue and white shirts, blue socks

Change colours: All red

Address and tel no of ground: St George's Lane, Worcester (Worcester 23003 – office; 25427 – club)

Founded: 1908

Tel no: Worcester 830549

Record attendance: 17,042 (1959)

Ground capacity: 15,000

Covered accommodation: 4,000

Seating capacity: 2,000

Floodlights: Yes

Clubhouse details: Two rooms – one with skittle alley, open every night, Saturday evening disco, Sunday live entertainment

Best season in F.A. Cup: 1958-59, lost 0-2 to Sheffield Utd 4th Rnd Proper

League clubs defeated in F.A. Cup: Millwall, Liverpool, Plymouth

Current players with Football League experience: L. Martin (Aston Villa); J. Cumbes (Aston Villa, West Bromwich, Coventry)

Major honours: Worcs Senior Cup winners more times than any other club; Birmingham Senior Cup winners; Staffordshire Senior Cup winners; Welsh Cup semi-finalists

Best seasons in F.A. Trophy: 1969-70 and 1973-74, Quarter-final

Programme: 15p

Local newspaper: Worcester Evening News

WORKINGTON (N.P.L.)

Chairman: A. G. Perry

Secretary: K. Nelson

Team manager: B. Endean

Previous league: Football League

Colours: Red shirts, white shorts

Founded: 1884

Tel no: Whitehaven 3438

Change colours: All blue

Address and tel no of ground: Borough Park, Workington, Cumbria (Workington 2871)

Record attendance: 20,000 (1958)

Ground capacity: 20,000

Covered accommodation: 10,000

Seating capacity: 1,500

Floodlights: Yes

Clubhouse details: Open match days and for private functions

Best season in F.A. Cup: 1934, 4th Rnd

League clubs defeated in F.A. Cup: Numerous when in Football League

Current players with Football League experience: M. Leng; I. Johnston; B. Brown; B. Donaghy; K. Armstrong; N. McDonald

Major honours: Promotion to Football League 3rd Div 1963–64

Best season in F.A. Trophy 1977-78, 1st Rnd

Club nickname: The Reds

Programme: 16 pages, 10p

Local newspaper: Workington Times & Star

WORKSOP TOWN (N.P.L.)

Chairman: G. E. Wheatley

Secretary: K. M. Wright

Team manager: Ron Reid

Founded: 1893

Tel no: Doncaster 744022

Previous leagues: Midland Counties, Yorkshire
Colours: Black and amber stripes   Change colours: Blue and white
Address and tel no of ground: Central Avenue, Worksop, Notts
  (Worksop 87641)   Record attendance: 7,500 (1924-25)
Ground capacity: 8,000   Seating capacity: 500
Covered accommodation: 2,000   Floodlights: Yes
Clubhouse details: Open every lunchtime and evening, light snacks available, weekend discos
Best seasons in F.A. Cup: 1956 and 1978-79, 3rd Rnd Proper
Major honours: Midland Counties League champions 1921-22, 1965-66, 1972-73; Sheffield & Hallam Senior Cup winners 1970, 1973
Best season in F.A. Trophy: 1971, 2nd Rnd
Club nickname: The Tigers   Programme: 12 pages, 10p
Local newspaper: Worksop Guardian

WORTHING   (B.I.L. DIV 2)

Chairman: M. L. Hollis   Founded: 1886
Secretary: W. Gibb   Tel no: Worthing 201588
Team manager: D. Cooke
Previous leagues: West Sussex, Sussex County, Athenian
Colours: Red shirts with white and blue trim, white shorts, red socks
Change colours: Yellow shirts with blue trim, yellow shorts, yellow socks
Address and tel no of ground: Woodside Road, Worthing, West Sussex
  (Worthing 39575)   Record attendance: 5,000 (1907)
Ground capacity: 6,000   Seating capacity: 700
Covered accommodation: 100   Floodlights: Yes
Clubhouse details: Open every night, various entertainments, steward: D. Steer (Worthing 33551)
Best season in F.A. Cup: 1936-37, 1st Rnd Proper
Current players with Football League experience: D. Cooke; D. Busby; T. Stanley
Major honours: Sussex County League champions eight times; Sussex Senior Cup winners 20 times; Athenian League Div. 1 runners-up 1963-64, Div. 2 runners-up 1971–72; Challenge Cup finalists 1972–73
Best season in F.A. Vase: 1978-79, 5th Rnd
Club nickname: The Rebels   Programme: 20 pages, 10p
Local newspapers: Worthing Gazette, Worthing Herald, Evening Argus

WREN ROVERS   (LANCS COMB.)

Chairman: G. Smales   Founded: 1931
Secretary: T. Mitchell   Tel no: Blackpool 43591
Team manager: Jimmy Sutton
Previous leagues: Blackpool Amateur, West Lancashire
Colours: Red shirts with white trim, black shorts, red socks with white trim
Change colours: White shirts, black shorts, white socks
Address and tel no of ground: School Road, Marton, Blackpool, Lancs
  (Blackpool 68425)   Record attendance: 700 (1979)
Ground capacity: 2,000   Seating capacity: Limited
Covered accommodation: 200   Floodlights: No
Clubhouse details: Open on match days and special occasions

Current players with Football League experience: J. Sutton (Newcastle);
P. Brown (Blackpool)
Major honours: Lancashire Combination League champions 1978-79;
Lancashire Combination Challenge Cup winners 1978-79
Best season in F.A. Vase: 1978-79, Prelim Rnd
Club nickname: The Wrens
Local newspaper: Blackpool Evening Gazette

WYCOMBE WANDERERS
(B.I.L. P. DIV.)

Chairman: R. H. Williams   Founded: 1884
Secretary: J. Goldsworthy   Tel no: High Wycombe 38042
Team manager: Andy Williams
Previous leagues: Berks & Herts Contiguous, Southern, Great Western
Suburban, Spartan
Colours: Light blue shirts, dark blue shorts
Change colours: Yellow shirts, light blue shorts
Address and tel no of ground: Loakes Park, High Wycombe, Bucks
(High Wycombe 26567)   Record attendance: 15,500 (1956-57)
Ground capacity: 12,000   Seating capacity: 1,000
Covered accommodation: 4,000   Floodlights: Yes
Clubhouse details: Available for private functions
Best season in F.A. Cup: 1974-75, 3rd Rnd Proper
League clubs defeated in F.A. Cup: Newport, Bournemouth
Major honours: Isthmian League champions six times; Berks & Bucks
Senior Cup winners 15 times
Best season in F.A. Trophy: 1978-79, 3rd Rnd Proper
Club nickname: The Blues   Programme: 16 pages, 10p
Local newspaper: Bucks Free Press

YEOVIL TOWN
(A.P.L.)

Chairman: D. J. Hawker   Founded: 1921
Secretary: Mrs U. O. Masters   Tel no: Yeovil 26183
Team manager: B. Lloyd
Previous league: Western
Colours: Green and white
Change colours: All white with green flashes
Address and tel no of ground: Huish, Yeovil, Somerset
(Yeovil 23662)   Record attendance: 17,501 (1948)
Ground capacity: 15,000   Seating capacity: 2,352
Covered accommodation: 9,000   Floodlights: Yes
Clubhouse details: Two bars, supporters' club, long room, lottery office
Best season in F.A. Cup: 1948-49, 5th Rnd
League clubs defeated in F.A. Cup: 13
Current players with Football League experience: All 16
Major honours: Southern League Cup winners 4 times; County Cup win-
ners 15 times; Southern League champions 3 times
Best seasons in F.A. Trophy: 1970-71 and 1971-72, Semi-final
Club nickname: The Glovers   Programme: 10p
Local newspapers: Western Gazette, Western Daily Press, Evening Post

SENIOR LEAGUE OFFICIALS

League	Chairman	Secretary	Sec's tel no
Alliance Premier	J. Thompson	G. E. Readle	0253 729421
Athenian	W. Jenkins	G. Dell	Chalfont St Giles 3819
B. Isthmian	B. East	A. C. F. Turvey	(Basingstoke 61789)
Cheshire Co.	J. Hinchcliffe	C. Mahood	Rufford 822688
Hellenic	N. Matthews	A. Harrison	Aylesbury 82865
Kent	N. Miles	D. Baker	Sittingbourne 25105
Lancs Comb.	J. Halliwell	K. Dean	Blackburn 62644
Midland Co.	W. Stanwell	A. A. Ridsdale	Worksop 5008
Midland Comb.	R. Timmings	L. James	Kingswinford 3459
Northern	A. Clarke	G. Nicholson	Bishop Auckland 2176
Northern Premier	K. Marsden	R. D. Bayley	061-980 7007
Southern	D. Settersfield	W. Dellow	Redhill 62585
South Midlands	K. Williamson	C. Moyse	Dunstable 64682
South Western	T. H. Scott	G. Gazzard	Penzance 61397
Town & Co.	A. E. Westwood	A. Rudd	Lowestoft 65996
United Counties	M. E. Pay	E. Evans	Kettering 710108
Wearside	P. Ramsey	J. Walsh	Sunderland 75513
Welsh	S. Jenkins	A. Griffiths	Maesteg 734096
Western	L. Phillips	J. Veale	Bristol 652699
West Midlands	R. Juggins	C. G. Davis	Stourbridge 73241
Yorkshire	C. Morris	B. Wood	Guiseley 74558

ALLIANCE PREMIER LEAGUE

Semi-professional football has always taken a back seat in Britain, with recognition being given chiefly to those leagues and clubs involved in important cup competitions, internationals and representative games. However, there have been three major moves to achieve recognition for semi-professional football. Firstly, in 1970 the Football Association introduced the Challenge Trophy with the attraction of its final at Wembley; secondly, there has been the introduction of international games for players at semi-professional level; and recently there has been the formation of the Alliance Premier League.

It has always been widely recognised that there are many clubs playing high-quality football with aspirations to be elected to the Football League. Over the past two years, excellent examples of this can be seen in the promotion of both Wimbledon and Wigan Athletic to the Football League – Wimbledon gaining promotion to the Third Division in their second year, and Wigan almost doing it in their first year.

For many years, talks were held between the Northern Premier League and the Southern League to explore the possibility of trying to establish a more direct access for semi-professional clubs to the higher echelons but, unfortunately, no real progress was made in this area until March 1978 when it was resolved to formulate plans to amalgamate the two Leagues. In April 1979 the plans were finally approved to form a two-tiered pyramid system at semi-professional level – the Alliance Premier League – consisting of 20 clubs. Seven of these clubs were to be culled from the Northern Premier League and 13 from the Southern League, with three feeder leagues below in the form of the Northern Premier League and Southern League's Midland and Southern Divisions.

Membership of the Alliance for the first season would be based on the following criteria:
1. Suitable grading of the club in respect of ground, facilities and organisation, and

2. Promotion, on merit, by use of a points system for league positions over the 1977–78 and 1978–79 seasons as follows: league champions one point, runners-up two points, third club three points, etc.

The end of the 1978–79 season showed that these clubs would qualify for the new Alliance Premier League: Altrincham, Bangor City, Barrow, Boston United, Northwich Victoria, Scarborough, and Stafford Rangers (all from the Northern Premier League); and A.P. Leamington, Barnet, Bath City, Gravesend and Northfleet, Kettering Town, Maidstone United, Nuneaton Borough, Redditch United, Telford, Wealdstone, Weymouth and Worcester City (all from the Southern League). Promotion and relegation between the Alliance Premier League and the Northern Premier League and Southern League (Midland Division and Southern Division) will operate at the end of the 1979–80 season.

A committee is to be established to advise and make recommendations on such matters as grading of clubs, insurance of players and geographical adjustments to boundaries for promotion and relegation. A travel cost equalisation scheme is to be introduced to subsidise those clubs incurring vast expenses for long-distance travel.

It is hoped that eventually a situation will be established similar to that in other European countries, where clubs in the lower reaches of football can, by progress, reorganisation improvements and team success, eventually be promoted to the Alliance and even to the Football League.

BERGER ISTHMIAN FOOTBALL LEAGUE

Final Tables 1978-79

PREMIER DIVISION

	P	W	D	L	F	A	Pts.	Penalty points C	Penalty points D
Barking	42	28	9	5	92	50	93	11	—
Dagenham	42	25	6	11	83	63	81	12	—
Enfield	42	22	11	9	69	37	77	12	—
Dulwich Hamlet	42	21	13	8	69	39	76	8	—
Slough Town	42	20	12	10	61	44	72	14	—
Wycombe Wanderers	42	20	9	13	59	44	69	8	—
Woking	42	18	14	10	79	59	68	13	3
Croydon	42	19	9	14	61	51	66	6	—
Hendon	42	16	14	12	55	48	62	7	8
Leatherhead	42	17	9	16	57	45	60	5	—
Sutton United	42	17	9	16	62	51	60	4	—
Tooting & Mitcham	42	15	14	13	52	52	59	15	5
Walthamstow Avenue	42	15	6	21	61	69	51	3	—
Tilbury	42	13	11	18	60	76	50	30	5
Boreham Wood	42	13	10	19	50	67	49	13	5
Hitchin Town	42	12	11	19	59	71	47	11	—
Carshalton Athletic	42	10	16	16	49	69	46	16	10
Hayes	42	9	18	15	45	58	45	15	5
Oxford City	42	12	7	23	50	80	43	17	—
Staines Town	42	6	16	20	40	64	34	13	10
Leytonstone	42	8	7	27	36	75	31	13	15
Kingstonian	42	3	15	24	35	72	24	9	—

206

FIRST DIVISION

	P	W	D	L	F	A	Pts.	C	D
Harlow Town	42	31	7	4	93	32	100	9	—
Harrow Borough	42	26	8	8	85	49	86	19	—
Maidenhead United	42	25	6	11	72	50	81	9	3
Bishop's Stortford	42	22	11	9	68	40	77	20	5
Hertford Town	42	21	11	10	62	41	74	24	—
Horsham	42	22	8	12	62	47	74	14	—
Harwich & Parkston	42	22	5	15	90	57	71	15	5
Bromley	42	18	12	12	76	50	66	19	5
Hampton	42	17	11	14	59	47	62	10	—
Epsom & Ewell	42	18	7	17	69	57	61	6	—
Wembley	42	15	14	13	57	50	59	23	14
Aveley	42	17	7	18	57	66	58	15	—
Wokingham Town	42	17	8	17	64	68	56*	11	10
Clapton	42	15	8	19	67	80	53	26	8
Metropolitan Police	42	12	13	17	58	55	49	19	—
Walton & Hersham	42	12	9	21	47	71	45	15	—
Ilford	42	13	5	24	48	80	44	16	—
Ware	42	11	10	21	46	69	43	21	—
Chesham United	42	11	9	22	46	66	42	15	5
Finchley	42	7	15	20	43	74	36	9	11
St Albans City	42	7	7	28	43	90	28	16	5
Southall & E.B.	42	5	5	32	41	114	20	11	5

* Three points deducted

SECOND DIVISION

	P	W	D	L	F	A	Pts.	C	D
Farnborough Town	34	26	3	5	77	34	81	13	5
Camberley Town	34	21	8	5	71	32	71	16	10
Molesey	34	19	11	4	55	33	68	20	—
Lewes	34	19	6	9	66	50	63	3	5
Feltham	34	16	7	11	47	36	55	9	5
Letchworth G.C.	34	14	10	10	56	48	52	18	8
Eastbourne United	34	16	4	14	47	46	52	3	—
Hemel Hempstead	34	13	11	10	46	37	50	7	—
Epping Town	34	14	7	13	49	44	49	14	—
Rainham Town	34	13	10	11	42	41	49	14	14
Cheshunt	34	11	8	15	43	49	41	14	10
Hungerford Town	34	11	8	15	48	58	41	8	—
Worthing	34	9	8	17	40	50	35	5	5
Hornchurch	34	9	8	17	38	61	35	16	—
Egham Town	34	7	12	15	49	54	33	7	10
Tring Town	34	6	8	20	33	56	26	3	—
Willesden	34	6	8	20	41	77	26	11	—
Corthinian Casuals	34	4	7	23	23	65	19	9	—

BERGER ISTHMIAN LEAGUE

PREMIER DIVISION RESULTS 1978-79	Barking	Boreham Wood	Carshalton A.	Croydon	Dagenham	Dulwich H.	Enfield	Hayes	Hendon	Hitchin T.
Barking	–	3–1	2–0	1–0	2–3	1–1	2–3	5–3	1–0	5–2
Boreham Wood ...1–2		–	1–1	0–2	0–1	0–2	0–2	1–0	3–1	2–0
Carshalton A. ...1–1		2–2	–	1–0	0–3	1–1	0–3	0–5	1–0	0–0
Croydon 0–4		1–2	0–0	–	3–2	2–3	2–6	4–1	1–3	1–1
Dagenham 0–3		0–0	4–3	3–0	–	0–2	2–6	4–1	1–1	3–1
Dulwich H. 0–0		9–2	1–1	1–0	0–1	–	0–2	2–1	2–1	2–2
Enfield 1–1		0–0	2–0	2–1	2–0	2–0	–	1–1	1–2	4–0
Hayes 2–2		2–1	1–1	0–2	1–3	0–0	1–1	–	1–0	1–1
Hendon 0–1		1–1	1–1	5–2	3–0	0–1	1–1	2–0	–	3–2
Hitchin T. 6–2		1–1	0–1	0–0	1–3	1–1	2–1	5–1	0–1	–
Kingstonian ...1–1		1–2	2–2	1–3	1–1	0–0	0–1	0–1	1–1	1–1
Leatherhead ...2–0		0–1	1–2	0–2	1–1	1–2	0–1	1–1	0–0	3–1
Leytonstone ...1–3		1–2	3–0	0–1	0–3	0–1	0–3	1–2	0–1	2–3
Oxford C 1–2		0–1	3–0	0–3	2–3	3–2	0–1	1–0	1–0	1–3
Slough T. 2–4		2–0	2–0	0–0	2–0	3–2	2–1	0–0	2–1	4–1
Staines T. 0–2		4–0	1–0	0–2	0–2	1–1	1–0	0–0	0–0	4–1
Sutton Utd. ...1–2		2–2	2–0	3–0	0–2	0–3	1–1	2–0	2–0	1–0
Tilbury 2–3		2–1	4–3	3–3	2–2	2–0	0–2	0–1	1–1	3–2
Tooting & M. ...0–2		2–0	1–1	0–0	3–1	1–1	1–2	0–0	1–3	3–0
Walthamstow A. 1–4		1–2	4–1	1–0	4–1	1–2	2–1	1–1	1–2	0–1
Woking 2–3		1–0	3–2	3–1	3–4	1–1	1–0	1–1	2–2	3–1
Wycombe W. ...1–4		1–0	0–2	0–0	1–1	1–0	0–0	3–2	5–0	2–0

	Kingstonian	Leatherhead	Leytonstone	Oxford C.	Slough T.	Staines T.	Sutton Utd.	Tilbury	Tooting & M.	Walthamstow A.	Woking	Wycombe W.
Kingstonian	–	2-0	1-0	3-1	4-1	1-1	2-1	2-2	4-2	1-2	1-0	2-0
Leatherhead	2-1	–	1-3	2-4	1-0	1-1	0-1	5-0	1-1	3-1	2-4	1-1
Leytonstone	1-1	1-1	–	3-0	1-1	2-2	3-2	2-0	0-0	1-0	0-4	2-3
Oxford C.	1-0	2-1	3-1	–	4-2	2-1	4-0	4-1	1-1	2-0	1-3	3-0
Slough T.	3-2	2-1	0-1	5-0	–	3-1	0-2	2-0	1-0	5-4	5-3	1-0
Staines T.	4-0	0-0	1-0	5-2	2-0	–	2-0	1-1	1-2	0-0	4-1	3-1
Sutton Utd.	4-1	2-0	1-1	0-1	3-0	1-0	–	2-1	0-2	4-4	1-1	1-4
Tilbury	2-0	1-0	2-2	3-1	1-1	0-0	1-1	–	2-5	1-1	1-1	0-1
Tooting & M.	2-2	1-1	3-0	0-0	3-2	1-1	1-0	1-1	–	1-1	1-2	1-0
Walthamstow A.	1-1	1-0	5-1	2-2	1-2	1-2	0-2	4-1	0-1	–	1-0	2-1
Woking	2-0	0-0	2-2	4-1	0-0	2-0	3-3	2-2	2-2	1-1	–	1-1
Wycombe W.	2-1	2-0	2-0	2-0	0-1	1-1	1-2	2-0	3-1	1-2	3-1	–

DIVISION ONE RESULTS 1978-79

	Aveley	Bishop's Stortford	Bromley	Chesham Utd.	Clapton	Epsom & Ewell	Finchley	Hampton	Harlow Town	Harrow Borough
Aveley	–	1–1	2–1	3–2	4–1	0–1	1–0	0–2	3–0	1–3
Bishop's S.	1–0	–	1–1	2–1	3–0	2–1	2–3	0–2	2–0	1–0
Bromley	1–1	2–1	–	4–0	4–3	3–0	1–1	4–2	0–0	0–0
Chesham Utd.	0–1	1–2	1–1	–	3–0	2–0	1–0	2–1	1–3	0–0
Clapton	3–1	0–1	1–4	3–1	–	1–3	3–1	1–2	2–4	3–1
Epsom & Ewell	3–0	0–2	0–4	3–0	1–1	–	4–0	1–1	1–2	4–1
Finchley	2–2	0–0	0–0	2–1	3–5	3–2	–	1–1	1–2	1–4
Hampton	1–2	0–0	1–2	1–1	1–0	4–0	2–2	–	0–1	1–3
Harlow Town	3–1	4–1	2–0	2–1	0–0	0–0	2–1	0–0	–	4–0
Harrow Borough	4–2	1–1	2–1	1–1	3–0	3–1	3–1	2–1	1–2	–
Harwich & Park.	3–0	2–1	4–1	1–2	0–1	5–1	4–0	2–1	0–1	0–1
Hertford Town	1–0	2–0	1–1	0–2	1–2	1–0	3–0	2–1	1–2	0–4
Horsham	2–1	2–1	2–1	2–0	2–2	1–0	2–1	2–0	0–2	1–1
Ilford	1–1	1–0	0–2	1–2	1–6	2–1	0–1	2–4	2–3	3–4
Maidenhead U.	0–1	1–1	1–4	2–0	3–1	1–0	1–1	1–2	1–4	1–1
Met. Police	2–0	2–3	0–1	2–2	1–1	1–3	0–0	2–3	1–2	0–1
Southall & E.B.	3–1	1–1	0–2	3–1	0–3	3–2	1–2	0–1	0–6	2–3
St Albans City	2–2	0–3	1–3	3–1	1–2	2–2	5–4	1–3	1–1	0–3
Walton & Her.	4–1	0–3	1–1	2–3	0–2	2–4	2–0	1–1	0–2	1–3
Ware	2–1	1–1	2–1	1–3	0–1	1–1	0–0	0–1	0–2	0–4
Wembley	0–1	1–1	1–1	2–1	0–0	2–1	1–1	0–0	0–2	0–3
Wokingham T.	2–2	0–0	4–0	3–1	5–2	0–2	1–1	1–1	2–1	1–3

Harwich & Park.	Hertford Town	Horsham	Ilford	Maidenhead Utd.	Met. Police	Southall & E.B.	St Albans City	Walton & Hersham	Ware	Wembley	Wokingham T.
2-1	0-2	1-2	3-0	2-0	1-5	2-0	2-1	2-0	3-2	1-2	2-1
2-1	1-1	5-1	3-0	2-0	3-1	3-1	5-1	0-2	1-0	2-0	3-2
1-4	1-1	1-2	1-2	1-2	3-1	5-1	1-1	4-0	3-0	4-0	0-1
0-2	0-2	0-2	1-2	0-0	0-1	2-0	1-1	0-2	0-0	2-2	3-1
2-3	1-4	0-3	2-1	2-5	0-1	1-1	1-0	3-2	1-1	2-3	1-2
1-1	3-1	1-2	3-1	1-0	3-1	4-0	4-0	2-0	4-1	0-0	1-0
1-1	1-2	1-3	1-0	1-4	1-1	3-2	1-0	0-1	0-0	0-1	0-2
4-0	1-3	0-2	3-0	0-1	2-1	2-1	1-0	3-0	2-2	0-0	0-1
2-2	2-1	2-0	5-1	3-0	0-0	8-0	3-0	3-0	3-1	3-1	0-3
4-3	1-1	3-1	2-2	2-1	0-2	1-2	2-1	2-0	2-0	0-2	3-0
–	0-1	1-0	1-1	2-3	4-1	6-1	3-0	4-0	3-2	1-0	1-2
3-1	–	1-1	2-0	1-3	0-0	2-0	2-0	4-0	0-0	1-2	2-1
1-2	1-1	–	2-0	0-1	1-0	0-0	1-2	3-3	3-1	1-0	2-0
1-3	2-0	2-1	–	0-5	0-2	5-1	2-1	1-1	1-2	1-0	0-3
3-1	1-2	3-2	1-0	–	1-0	3-2	1-0	1-1	3-0	2-1	3-1
2-0	1-1	1-0	1-2	1-2	–	3-0	1-2	0-0	2-1	1-1	6-0
0-4	1-1	1-2	1-2	1-2	1-5	–	5-2	1-2	1-6	0-2	2-3
1-5	1-2	1-2	1-0	1-1	5-0		–	0-1	0-1	3-1	1-1
1-2	1-1	1-3	0-1	0-1	2-2	1-0	5-0	–	2-0	0-3	1-1
2-1	1-0	1-1	1-1	0-1	0-0	4-0	3-2		–	4-3	2-3
4-4	0-1	1-0	3-1	2-2	5-1	1-1	1-0	0-1	6-0	–	1-1
0-2	1-4	1-1	0-3	3-2	1-2	3-1	2-0	1-2	1-0	2-2	–

DIVISION 2
RESULTS
1978–79

	Camberley Town	Cheshunt	Corinthian C.	Eastbourne Utd.	Egham Town	Epping Town	Farnborough Town
Camberley Town.............	–	2–0	3–0	4–0	2–0	2–2	1–0
Cheshunt	2–0	–	2–0	1–0	2–2	1–0	0–2
Corinthian C.	1–5	1–1	–	1–0	0–0	1–1	2–0
Eastbourne Utd.	2–3	3–1	4–1	–	0–0	1–0	1–0
Egham Town	1–1	1–3	4–0	6–0	–	0–1	1–2
Epping Town	1–2	1–0	3–1	1–2	0–0	–	1–2
Farnborough Town	3–4	4–1	2–1	2–0	3–2	3–1	–
Feltham	2–1	4–5	0–2	3–1	0–1	2–0	1–3
Hemel Hempstead	0–2	2–2	3–2	0–1	2–1	2–0	1–2
Hornchurch	2–1	1–1	2–1	3–1	1–0	2–1	0–3
Hungerford Town	0–1	2–1	2–1	1–1	2–2	1–2	0–3
Letchworth G.C.............	2–1	2–1	3–0	1–3	4–1	2–2	1–1
Lewes	1–2	4–1	0–0	2–1	1–1	2–0	2–5
Molesey	1–1	2–1	1–0	2–0	4–1	1–2	0–0
Rainham Town	1–1	1–0	1–0	0–0	3–3	3–0	2–0
Tring Town	2–3	1–0	0–0	1–3	2–1	0–1	0–1
Worthing	2–2	2–2	2–1	2–3	1–1	1–0	0–2
Willesden	2–5	0–1	1–0	1–4	2–5	2–2	1–2

Feltham	Hemel Hempstead	Hornchurch	Hungerford Town	Letchworth G.C.	Lewes	Molesey	Rainham Town	Tring Town	Worthing	Willesden
1–0	0–0	4–0	2–1	0–0	1–2	2–2	1–0	2–0	2–0	7–0
0–1	0–1	1–1	1–1	2–0	4–2	2–3	1–0	2–2	0–1	1–0
0–3	0–3	1–3	1–3	0–3	2–4	0–1	0–3	3–0	1–1	2–1
0–0	1–0	0–1	3–0	3–0	1–3	0–1	1–0	0–1	2–1	2–3
0–1	3–2	2–1	2–1	1–3	1–3	2–1	2–2	2–2	2–3	1–1
2–0	2–0	2–0	4–0	2–4	2–0	2–2	2–2	4–3	3–0	2–0
1–1	2–1	3–2	4–1	3–0	1–0	1–0	4–0	2–1	6–1	4–3
–	2–2	1–1	1–2	1–1	1–3	1–0	1–2	2–0	1–0	2–0
0–1	–	3–3	3–3	3–1	1–0	2–2	1–0	1–2	2–0	0–0
0–2	0–1	–	1–0	1–1	2–3	1–1	0–3	2–1	2–3	1–1
1–3	1–3	3–1	–	3–1	4–0	0–2	1–4	3–0	1–0	5–3
2–1	1–0	2–2	1–0	–	3–1	3–4	1–1	2–0	2–1	4–0
3–2	2–2	3–1	3–1	1–2	–	2–2	3–2	2–0	1–0	4–2
1–1	1–0	3–2	0–0	1–1	1–1	–	2–0	1–0	1–0	1–2
0–3	0–0	1–1	2–1	0–0	0–3	1–1	–	2–1	3–1	0–5
0–1	1–1	3–0	2–3	3–2	1–1	1–3	0–1	–	2–2	1–2
0–1	0–0	4–0	0–0	3–1	0–1	0–1	2–0	2–2	–	1–2
1–1	2–4	2–1	0–0	2–2	1–3	0–2	0–2	0–0	0–4	–

HITACHI CUP 1978-79

	1st Rnd £25	D	3rd Rnd £40	D	4th Rnd £70	D	5th Rnd £150	D	S-f. £300	D	Final £600	D	Total	D
Premier Div.														
Enfield			40		70		150		300	(90)	600		1,160	(90)
Hayes			40		70	(10)	150		300	(30)			560	(40)
Dulwich H.			40		70		150			(90)			260	(90)
Croydon			40		70	(10)							110	(10)
Sutton U.			40		70								110	
Tilbury			40		70								110	
Boreham W.			40										40	
Barking			40			(20)							40	(20)
Dagenham			40										40	
Leatherhead			40			(10)							40	(10)
Slough T.			40										40	
Tooting & M.			40										40	
			480	—	420	(50)	450	—	600	(210)	600	—	2,550	(260)
Division One														
Harrow B.	25	(10)	40	(10)	70	(30)	150			(60)			285	(80)
Bromley	25		40	(10)	70	(10)							135	(30)
Ilford	25		40	(10)									65	(10)
Wokingham T.	25		40										65	
B. Stortford	25												25	
Chesham U.	25												25	
Epsom & E.	25												25	
Finchley	25	(15)											25	(15)
Harlow T.	25	(5)											25	(15)
Harwich & P.	25	(15)											25	(15)
Hertford T.	25												25	
Horsham	25												25	(10)
Met. Police	25	(5)											25	(5)
Southall & E.B.	25	(10)											25	(10)
Wembley	25												25	
	375	(60)	160	(30)	140	(40)	150	—		(60)	—		825	(190)

214

	25	(10)	
	25		
	25	(10)	
	25		
	125	(20)	

Division Two

Egham	25	(10)	
Farnborough T.	25		
Feltham	25		(10)
H. Hempstead	25		
Molesey	25		(10)
	125	(10)	(10)

Totals in brackets represent amounts deducted for cautions or dismissals.

HITACHI CUP 1978-79

Quarter-finals		Semi-finals	Final
Bromley	0		
Enfield	4	Enfield	
			003
Dulwich Hamlet	4		Enfield 2
Sutton United	3	Dulwich Hamlet 002	
			Enfield
Croydon	0		
Harrow Borough	3	Harrow Borough 1	
			Hayes 1
Tilbury	1		
Hayes	3	Hayes 2	

Premier Division	Champions	Barking
	Runners-up	Dagenham
	Relegated	Leytonstone and Kingstonian
Division 1	Champions	Harlow Town
	Runners-up	Harrow Borough
	Relegated	Southall and Ealing Borough
Division 2	Champions	Farnborough Town
	Runners-up	Camberley Town
Hitachi Cup	Winners	Enfield
	Finalists	Hayes
Anglo-Italian Tournament	Winners	Sutton United
Berks & Bucks Senior Cup	Winners	Wycombe Wanderers
	Finalists	Hungerford Town
Essex Senior Cup	Winners	Harlow Town
	Finalists	Tilbury
Essex Senior Trophy	Finalists	Clapton
Hants Senior Cup	Finalists	Farnborough Town
Herts Senior Cup	Finalists	St Albans City
London Senior Cup	Winners	Barking
	Finalists	Croydon
Middlesex Senior Cup	Winners	Enfield
	Finalists	Wembley
Surrey Senior Cup	Winners	Camberley Town
	Finalists	Leatherhead
Sussex Senior Cup	Finalists	Horsham

THE BERGER YOUTH
KNOCK-OUT COMPETITION 1978-79

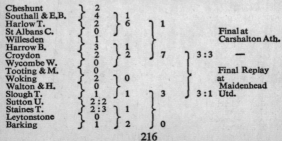

Cheshunt	2			
Southall & E.B.	4	1		
Harlow T.	2	6	1	
St Albans C.	0			
Willesden	1			Final at
Harrow B.	3	1		Carshalton Ath.
Croydon	2	2	7	3:3
Wycombe W.	0			—
Tooting & M.	0			
Woking	2	0		Final Replay
Walton & H.	0	1	3	at
Slough T.	1			Maidenhead
Sutton U.	2:2			3:1 Utd.
Staines T.	2:3	1		
Leytonstone	0	2		
Barking	1		0	

216

WINNERS OF CHAMPIONSHIP
SENIOR SECTION

Season	Champions	Runners-up
1905-06	London Caledonians	Clapton
1906-07	Ilford	London Caledonians
1907-08	London Caledonians	Clapton
1908-09	Bromley	Leytonstone
1909-10	Bromley	Clapton
1910-11	Clapton	Leytonstone
1911-12	London Caledonians	Ilford
1912-13	London Caledonians	Leytonstone
1913-14	London Caledonians	Nunhead
1919-20	Dulwich Hamlet	Nunhead
1920-21	Ilford	London Caledonians
1921-22	Ilford	Dulwich Hamlet
1922-23	Clapton	Nunhead
1923-24	St Albans City	Dulwich Hamlet
1924-25	London Caledonians	Clapton
1925-26	Dulwich Hamlet	London Caledonians
1926-27	St Albans City	Ilford
1927-28	St Albans City	London Caledonians
1928-29	Nunhead	London Caledonians
1929-30	Nunhead	Dulwich Hamlet
1930-31	Wimbledon	Dulwich Hamlet
1931-32	Wimbledon	Ilford
1932-33	Dulwich Hamlet	Leytonstone
1933-34	Kingstonian	Dulwich Hamlet
1934-35	Wimbledon	Oxford City
1935-36	Wimbledon	The Casuals
1936-37	Kingstonian	Nunhead
1937-38	Leytonstone	Ilford
1938-39	Leytonstone	Ilford
1945-46	Walthamstow Avenue	Oxford City
1946-47	Leytonstone	Dulwich Hamlet
1947-48	Leytonstone	Kingstonian
1948-49	Dulwich Hamlet	Walthamstow Avenue
1949-50	Leytonstone	Wimbledon
1950-51	Leytonstone	Walthamstow Avenue
1951-52	Leytonstone	Wimbledon
1952-53	Walthamstow Avenue	Bromley
1953-54	Bromley	Walthamstow Avenue
1954-55	Walthamstow Avenue	St Albans City
1955-56	Wycombe Wanderers	Bromley
1956-57	Wycombe Wanderers	Woking
1957-58	Tooting & Mitcham Utd.	Wycombe Wanderers
1958-59	Wimbledon	Dulwich Hamlet
1959-60	Tooting & Mitcham Utd.	Wycombe Wanderers
1960-61	Bromley	Walthamstow Avenue
1961-62	Wimbledon	Leytonstone
1962-63	Wimbledon	Kingstonian
1963-64	Wimbledon	Hendon
1964-65	Hendon	Enfield

1965-66	Leytonstone	Hendon
1966-67	Sutton United	Walthamstow Avenue
1967-68	Enfield	Sutton United
1968-69	Enfield	Hitchin Town
1969-70	Enfield	Wycombe Wanderers
1970-71	Wycombe Wanderers	Sutton United
1971-72	Wycombe Wanderers	Enfield
1972–73	Hendon	Walton & H.

RETITLED DIVISION ONE

1973–74	Wycombe Wanderers	Hendon
1974–75	Wycombe Wanderers	Enfield
1975–76	Enfield	Wycombe Wanderers
1976–77	Enfield	Wycombe Wanderers

RETITLED PREMIER DIVISION

1977–78	Enfield	Dagenham
1978–79	Barking	Dagenham

YOUTH CUP COMPETITION 1978-79

	1st Rnd		2nd Rnd		3rd Rnd		S-F		Final		Total	
	£50	D	£150	D	£300	D	£400	D	£500	D		
	£	£	£	£	£	£	£	£	£	£	£	£
Cheshunt	50	—									50	—
Southall & E. B.		(15)	150								150	(15)
Harlow T.		(5)			300			(20)			300	(25)
St Albans C.	50	—									50	—
Willesden	50	(15)									50	(15)
Harrow B.		(10)	150								150	(10)
Croydon		(35)							500		500	(35)
Wycombe W.	50	(5)									50	(5)
Tooting & M.	50	(10)									50	(10)
Woking		(10)	150								150	(10)
Walton & H.	50	(15)									50	(15)
Slough T.		(15)					400				400	(15)
Sutton U.	50	(5)									50	(5)
Staines T.		(5)	150								150	(5)
Leytonstone	50	(25)									50	(25)
Barking		(20)			300						300	(20)
	400	(190)*	600	—	600	—	400	(20)	500	—	2,500	(210)

*Disciplinary points 1st Rnd or earlier.

To Clubs £2,290

218

DETAILS OF SPORTSMANSHIP POOL

Each club started the season with eight sportsmanship points and lost
them for a dismissal (four points) or a caution (one point).

Premier Division (43 shares @ £100 each)	Shares	£
Walthamstow A.	9	900.00
Sutton U.	8	800.00
Leatherhead	7	700.00
Croydon	6	600.00
Dulwich H.	4	400.00
Wycombe W.	4	400.00
Kingstonian	3	300.00
Barking	1	100.00
Hitchin T.	1	100.00
	43	£4,300.00

*Note: Enfield were successful with a late appeal against a caution so they
finished the season with one share and consequently there were 44 shares in
the Premier Division.*

Division One (12 shares @ £256.67 each)	Shares	£
Epsom & Ewell	6	1,540.02
Harlow T.	4	1,026.64
Hampton	2	513.38
	12	3,080.04

Division Two (38 shares @ £67.89 each)	Shares	£
Eastbourne U.	9	611.01
Tring T.	9	611.01
H. Hempstead	5	339.45
Hungerford T.	4	271.56
Lewes	4	271.56
Corinthian C.	3	203.67
Worthing	3	203.67
Willesden	1	67.89
	38	2,579.82

*Note: In the five years the sportsmanship pool has existed, Sutton United
have lost a total of only 13 points and Wycombe Wanderers only 14 points.*

SPONSORSHIP PAYMENTS TO CLUBS 1978-79

Club	£ Champions	£ Annual goal awards	£ 3—0 goal awards	£ B, Youth Cup	£ Sp'ship Pool	£ Hitachi Cup	£ Total
Harlow T.	1,000		270	275	1,026.68	10	2,606.36
Barking	1,500		240	280	100.00	20	2,164.68
Epsom & E.			210		1,540.02	25	1,799.70
Croydon			160	465	600.00	100	1,349.68
Enfield			240			1,070	1,334.68
Sutton U.			240	45	800.00	110	1,219.68
Walthamstow A.			200		900.00		1,124.68
Leatherhead			240		700.00	40	1,004.68
Dulwich H.			200		400.00	170	794.68
Eastbourne U.			100		611.01		735.69
Hampton			120		513.34		658.02
Tring T.			20		611.01		655.69
Wycombe W.			120	45	400.00		589.68
Hayes			40			520	584.68
Harrow B.			210	140		205	579.68
Slough T.			120	385		30	559.68
Lewes	200		40		271.56		536.24
Bromley			70			105	399.68
H. Hempstead			220		339.45	15	399.13
Harwich & P.			330			10	364.68
Hungerford T.			40		271.56		336.24
Kingstonian					300.00		324.68
Hitchin T.			160		100.00		284.68
Woking			120	140			284.68
Dagenham			200			40	264.68
Worthing			40		203.67		268.35
Staines T.			80	145			249.68
B. Stortford			180			25	229.68
Corinthian C.					203.67		228.35
Tooting & M.			120	40		40	224.68
Farnborough T.			160			25	209.68
Southall & E.			30	135		20	209.68
Wokingham T.			120			55	199.68
Tilbury			40			110	174.68
Hertford T.			120			25	169.68
Met. Police			120			15	159.68
Ilford			60			65	149.68
Willesden			20	35	67.89		147.57
Camberley T.			120				144.68
Hendon			120				144.68
Maidenhead U.			120				144.68

Wembley	90			15		129.68
Walton & H.	60	35				119.68
Aveley	90					114.68
Boreham W.	40			40		104.68
Carshalton A.	80					104.68
Letchworth G.C.	80					104.68
Oxford C.	80					104.68
Rainham T.	80					104.68
St Albans C.	30	50				104.68
Egham T.	60			15		99.68
Feltham	40			25		89.68
Leytonstone	40	25				89.68
Clapton	60					84.68
Ware	60					84.68
Chesham U.	30			25		79.68
Horsham	30			25		79.68
Cheshunt		50				74.68
Molesey	20			25		69.68
Epping T.	40					64.68
Finchley				10		34.68
Hornchurch						24.68
	2,500 200	6,370	2,290	9,959.86	3,030	25,880.02

Note: Each club received £24.68 towards the Berger Isthmian League News, totalling £1,530.16. Sportsmanship Pool details were slightly amended due to Enfield winning a late appeal against a caution and consequently retaining one share of the Sportsmanship Pool, thus reducing the amount each share was worth.

CHESHIRE COUNTY
FOOTBALL LEAGUE

Final Tables 1978-79

FIRST DIVISION

	P	W	D	L	F	A	Pts.	G.D.
Horwich R.M.I.	42	35	2	5	89	45	72	+44
Witton Albion	42	30	4	8	114	38	64	+76
Marine	42	29	5	8	104	38	63	+66
Stalybridge Celtic	42	25	5	12	93	47	55	+46
Burscough	42	19	15	8	59	31	53	+28
Winsford United	42	21	11	10	74	49	53	+25
Chorley	42	21	8	13	66	43	50	+23
Formby	42	20	9	13	73	57	49	+16
Leek Town	42	19	10	13	62	43	48	+19
Droylsden	42	18	9	15	62	61	45	+ 1
Nantwich Town	42	18	8	16	76	72	44	+ 4
Fleetwood Town	42	17	10	15	70	68	44	+ 2
Hyde United	42	15	12	15	59	57	42	+ 2
St Helens Town	42	16	9	17	59	57	41	+ 2
Darwen	42	15	9	18	52	53	39	— 1
Rhyl	42	15	8	19	53	60	38	— 7
Ashton United	42	13	5	24	63	94	31	—31
New Mills	42	9	11	22	58	82	29	—24
Rossendale United	42	11	6	25	51	108	28	—57
Radcliffe Borough	42	4	7	31	37	115	15	—78
New Brighton	42	3	5	34	36	115	11	—79
Middlewich Athletic	42	3	4	35	43	120	10	—77

LEADING GOALSCORERS (League and League Cup)

	Total
P. Meachin (Marine)	30
D. McClatchey (Marine)	29
K. Keelan (Stalybridge Celtic)	24
T. Cooke (Stalybridge Celtic)	23
J. Walker (Witton Albion)	22
W. Jaycock (Burscough)	20
J. Pearson (Horwich R.M.I.)	20
J. Garrett (Chorley)	19
R. Fraser (Winsford United)	18
S. Morris (Rhyl)	18

SECOND DIVISION

	P	W	D	L	F	A	Pts.	G.D.
Bootle	34	19	9	6	61	35	47	+26
Curzon Ashton	34	18	9	7	57	32	45	+25
Prescot Town*	34	20	5	9	68	37	43	+31
Kirkby Town	34	18	6	10	66	42	42	+24
Accrington Stanley	34	18	6	10	65	43	42	+22
Irlam Town	34	16	10	8	47	33	42	+14
Congleton Town	34	14	13	7	52	31	41	+21
Prescot B.I.	34	15	11	8	55	42	41	+13
Eastwood Hanley	34	15	9	10	60	47	39	+13
Prestwich Heys*	34	17	5	12	53	41	37	+12
Maghull	34	11	7	16	41	50	29	— 9
Ford Motors	34	9	10	15	38	52	28	—14
Anson Villa	34	10	7	17	39	60	27	—21
Warrington Town	34	11	5	18	45	69	27	—24
Atherton Collieries	34	8	9	17	43	56	25	—13
Skelmersdale United	34	9	6	19	36	53	24	—17
Glossop	34	6	6	22	42	83	18	—41
Ashton Town	34	3	5	26	22	84	11	—62

Two points each deducted for fielding ineligible players.

LEADING GOALSCORERS (League and League Cup)

	Total
D. Hargreaves (Accrington Stanley)	32
K. Crosswaite (Curzon Ashton)	20
A. Galway (Congleton Town)	19
R. Brunt (Prescot B.I.)	17
G. Howarth (Prestwich Heys)	17
S. Lennon (Glossop)	17
R. Nesbitt (Prestwich Heys)	17
D. Farnsworth (Kirkby Town)	16
P. Theckston (Atherton Collieries)	15
M. Wagstaffe (Irlam Town)	15

HONOURS LIST
League Cup Final: Winsford United 3 Witton Albion 1
Challenge Shield: (Champions v Runners-up) Horwich R.M.I. 2 Witton Albion 0
Lancashire Junior Cup: Marine 4 Chorley 2 (in replay)
Liverpool Senior Cup: Marine 1 South Liverpool 0 (in replay)
Manchester Senior Cup: Droylsden 4 Mossley 1 (on aggregate)

223

ESSEX SENIOR FOOTBALL LEAGUE

Final Table 1978-79

SENIOR SECTION

	P	W	D	L	F	A	Pts.
Basildon	32	26	5	1	86	14	57
Canvey Island	32	22	8	2	73	21	52
Eton Manor	32	19	6	7	68	37	44
Heybridge	32	17	9	6	50	32	43
Brentwood	32	15	9	8	64	49	39
East Ham	32	16	6	10	57	42	38
Witham	32	14	7	11	47	43	35
Tiptree	32	11	11	10	42	32	33
Brightlingsea	32	12	9	11	53	51	33
Bowers	32	12	8	12	41	47	32
Chelmsford Res	32	11	6	15	41	47	28
Maldon	32	7	14	11	43	60	28
Woodford	32	10	7	15	46	62	27
Ford	32	4	9	19	28	47	17
Stansted	32	7	2	23	34	72	16
Coggeshall	32	2	10	20	40	82	14
Sawbridgeworth	32	3	2	27	29	104	8

LEADING GOALSCORER
Cullen (Brentwood) 33

HONOURS LIST
League Cup Final: Brentwood 2 Brightlingsea 0

GLOUCESTERSHIRE COUNTY LEAGUE

Final Table 1978-79

	P	W	D	L	F	A	Pts.
Almondsbury Greenway ...	32	23	3	6	112	36	49
Hambrook	32	22	4	6	73	44	48
Worrall Hill	32	18	7	7	64	45	43
Port of Bristol	32	16	10	6	72	45	42
Matson Athletic.........	32	16	9	7	67	44	41
Sharpness	32	16	3	13	64	48	35
Yate Town	32	13	9	10	58	44	35
Hanham Athletic	32	15	5	12	55	44	35
Old Georgians	32	13	9	10	53	48	35
Stonehouse	32	12	10	10	47	55	34
Bristol St George	32	10	5	17	45	54	25
Lydbrook Athletic.......	32	8	9	15	42	69	25
Patchway	32	7	9	16	39	75	23
Wilton Rovers	32	9	4	19	33	68	22
Oldland	32	6	9	17	33	61	21
Shortwood United........	32	3	10	19	43	88	16
Gloucester City Reserves ..	32	3	9	20	33	65	15

LEADING GOALSCORERS 1978-79

	Total
S. Price (Almondsbury Greenway)	33
A. Kerr (Almondsbury Greenway)	22
M. Brown (Port of Bristol)	20
S. Moore (Yate Town)	20

HONOURS LIST

Gloucestershire F.A. Challenge Trophy Final : Almondsbury Greenway 3 Yate Town 0

HAMPSHIRE LEAGUE

Final Tables 1978-79
FIRST DIVISION

	P	W	D	L	F	A	Pts.
Newport	30	23	5	2	64	11	51
Fareham Town	30	18	7	5	75	34	43
Brockenhurst	30	14	9	7	46	35	37
Waterlooville Reserves	30	14	8	8	41	34	36
Swaythling	30	13	9	8	42	35	35
Pirelli General	30	10	12	8	44	30	32
Sholing Sports	30	14	3	13	47	37	31
Southampton 'A'	30	10	10	10	43	37	30
East Cowes Vics	30	12	4	14	38	52	28
B.A.T.*	30	11	6	13	34	38	27
Netley Centre Sports	30	11	3	16	39	44	25
Gosport Borough Reserves	30	9	6	15	39	60	24
Moneyfield Sports	30	7	9	14	27	48	23
Brading Town	30	8	7	15	22	47	23
Portsmouth R.N.*	30	7	5	18	25	53	18
Havant Town	30	5	7	18	41	69	17

One point each deducted for playing an ineligible player.

SECOND DIVISION

	P	W	D	L	F	A	Pts.
Romsey Town	30	19	7	4	47	21	45
Bournemouth	30	17	9	4	48	20	43
Horndean	30	17	6	7	49	29	40
Cove	30	16	6	8	45	36	38
Ringwood Town	30	14	9	7	40	20	37
A.F.C. Totton	30	16	3	11	49	38	35
New Street	30	14	7	9	36	25	35
Portals Athletic	30	11	7	12	38	36	29
Warsash	30	13	3	14	46	51	29
Cowes	30	9	10	11	27	34	28
Sholing Sports Reserves	30	9	9	12	38	45	27
Overton United	30	11	3	16	44	53	25
Swaythling Reserves	30	8	7	15	37	47	23
Fareham Town Reserves	30	8	6	16	37	45	22
Pirelli General Reserves	30	4	6	20	29	63	14
Winchester City	30	2	6	22	22	71	10

HELLENIC FOOTBALL LEAGUE

Final Table 1978-79
PREMIER DIVISION

	P	W	D	L	F	A	Pts.
Newbury Town	26	14	8	4	52	31	36
Fairford Town	26	14	7	5	53	39	35
Forest Green Rovers	26	15	4	7	52	35	34
Thame United	26	15	3	8	37	26	33
Bicester Town	26	12	9	5	47	38	33
Chipping Norton Town	26	14	4	8	51	27	32
Moreton Town	26	12	7	7	42	31	31
Flackwell Heath	26	10	8	8	37	33	28
Clanfield	26	9	4	13	36	47	22
Wallingford Town	26	8	4	14	41	48	20
Abingdon Town	26	6	7	13	34	51	19
Didcot Town	26	4	9	13	33	52	17
Garrard Athletic	26	4	8	14	35	51	16
Abingdon United	26	2	4	20	24	65	8

HONOURS LIST
    League Cup Final: Fairford Town 3 Thame United 1
    Cold Shield Jubilee Cup: Chipping Norton Town 3 Bicester Town 2

KENT FOOTBALL LEAGUE

Final Table 1978-79

	P	W	D	L	F	A	Pts.
Sheppy United	34	22	11	1	73	28	55
Hythe Town	34	21	7	6	71	34	49
Faversham	34	22	5	7	71	37	49
Medway	34	18	10	6	64	27	46
Whitstable	34	18	7	9	52	35	43
Sittingbourne	34	16	7	11	57	42	39
Tunbridge Wells	34	15	6	13	51	52	36
Darenth Heathside	34	10	12	12	42	38	32
Deal Town	34	13	6	15	40	50	32
Ramsgate	34	14	4	16	42	59	32
Slade Green	34	8	13	13	46	47	29
Dartford Glentworth	34	10	8	16	45	52	28
Herne Bay*	34	10	10	14	47	59	28
Cray Wanderers	34	9	9	16	50	65	27
Erith & Belvedere	34	8	9	17	49	48	25
Kent Police	34	10	4	20	46	67	24
Crockenhill	34	7	7	20	43	73	21
Snowdon	34	4	7	23	29	102	15

* Two goals and two points deducted for playing an ineligible player.

KINGSMEAD ATHENIAN FOOTBALL LEAGUE

Final Table 1978-79

	P	W	D	L	F	A	Pts.	C	D
Billericay Town	36	26	5	5	86	29	57	9	4
Burnham	36	22	10	4	86	37	54	5	—
Edgware	36	19	11	6	83	34	49	8	4
Windsor & Eton	36	21	6	9	62	30	48	4	—
Haringey Borough	36	16	15	5	60	42	47	14	8
Uxbridge	36	17	12	7	45	22	46	7	—
Welling United	36	17	9	10	60	46	43	11	4
Leyton-Wingate	36	16	10	10	67	48	42	11	4
Grays Athletic	36	17	8	11	55	46	42	3	—
Alton Town	36	15	9	12	51	45	39	13	4
Hoddesdon Town	36	13	7	16	63	60	33	11	—
Chalfont St Peter	36	12	8	16	41	58	32	6	—
Harefield United	36	11	7	18	53	70	29	15	4
Dorking Town	36	10	7	19	39	64	27	7	—
Marlow	36	9	4	23	48	92	22	9	8
Ruislip Manor	36	8	4	24	35	71	20	7	—
Fleet Town	36	6	7	23	37	73	19	5	8
Redhill	36	6	7	23	29	79	19	10	4
Chertsey Town	36	4	8	24	36	90	16	6	—

New clubs next season will be Banstead and Woodford Town.

LEADING GOALSCORERS

	Total
J. Bartlet (Welling)	30
D. Young (Billericay)	22
F. Clayden (Billericay)	21
P. Shodeinde (Edgware)	20
A. Warwick (Edgware)	20
L. Codogin (Windsor & Eton)	18

HONOURS LIST

League Cup Final: Alton Town 2   Windsor & Eton 1

SPORTMANSHIP DETAILS 1978-79

Champions	Billericay	500.00	
3rd place	Edgware	125.00	
Top goalscorer	Leyton-Wingate	100.00	
2nd goalscorer	Hoddesdon	75.00	
		800.00	
	Less 10% to League	80.00	720.00
			£1,620.00

Pen. Points Lost	Eligible clubs	Share of award	
3	Grays	5	426.32
4	Windsor & E.	4	341.05
5	Burnham	3	255.79
6	Chalfont St P.	2	170.53
6	Chertsey	2	170.53
7	Uxbridge	1	85.26
7	Dorking	1	85.26
7	Ruislip	1	85.26
		19	£1,620.00

£,1620.00 ÷ 19 = £85.26 per point.

		League awards	Goalscoring awards	Sport'ship awards	Total
Burnham	Runners-up	250.00		255.79	505.79
Grays				426.32	426.32
Windsor & E.	3rd Goalscorer		50.00	341.05	391.05
Chalfont St P.				170.53	170.53
Chertsey				170.53	170.53
Dorking				85.26	85.26
Ruislip				85.26	85.26
Uxbridge				85.26	85.26
		£250.00	£50.00	£1,620.00	£1,920.00
		10% of forfeits to League			80.00
					£2,000.00

Clubs losing 8 or more points not only forfeit any share in the sportsmanship award but also any share in League and Goalscoring awards. The amount(s) thus forfeit to be added to the sportsmanship award totals after deduction of 10% of the forfeitures towards League funds. Cautions and Send Offs in the Athenian League Cup are not included in this scheme.

LANCASHIRE FOOTBALL COMBINATION

Final Table 1978-79

	P	W	D	L	F	A	Pts.
Wren Rovers	28	21	5	2	51	10	47
Leyland Motors	28	18	6	4	63	26	42
Whitworth Valley	28	15	8	5	49	35	38
Colne Dynamoes	28	13	8	7	50	32	34
Bacup Borough	28	14	6	8	48	36	34
Padiham	28	14	5	9	40	35	33
Lytham	28	11	8	9	41	34	30
Nelson	28	7	10	11	31	33	24
Blackpool Mech	28	7	10	11	21	33	24
Chorley Reserves	28	6	11	11	34	37	23
Wigan Rovers	28	6	9	13	25	40	21
Barrow Reserves	28	6	8	14	25	39	20
Daisey Hill	28	5	10	13	26	45	20
Clitheroe	28	7	5	16	31	46	19
Ashton Athletic	28	3	5	20	17	67	11

LEICESTERSHIRE SENIOR FOOTBALL LEAGUE

Final Table 1978-79

FIRST DIVISION

	P	W	D	L	F	A	Pts.
Shepshed Charterhouse	30	21	5	4	64	15	47
Anstey Nomads	30	17	9	4	63	18	43
Friar Lane Old Boys	30	17	6	7	57	27	40
Oadby Town	30	14	11	5	58	37	39
Hinckley Town	30	17	4	9	59	37	38
Stapenhill	30	15	7	8	59	40	37
Wigston Fields	30	12	10	8	30	31	34
Hillcroft	30	14	3	13	44	58	31
Newfoundpool W.M.C.	30	11	8	11	42	42	30
Endbury Reserves	30	10	9	11	33	36	29
Melton Town	30	11	5	14	31	40	27
Birstall United Society	30	7	8	15	34	41	22
Thringstone M.W.	30	8	6	16	31	53	22
Lutterworth Town	30	6	7	17	35	63	19
Earl Shilton Albion	30	3	7	20	26	65	13
Corby Reserves	30	2	5	23	28	91	9

LEADING GOALSCORER

	Total
C. Attwood (Rolls Royce)	26

HONOURS LIST

League Cup Final (Tebbutt Brown Cup): Anstey Nomads 1 Shepshed
Charterhouse 0

MIDLAND FOOTBALL COMBINATION

Final Table 1978-79

FIRST DIVISION

	P	W	D	L	F	A	Pts.
Sutton Coldfield Town	38	26	9	3	104	30	61
Oldbury United	38	20	11	7	49	29	51
Bridgnorth Town	38	19	11	8	54	31	49
Boldmere St Michaels	38	20	9	9	44	35	49
Walsall Sportsco	38	18	11	9	58	41	47
Blakenall	38	17	10	11	57	38	44
Solihull Borough	38	18	8	12	59	46	44
Paget Rangers	38	16	10	12	50	41	42
Knowle	38	17	7	14	51	44	41
Mile Oak Rovers	38	15	10	13	42	37	40
Moor Green	38	16	7	15	70	55	39
Highgate United	38	13	7	18	46	54	33
Malvern Town	38	9	15	14	39	51	33
West Midlands Police	38	11	11	16	32	46	33
Racing Club Warwick	38	11	10	17	41	46	32
Walsall Wood	38	10	11	17	43	65	31
Cinderford Town	38	10	10	18	36	64	30
Northfield Town	38	12	5	21	41	62	29
Evesham United	38	7	5	26	29	80	19
Coleshill Town	38	1	11	26	22	72	13

MIDLAND COUNTIES FOOTBALL LEAGUE

Final Table 1978-79

PREMIER DIVISION

	P	W	D	L	F	A	Pts.
Boston	36	24	6	6	71	27	54
Skegness Town	36	23	8	4	65	31	54
Mexborough Town Athletic	36	21	8	7	57	35	50
Eastwood Town..............	36	19	10	7	56	35	48
Bridlington Trinity	36	15	11	9	76	43	43
Arnold	36	14	14	8	56	50	42
Sutton Town	36	16	7	13	53	50	39
Long Eaton United	36	16	6	14	51	40	38
Brigg Town	36	12	9	15	52	54	33
Ashby	36	13	7	16	36	48	33
Retford Town	36	12	8	16	49	49	32
Appleby Frodingham Ath.	36	13	6	17	55	63	32
Ilkeston Town	36	11	9	16	52	61	31
Kimberley Town	36	7	16	13	46	54	30
Louth United	36	10	7	19	43	72	27
Spalding United..............	36	7	12	17	44	68	26
Alfreton Town	36	6	13	17	39	61	25
Heanor Town	36	7	10	19	37	64	24
Belper Town	36	6	11	19	43	76	23

LEADING GOALSCORER
N. Mallinder (Boston) 32

HONOURS LIST

League Cup	Winners	Appleby Frodingham (5-4 on aggregate)
	Runners-up	Skegness
Notts Senior Cup	Winners	Eastwood Town
Derbys Senior Cup	Winners	Heanor Town

NORTHERN FOOTBALL LEAGUE

Final Table 1978-79

	P	W	D	L	F	A	Pts.
Spennymoor United	38	25	6	7	96	43	81
Ashington	38	23	7	8	79	47	76
Crook Town	38	21	10	7	63	38	73
Blyth Spartans	38	19	12	7	81	39	69
Consett	38	21	9	8	84	52	*69
North Shields	38	21	4	13	76	55	67
South Bank	38	16	11	11	58	47	59
Horden Colliery Welfare	38	17	8	13	64	56	59
Durham City	38	15	9	14	63	62	54
Bishop Auckland	38	25	5	8	96	38	48
Billingham Synthonia	38	12	12	14	60	55	48
Tow Law Town	38	12	8	18	54	63	44
Shildon	38	11	10	17	52	69	43
Whitby Town	38	11	12	15	55	68	*42
Whitley Bay	38	9	9	20	54	77	36
West Auckland Town	38	9	9	20	54	87	36
Ferryhill Athletic	38	10	5	23	43	74	35
Willington	38	7	10	21	41	75	31
Penrith	38	8	7	23	35	82	31
Evenwood Town	38	4	5	29	31	112	*14

Denotes three points deducted.

DRYBROUGH SPONSORSHIP

Drybroughs, the Edinburgh-based brewery, recently announced that, for the next three seasons from 1979-80, they will be sponsoring the Northern League. The value placed on the sponsorship is around £55,000 over the three years, of which £30,000 will be in cash awards to the most successful of the League's 20 clubs. The venture is a major continuation of the Drybrough policy of football sponsorship, in which they have been involved in Scotland at both senior and junior level over the past 10 years.

Iain Nelson, the firm's marketing director, announcing the sponsorship of Drybroughs Northern League, stated: 'This new venture is directly related to Drybroughs encouraging growth in the North-east of England. We are delighted to be able to give our support to the North's 90-year-old senior competition. As sponsors, we hope to benefit from the good-will and publicity of the Drybrough name, while the clubs themselves will be able to improve their facilities as a result of our cash sponsorship. With our experience in promoting football, we are anxious that the emphasis in Drybroughs Northern League should be placed on goalscoring. The game of football is all about goals and our sponsorship of the League includes cash rewards for goalscoring in addition to individual prizes for the leading goal scores. Drybroughs Northern League will promote attractive attacking football. We are confident that the clubs and players alike will participate in this spirit.'

SPONSORSHIP DETAILS 1979-80

League championship incentive   *Total*
Champions £1,000; 2nd £600; 3rd £500; 4th £400   £2,500
Goalscoring – weekly club awards
Matches won by 3 clear goals in a Drybroughs
Northern League match at £30 per club achieving,
estimated at   £2,400
Goalscoring – seasonal club awards
For the clubs who have scored most goals but have not
received awards under League Championship incentive.
Highest scorer £400; 2nd £300; 3rd £200; 4th £100   £1,000
Goalscoring – seasonal player awards
For the top individual goalscorers of Drybroughs
Northern League. Top goalscorer £300; 2nd £200;
3rd £100   £600
Drybroughs Northern League – administrative costs
To be shared amongst member clubs   £3,500

                                                        Total sponsorship £10,000

HONOURS LIST

League Cup	Winners	Blyth Spartans
	Finalists	Consett
Durham Challenge Cup	Winners	Spennymoor United
	Finalists	Horden Colliery Welfare
North Riding Cup	Winners	Billingham Synthonia
Northumberland Senior Cup	Winners	North Shields

NORTHERN PREMIER FOOTBALL LEAGUE

Final Table 1978-79

	P	W	D	L	F	A	Pts.
Mossley	44	32	5	7	117	48	69
Altrincham	44	25	11	8	93	39	61
Matlock Town	44	24	8	12	100	59	56
Scarborough	44	19	14	11	61	44	52
Southport	44	19	14	11	62	49	52
Boston United	44	17	18	9	41	34	52
Runcorn	44	21	9	14	59	54	51
Stafford Rangers	44	18	14	12	67	41	50
Goole Town	44	17	15	12	56	61	49
Northwich Victoria	44	18	11	11	64	52	47
Lancaster City	44	17	12	15	62	54	46
Bangor City	44	15	14	15	65	66	44
Worksop Town	44	13	14	17	55	67	40
Workington	44	15	7	21	62	74	39
Netherfield	44	16	7	21	62	74	39
Barrow	44	13	11	20	39	69	37
Gainsborough Trinity	44	14	9	21	47	78	37
Morecambe	44	12	12	20	52	67	36
Frickley Athletic	44	11	13	20	55	65	35
South Liverpool........	44	13	9	22	58	70	35
Gateshead	44	12	10	22	48	85	34
Buxton	44	11	11	22	42	63	33
Macclesfield	44	11	9	24	50	84	31
	44	8	10	26	40	92	26

1978–79

	Altrincham	Bangor City	Barrow	Boston United	Buxton	Frickley Ath.	Gainsborough T	Gateshead	Goole Town	Lancaster C.
Altrincham	–	3-2	4-0	3-0	0-1	1-2	3-0	2-0	2-1	0-0
Bangor City	1-1	–	1-3	1-1	2-0	4-2	1-1	1-2	2-2	2-1
Barrow	1-6	0-1	–	0-0	1-0	1-0	2-1	4-2	0-0	2-1
Boston United	1-4	1-1	2-0	–	1-0	2-0	1-0	1-1	0-0	0-0
Buxton	0-4	5-1	2-1	0-0	–	1-0	1-1	0-1	2-1	3-1
Frickley Ath.	0-4	1-3	1-2	1-1	2-1	–	4-0	1-1	1-2	3-2
Gainsborough T.	2-4	1-1	1-2	2-0	1-2	1-1	–	0-1	1-2	1-0
Gateshead	0-3	2-4	1-2	0-1	0-0	1-0	1-0	–	0-1	0-1
Goole Town	1-1	3-1	3-1	0-0	3-3	2-0	0-0	0-0	–	0-0
Lancaster C.	0-4	3-1	0-1	0-2	4-1	1-3	3-0	1-0	1-2	–
Macclesfield T.	1-5	0-0	1-1	0-2	2-2	0-2	2-2	0-1	1-2	0-1
Matlock T.	2-0	1-2	0-1	1-0	4-1	1-0	2-3	4-1	2-2	2-0
Morecambe	2-4	3-1	0-0	0-0	3-1	1-1	2-2	1-2	3-2	2-0
Mossley	1-1	3-0	6-1	1-1	3-1	4-3	2-0	3-3	5-1	3-1
Netherfield	0-0	1-0	0-1	0-2	2-4	1-0	0-2	0-0	3-0	0-0
Northwich Vic.	1-0	1-2	3-0	3-0	0-0	4-0	1-2	3-1	0-0	2-2
Runcorn	0-0	0-0	2-1	4-2	6-0	0-1	3-0	2-0	4-0	1-3
Scarborough	1-2	1-1	1-0	0-0	1-1	2-0	3-0	2-1	3-1	1-3
South Liverpool	1-1	1-1	2-0	3-1	1-0	3-0	2-2	0-1	2-0	0-2
Southport	3-1	0-0	1-2	1-0	1-0	0-0	3-3	0-2	1-1	2-2
Stafford R.	1-1	3-2	4-2	0-0	4-3	1-0	0-1	1-1	3-0	1-1
Workington	0-4	3-1	3-0	1-2	2-1	2-2	0-0	3-2	3-3	0-0
Worksop Town	1-2	1-3	3-1	1-1	0-1	3-3	1-1	2-1	0-1	0-1

Macclesfield T.	Matlock T.	Morecambe	Mossley	Netherfield	Northwich Vic.	Runcorn	Scarborough	South Liverpool	Southport	Stafford R.	Workington	Worksop Town
0-1	3-1	1-1	0-1	1-0	1-1	2-1	2-0	5-1	1-3	0-0	3-2	4-1
2-1	3-3	4-0	3-1	1-1	1-0	1-2	0-0	3-0	0-2	0-2	2-0	2-4
1-2	3-2	0-0	2-5	3-3	2-4	0-3	0-1	0-0	0-2	1-1	1-2	1-1
2-0	2-1	3-0	1-0	0-0	1-0	0-0	1-0	1-0	0-1	2-1	2-2	
2-1	1-3	1-6	1-3	1-1	0-2	0-2	0-3	4-1	1-1	0-1	0-4	1-1
3-1	1-3	1-1	0-2	5-0	1-3	1-0	1-0	6-0	1-3	0-3	3-1	1-1
2-2	3-3	2-1	2-1	0-1	0-1	2-3	1-2	1-2	3-0	1-0	3-0	1-2
0-1	1-2	2-0	1-3	1-3	2-2	1-1	1-2	1-1	2-1	1-1	0-1	0-2
2-0	1-1	3-2	0-4	1-0	1-0	3-0	2-2	2-1	0-2	2-1	2-1	1-2
5-3	0-0	4-2	2-3	1-0	2-3	1-0	4-0	2-2	1-0	4-1	1-1	
–	0-4	1-3	1-1	1-1	1-0	3-2	1-1	3-2	1-1	0-2	3-0	1-0
5-0	–	1-1	2-4	2-1	3-2	2-3	6-0	3-1	1-1	3-2	5-1	1-0
4-0	0-1	–	1-2	3-1	0-0	1-0	1-3	2-1	0-1	0-1	2-0	1-4
5-0	3-1	3-2	–	2-0	2-3	4-2	2-2	6-0	1-2	2-1	4-1	4-0
2-0	1-6	0-0	1-3	–	3-1	0-2	1-1	3-1	1-1	1-1	0-2	1-1
3-0	2-0	2-0	0-2	3-0	–	2-3	2-0	0-2	2-2	2-0	2-1	1-1
6-0	2-3	2-0	0-2	4-0	1-2	–	0-0	4-1	0-0	3-2	0-0	2-0
2-2	0-1	0-0	2-1	5-0	4-0	3-0	–	2-0	1-0	1-1	2-1	2-0
1-1	0-3	3-1	0-1	2-1	2-1	4-1	2-0	–	0-1	0-2	1-1	1-0
3-2	2-1	1-0	0-1	2-2	0-3	1-2	2-2		–	1-2	3-1	2-0
2-0	1-2	0-0	0-2	7-0	3-0	4-0	0-0	5-1	1-1	–	0-2	0-0
2-0	1-0	3-1	0-6	0-1	4-1	1-1	3-2	6-1	0-2	1-0	–	3-0
3-1	2-5	3-2	1-2	1-0	2-0	1-1	2-2	1-1	0-2	2-2	1-0	–

LEADING GOALSCORERS

D. Moore (Mossley) 38　　　　　L. Skeet (Mossley) 24
I. Smith (Mossley) 33　　　　　J. Johnson (Altrincham) 22
E. O'Keefe (Mossley) 30　　　　B. Whitbread (Runcorn) 21
J. Rogers (Altrincham) 29　　　G. Heathcote (Altrincham) 19
M. Cullerton (Stafford Rangers) 24　　I. Thompson (Goole Town) 19

HONOURS LIST

Best performances in F.A. competitions:
F.A. Trophy winners: Stafford Rangers
Team through to F.A. Cup 3rd Round: Altrincham

John Smith Cup winners (League Cup): Mossley
Challenge Shield winners: Matlock Town
Clubs with most victories: Mossley (32), Altrincham (25)
Clubs with most drawn games: Boston United (18)
Biggest home win in League: Stafford Rangers 7 Netherfield 0
Biggest away win in League: Workington 0 Mossley 6
Highest number of consecutive wins: Scarborough (7)

SOUTHERN FOOTBALL LEAGUE

Final Tables 1978-79

PREMIER DIVISION

	P	W	D	L	F	A	Pts.
Worcester City	42	27	11	4	92	33	65
Kettering Town	42	27	7	8	109	43	61
Telford United	42	22	10	10	60	39	54
Maidstone United	42	18	18	6	55	35	54
Bath City	42	17	19	6	59	41	53
Weymouth	42	18	15	9	71	51	51
A.P. Leamington	42	19	11	12	65	53	49
Redditch United	42	19	10	13	70	57	48
Yeovil Town	42	15	16	11	59	49	46
Witney Town	42	17	10	15	53	52	44
Nuneaton Borough	42	13	17	12	59	50	43
Gravesend & Northfleet	42	15	12	15	56	55	42
Barnet	42	16	10	16	52	64	42
Hillingdon Borough	42	12	16	14	50	41	40
Wealdstone	42	12	12	18	51	59	36
Atherstone Town	42	9	17	16	46	65	35
Dartford	42	10	14	18	40	56	34
Cheltenham Town	42	11	10	21	38	72	32
Margate	42	10	9	23	44	75	29
Dorchester Town	42	7	11	24	46	86	25
Hastings United	42	5	13	24	37	85	23
Bridgend Town	42	6	6	30	39	90	18

FIRST DIVISION SOUTH

	P	W	D	L	F	A	Pts.
Dover	40	28	9	3	88	20	65
Folkstone & Shepway	40	22	6	12	84	50	50
Gosport Borough	40	19	11	10	62	47	49
Chelmsford City	40	20	7	13	65	61	47
Minehead	40	16	13	11	58	39	45
Poole Town	40	15	15	10	48	44	45
Hounslow	40	16	12	12	56	45	44
Waterlooville	40	17	10	13	52	43	44
Trowbridge Town	40	15	12	13	65	61	42
Aylesbury United	40	16	9	15	54	52	41
Taunton Town	40	16	9	15	53	51	41
Bognor Regis Town	40	17	7	16	58	58	41
Dunstable	40	18	4	18	57	55	40
Tonbridge AFC	40	15	10	15	43	47	40
Salisbury	40	13	10	17	47	51	36
Basingstoke Town	40	12	11	17	49	62	35
Addlestone	40	12	9	19	56	64	33
Andover	40	12	6	22	47	69	30
Ashford Town	40	10	10	20	28	53	30
Crawley Town	40	9	9	22	44	75	27
Canterbury City	40	6	3	31	31	98	15

FIRST DIVISION NORTH

	P	W	D	L	F	A	Pts.
Grantham	38	21	10	7	70	45	52
Merthyr Tydfil	38	22	7	9	90	53	51
Alvechurch	38	20	10	8	70	42	50
Bedford Town	38	19	9	10	74	49	47
King's Lynn	38	17	11	10	57	46	45
Oswestry Town	38	18	8	12	63	43	44
Gloucester City	38	18	8	12	76	59	44
Burton Albion	38	16	10	12	51	40	42
Kidderminster Harriers ...	38	13	14	11	70	60	40
Bedworth United	38	13	14	11	41	34	40
Tamworth	38	15	8	15	47	45	38
Stourbridge	38	15	7	16	64	61	37
Barry Town	38	14	9	15	51	53	37
Enderby Town	38	14	8	16	46	55	36
Banbury United	38	10	13	15	42	58	33
Wellingborough Town	38	13	6	19	50	71	32
Cambridge City	38	9	9	20	37	62	27
Bromsgrove Rovers	38	6	14	18	33	61	26
Milton Keynes City	38	7	9	22	37	87	23
Corby Town	38	5	6	27	40	85	19

SOUTHERN LEAGUE PREMIER DIVISION

1978-79 Home Team	A.P. Leamington	Atherstone	Barnet	Bath City	Bridgend	Cheltenham	Dartford	Dorchester	Gravesend	Hastings
A.P. Leamington	–	0–1	1–3	1–1	5–1	1–0	2–0	3–2	1–0	3–1
Atherstone	1–3	–	2–1	1–1	2–0	2–2	1–1	0–1	0–1	2–2
Barnet	2–1	1–1	–	1–1	0–0	2–0	1–0	3–3	0–0	4–0
Bath City	1–1	1–1	4–0	–	5–0	2–1	2–0	2–0	1–0	1–0
Bridgend	3–2	1–0	0–2	1–2	–	0–1	0–2	1–2	1–2	2–3
Cheltenham	0–0	4–2	1–0	0–2	2–0	–	1–0	2–1	0–2	1–0
Dartford	0–2	1–2	2–1	1–1	0–1	1–0	–	2–1	3–1	0–0
Dorchester	0–0	0–1	0–1	1–1	1–1	3–3	3–2	–	1–1	2–1
Gravesend	2–1	3–3	1–4	2–2	5–1	3–0	0–1	3–1	–	0–0
Hastings	2–3	1–4	0–0	2–2	0–0	3–1	1–1	4–0	1–1	–
Hillingdon	1–1	2–0	0–0	4–0	3–0	2–0	1–1	2–4	1–1	3–0
Kettering	4–2	5–0	4–0	6–1	5–0	2–1	0–0	3–1	3–0	5–0
Maidstone	1–0	1–1	1–1	0–0	1–0	3–1	2–2	3–0	1–0	3–1
Margate	4–2	0–3	0–2	1–4	1–0	2–3	1–1	3–1	1–3	2–2
Nuneaton	1–0	2–0	0–1	2–1	3–1	3–0	1–1	3–0	0–0	3–0
Redditch United	3–5	2–1	5–0	1–1	2–1	5–1	3–0	1–0	0–0	1–1
Telford United	4–0	0–0	1–2	1–1	0–0	1–0	1–0	0–0	1–2	2–0
Wealdstone	0–1	1–1	1–1	0–0	3–0	0–0	3–4	2–2	2–1	1–2
Weymouth	2–1	1–1	4–1	1–3	4–1	3–0	3–0	2–1	2–1	3–0
Witney Town	2–3	1–1	4–3	1–2	2–2	0–0	2–0	2–1	1–0	5–0
Worcester	1–2	7–1	2–1	0–1	2–1	5–0	3–3	3–0	1–1	4–1
Yeovil Town	3–1	0–0	0–1	1–1	1–0	0–0	2–1	3–0	4–0	3–1

LEADING GOALSCORERS

PREMIER DIVISION

Kellock (Kettering Town)	31
Phipps (Kettering Town)	25
Henderson (Weymouth)	22
Clayton (Kettering Town)	21

FIRST DIVISION NORTH

Cooke (Grantham)	34
Pratt (Merthyr Tydfil)	29
Mullen (Kidderminster Harriers)	26
Cunningham (Stourbridge)	25
Mortimore (Bedford Town)	19

Hillingdon	Kettering	Maidstone	Margate	Nuneaton	Redditch United	Telford United	Wealdstone	Weymouth	Witney Town	Worcester	Yeovil Town
2-2	2-1	1-0	2-0	0-0	1-1	1-0	0-0	2-2	2-0	1-1	3-0
1-0	0-2	2-2	1-1	2-2	1-3	0-2	2-2	1-0	0-1	1-3	1-1
0-2	0-4	0-2	2-0	0-2	2-1	1-4	3-2	0-4	1-0	2-3	1-1
0-2	0-0	0-1	1-1	3-2	1-1	1-2	1-0	1-1	1-0	0-0	3-0
0-1	1-2	1-2	1-2	1-5	0-1	1-0	3-1	3-1	3-5	3-3	1-1
0-0	0-4	1-1	3-2	1-0	3-1	2-1	2-4	2-4	1-1	0-2	0-0
0-1	0-1	0-2	1-2	1-0	2-3	0-0	1-0	1-3	2-1	1-1	1-1
1-4	0-6	0-0	1-2	1-1	0-2	1-1	5-1	0-0	0-1	1-5	3-1
1-1	1-4	2-2	2-1	3-1	2-1	1-0	5-2	2-1	2-0	0-1	0-1
0-0	0-3	1-1	0-2	2-2	1-2	1-0	2-4	1-2	0-1	0-4	0-2
-	1-3	0-1	1-1	1-1	2-0	1-1	0-1	0-0	3-0	0-1	0-0
2-2	-	1-2	3-0	2-1	2-3	1-3	1-0	4-3	2-1	3-5	5-1
3-2	1-0	-	3-0	1-1	1-1	0-1	0-1	1-1	1-1	1-2	2-2
4-1	3-2	0-2	-	1-1	1-3	0-1	1-0	2-3	0-2	0-2	0-0
0-0	0-3	3-3	4-1	-	1-1	0-1	4-0	2-2	1-2	1-1	0-0
3-2	1-1	3-0	4-1	0-2	-	0-2	1-0	2-2	1-2	0-1	3-1
2-0	0-5	0-2	2-1	1-0	1-0	-	2-2	1-1	3-1	0-0	2-0
1-0	1-1	2-1	1-0	0-0	3-0	3-0	-	0-0	0-1	0-0	4-0
1-0	2-2	0-1	0-0	4-0	2-2	0-1	2-1	-	1-0	1-0	3-3
1-1	1-1	1-0	0-0	1-1	2-1	0-2	3-1	0-0	-	1-2	3-2
1-0	3-0	0-0	3-0	1-2	5-2	3-1	3-0	3-0	3-0	-	1-0
2-1	0-1	0-0	2-0	3-1	4-0	3-3	4-1	4-0	2-0	1-1	-

FIRST DIVISION SOUTH

Ovard (Folkestone & Shepway) 31
Coulbert (Gosport Borough) 23
Green (Andover) 19
Morris (Addlestone) 19
Unit (Bognor Regis Town) 19

CHALLENGE CUP FINAL

FIRST LEG
Bath City   1   Yeovil Town   0

SECOND LEG
Yeovil Town   0   Bath City   0

SOUTHERN LEAGUE DIVISION 1 SOUTH

1978-79
Home Team

	Addlestone	Andover	Ashford	Aylesbury	Basingstoke	Bognor	Canterbury	Chelmsford	Crawley	Dover
Addlestone	–	4–1	1–3	2–0	5–1	2–0	3–0	2–3	1–2	0–1
Andover	3–0	–	1–1	2–3	2–5	0–2	2–1	1–2	0–1	1–1
Ashford	0–2	2–1	–	2–0	1–0	0–2	1–0	1–1	1–0	0–1
Aylesbury	3–3	1–1	3–1	–	1–0	1–1	3–2	2–0	4–0	1–2
Basingstoke	2–0	2–1	0–1	1–1	–	1–0	3–1	0–1	0–0	0–2
Bognor	2–1	2–0	1–0	1–3	5–2	–	0–2	1–2	3–1	2–1
Canterbury	0–2	0–1	2–0	1–0	0–1	0–1	–	1–3	1–3	0–2
Chelmsford	3–1	1–1	4–0	2–3	1–0	4–1	2–0	–	2–1	2–1
Crawley	0–3	1–2	1–1	0–0	2–4	0–1	3–1	1–1	–	2–1
Dover	7–1	4–2	2–1	0–0	2–0	4–0	7–0	5–0	7–1	–
Dunstable	2–1	3–1	1–0	0–0	2–0	4–2	4–0	2–0	3–0	1–3
Folkestone	2–4	4–0	4–1	2–2	3–1	4–2	1–2	0–1	3–0	0–1
Gosport	4–0	2–0	3–0	0–3	0–0	2–2	4–0	3–1	1–1	0–2
Hounslow	1–1	1–3	2–0	1–2	2–2	2–2	5–0	2–1	0–0	0–1
Minehead	2–2	0–0	2–1	4–0	2–0	0–1	1–1	4–0	0–0	0–2
Poole Town	0–0	1–4	1–1	1–0	2–1	3–2	2–2	3–1	2–1	1–1
Salisbury	1–0	1–2	3–0	4–1	0–0	1–0	1–0	1–1	2–0	0–2
Taunton	0–1	0–1	1–0	1–0	1–1	1–1	3–0	4–0	2–0	0–2
Tonbridge	0–3	2–0	1–0	1–0	1–2	0–3	2–0	2–1	1–3	0–2
Trowbridge	4–2	3–2	1–1	2–2	3–3	3–0	3–1	1–2	4–2	0–0
Waterlooville	2–0	3–0	1–1	3–0	0–0	1–2	4–1	1–4	0–1	0–0

Dunstable	Folkestone	Gosport	Hounslow	Minehead	Poole Town	Salisbury	Taunton	Tonbridge	Trowbridge	Waterlooville
0-0	1-3	1-0	1-1	2-3	0-0	0-0	1-2	1-1	1-3	1-2
0-2	1-3	0-1	0-2	3-1	0-0	2-1	0-2	2-1	3-1	1-2
2-1	1-0	0-0	0-2	0-3	0-1	1-1	0-1	1-1	0-0	2-0
2-0	3-2	4-0	0-1	0-1	2-1	2-1	0-2	0-2	2-0	0-2
1-2	2-1	3-0	1-3	0-6	1-3	1-1	2-2	0-0	2-1	4-1
2-0	3-3	2-2	2-0	2-1	0-1	1-2	0-1	0-1	2-0	2-1
1-3	2-5	1-1	2-1	1-0	1-4	0-3	1-3	3-3	1-3	0-2
2-1	3-2	2-3	0-1	2-0	3-3	0-3	1-3	3-2	1-1	2-1
2-3	0-3	0-2	0-1	0-2	1-2	4-3	4-1	2-2	1-2	1-1
2-0	1-0	4-1	0-0	1-1	0-0	4-0	4-0	2-1	1-1	3-1
–	1-0	2-0	3-1	0-1	2-1	1-3	1-2	1-1	0-1	1-0
2-1	–	6-2	2-1	0-0	1-0	2-1	4-0	1-0	3-2	2-0
2-1	5-2	–	2-1	1-0	2-1	1-0	3-0	5-0	1-1	1-1
2-3	0-3	0-1	–	2-0	0-0	2-0	1-1	2-0	2-1	4-2
7-3	0-0	1-0	1-3	–	2-1	0-2	1-1	2-0	5-2	1-1
2-1	0-2	0-0	2-2	1-1	–	1-1	1-0	0-0	2-2	2-1
3-1	0-4	0-3	1-1	1-0	0-1	–	2-4	0-1	1-1	0-0
2-1	2-3	2-2	0-1	0-0	1-2	0-0	–	0-2	3-0	1-0
2-0	1-1	0-0	0-0	2-0	0-1	4-2	2-1	–	2-0	0-1
2-0	1-1	1-2	2-2	0-1	2-1	2-1	3-1	2-0	–	1-3
0-0	2-0	2-0	3-1	0-0	3-0	1-0	2-1	0-2	1-3	–

SOUTHERN LEAGUE DIVISION 1 NORTH

1978-79 Home Team	Alvechurch	Banbury United	Barry Town	Bedford Town	Bedworth United	Bromsgrove	Burton Albion	Cambridge City	Corby Town	Enderby Town
Alvechurch	–	1–1	2–1	3–2	1–1	3–1	2–0	5–1	1–0	4–0
Banbury United	1–1	–	1–0	1–1	0–2	1–1	1–1	1–3	3–2	2–1
Barry Town	2–0	1–2	–	1–3	1–0	1–2	5–2	2–0	4–1	1–2
Bedford Town	1–2	1–0	1–1	–	0–0	3–2	3–1	2–0	3–1	2–3
Bedworth United	0–0	1–0	0–0	1–3	–	1–0	0–1	1–2	4–0	4–1
Bromsgrove	1–2	1–2	1–4	1–0	1–1	–	1–1	1–1	2–1	0–0
Burton Alb.	3–1	2–0	2–0	2–2	2–1	1–3	–	1–0	4–2	0–1
Cambridge City	1–0	0–0	1–1	1–3	0–2	2–2	1–1	–	4–0	1–3
Corby Town	0–1	4–1	0–2	2–3	0–2	0–0	0–0	0–0	–	1–1
Enderby Town	1–1	1–1	1–1	1–0	0–0	2–0	0–2	0–0	1–5	–
Gloucester City	0–3	3–1	3–1	3–1	1–2	1–1	1–1	0–2	4–1	4–1
Grantham	3–3	3–0	0–0	1–1	3–2	1–2	1–1	2–0	3–2	3–1
Kidderminster	1–0	1–1	4–0	1–3	2–2	3–0	1–1	1–2	6–1	1–1
King's Lynn	3–1	0–0	0–0	3–2	1–1		0–2	3–4	4–2	1–0
Merthyr Tydfil	4–2	3–1	2–1	2–1	0–0	3–0	0–1	6–2	9–0	3–2
Milton Keynes	0–2	1–2	0–0	1–4	0–0	0–0	1–0	2–0	1–4	1–0
Oswestry Town	0–0	3–0	4–0	0–0	0–1	1–0	1–0	0–1	1–1	3–0
Stourbridge	0–3	1–1	3–0	1–3	4–2	0–1	1–0	4–1	2–0	1–1
Tamworth	1–2	2–0	0–1	1–1	1–0	0–0	2–1	2–1	2–0	2–0
Wellingboro'	1–2	1–3	4–1	1–1	0–1	5–0	3–1	5–1	3–2	0–2

Gloucester City	Grantham	Kidderminster	King's Lynn	Merthyr Tydfil	Milton Keynes	Oswestry Town	Stourbridge	Tamworth	Wellingboro'
1–1	1–1	4–2	2–2	1–0	6–0	1–2	2–1	1–2	3–1
2–2	1–3	3–3	2–1	2–1	3–0	1–4	1–2	0–0	0–1
3–1	3–1	1–4	4–1	1–0	3–1	2–0	0–2	0–2	2–2
2–0	5–0	5–2	2–3	1–1	0–3	2–1	2–0	2–1	3–1
0–2	1–2	1–1	0–0	1–1	1–1	0–2	2–1	2–0	1–0
2–3	0–1	2–2	1–4	1–3	2–2	0–3	1–1	0–1	0–0
1–1	0–1	2–2	1–0	0–1	4–0	3–1	1–0	3–0	2–0
0–1	0–0	0–2	0–1	3–1	0–1	1–0	0–1	1–0	2–3
1–2	0–1	0–0	0–3	1–2	2–3	2–1	0–1	3–0	0–2
3–1	1–2	2–0	3–0	0–2	2–1	4–1	3–4	0–1	0–1
–	1–2	2–3	3–0	5–0	2–1	4–3	2–2	1–0	0–3
3–0	–	2–2	0–3	3–0	3–0	1–1	1–1	1–0	6–0
1–3	1–3	–	0–3	2–5	5–1	1–2	4–2	0–2	3–0
4–1	2–4	0–0	–	0–3	1–1	0–0	1–2	0–0	0–1
3–2	2–2	0–0	2–1	–	4–2	4–0	1–3	5–0	5–2
0–7	0–3	1–2	1–2	3–6	–	1–5	2–5	0–0	0–0
1–0	2–0	0–2	0–2	1–1	3–1	–	3–1	3–2	5–0
3–4	1–2	2–2	1–3	5–3	1–2	1–1	–	2–1	2–0
4–3	4–2	1–3	1–1	0–1	3–2	1–1	2–0	–	5–0
1–2	1–0	0–2	1–1	1–2	0–0	3–2	3–2	3–2	–

SOUTH MIDLANDS FOOTBALL LEAGUE

Final Table 1978-79

PREMIER DIVISION

	P	W	D	L	F	A	Pts.
Barton Rovers	30	25	4	1	81	12	54
Pirton	30	23	4	3	63	23	50
Arlesey Town	30	17	9	4	49	32	43
Royston Town	30	16	6	8	50	37	38
Stotfold	30	12	10	8	32	18	34
Selby	30	12	7	11	48	43	31
Electrolux	30	11	9	10	35	32	31
Sandy Albions	30	11	7	12	41	50	29
Baldock Town	30	10	8	12	32	33	28
Shillington	30	10	7	13	43	35	27
Winslow United	30	9	7	14	40	44	25
New Bradwell St Peter	30	5	13	12	35	49	23
Waterlows	30	7	5	18	31	51	19
Langford	30	6	7	17	33	69	19
Harpenden Town	30	7	4	19	30	68	18
Eaton Bray United	30	4	3	23	26	73	11

New clubs in Division 1: Hatfield Town, Milton Keynes Borough and Vauxhall Motors
Division 1 promoted clubs: B.A.C. and Leighton Town

HONOURS LIST
League Challenge Trophy Final: First Leg: Royston Town 1 Barton Rovers 3
Second Leg: Barton Rovers 2 Royston Town 2
Bedfordshire Senior Cup Final: Arlesey Town 2 Stotfold 1
Herts Charity Shield Final: Hoddesdon Town 4 Royston Town 1

Final Table 1978-79

	P	W	D	L	F	A	Pts.
Liskeard	36	26	5	5	98	42	57
Wadebridge	36	23	7	6	91	36	53
Newquay	36	22	9	5	74	33	53
Plymouth Civil Service	36	20	7	9	71	45	47
St Blazey	36	17	7	12	60	49	41
Torpoint Athletic	36	16	9	11	73	69	41
Louis International	36	15	10	11	57	52	40
Truro City	36	15	9	12	69	57	39
Holsworth	36	15	8	13	66	59	38
St Austell	36	15	7	14	57	59	37
Tavistock	36	11	11	14	61	64	33
Penzance	36	11	10	15	63	65	32
Bugle	36	11	7	18	43	71	29
Appledore	36	10	8	18	47	58	28
Bodmin	36	9	7	20	43	81	25
Illogan RBL	36	6	12	18	58	88	24
Torrington	36	8	9	19	50	80	*23
Newton Abbot Dynamos	36	8	6	22	33	59	22
Plymouth Command	36	6	8	22	34	82	20

*Points deducted.

HONOURS LIST

League Challenge Cup Final		Liskeard 1
		Plymouth Civil Service 0
Devon Premier Cup	Winners	Holsworth
Cornwall Charity Cup	Winners	St Blazey
Devon Charity Cup	Winners	Tavistock
Pratten Cup	Winners	Liskeard
	Runners-up	Wadebridge

SUSSEX COUNTY FOOTBALL LEAGUE

Final Table 1978-79

FIRST DIVISION

	P	W	D	L	F	A	Pts.
Peacehaven & Telscombe	30	18	9	3	61	28	45
Southwick	30	16	9	5	60	33	41
Horsham YMCA	30	18	5	7	58	33	41
Steyning	30	15	7	8	56	45	37
Littlehampton Town	30	14	7	9	54	34	35
Ringmer	30	13	8	9	41	44	34
Arundel	30	13	7	10	44	37	33
Shoreham	30	10	10	10	43	40	30
Haywards Heath	30	9	12	9	44	47	30
Bexhill Town	30	11	5	14	56	56	27
Eastbourne Town	30	10	6	14	47	51	26
Chichester City	30	10	5	15	51	64	25
Burgess Hill Town	30	8	6	16	34	56	22
Rye United	30	8	5	17	31	42	21
East Grinstead	30	5	8	17	40	65	18
Sidley United	30	5	5	20	22	67	15

HONOURS LIST

League Challenge Cup
Winners Steyning   Runners-up Arundel
Sussex Royal Ulster Rifles Charity Cup
Winners Arundel   Runners-up Ringmer

SPONSORSHIP DETAILS

£2,000 per annum by the Sx. Co. Building Society. £1,000 goes towards League running expenses. League Cup winners £100, runners-up £50, Division Two Cup £50, runners-up £25. In addition a merit table is used allying results and misconduct (cautions, send-offs) Winners receive £275 2nd £200, 3rd £150, 4th £100, 5th £50.
Results of Merit table: 1. Pagham, 2. Horsham YMCA, 3. Littlehampton, 4. Peacehaven, Southwick.

TEESSIDE FOOTBALL LEAGUE

Final Table 1978-79

	P	W	D	L	F	A	Pts.
Billingham SC	34	23	8	3	71	22	54
Smiths Dock	34	23	6	5	83	36	52
Hartlepool BWO	34	23	4	7	92	41	50
Redcar Albion	34	20	9	5	71	32	49
Darlington RA	34	20	7	7	65	35	47
ICI Cassel Works	34	17	9	8	66	35	43
Norton CCT	34	18	6	10	78	55	42
Stockton Buffs SC	34	17	6	11	63	42	40
Head Wrightson	34	16	4	14	56	43	36
Nunthorpe Athletic	34	14	4	16	66	53	32
Marske United	34	13	4	17	47	67	30
Teesside Polytechnic.........	34	10	7	17	48	62	27
ICI Wilton...................	34	10	2	22	48	68	22
Redcar Works BSC	34	8	8	18	45	79	*22
Dormans Athletic............	34	8	4	22	36	82	20
Acklam Works	34	6	7	21	39	69	19
Brotton	34	5	7	22	27	69	17
Boosbeck United	34	3	2	29	22	133	8

Two points deducted.

TOWN & COUNTRY FOOTBALL LEAGUE
Final Table 1978-79

	P	W	D	L	F	A	Pts.
Haverhill Rovers	42	29	9	4	90	36	67
Gt Yarmouth Town	42	28	10	4	112	44	66
Lowestoft Town	42	24	15	3	89	40	63
Bury Town	42	27	7	8	99	56	61
Sudbury Town	42	19	11	12	78	50	49
Ely City	42	18	11	13	50	57	47
Gorleston	42	21	4	17	74	67	46
Braintree & Crittall Ath.	42	18	9	15	78	72	45
Wisbech Town	42	17	11	14	68	69	45
Brantham Ath.	42	16	11	15	62	61	43
March Town Utd	42	16	9	17	65	69	41
Cambridge Utd Res.	42	16	9	17	58	67	41
Soham Town Rangers	42	18	4	20	70	74	40
Thetford Town	42	14	9	19	73	78	37
Histon	42	15	6	21	61	73	36
Saffron Walden	42	13	9	20	64	68	35
Felixstowe Town	42	11	10	21	43	64	32
Colchester Utd Res.	42	11	8	23	54	78	30
Stowmarket	42	10	9	23	62	84	29
Clacton Town	42	8	13	21	38	62	29
Chatteris Town	42	10	7	25	80	120	27
Newmarket Town	42	5	4	33	34	107	14

LEADING GOALSCORERS

	Total
R. Knight (Bury Town)	43
J. Thomson (Haverhill Rovers)	36
N. Hart (Gt Yarmouth Town)	30

HONOURS LIST

League KO Cup	Winners	Cambridge United Reserves
Suffolk Premier Cup	Winners	Lowestoft Town
Norfolk Senior Cup	Winners	Great Yarmouth Town

SPONSORSHIP AWARDS

League Winners	Haverhill Rovers	£300
Runners-up	Gt Yarmouth Town	£150
Third	Lowestoft Town	£100
Fourth	Bury Town	£50
K.O. Cup Semi-finalists	Gorleston	£50
	Cambridge United	£50
	Soham Town Rangers	£50
	Sudbury Town	£50
K.O. Cup Winners	Cambridge United	£100
Runners-up	Gorleston	£50

GOAL SCORING AWARDS

Yarmouth £48, Bury £36, Haverhill £32, Sudbury £32, Lowestoft £32, March £24, Gorleston £20, Saffron Walden £20, Chatteris £20 Braintree £16, Stowmarket £16, Thetford £16, Soham £16, Wisbech £12, Colchester £12, Brantham £8, Cambridge £8, Histon £8, Ely £4, Clacton £12. *Each club received four match footballs.*

UNITED COUNTIES FOOTBALL LEAGUE

Final Table 1978-79

PREMIER DIVISION

	P	W	D	L	F	A	Pts.
Irthlingborough Diamonds	36	25	5	6	88	31	55
Rushden Town	36	22	7	7	72	29	51
Kempston Rovers	36	20	7	9	55	23	47
Desborough Town	36	20	3	13	82	59	43
Potton United	36	18	7	11	59	49	43
Wolverton Town	36	17	9	10	61	52	43
Rothwell Town	36	14	12	10	56	50	40
Stamford	36	15	9	12	61	47	39
St Neots Town	36	16	7	13	59	51	39
Wootton Blue Cross	36	15	8	13	77	63	38
Stewart & Lloyds (Corby)	36	16	5	15	48	46	37
Olney Town	36	14	9	13	36	43	37
Buckingham Town	36	10	11	15	46	52	31
Long Buckby..................	36	12	6	18	41	58	30
Ampthill Town	36	10	5	21	44	74	25
Bourne Town..................	36	9	6	21	51	86	24
Northampton Spencer O.B.	36	7	9	20	47	76	23
Holbeach United	36	9	4	23	51	94	22
Eynesbury Rovers	36	6	5	25	28	79	17

WEARSIDE FOOTBALL LEAGUE

Final Table 1978-79

	P	W	D	L	F	A	Pts.
Wallsend Town	32	21	5	6	88	42	47
Wingate	32	21	4	7	81	46	46
Whickham	32	17	10	5	66	36	44
Boldon CA...................	32	18	7	7	77	43	43
South Shields	32	16	11	5	80	50	43
Hartlepool Reserves	32	15	5	11	61	52	37
Chester le Street Town......	32	13	10	9	55	48	36
Blue Star*	32	20	5	8	90	42	35
Annfield Plain	32	13	6	13	67	69	32
Easington CW	32	11	8	13	50	73	30
Ryhope CW	32	8	11	13	49	50	27
Eppleton CW...............	32	8	6	18	52	71	22
Washington**	32	7	8	17	32	59	20
Reyrolles	32	8	4	20	52	90	20
Roker	32	5	8	19	38	79	18
Heaton Stannington	32	6	5	21	43	86	17
Murton CW	32	4	9	19	27	75	17

*Ten points deducted; **two points deducted.*

LEADING GOALSCORERS

	Total
G. Hogan (Wingate)	24
M. Carr (South Shields)	23

HONOURS LIST

League Challenge Cup: Wingate 1 Eppleton C.W. 4

WELSH FOOTBALL LEAGUE

Final Tables 1978-79

PREMIER DIVISION

	P	W	D	L	F	A	Pts.
Pontllanfraith	34	23	7	4	73	37	53
Cardiff Corinthians	34	20	4	10	77	45	44
Newport County	34	14	13	7	55	25	41
Afan Lido	34	17	7	10	43	37	41
Ton Pentre	34	16	8	10	62	42	40
Swansea City	34	15	9	10	61	47	39
Ammanford Town	34	14	11	9	47	42	39
Pembroke Borough	34	16	6	12	63	50	38
Merthyr Tydfil	34	15	7	12	61	58	37
Barry Town	34	12	11	11	54	45	35
Caerau Athletic	34	13	8	13	45	55	34
Sully	34	13	7	14	42	41	33
Milford United	34	12	8	14	55	45	32
Llanelli	34	11	9	14	41	55	31
Pontlottyn	34	9	10	15	41	57	28
Treharris Athletic	34	9	8	17	43	65	26
Ferndale Athletic	34	3	6	25	36	90	12
Cardiff College	34	1	7	26	25	88	9

NORTHERN SECTION

	P	W	D	L	F	A	Pts.
Caernarfon Town	20	15	5	0	77	11	35
Pwllheli & District	20	14	4	2	47	20	32
Porthmadog	20	13	4	3	85	21	30
Colwyn Bay	20	9	6	5	51	30	24
Nantlle Vale	20	10	3	7	58	21	23
Conway United	20	8	5	7	40	38	21
Bl Ffestiniog	20	6	6	8	32	40	18
Bangor City	20	5	6	9	34	42	16
Rhos United	20	6	1	13	24	55	13
Rhyl	20	0	3	17	11	78	3
Llandudno Swifts*	20	1	3	16	11	114	3

Two points deducted for playing an ineligible player.

HONOURS LIST

The Welsh League S. A. Brain Challenge Cup Final: Barry Town 0
(5 pens.) Pontllanfraith 0 (4 pens.)

The South Wales F.A. Senior Cup: Winners Maesteg Park Athletic
Runners-up Lake United

The West Wales F.A. Senior Cup: Winners Milford United Runners-up
Llanelli

253

WESTERN FOOTBALL LEAGUE

Final Tables 1978-79

PREMIER DIVISION

	P	W	D	L	F	A	Pts.
Frome Town	38	21	12	5	60	29	75
Bideford	38	22	8	8	76	39	74
Saltash United	38	19	10	9	65	39	67
Barnstaple Town	38	18	10	10	65	35	64
Tiverton Town	38	17	9	12	71	60	60
Clandown	38	16	11	11	58	49	59
Weston-super-Mare	38	14	15	9	65	48	57
Falmouth Town	38	15	9	14	51	47	54
Paulton Rovers	38	15	9	14	40	48	54
Bridport	38	13	13	12	54	50	52
Bridgwater Town	38	14	9	15	57	53	51
Keynsham Town	38	13	12	13	47	57	51
Mangotsfield PF	38	15	2	21	53	64	47
Ilminster Town	38	11	12	15	45	55	45
Welton Rovers	38	11	8	19	44	59	41
Exeter City	38	12	5	21	48	75	41
Clevedon Town	38	11	7	20	50	64	40
Dawlish	38	10	10	18	43	61	40
Shepton Mallet Town	38	10	10	18	48	74	40
Glastonbury	38	8	9	21	42	76	33

FIRST DIVISION

	P	W	D	L	F	A	Pts.
AFC Bournemouth	36	25	6	5	101	41	81
Portway-Bristol	36	23	5	8	81	43	74
Bristol Manor Farm	36	20	5	11	59	47	65
Chippenham Town	36	19	7	10	56	43	64
Torquay United	36	20	4	12	82	47	**62
Melksham Town	36	18	4	14	58	57	58
Devizes Town	36	16	9	11	71	54	57
Wellington	36	18	3	15	48	46	57
Chard Town	36	15	6	15	57	58	51
Brixham United	36	15	5	16	55	61	50
Elmore	36	15	3	18	48	65	48
Ottery St Mary	36	13	5	18	51	60	*43
Larkhall Athletic	36	12	6	18	52	56	42
Westland-Yeovil	36	11	9	16	43	53	42
Heavitree United	36	12	5	19	39	61	41
Swanage Town & Herston	36	11	6	19	51	60	39
Odd Down	36	10	5	21	38	71	35
Exmouth Town	36	8	9	19	41	72	*33
Yeovil Town	36	5	10	21	30	65	*24

*One point each deducted for playing an ineligible player; **two points deducted for playing an ineligible player.

WEST MIDLANDS (REGIONAL) LEAGUE

Final Table 1978-79

PREMIER DIVISION

	P	W	D	L	F	A	Pts.
Willenhall Town	34	23	7	4	82	32	53
Lye Town	34	21	11	2	62	33	53
Dudley Town	34	21	8	5	53	23	50
Hednesford Town	34	19	10	5	59	26	48
Tividale	34	19	6	9	63	40	44
Bilston	34	15	10	9	50	34	40
Brierley Hill Alliance	34	17	5	12	67	47	39
Brereton Social	34	17	5	12	48	40	39
Darlaston	34	15	5	14	52	51	35
Coventry Sporting	34	12	6	16	39	48	30
Hinckley Athletic	34	12	5	17	42	52	29
Ledbury Town	34	10	7	17	57	63	27
V.S. Rugby	34	9	9	16	29	41	27
Wednesfield Social	34	7	12	15	27	45	26
Halesowen Town	34	8	8	18	35	55	24
Armitage	34	7	6	21	44	69	20
Gresley Rovers	34	4	7	23	27	67	15
Gornal Athletic	34	4	5	25	21	91	13

WILTSHIRE COUNTY FOOTBALL LEAGUE

Final Table 1978-79

FIRST DIVISION

	P	W	D	L	F	A	Pts.
Park	30	22	6	2	73	22	50
Amesbury	30	21	7	2	63	15	49
Vickers	30	15	7	8	51	45	37
Penhill YC	30	14	6	10	51	43	34
Bromham	30	11	10	9	48	42	32
Sanford	30	13	5	12	62	47	31
Westbury	30	13	5	12	49	48	31
Warminster	30	14	2	14	47	54	30
Salisbury Res	30	9	10	11	36	50	28
Malmesbury	30	8	9	13	37	42	25
Corsham Town	30	10	5	15	35	62	25
Avon Bradford	30	8	8	14	39	47	24
Marlborough	30	7	7	15	55	64	23
Bemerton	30	8	7	15	45	58	23
Calne Town	30	8	6	16	33	64	22
Highworth	30	4	8	18	36	57	16

LEADING GOALSCORERS

	Total
S. Burson (Park)	21
P. Laggett (Sanford)	21
O. Murphy (Park)	20

YORKSHIRE FOOTBALL LEAGUE

Final Tables 1978-79

FIRST DIVISION

	P	W	D	L	F	A	Pts.
Winterton Rangers	30	19	5	6	54	21	43
Emley	30	18	5	7	58	31	41
North Ferriby	30	16	9	5	55	31	41
Guiseley	30	11	9	10	35	32	31
Thackley	30	13	5	12	41	39	31
Ossett Town	30	14	2	14	42	37	30
Scarborough	30	10	10	10	34	36	30
Sheffield	30	9	11	10	26	28	29
Leeds Ashley Road	30	10	8	12	34	37	28
Hallam	30	12	4	14	33	42	28
Bridlington Town	30	11	6	13	36	48	28
Frecheville CA	30	7	13	10	33	42	27
Tadcaster Albion	30	9	8	13	33	39	26
Bentley VW	30	9	7	14	34	38	25
Kiveton Park	30	8	7	15	44	54	23
Lincoln United	30	5	9	16	28	65	19

SECOND DIVISION

	P	W	D	L	F	A	Pts
Ossett Albion	30	17	9	4	37	18	43
Fryston CW	30	15	6	9	56	36	36
Thorne Colliery	30	12	12	6	45	34	36
Liversedge	30	13	9	8	39	33	35
Brook Sports	30	12	8	10	45	48	32
Farsley Celtic	30	10	11	9	49	38	31
Hatfield Main	30	11	9	10	39	36	31
Maltby MW	30	8	12	10	37	38	28
Denaby United	30	10	7	13	47	51	27
Norton Woodseats	30	10	7	13	38	47	27
Yorkshire Amateur	30	9	9	12	44	46	27
Barton Town	30	10	6	14	43	47	26
Rawmarsh Welfare	30	8	10	12	45	51	26
Worsbrough Bridge MW	30	11	4	15	39	48	26
Leeds Carnegie Polytechnic	30	11	3	16	55	58	25
Wombwell SA	30	9	6	15	33	52	24

ADDITIONAL LEAGUE DETAILS

Competition	Champions	Secretary
Anglian Combination	Diss	J. Harpley (Norwich 408803)
Bristol & Suburban	Glenside St Gabriels	O. L. England (Bristol 652853)
Carlisle & District	Gretna	P. Woods (Carlisle 22475)
Gloucestershire Northern	St Marks C.A.	L. James (Gloucester 68671)
Hertfordshire	Cockfosters	E. Dear (Welwyn 5415)
Home Counties	Bac (Weybridge)	G.A. Hall (01-399 0673)
Lancashire Amateur	Burnley Belvedere	H. Heap (061-980 2344)
Lincs. & S. Humberside	Brewery Sports	E. Turner (Scunthorpe 2321)
Liverpool County	Waterloo Dock	F. Hunter (051-427 1719)
Manchester Amateur	Salford Amateurs	T. Gilchrist (061-764 5807)
Mid Cheshire	Kidsgrove Athletic	R. Darlington (Runcorn 74289)
Notts Alliance	Rainworth M.W.	E.R. Rudd (Sandyacre 216382)
Peterborough & District	Downham	A. Brown (Peterborough 67765)
Somerset Senior	Radstock Town	L. Webb (Midsomer Norton 413176)
Westmorland	Appleby	N. Braithwaite (Kendal 20446)
West Yorkshire	Bradley Rangers	W. Keyworth (Pudsey 574465)

COUNTY DETAILS

County	Senior cup winners	Chairman	Secretary	Address	Tel no
Bedfordshire	Arlesey Town	R.R. Cox	P.Burns	13 Wendover Way, Luton, Beds, LU27LS	Luton 30829
Berks & Bucks	Wycombe Wanderers	D.R. Goodchild	C.Twelftree	42 Bourtonville, Buckingham, Bucks	Buckingham 2137
Birmingham	Bedworth United	W.Goodman	W.F.Pennick	Ray Hall Lane, Great Barr, Birmingham	021-357 4278
Cambridgeshire	Great Shelford	C. Andrews	R.Rogers	20 Aingers Road, Histon, Cambs	Histon 2803
Cheshire	Northwich Victoria	A.Burbridge	F.Foden	549 Crewe Road, Wistaston, Crewe, Cheshire, CW2 6PW	Crewe 69429
Cornwall	Falmouth Town	D.Champion	W.Parnell	12 Higher Tremena, St Austell, Cornwall, PL25 5QQ	St Austell 3236
Cumberland County	Cleator Celtic	W.Hodgson	E.D.Smith	4 High Rigg, Brigham, Cockermouth, Cumbria	Cockermouth 825242
Derbyshire	Heanor Town	W.Screen	H.Holmes	82 Friar Lane, Derby, DE1 1FL	Derby 361422
Devon	Holsworthy	B.Williams	C.Norsworthy	8 Belair Road, Peverell, Plymouth, Devon	Plymouth 773550
Dorset	Bridport	B.White	G. Mitchell	8 Beaufoys Close, Ferndown, Wimborne, Dorset	Ferndown 874131
Durham	Spennymoor United	A.Askew	A.D.Lyons	'Codeslaw', Ferens Park Durham, CH1 1JZ	Durham 3653
East Riding	North Ferriby United	H.Padget	C.Branton	83 Belvedere Road, Hessle, N. Humberside, HU13 9JH	Hull 649294
Essex	Harlow Town	A.Barrett	M.Jeffers	54a Eastwood Road, Goodmayes, Ilford, Essex	01-590 7893
Gloucestershire	Almondsbury Greenway	C.Wilcox	E.Marsh	46 Douglas Road, Horfield, Bristol	Bristol 46430

County	Club			Address	Phone
Hampshire	Romsey Town	J.Barter	R.Barnes	367 Winchester Road, Southampton, Hampshire	Southampton 766884
Herefordshire	Hinton Y.C.	C.W.Jones	R.A.Doody	Longwind, Paradise Green, Marden, Hereford	Sutton St Nicholas 674
Hertfordshire	Watford	P.W. Poulter	F.Holloway	115 Tile Kiln Lane, Leverstock Green, Hemel Hampshire, SO9 2UA	Hemel Hempstead 54131
Huntingdonshire	Phopres Sports	F.E.Rooke	M.M. Armstrong	1 Chapel Lane, Great Glodings, Huntingdon, Cambs	Winwick 262
Kent	Maidstone United	J.E. Blackburn	K.Masters	69 Maidstone Road, Maidstone, Kent	Medway 43824
Lancashire	Marine (Junior cup winners)	R.W.Lord	J.Kenyon	31a Wellington Street, Blackburn, Lancs, BB1 8AU	Blackburn 64333
Leics & Rutland	Enderby Town	I.Finn	J.Holmes	492 Melton Road, Leics	Leicester 64212
Lincolnshire	Boston United	G. Dorrington	B.Webster	31 Chantry Lane, Grimsby, S. Humberside	Grimsby 57709
Liverpool	Marine	J.H.Allen	S.Rudd	23 Greenfield Road, Old Swan, Liverpool 13	051-220 6089
London	Barking	L.A.M. MacKay	A.F.Monger	Association House, 88 Lewisham High Street, London, S.E.13	01-852 4777
Manchester	Droylsden	F.Hannah	S.Holliday	87 Hart Road, Fallowfield, Manchester 14	061-224 5185
Middlesex	Enfield	D.Jenkins	A.Smith	68 Squires Lane, London, N3 2AP	01-346 7565
Norfolk	Great Yarmouth Town	S.Latimer	B.Smith	'Mon Reve', 64 Gunton Lane, Costessey, Norwich, Norfolk	Norwich 742894
Northamptonshire	Kettering Town	F.Deeley	N.Hillier	36 Watkin Terrace, Northampton, NN1 3ER	Northampton 37071

County	Club			Address	Telephone
North Riding	Billingham Synthonia	W.Cotton	T.H.Harper	125 Westbury Street, Thornaby, Stockton-on-Tees, Cleveland, TS17 6NF	Stockton-on-Tees 67866
Northumberland	North Shields	G.S. Seymour	J.Laidler	80 Riding Dene, Mickley, Stocksfield, Northumberland	Stocksfield 2360
Nottinghamshire	Eastwood Town	J.Williams	W.Annable	7 Clarendon Street, Nottingham	Nottingham 48954
Oxfordshire	Banbury United	J.Roughton	S.Jacobs	9 Burrows Close, Headington, Oxford	Oxford 61187
Sheffield & Hallamshire	Frickley Athletic	A.Engledon	G. Thompson	Clegg House, 253 Pittsmore Road, Sheffield	Sheffield 7817
Shropshire	Telford United	S.Rogers	W.Jones	146 Whitchurch Road, Shrewsbury, Shropshire	Shrewsbury 3243
Somerset & Avon (South)	Radstock Town	D.Cummins	L.Webb	32 North Road, Midsomer Norton, Bath, Avon, BA3 2QQ	Midsomer Norton 413176
Staffordshire	Northwich Victoria	G.H.Goode	T.Myatt	Miller Street, Newcastle-under-Lyme, Staffs	Newcastle-under-Lyme 622585
Suffolk	Lowestoft Town	J.O'Dwyer	E.Brown	'Shobdon', 68 Fairfield Road, Saxmundham, Suf.	Saxmundham 2165
Surrey	Camberley Town	J.Hewlett	L.Smith	2 Fairfield Avenue, Horley, Surrey	Horley 4945
Sussex	Hastings United	S.Vicars	R.Reeve	56 Hawkins Crescent, Shoreham-by-Sea, Sussex	Brighton 593444
Westmorland	Staveley	J.Rigg	J.Plumbe	24 Crescent Green, Kendal, Cumbria	Kendal 23227
West Riding	Guiseley	J. Fletcher	R. Robin	77 Great George Street, Leeds, LS1 3BR	Leeds 452444
Wiltshire	Devizes Town	W. Humphries	F. Peart	161 Grange Drive, Stratton St Margaret, Swindon, Wilts	Swindon 822239
Worcestershire	Kidderminster Harriers	R. Bannister	P. Rushton	84 Windermere Drive, Worcester	Worcester 51166

First class coverage daily.

The Daily Telegraph
Sports Pages

LEADING GOALSCORERS AND MOST APPEARANCES 1978-79

The following tables depict clubs now playing in the leagues as shown. However, it does not follow that the clubs necessarily belonged to those leagues when the goals were scored and the appearances were made.

ALLIANCE PREMIER LEAGUE
LEADING GOALSCORERS

Altrincham	J. Rogers ____35	J. Johnson ____31	G. Heathcote ____22	
A. P. Leamington	D. Gardner ____	R. Vincent ____	T. Gorman ____	
Bangor City	M. Owen ____20	A. Broadhead 16		
Barnet	G. Cleary ____26	J. Fairbrother 12	J. Greaves ____11	
			D. Brown ____11	
Barrow	C. Cowperthwaite	R. Thomas ____	A. Suddick ____	
Bath City	J. Jenkins ____23	G. Gibbs ____13	P. Rogers ____ 13	
Boston Utd.	J. Kabia ____22	D. Poplar ____10	D. Adamson ____ 8	
Gravesend N.	A. Noon ____18	B. Woolfe ____15	S. Brown ____14	
Kettering Town	W. Kellock ____40	P. Phipps ____29	R. Clayton ____28	
Maidstone Utd.	B. Gregory ____23	G. Coupland 19	P. Silvester ____10	
Northwich V.	C. Williams ____29	T. O'Connor 24	L. Garrity ____15	
Nuneaton B.	C. Campbell 22	G. Dale ____21	T. Smithers ____13	
Redditch Utd.	G. Bastable ____24	M. Tuohy ____23	C. Cotton ____ 9	
Scarborough	D. Abbey ____15	H. Dunn ____11	R. Gauden ____ 9	
Stafford R.	M. Cullerton 31	A. Wood ____15	B. Seddon ____14	
Telford Utd.	D. Hickton ____13	F. Stromer ____ 9	J. Steele ____ 8	
Wealdstone				
Weymouth	A. Leitch ____27	T. Henderson 24	P. Hawkins ____19	
Worcester C.	M. Phelps ____26	J. Williams ____25	B. Williams ____21	
Yeovil T.	D. Platt ____	T. Cotton ____	C. Green ____	

ALLIANCE PREMIER LEAGUE
MOST APPEARANCES

Altrincham	B. Howard ____59	J. Johnson ____58	G. Heathcote ____57	
			J. Davison ____57	
A. P. Leamington	Taylor ____	Dulleston ____	D. Gardner ____	
Bangor C.	K. Charlton ____	P. Lunn ____	P. Olney ____	
Barnet	L. McCormack 57	T. Townsend 55	S. Oliver ____50	
Barrow	C. Cowperthwaite	K. Thomas ____	D. Large ____	
Bath City	M. Rogers ____59	N. Ryan ____57	J. Jenkins ____53	
			K. Book ____53	
Boston Utd.	G. Stewart ____44	A. Phelan ____44	D. Poplar ____44	
Gravesend N.	L. Smelt ____42	R. Grozier ____39	G. Idle ____38	
			P. Osborne ____38	
Kettering Town	R. Clayton ____56	R. Ashby ____55	R. Dixey ____55	
Maidstone Utd.	N. Merrick ____66	W. Edwards ____65	N. Fusio ____62	
Northwich V.	K. Jones ____65	M. Brennan ____61	T. Bailey ____58	
Nuneaton B.	T. Smithers ____60	T. Peake ____53	B. Phillips ____53	
Redditch Utd.	R. Edwards ____44	J. Jones ____42	M. Tuohy ____43	
Scarborough	H. Dunn ____40	D. Abbey ____39	G. Donoghue ____38	
			S. Marshall ____38	

Stafford R.	B. Seddon	59	J. Arnold	57	J. Sargeant	37
Telford Utd	K. Malcolm	47	E. Hogan	46	M. Gavin	41
Wealdstone						
Weymouth	K. Dove	66	S. Dyer	64	A. Iannone	62
Worcester C.	M. Phelps	66	G. Stevens	65	K. Lawrence	63
Yeovil T.	B. Parker		T. Cotton		B. Thompson	

BERGER ISTHMIAN LEAGUE
PREMIER DIVISION
LEADING GOALSCORERS

Barking	B. Key	36	P. Burton	31	N. Ashford	26
Boreham Wood	N.O'Donaghie	24	P. Watson	16	J. Batten	10
Carshalton Ath.	G. Allen		A. Walker		G. Dennis	
Croydon	C. Pooley	23	A. Jackson	16	R. Ward	14
Dagenham	R. Kidd	30	J. Dunwell	26	M. Harkins	19
Dulwich Hamlet	O. Bayram	29	A. James	16	K. Connett	12
Enfield	K. Searle	22	N. Glover	17	R. Howells	16
					S. King	16
Harlow T.	P. Twige	31	J. McKenzie	19	M. Springett	19
Harrow B.	P. Sharratt	44	P. Caines	18	H. Manoe	16
Hayes	P. Morrisey	13	R. Nelson	10	G. Gilbert	9
Hendon	M. Garrini		R. Butler		G. Sewell	
Hitchin T.	P. Giggle	19	G. Harthill	12	J. McCarthy	9
Leatherhead	J. Baker		S. Camp		C. Kelly	
Oxford City	P. Dallaway	14	M. Boyland	12	A. Sinnott	10
Slough Town	M. Kiely	14	P. Lee	14	B. Metcalfe	14
Staines Town	J. Williams	19	E. Bissett	14	B. Greenhaigh	10
Sutton Utd.	T. Harris	18	P. McKinnon	18	J. Rains	13
Tilbury	K. Gray	19	N. Smith	14	S. Coventry	9
Tooting & Mitcham	A. Ives	14	P. Basey	10	D. Dennis	9
Walthamstow A.	R. Sedgwick	25	B. Walder	14	R. Tappin	13
Woking	A. Morton	39	R. James	33	S. Cosham	18
Wycombe W.	S. Atkins	21	S. Long	18	T. Scott	18

BERGER ISTHMIAN LEAGUE
PREMIER DIVISION
MOST APPEARANCES

Barking	P. Burton	64	R. Makin	62	C. Ballard	61
Boreham Wood	S. Waller		N. O'Donaghue		J. Sneddon	
Carshalton	P. Gaydon	52	I. Finch	50	T. Coombe	47
Croydon	A. Ward	58	A. Jackson	58	B. Walker	57
Dagenham	J. Dunwell	63	I. Huttley	63	D. Moore	60
Dulwich Hamlet	C. Lewington	59	G. Borg	58	M. Lewis	58
Enfield	T. Jennings	73	J. Tone	71	T. Moore	70
Harlow	P. Kitson	55	P. Twigg	48	T. Gough	49
Harrow B.	H. Manoe	64	P. Sharratt	64	L. Currell	57
Hayes	A. Jarrett	61	V. Akers	58	M. McGovern	58
Hendon	R. Haider		G. Hand		R. Butler	
Hitching T.	R. Bradwell	53	K. Hammond	51	P. Giggle	50
Leatherhead	J. Swannel	60	B. Salkeld	59	D. Reid	58
Oxford City	S. Massey	50	M. Prescott	45	A. Glass	45

Slough Town	R. Teale ____	R. McKay ____	J. Beyer ____
Staines Town	E. Bissett ____48	P. Beasant____45	B. Steep ____42
Sutton Utd.	D. Collyer____66	L. Pritchard____65	J. Rains ____65
Tilbury	M. Binks ____53	M. Linton ____52	S. Coventry ____51
			K. Gray ____51
Tooting & Mitcham	R. Pittaway ____54	K. Highland____53	R. Green ____52
Walthamstow A.	B. Willson____52	D. Wells ____55	R. Sedgwick ____57
Woking	F. Parsons ____63	J. Love ____62	A. Martin ____61
Wycombe W.	M. Holifield ____63	D. Evans ____59	P. Birdseye____58

BERGER ISTHMIAN LEAGUE
DIVISION ONE
LEADING GOALSCORERS

Aveley	A. Noonan ____12	M. Hanson ____11	A. Butler ____ 7
Bishop's Stortford	D. Worrell ____22	P. Ferry ____19	L. Eason____17
Bromley	B. Dunn ____39	D. Waight ____12	J. Crooks ____10
Camberley T.	M. Clarke____39	G. Hawkett ____16	R. Parkin ____15
Chesham Utd.	J. Watt ____11	G. Nash ____10	R. Martell ____ 7
Clapton	J. Gormley ____	B. McPherson ____	T. Dormen ____
Epsom & Ewell	T. Tuite____36	G. Archer____16	G. Hunn ____12
Farnborough T.	R. Saunders ____24	A. Gunn ____18	D. Sheedy ____17
Finchley	____	____	____
Hampton	____	____	____
Harwich & P.	J. Wallace____31	M. Crissell ____25	M. Stanford ____17
Hertford	____	____	____
Horsham	____	____	____
Ilford &	T. Glynn ____19	R. Wade ____14	R. Harding ____ 9
Leytonstone	G. Parker ____11	B. Reeves ____ 8	P. Powell____ 6
Kingstonian	____	____	____
Maidenhead Utd.	____	____	____
Met. Police	Oliver ____28	Ward____11	Docherty ____ 8
St Albans C.	____	____	____
Walton H.	M. Bennett ____14	M. Heath ____ 4 T. Addinall ____ 4	G. Woolbridge 4
Ware	J. Vintinner ____24	S. Archer ____ 6	J. Reading ____ 6
Wembley	____	____	____
Wokingham T.	J. Griffiths ____13	T. Bell ____10	B. McKevitt ____10

BERGER ISTHMIAN LEAGUE
DIVISION ONE
MOST APPEARANCES

Aveley	M. Hanson ____46	J. O'Sullivan____46	J. Swan ____39
Bishop's Stortford	W. Carrick ____59	L. Eason ____59	P. Ferry ____55
Bromley	M. Broadway 63	D. Waight____61	R. Clarke ____58
Camberley T.	R. Barnforth ____41	A. Turner ____41	P. Dodds ____39
Chesham Utd.	J. Watt ____47	R. Martell ____47	P. Griffiths ____46
Clapton	S. Shorey ____	J. Gormley ____	A. Shirley ____
Epsom & Ewell	A. Hill ____54	T. Tuite ____54	D. Turner ____54
Farnborough T.	H. Richardson 48	R. Saunders ____48	T. Waughman 46
Finchley	____	____	____

Hampton			
Harwich & P.	J. Wallace 54	M. Clarke 53	G. Wallace 53
Hertford			
Horsham			
Ilford & Leytonstone	R. Wade 55 M. McCayna 48	T. Glynn 47 P. Powell 43	S. Barrett 46 B. Newman 42
Kingstonian	D. Vaughan 53	G. Stille 48	M. Whartford 47
Maidenhead Utd.			
Met. Police	Rees 57	Thomas 56	Oliver 55 Docherty 55
St Albans C.			
Walton & H.	G. Bloom 46	M. Heath 38	A. Hawlett 37 K. Weaver 37
Ware	J. Vintinner 49	P. Young 46	W. Morgan 45
Wembley			
Wokingham T.	M. Dixon 51	B. McKevitt 44	J. Richardson 42

BERGER ISTHMIAN LEAGUE
DIVISION TWO
LEADING GOALSCORERS

Barton Rovers ...	S. Turner 16	R. Singfield 13	P. Smith 13
Billericay T.	F. Clayden 33	D. Young 33	J. Reeves 15
Cheshunt	E. Sedgwick 23	J. Shaffer 14	K. Hook 13
Corinthian C. ...	J. McElligott 9	K. East 7	P. Wilson 5
Eastbourne Utd.	J. Daubney 39	J. Kemp 19	R. Saunders 9
Egham Town ...	J. Carter 9	S. Webb 7	S. Atkins 7
Epping Town ...	D. Keefe 13	G. Cole 8	A. Howe 5
Feltham	G. Drake 25	G. Rossiter 14	B. Drake 7
Hemel Hempstead	S. Woolfrey	E. Dillsworth ...	P. Fairclough
Hornchurch	K. Gaine 14	T. Moorcroft ...6	G. Cole 5
Hungerford T.	D. Ingram 16	I. Farr 14	A. Young 13
Letchworth G.C.	R. Chandler ...20	S. Hodge 20	D. Dance 13
Lewes	P. Parris 22	R. Holder 16	D. Harding 15
Molesey			
Rainham T.	S. Plant 22	J. Phillips 15	J. Coates 11
Southall	C. Hutchings 12	D. Doyle 9	G. Jones 8
Tring Town	B. Mapp	J. Delaney	G. Rotherham
Willesden			
Worthing	D. Busby 26	W. Cairns 12	M. Streeter 8

BERGER ISTHMIAN LEAGUE
DIVISION TWO
MOST APPEARANCES

Barton Rovers ...	P. Fossey 30	A. Dunn 29	S. Norris 28
Billericay T.	P. Whettell 57	J. Pullin 55	W. Bingham 51
Cheshunt	E. Sedgwick 52	C. Gilbery 47	J. Burling 46
Corinthian C. ...	C. Booth 46	J. McElligott 44	P. Wilson 42
Eastbourne Utd.	P. Stephens 52	N. Ivemy 52	A. Noakes 51
Egham Town ...	S. Webb 38	D. Haslegrave 37	M. Wright 34
Epping Town ...	G. Stack 47	D. Townshend 46	D. Keefe 42
Feltham	J. Greenwood	P. Mason	I. Wenlock
Hemel Hempstead	E. Dillsworth ...	D. Johnson	P. Fairclough ...

Hornchurch	K. Gaine	D. Pedder	T. Moorcroft ....
Hungerford T...	J. Ashton 46	W. Angell 46	D. Reilly 43
Letchworth G.C.	L. Adcroft 45	D. Dance 43	H. Wilson 42
Lewes	R. Smith	M. Fountain	R. Holder ....
Molesey			
Rainham T.	S. Plant 60	P. Dawkins 54	M. Taylor 52
Southall	P. Griffiths ...53	D. Doyle 46	J. Dudman 40
Tring Town ...	S. Byrne	T. Warren	D. Holt ....
Willesden			
Worthing	N. Cairns 56	T. Barden 54	R. Sopp 52

CHESHIRE COUNTY LEAGUE
DIVISION ONE
LEADING GOALSCORERS

Ashton Utd.			
Bootle	P. Wilkinson ...	R. Wilkinson ...	J. Baker ....
Burscough	W. Jaylock ...23	S. Nolan 10	A. Duffy 10
Chorley	M. Telfer 29	J. Garrett 28	A. Grimshaw ...10
Curzon Ashton	K. Crosswaite 23		
Darwen.............	C. Smith 12	G. Isherwood 9	G. Johnston ... 8
Droylsden.........	N. Nicklin	L. Hughes	J. Gannon ....
Fleetwood	S. Brooks 10	N. Moran 9	B. Berry 8
Formby	C. Culley	C. Lam	R. Pascoe ......
Horwich R.M.I.	J. Pearson......	G. Baker.......	P. Burrows ......
Hyde United ...	D. Holt 16	S. Johnson ... 9	J. Golder....... 8
Leek Town	J. Key 12	K. Braithwaite11	G. Hamlets 11
Nantwich T.	P. Reid 17	I. Challinor ...14	K. Westwood 10
New Brighton ...			
New Mills	A. Clerk	B. Burch	
Radcliffe B.	J. Denham ...13	D. Norbury ...6	M. Capstick ... 5
Rhyl	S. Morris 28	K. Lewis 11	L. Lommand ... 6
Rossendale Utd			
St Helens T.......	G. Robinson 18	J. McGuire ... 8	A. Richardson 7
Stalybridge C. ...	T. Cook.......	K. Kielan	K. Mason ......
Winsford Utd. ...	R. Fraser 19	G. Smith 14	J. Flaherty 10

CHESHIRE COUNTY LEAGUE
DIVISION ONE
MOST APPEARANCES

Ashton Utd.			
Bootle	D. Mortimer	J. Day	J. Mortimer ......
Burscough	A. Bowen 40	A. Duffy 39	J. Moran ... 36
Chorley.............	C. Hope 58	J. Wood 58	J. Garrett 57
Curzon Ashton	C. Matthews...43	J. Lumas 41	K. Crosthwaite 41
Darwen.............	F. Roberts 41	B. Redhead ...39	B. Fox 36
			R. Brooks 36
Droylsden.........	N. Nicklin	W. Roberts	S. Wilkinson ...
Fleetwood	A. Tuson 50	S. Brooks 43	N. Moran 41
Formby	K. Skupski	A. Cahill	L. Cray ......
Horwich R.M.I.	B. Kershaw	W. Greenan	G. Foster ......
Hyde United ...	N. Colbourne 50	D. Holt 48	A. Steenson ...47

Leek Town ...... M. Brindley ...43 K. Braithwaite 42 G. Hamlets ...41
Nantwich T. ... P. Mayman ...46 K. Roche ...44 K. Westwood 44
New Brighton ...
New Mills ... M. Stevens ... D. Bell .... C. Hudders ......
Radcliffe B. ...... B. Tonge ......42 J. Heyes ......41 J. Denham 40
            I. Edwards 40
Rhyl .... S. Morris ... J. Crinigan ...... K. Lewis ......
            L. Lomman ......
Rossendale Utd. ...
St Helens T. ...... A. Sharrock ...41 S. Tickle ...40
      A. Richardson 41
Stalybridge C. ... T. Cook ...... K. Kielan .... K. Mason ....
            G. Forshaw ......
Winsford Utd. ... M. Roberts ...52 D. Elder ......50 G. Carr 49

DRYBROUGH NORTHERN LEAGUE
LEADING GOALSCORERS

Ashington	D. Brown 27	B. Pringle 19	I. Donaldson 4	
Billingham S.	A. McKinnell 18	P. Cook......15	T. Gaffney ...12	
Bishop Auckland	T. Sword 35	M. Gooding ...19	T. Waugh ...13	
Blyth Spartans ...	T. Johnson ...18	P. Davies 15	L. Mutrie ...14	
Consett	K. Cross 38	D. Rutherford 33	A. Foggon ...17	
			G. Hindson ...17	
Crook Town	P. Bailes 17	D. Newton ... 9	S. Ogden 7	
Durham City	C. Marshall ...22	M. Bell 6	I. Greener...... 6	
Evenwood T.	R. Beecham ...	K. Close	B. Fowler	
Ferryhill A.W.	J. Grady 12	D. Blades 7	D. Christie	
Horden C.W.	J. Gates	J. Hather	C. Cain	
North Shields ...	M. Moore......24	R. Holmes ...16	I. Mutrie 13	
Penrith	M. Wilson ... 7	G. Rayson ... 5	A. Warner ... 5	
Shildon	K. Stonehouse 18	P. Main 15	C. Smith 8	
South Bank	G. Foster 21	P. Sawden ...16	D. Hume 6	
Spennymoor Utd.	K. Reilly 26	J. Davies 22	G. Hart 14	
Tow Law Town...	T. Mason	A. Liddane	K. Ross	
West Auckland T.	C. Mills......15	G. Richardson10	D. Foster 10	
Whitby Town	B. Ward 18	D. Burluraux 9	C. Gittins 8	
Whitley Bay	Scope 11	Anderson 9	Rafferty 7	
Willington	G. Parnaby ... 9	D. Purdie	R. Pardew...... 7	

DRYBROUGH NORTHERN LEAGUE
MOST APPEARANCES

Ashington	J. Harmeson 44	R. Scott 43	D. Brown 40	
Billingham S.	J. Alderson ...52	M. O'Neill ...49	E. Chamberlin 47	
Bishop Auckland	A. Garron......	M. Gooding ...	T. Waugh	
Blyth Spartans ...	T. Dixon 49	D. Clarke 47	D. Varty 47	
Consett	G. Hindson ...59	T. Dixon Cave 58	J. Swinburn ...58	
			D. Rutherford ...58	
Crook Town	J. Rooney 43	J. Foster 42	A. Butterfield 40	
			M. Newton ... 40	

Durham City	S. Birkenhead 45	J. Raine..........44	D. Parnaby ...41
Evenwood T.	R. Evans	Fowler	K. Anderson ...
Ferryhill A.	K. Ross	W. Langford ...	T. English..........
			D. Christie ......
Horden C.W.	B. McGee	J. Hather	J. Gates ......
North Shields	A. Barker 49	R. Young 48	R. Holmes ...43
Penrith	M. Wilson 30	M. Herding ...27	J. Rayson 26
Shildon	G. Reed 43	C. Dunn 42	B. Dale 42
South Bank	G. Burke 46	R. Robinson...46	A. Lucas 46
Spennymoor Utd.	A. Hickman ...38	K. Reilly	G. Simpson ...37
			D. Curry 37
			A. Porter 37
Tow Law Town...	D. Longstaff ...	R. Ellison	T. Mason ......
West Auckland T.	B. Hardy 44	E. Sharp 43	D. Foster 42
Whitby Town	B. Ward 44	D. Hampton...42	R. Walker ...42
Whitley Bay	I. McDonald 35	T. Young 31	M. Anderson 31
Willington	G. Parnaby ...33	R. Pardew......32	D. Purdie 30

NORTHERN PREMIER LEAGUE
LEADING GOALSCORERS

Burton A.	P. Annable ...10	J. McCann ... 9	G. Fearn....... 9
Buxton	L. Yates 10	D. Herbert ... 8	S. Guest 6
Frickley A.	M. Wadsworth 12	R. Barrett ...10	A. Murray ... 8
Gainsborough T.	M. Boyers 18	S. Downes ...11	
Gateshead	R. Topping ...20	L. Mutrie ...12	K. Heslop ... 9
Goole T.	M. Thompson		
Grantham	R. Cooke 46	R. Norris ...12	D. Benskin ...10
Lancaster C.	K. Dyson 10	G. Cooper ...10	I. Innes 9
			K. Brindle ... 9
Macclesfield T.	J. Fletcher ... 6	N. Boodlen ... 4	C. Skillen ... 4
Marine	D. McClatchley 38	P. Meachin ...33	A. Windsor ...17
			P. Smith 17
Matlock T.	P. Scott 19	N. Fenoughty 17	M. Palmer ...12
Morecambe	N. McLachlan 13	M. Darling ...13	M. Parry ... 7
Mossley	D. Moore 42	I. Smith 39	E. O'Keefe ...31
Netherfield	K. Galley	P. Handley ...	E. Banks ......
Oswestry T.	W. Telford	P. Wilkey	P. Hampson......
Runcorn	B. Whitbread 34	J. Kenyon ...23	M. Scott 15
South Liverpool.	J. Aldridge ...15	S. Smith 13	P. McFerran...11
Southport	J. Beesley ... 8	J. Turner ... 8	J. Gerrard ... 7
Tamworth	R. Miller 13	A. Bourton ...10	P. Langan...... 9
Witton Albion	P. Henderson 33	J. Walker 23	J. White 22
Workington	Gillott 19	Armstrong ...12	D. Irving 12
Worksop T.	P. Fisher	G. Vardy	P. Webb ....

NORTHERN PREMIER LEAGUE
MOST APPEARANCES

Burton A.			
Buxton	W. Boslem ...41	L. Yates 38	K. Deakin ...36
			S. Guest ...36
Frickley A.	T. Meeham	K. Whiteley	M. Long ....

269

Gainsborough T. D. Finch ......55 | B. Williams ...53 | G. Jones 52
L. Harris.......52
Gateshead .... R. McLeod ...53 | K. Heslop ...50 | S. Holbrook 45
Goole T. .... M. Thompson ... | M. Broughton ... | N. Sellers ....
Grantham .... N. Jarvis .... | C. Chamber-lain .... | C. Gardiner ....
Lancaster C. ...... I. Innes ......54 | G. Benfold ...53 | S. Cox 52
Macclesfield T. . J. Fletcher ...35 | L. Morrell ...30 | R. Higham ...30
Marine .... D. Hughes ...64 | D. McClatchley | P. Smith 62
Matlock T. ...... M. Fen-noughty ...43 | A. Lukasir ...42 | P. Scott..........41
Morecambe ...... M. Eatough ...44 | J. Street ......42 | M. Parry 42
Mossley .... D. Vaughan ...61 | A. Brown ......60 | J. Fitton 59
I. Smith 59
Netherfield ...... M. Burgess ...... | N. Tomlinson ... | P. Handley ......
Oswestry T. ...... R. Edwards ...... | I. Fraser .... | S. Blakemore ...
Runcorn .... T. Rutter ......65 | B. Whitbread 64 | Kenyon 62
South Liverpool.. R. Perkins....54 | P. Long ......51 | L. Koo 45
Southport .... R. Pickering 43 | B. Knowles ...41 | N. Halsall ...33
Tamworth .... G. Taylor ...... | K. Lane......... | D. Devline ......
Witton Albion ... R. Fletcher ...64 | A. Keyes ......61 | B. Griffin 60
Workington ...... Johnson ......55 | McDonald ...52 | Leng 52
Worksop T. ...... J. Conroy ...... | P. Evans .... | K. Woods ......

SOUTHERN LEAGUE (SOUTH)
LEADING GOALSCORERS

Addlestone.........
Andover .... A. Green ......24 | J. Howarth ...14 | A. Kebby 6
Ashford .... D. Clay ...... 8 | P. McRobert 7 | A. Smith 6
E. Wynton 6
Aylesbury Utd. .... V. Melisi ......17 | G. Harthill ... 9 | D. O'Reilly ... 6
Basingstoke ...... P. Simpson ...... | D. Eddie .... | A. Cooper............
Bognor Regis ...... A. Unitt ......22 | K. Clements ... 12 | D. Loney 6
S. Chappell 6
Canterbury C. ... J. Young ......10 | P. Wordall ... 7 | G. Vincer 6
Chelmsford C. .. F. Peterson ...19 | C. Damudas... 9 | D. Mandell ... 8
Crawley .... B. Roberts ...12 | M. Elliott ......10 | R. Fitzgerald 8
Dartford .... G. Williams ...10 | P. Hunt......... 9 | G. Bray 8
Dorchester T. ...
Dover .... I. Cook ......16 | P. Hilton ......13 | T. Horsfall ...12
K. Rogers.......12
Dunstable T. ...... A. Cowan ...12 | G. Ward ...... 9 | D. Martin 8
Fareham T. ...... K. Albury ...24 | A. Stewart ... 14 | K. Smart 10
Folkestone S. ...... F. Ovard ......31 | R. Summers...11 | K. Robinson 11
Gosport B. ...... R. Coulbert ...28 | J. Hawes ......19 | K. Warren ......
Hastings Utd. ...... S. Gill ......16 | W. Peacock ...13 | C. Harris 10
Hillingdon B. ...... E. Reeve ......20 | S. Melledew ...16 | A. Davies 10
Hounslow T. ...... M. Francis ...19 | T. Burge ......11 | J. Auguste...... 6
Margate ....
Poole T. .... C. Guy ......12 | J. Olsen ...... 9 | M. Barber 8
Salisbury.............
Tonbridge .... R. Haies ......13 | I. Hamilton ... 9 | K. Walsh 9

| Waterlooville | ... | J. Robson | ...14 | M. Mellows | ...10 | M. Seymour... 10 |
| | | | | | | M. Bennett ...10 |

Addlestone	......					
Andover	....	A. Green	...50	P. Pollard	42	B. Humphries 40
Ashford	....	P. Nash	...46	P. Carmen	...44	D. Partington 44
						P. McRobert 44
Aylesbury Utd.	...	D. O'Reilly	...44	R. Lucas	37	C. Austin 37
Basingstoke	......	J. Armon	....	D. Husbands	...	P. Simpson .....
Bognor Regis...	...	M. Pullen	...50	K. Clements	48	P. Pullen 48
Canterbury C.	...	D. Walton	...46	G. Vincer	...45	J. Young 43
Chelmsford C.	...	P. Coker	...39	F. Peterson	...38	B. Penn 37
Crawley	....	J. Leedham	...53	B. Roberts	...52	S. Breach 51
						R. Fitz-
						gerald 51
Dartford	......	R. Tumbridge	59	R. Keen	45	A. Durney ...45
Dorchester T.	......					
Dover	....	A. Knight	......	C. Hamshare	...	P. Brooks .....
Dunstable T.	...	N. Blackwell...43		A. Malcolm	...39	A. Cowan 31
Fareham T.	...	P. Grant	...43	S. Brown	42	K. Albury ...35
Folkestone S.	...	K. Robinson	......	J. Smith.........		M. Goodburn ...
Gosport B.	......	A. Maloney	...48	R. Coulbert	...48	N. Wood 48
Hastings Utd.	...	S. Gill	...39	G. Armstrong	40	M. Westburgh 37
Hillingdon B.	...	K. Millett	...58	R. Wain-		G. Williams ...55
				wright	58	
Hounslow T.	...	R. Noad	48	M. Francis	...45	D. Pipe 42
Margate	....					
Poole T.	......	D. Burns	38	P. Reader	37	B. Collie 35
Salisbury...	......					
Tonbridge	......	B. Richardson	53	S. Briggs	51	K. Waish 50
Waterlooville...	...	M. Seymour...55		M. Mellows	...52	A. Stones 50

Alvechurch	......	P. Harper	19	J. Chester	16	R. Cope	11
Banbury Utd.	......	Worthington	18	K. Wilson	...11	Slaughter	 8
Barry Town	......	R. Smith	......	P. Lents.........		J. O'Brien	......
Bedford Town	......	E. Roberts	...24	T. Mortimer...23		J. Brown	21
Bedworth	......	D. Connay	...22	R. Palmer	... 9	S. Lee	 7
Bridgend	......	G. Bennett	...21	J. McInch	...12	P. Bannon...	...
Bromsgrove R.	......	S. Smith	... 9	N. Fagan	... 6	G. Smith	... 5
Cambridge C.	...	D. Simmons	... 15	S. Kearns	... 7	K. Herridge	... 7
Cheltenham T.	...	D. Lewis	...26	J. Davies	...16	D. Browns	... 8
Corby	......	W. McCowatt	...	J. Powell	......	T. Veasey	......
Enderby T.	......						
Gloucester C.	......	T. Paterson	...13	J. Evans	10	K. Griffin	10
Kidderminster H.	...	P. Mullen	...42	J. Griffiths	...12	D. Foxwell	...11
King's Lynn	......	R. Rudd	...17	D. Wiles	...17	R. McManus	8
Merthyr Tydfil	...	R. Pratt	...34	P. Caviel	...19		
Milton Keynes	...	K. King	17	D. Earl	... 9	G. Collier	... 6
Minehead	......	W. Brown	...22	R. Guscott	... 8	S. Whitmore...	8
Stourbridge	......						

Taunton T.	.... C. Callaway ...26	E. Aherne......13	S. Summers... 10
Trowbridge T.	... R. Legg..........21	A. Gilligan ... 9	K. Griffin 8
Wellingborough T.	....		
Witney T.	.... C. Daley 12	P. Dallaway ... 8	T. Stokes 8

SOUTHERN LEAGUE (MIDLAND)
MOST APPEARANCES

Alvechurch	...... A. Travis 40	S. O'Driscoll 40	C. Birch 39
Banbury Utd.	... J. Hastie	A. Hyatt	D. Evans ......
Barry Town	.... J. Emmanuel ...	T. Nott	M. Donovan ...
Bedford Town	... R. Folds	E. Roberts ...	T. Gould ......
Bedworth	.... W. Moore......54	D. Conway ...48	A. Ashley 45
Bridgend	.... G. Bennett ...37	J. McInch......33	J. Humphries 32
Bromsgrove R.	... A. Parsons ...46	S. O'Mearr ...46	A. Lloyd 42
Cambridge C	.... M. Green 41	K. Herridge ...40	D. Hill 40
			A. Tuddenham 40
Cheltenham T.	... J. Murphy......52	D. Lewis 51	J. Davies 50
Corby T.	.... A. McIlwain ...	D. Dall	D. Gill ......
Enderby T.	....		
Gloucester C.	.... J. Turner	G. Mockridge ...	J. Evans ......
Kidderminster H.	P. Mullen 58	J. Chambers ...55	D. Seddon 47
King's Lynn	.... M. Wright 49	C. Watts 49	R. McManus 48
Merthyr Tydfil	.... D. Payne	I. Docherty ...	P. Caviel ......
Milton Keynes	... K. King..........52	R. Taylor 50	R. Goodman 49
Minehead	.... A. Impey	S. Carter	A. Clavsen ......
Stourbridge	....		
Taunton T.	.... E. Aherne......52	G. Smith 52	B. McAvley ...51
Trowbridge T.	... K. Tanner 53	R. Legg..........51	D. Moss 50
Wellingborough T.	....		
Witney T.	.... A. Jefferies ...54	K. Baker 52	R. Clark 50

CLUB CAREER
GOALSCORING RECORDS

QUALIFICATION: 250 GOALS

Don Spendlove	Rhyl	647
Tony Horseman	Wycombe Wanderers	525
George Brown	Bromley	510
Peter Wassall	Kidderminster Harriers	448
Jack Bentley	Telford United	431
Edgar Kail	Dulwich Hamlet	427
Arthur Morse	Bridgend Town	377
John Woodley	Oxford City	350
Billy Wright	Whitley Bay	331
Rodney Lawton	Curzon Ashton	328
Norman Dearlove	Carshalton Athletic	306
Dave Taylor	Yeovil Town	285
'Farmer' Haines	Weymouth	275
Mike Clausen	Maidenhead United	274
Dave Lewis	Cheltenham Town	256
Neville Fox	Barking	253

CLUB CAREER
APPEARANCES RECORDS

THE '600' CLUB

A. Hobson	Weymouth	1,060
M. Wright	King's Lynn	1,040
J. Woodley	Oxford City	896
D. Moore	Dagenham	853
J. Bentley	Telford United	835
C. Hooper	Bromsgrove Rovers	835
G. Brown	Bromley	820
A. Burns	Dartford	800
A. Clausen	Minehead	739
P. Giggle	Hitchin Town	736
J. Maggs	Crawley Town	720
R. Thorndale	Cheltenham Town	701
H. Dunn	Scarborough	700
S. Logan	Kidderminster Harriers	700
L. Harris	Yeovil Town	691
A. Payne	Taunton Town	684
M. Brown	Gainsborough Trinity	669
B. Oakley	Whitley Bay	657
D. Jones	Egham Town	652
H. Brockington	Sittingbourne	650
S. Page	Harwich & Parkeston	650
M. Davis	Buxton	620
R. Ashby	Kettering Town	616
T. Monkhouse	Evenwood Town	600

CLUB RECORDS 1978-79

Club	League	Leading Goal-scorers		Most Appearances	
Accrington Stanley	C.C. (Div 2)	D. Hargreaves	35	I. Wilcox	44
Alfreton Town ...	....	K. Greaves	......	K. Greaves	....
Almondsbury Greenway	G.C.	S. Price	50	P. Bowers	49
Basildon Utd.......	E. S. K. A.	A. Selwyn	43	S. Bettis	43
				K. Shields	43
Belper Town	M. Co.	P. Stone	7	P. Stone	....
		P. Bingham	7		
Bideford............	W.	P. Druce	22	A. Hooker	....
Bilston	W.M.	A. Price	......	D. Walker	....
Blakenall	W.M.	P. Walters	......	S. Taylor	....
Blue Star	We.	P. Dixon	16	K. Tweddle	45
Boston	M.Co.	N. Mallinder	36	R. Duncan	46
				F. Taylor	46
				J. McPherson	46

273

Club	League	Player 1	No.	Player 2	No.
Bourne Town	U.C.	M. Burrell	16	N. Mann	43
Brandon Utd.	N.A.	T. Holden	33	T. Holden	38
				C. Hallimond	38
				W. White	38
Bridgnorth T.	M.C.	V. Francis	16	W. Ball	50
Bridgwater T.	W.	N. Sutton	17	P. Charles	
Bridlington T.	Y.	Caldwell	10	Alderslade	24
Bridlington Trin.	M.Co.	P. Taylor	26	P. Blackburn	
Brierley Hill All.	W.M.	R. Ball	26	M. Rich	48
Burnham	K.A.	K. White	19	M. James	
Bury Town	T. & C.	R. Knights	43	R. Knights	42
				N, Garnham	42
				D. Dodds	42
Chalfont St Peter	K.A.	K. Shead		G. Lester	
Chatham T.	K.	B. Harrison	15	A. Hughes	44
(Medway T.)				S. Rennie	44
Chipping Norton Town	M.Co.	B. McCrae	29	S. Rennie	
Clacton Town	T. & C.	A. Talty	8	C. Hazelton	50
Clevedon Town	W.	J. Patch	21	R. Mabbutt	42
Crockenhill	K.	T. Elphick		T. Elphick	
Dawlish	W.	A. Jennings		S. Sullivan	
Dewby Utd.	Y.	R. Davidson	18	M. Ryan	30
Eastwood Town	M.Co.	M. Wright	24	K. Shaw	
Edgware	K.A.	A. Warwick	27	J. Rowland	32
Emley	Y.	J. Wilkinson	31	R. Dennis	42
Falmouth T.	W.	A. Leigh	19	D. Ferrett	37
Faversham T.	K.	D. Housden	41	D. Housden	
Frome Town	W.	S. Gay	12	S. Gay	42
Glastonbury	W.	A. Gould	7	L. Temel	
Glossop	C.C.(Div 2)	S. Lennon	21	S. Lennon	39
Gorleston	T. & C.	J. Blyth	31	R. Barrett	58
Great Yarmouth	T. & C.	N. Hart	34	P. Kirk	51
Guiseley	Y.	J. Waddilor	7	P. Barlow	
Halesowen	W.M.	G. Moss	19	P. Checkett	44
Harrogate	Y.	J. Hague		J. Hague	
Haverill Rov.	T. & C.	J. Thomson	39	S. Halls	
Hednesford T.	W.M.	J. Branch	21	B. Sweet	44
Hinckley Ath.	W.M.	S. Dean		S. Dean	
Hythe Town	K.	P. Prior	37	P. Prior	41
Irthlingborough D.	U.C.	K. Kettleborough	36	S. Payne	59
Kempston Rov.	U.C.	K. Parker	10	R. Shreeves	43
Kirkby T.	C.C.(Div 2)	D. Farnsworth		W. Broom	
				M. Smith	
Leyton Wingate	K.A.	L. Lynch	19	K. Moore	45
Liskeard	S.W.	B. Murphy	31	A. Coe	63
Long Eaton Utd.	U.C.	I. Muir	15	J. Inger	46
Lowestoft T.	T. & C.	T. Cheek	21	B. Bullen	57
Lye Town	W.M.	R. Sidaway	27	K. Morton	51
March Town Utd.	T. & C.	D. Eldred	16	M. Simmons	52
Marlow	K.A.	T. Staines		M. McKeown	
Mexborough T.	M.Co.	S. Kulic	20	A. Cooper	46

Club	Code				
Middlewich Ath.	C.C. (Div 2)	S. Beresford	...10	P. Newton	34
Newport (I.O.W.)	H.	R. Mussle-White	36	D. Young	......
North Ferriby Utd.	Y.	S. Cockin		P. Start	......
Peacehaven & T.	S.	N. Barrett		A. Plant	......
Prescott	C.C. (Div 2)	S. Malloy		M. Kinsella	......
Prestwich Heys	C.C. (Div 2)	G. Howarth	...18	P. Critchley	......
Pwllheli D.	W.L. (N)	J. Morgan	...28	A. Williams	......
Ruislip Manor	K.A.	J. Ashe		A. Stevens	......
Saffron Walden T.	T. & C.	L. Page	...17	K. Moore	48
St Neots Town	U.C.	T. Minett	...31	G. How	48
Saltash Utd.	W.	D. Rickard	...18	R. Swiggs	37
Sheffield	Y.	D. Lewis	7	C. Gilbody	34
Sheppey Utd.	K.	P. McKenna	...22	S. Williams	52
Shepshed C.'house	L.S.	W. Wilcox		D. Blockley	......
Sittingbourne	K.	A. Peploe	...12	W. Butler	......
Skegness T	M.Co.	P. Piggott	...34	D. Birkinshaw	50
Skelmersdale Utd.	C.C. (Div 2)	A. Gray	...14	A. Gray	39
				R. Goulbourne	39
Stonehouse	G.C.	C. Chivers	...20	D. Gallagher	......
Sutton Coldfield	M.C.	E. Pugh	...42	B. Kenning	47
Sutton Town	M.Co.	Bentley	...13	Fisher	45
Tiverton Town	W.	C. Venner	...16	N. Howe	45
				M. Howe	45
Tividale	W.M.	P. Wilkinson	...22	R. Porter	......
Ton Pentre	W.L.	K. Davies	...22	K. Davies	45
Tunbridge Wells	K.	T. Moss	...16	M. Crittendew	...47
Uxbridge	K.A.	D. Faulkes		R. Nichols	51
V. S. Rugby	W.M.	G. Smith	...10	C. Burton	39
Warrington Town	C.C. (Div 2)	E. Rathbone		D. Gleave	......
Welton Rovers	W.	G. Withey	...21	M. Bennett	56
Weston S. Mare	W.	R. Honiecombe	19	H. Thomas	44
Whickham	We.	D. Callaghan		T. Callaghan	47
Willenhall T.	W.M.	G. Matthews	...32	J. Newell	50
Windsor & Eton	K.A.	L. Cadogan	...20	K. Beckett	50
Winterton Rangers	Y.	R. Hughes	...17	N. Jackson	30
Wisbech Town	T. & C.	G. Rider	...12	D. Clarke	51
Wren Rovers	L.C.	V. Sheilds	...23	D. Roach	37
				V. Sheilds	37
Yorkshire Amateurs	Y.	P. Wormley	... 5	G. Hurst	29

The following codes apply to the league information above:
C.C. (Cheshire County); E.S. (Essex Senior); G.C. (Gloucestershire County); H. (Hampshire); K. (Kent); K.A. (Kingsmead Athenian); L.C. (Lancashire Combination); L.S. (Leicestershire Senior); M.C. (Midland Combination); M.Co. (Midland Counties); N.A. (Northern Alliance); S. (Sussex); S.W. (South Western); T. & C. (Town and Country); U.C. (United Counties); W. (Western); We. (Wearside); W.L. (Welsh League); W.M. (West Midlands); Y. (Yorkshire).

Rothmans Football Yearbook

PAST EDITIONS   The following past editions of *Rothmans Football Yearbook* are still available:

1973-74	(limp edition)	£1.30
1975-76	(limp edition)	£2.75
1975-76	(cased edition)	£3.75
1976-77	(limp edition)	£2.50
1977-78	(limp edition)	£2.95
1977-78	(cased edition)	£4.50
1978-79	(limp edition)	£3.25
1978-79	(cased edition)	£4.95
1979-80	(limp edition)	£3.75
1979-80	(cased edition)	£5.50

Orders for the above books should be sent to Queen Anne Press Cash Sales, 9 Partridge Drive, Orpington, Kent, with a cheque or Postal Order made out for the amount shown plus 40p postage and packing.

A limited number of last season's *F.A. Non-League Football Annual 1978-79* are still available from Tony Williams Football Promotions, 130 High Street, Hungerford, Berkshire, price 80p, inclusive of postage and packing.

ANGLO-ITALIAN FOOTBALL

ALITALIA CHALLENGE CUP 1979

Wednesday 14 March 1979

Chieti 2 (Luzi, Oliva)   Matlock Town 1 (Wilson)
Cremonese 1 (Mondonico)   Nuneaton Borough 0
Juniorcasale 1 (Moneta)   Sutton United 1 (Frazer)
Pisa 1 (Quarella)   Barnet 0

Saturday 17 March 1979

Chieti 3 (Jannillo, Beccaria,   Barnet 0
  (Riccardino)
Cremonese 0   Sutton United 1 (Waldon)
Juniorcasale 2 (Motta, Pozzi)   Nuneaton Borough 0
Pisa 2 (Barbana, Cannata)   Matlock Town 1 (Wilson)

Wednesday 11 April 1979

Barnet 5 (McCormack, Turner,   Cremonese 2 (Chigioni, Bonomi)
  O'Hare, Sperrin, Cleary)
Matlock Town 2 (Fenoughty 2)   Juniorcasale 0
Nuneaton Borough 0   Chieti 1 (Antignani)
Sutton United 1 (Mckinnon – pen.)   Pisa 0

Saturday 14 April 1979

Barnet 3 (O'Hare, Sperrin,   Juniorcasale 2 (Pozzi, Motta)
  Townsend)
Matlock Town 2 (Whiteley, Scott)   Cremonese 0
Nuneaton Borough 3 (Cooper,   Pisa 0
  Dale – pen., Dale)
Sutton United 0   Chiete 1 (Beccaria)

TABLES

English Clubs

	P	W	D	L	F	A	Pts.
Sutton Utd	4	2	1	1	3	2	7
Matlock T.	4	2	0	2	8	4	6
Barnet	4	2	0	2	8	8	6
Nuneaton B.	4	1	0	3	3	4	3

Italian Clubs

	P	W	D	L	F	A	Pts.
Chieti	4	4	0	0	7	1	12
Pisa	4	2	0	2	5	5	6
Juniorcasale	4	1	1	2	5	6	4
Cremonese	4	1	0	3	3	8	3

FINAL

Chieti 1 Sutton United 2 (Southam, Rains) (in Chieti, on Wednesday 25 April 1979)

F.A. AMATEUR CUP WINNERS 1894-1974

Year	Venue	Winners	Runners-up	Score	
1894	Richmond	Old Carthusians	Casuals	2-1	
1895	Leeds	Middlesbro'	Old Carthusians	2-1	
1896	Leicester	Bishop Auckland	RA (Portsmouth)	1-0	
1897	Darlington	Old Carthusians	Stockton	4-1	after 1-1 draw at Tufnell Park
1898	Crystal Palace	Middlesbro'	Uxbridge	2-1	
1899	Middlesbro'	Stockton	Harwich & Parkeston	1-0	
1900	Leicester	Bishop Auckland	Lowestoft T.	5-1	
1901	Ipswich	Crook T.	King's Lynn	3-0	after 1-1 draw at Harwich
1902	Leeds	Old Malvernians	Bishop Auckland	5-1	
1903	Darlington	Stockton	Oxford C.	1-0	after 0-0 draw at Reading
1904	Bradford	Sheffield	Ealing	3-1	
1905	Shepherds Bush	West Hartlepool	Clapton	3-2	
1906	Stockton	Oxford C.	Bishop Auckland	3-0	
1907	Chelsea	Clapton	Stockton	2-1	
1908	Bishop Auckland	Depot Bn. R.E.	Stockton	2-1	
1909	Ilford	Clapton	Eston U.	6-0	
1910	Bishop Auckland	RMLI (Gosport)	South Bank	2-1	
1911	Herne Hill	Bromley	Bishop Auckland	1-0	
1912	Middlesbro'	Stockton	Eston U.	1-0	after 0-0 draw at Middlesbro'
1913	Bishop Auckland	South Bank	Oxford C.	1-0	after 1-1 draw at Reading
1914	Leeds	Bishop Auckland	Northern Nomads	1-0	
1915	Millwall	Clapton	Bishop Auckland	1-0	
1920	Millwall	Dulwich Hamlet	Tufnell Park	1-0	after extra time
1921	Middlesbro'	Bishop Auckland	Swindon Vic.	4-2	

278

Year				Score	Notes
1922	Middlesbro'	Bishop Auckland	South Bank	5-2	after extra time
1923	C. Palace	London Caledonians	Evesham T.	2-1	after extra time
1924	Millwall	Clapton	Erith & Belvedere	3-0	
1925	Millwall	Clapton	Southall	2-1	
1926	Sunderland	Northern Nomads	Stockton T	7-1	
1927	Millwall	Leyton	Barking	3-1	
1928	Middlesbro'	Leyton	Cockfield	3-2	
1929	Arsenal	Ilford	Leyton	3-1	
1930	West Ham	Ilford	B'mouth Gasw'ks Ath.	5-1	
1931	Arsenal	Wycombe W.	Hayes	1-0	
1932	West Ham	Dulwich Hamlet	Marine (Liverpool)	7-1	
1933	Darlington	Kingstonian	Stockton	4-1 1-1	at Dulwich
1934	West Ham	Dulwich Hamlet	Leyton	2-1	
1935	Chelsea	Bishop Auckland	Wimbledon	2-1	
1936	West Ham	Casuals	Ilford	2-0	after 1-1 draw at Selhurst Park
1937	West Ham	Dulwich Hamlet	Leyton	2-0	
1938	Millwall	Bromley	Erith & Belvedere	1-0	
1939	Sunderland	Bishop Auckland	Willington	3-0	after extra time
1946	Chelsea	Barnet	Bishop Auckland	3-2	
1947	Arsenal	Leytonstone	Wimbledon	2-1	
1948	Chelsea	Leytonstone	Barnet	1-0	
1949	Wembley	Bromley	Romford	1-0	
1950	Wembley	Willington	Bishop Auckland	4-0	
1951	Wembley	Pegasus	Bishop Auckland	2-1	
1952	Wembley	Walthamstow Ave.	Leyton	2-1	after extra time
1953	Wembley	Pegasus	Harwich & Parkeston	6-0	
1954	Middlesbro'	Crook T.	Bishop Auckland	1-0	after two draws: at Wembley (2-2) Newcastle (2-2)
1955	Wembley	Bishop Auckland	Hendon	2-0	
1956	Middlesbro'	Bishop Auckland	Corinthian-Casuals	4-1 1-1	at Wembley
1957	Wembley	Bishop Auckland	Wycombe W.	3-1	
1958	Wembley	Bishop Auckland	Ilford	3-0	
1959	Wembley	Crook T.	Barnet	3-2	

Year	Venue			Score	
1960	Wembley	Hendon	Kingstonian	2-1	
1961	Wembley	Walthamstow Ave.	W. Auckland T.	2-1	
1962	Middlesbro'	Crook T.	Hounslow T.	4-0	1-1 at Wembley
1963	Wembley	Wimbledon	Sutton U.	4-2	
1964	Wembley	Crook T.	Enfield	2-1	
1965	Wembley	Hendon	Whitby T.	3-1	
1966	Wembley	Wealdstone	Hendon	3-1	
1967	Manchester	Enfield	Skelmersdale U.	3-0	0-0 at Wembley
1968	Wembley	Leytonstone	Chesham U.	1-0	
1969	Wembley	North Shields	Sutton U.	2-1	
1970	Wembley	Enfield	Dagenham	5-1	
1971	Wembley	Skelmersdale U.	Dagenham	4-1	
1972	Wembley	Hendon	Enfield	2-0	
1973	Wembley	Walton & Hersham	Slough Town	1-0	
1974	Wembley	Bishop's Stortford	Ilford	4-1	

SCOTTISH JUNIOR FOOTBALL

SCOTTISH JUNIOR CUP FINAL REVIEW

Bo'ness United 0 Cumnock Juniors 1 (Flynn – 78 mins)
    Attendance: 13,692 At Hampden Park, Glasgow. Saturday 19 May 1979.

Once again the Scottish Junior Cup Final provided better entertainment than that of the senior occasion. At one time this game looked as if it would also succumb to the jinx which had seemed to blight strikers in recent Hampden cup finals, but Flynn, with 12 minutes remaining, headed in a Docherty cross from the right and that effort from six yards out was the only time the ball entered the net although there were many near misses before and after the goal in a game which was a fine advertisement for Scottish Junior Football.

    Thus the Cup went to the small Ayrshire town for the first time and the team justly deserved it. With eight former senior players, Cumnock had a big advantage in experience, which was crucial. Reynolds had, in fact, been in the Airdrie team which lost a senior final to Celtic in 1975, whilst McAnespie had once faced Rangers at Hampden Park when playing for Ayr United in a semi-final. With Lawrence Docherty also outstanding it was a great day for Cumnock, but Bo'ness were far from outclassed and helped to make it a memorable match.

Bo'ness United Howie; Robertson, McQueen, Dunlevie (Ward) (Taylor), Stewart, Boyd, Shields, Masterton, Logan, Reid, MacDonald.

Cumnock Juniors Bently; Baton, Barrowman, Reynolds, McCulloch, McAnespie, Dickson, Doherty, Docherty, Flynn, Murray (Paton).

Referee Mr D. McVicar, Central.

OTHER SCOTTISH JUNIOR CUP FINALS

Cowdenbeath Cup Final
Halbeath 5   Oakley United 2
East of Scotland Junior Cup (Laidlaw Cup Final)
Haddington 3   Bonnybridge 2
Ayrshire League Cup Final (Jackie Scarlett Cup)
Cumnock Juniors 2   Irvine Meadow 0
Central League Cup Final
Pollok 2   Port Glasgow 0

HIGHLAND LEAGUE

	P	W	D	L	F	A	Pts.
Keith	30	21	6	3	67	25	48
Caley	30	20	5	5	59	26	45
Peterhead	30	19	5	6	62	32	43
Invern. Th.	30	18	2	10	91	43	38
Ross Co.	30	17	4	9	52	33	38
Elgin	30	14	7	9	64	49	35
Buckie Th.	30	14	6	10	61	49	34
Dev'vale	30	14	6	10	63	57	34
Rothes	30	9	10	11	47	60	28
Fraserb'gh	30	10	7	13	45	50	27
Nairn Co.	30	9	6	15	47	56	24
Brora Ran.	30	9	4	17	45	51	22
Clach	30	8	3	19	45	75	19
Huntly	30	7	4	19	51	66	18
Forres	30	6	3	21	52	94	17
Lossie	30	3	4	23	24	109	10

TAYSIDE JUNIOR LEAGUE

DIVISION ONE

	P	W	D	L	F	A	Pts.
Carnoustie	26	19	3	4	65	33	41
Stobswell	26	19	3	4	57	26	41
Lochee Utd	26	14	6	6	72	41	34
Brechin Vics	26	9	8	9	55	48	26
Blairgowrie	26	9	8	9	53	46	26
Arbroath Vics	26	11	6	10	46	51	26
Downfield	26	11	4	11	51	57	26
Kirrie Thistle	26	8	10	8	37	43	26
Violet	26	11	3	12	44	48	25
Osborne	26	9	6	11	40	46	24
Kinnoull	26	9	5	12	58	56	23
Crieff E'grove	26	6	7	13	35	55	19
Bankfoot	26	2	10	14	34	68	14
Forfar Albion	26	3	7	16	39	68	13

DIVISION TWO

	P	W	D	L	F	A	Pts.
North End	26	18	5	3	69	33	41
Harp	26	17	5	4	52	23	39
Forfar W.E.	26	15	4	7	55	39	34
Luncarty	26	14	5	7	53	30	33
Coupar Angus	26	11	5	10	48	46	27
St Josephs	26	10	7	9	47	51	27
Jeanfield Sw'ts	26	9	8	9	40	35	26
Arbroath S.C.	26	7	11	8	48	46	25
Perth Celtic	26	8	8	10	43	43	24
Broty Athletic	26	7	8	11	47	53	22
East Craigie	26	7	8	11	36	52	22
Montrose R'lea	26	6	6	14	50	64	18
Balbeggie	26	6	6	14	40	64	18
Alyth Utd	26	2	4	20	31	80	8

FIFE JUNIOR LEAGUE
A DIVISION

	P	W	D	L	F	A	Pts.
Oakley United	14	9	5	0	40	19	21
Glenrothes	14	8	5	1	27	7	21
Newburgh	14	6	5	3	31	23	17
Lochgelly A.	14	5	2	7	28	35	14
Dundonald B.	14	3	6	5	27	29	12
Halbeath	14	5	2	7	27	31	12
Thornton Hibs	14	4	1	9	20	34	9
Clackmannan	14	3	0	11	21	43	6

Two points deducted from Oakley United and awarded to Lochgelly Albert.

B DIVISION

	P	W	D	L	F	A	Pts.
St Andrews U.	16	10	4	2	32	15	24
Lochore W.	16	10	3	3	32	15	23
Leven	16	9	3	4	42	22	21
K'Caldy Y.M.	16	9	3	4	39	25	21
Jubilee Ath.	16	6	5	5	32	29	17
Tulliallan Th.	16	5	5	6	34	35	15
Comrie Col.	16	6	3	7	28	35	15
North Fife	16	1	4	11	19	39	6
Frances Col.	16	0	2	14	15	58	2

FIFE REGION HONOURS LIST
FIFE REGION LEAGUE AND CUP WINNERS

Tennent Caledonian League A Division
winners Oakley United   runners-up Glenrothes
B Division winners St Andrews United   runners-up Lochore Welfare
Fife Cup winners Glenrothes
Cowdenbeath Cup winners Halbeath
Fife Drybrough Cup winners Glenrothes
Haigs Whisky League Cup winners Halbeath
Clackmannan and Thornton Hibs are relegated from the A Division and
St Andrews United and Lochore Welfare being promoted.

NON-LEAGUE FOOTBALL PROGRAMMES

Once again interest in club programmes at this level of the game has increased, possibly because many clubs now sell productions which resemble magazines rather than the old-fashioned team sheets. Of the issues received during the season, the programmes of Nuneaton Borough, Worthing, Altrincham, Farnborough Town, Kettering and Northwood and many others were very impressive. The standard was superb and no doubt, knowing the number of journalists involved in the editorial work at clubs across the country, it will improve yet again this season.

The official results of The Wirral Programme Club Non-League survey, supervised by Ian Runham, are as follows:

Best Non-League Programme 1978-79
1st Farnborough Town (Berger Isthmian League, Div 2)
2nd Andover (Southern League Div 1 South)
3rd Northwood (Hellenic League)
Best Special Issue
Threave Rovers v E. Stirling
Top Thirty in Britain
1 Farnborough T. 84 pts; 2 Andover 83 pts; 3 Northwood 82 pts; 4 Gateshead 80 pts; 5 Guisborough T. 78 pts; 6 Altrincham 77 pts; 7 Southwick 76 pts; 8 Nuneaton B. 74 pts; 9 Basingstoke T. and Marine 72 pts each; 11 Hungerford T.; 12 Braintree and Dover; 14 Barnet; 15 Grantham; 16 Addlestone; 17 Hillingdon B. and Saltash U.; 19 Dartford; 20 Lancaster C. and Maidstone U.; 22 Dagenham and Worthing; 24 Southall and Ealing B.; 25 Buckie T. and Oxford C.; 27 Aylesbury U. and Chelmsford C. and Chorley; 30 Barnstaple T.

Senior League Placings			
Berger Isthmian	Farnborough T. (1)	Hungerford T. (11)	Dagenham (22)
Cheshire County	Marine (9)	Chorley (27)	Stalybridge C. Winsford
Northern	North Shields	Blyth Spartans	Durham City
Northern Premier	Gateshead (4)	Altrincham (6)	Lancaster City (20)
Southern	Andover (2)	Nuneaton B. (8)	Basingstoke T. (9)
Western	Saltash Utd. (17)	Barnstaple T. (30)	Bideford
West Midlands	Coventry Sporting	Shifnal T.	Hednesford

Some small awards will be presented to a number of the winners by *The F.A. Non-League Football Annual* in conjunction with The Wirral Programme club at the beginning of the 1979-80 season.

Non-League Football still doesn't receive the national Press coverage it deserves but great service was given to the game by *Netstretcher*, that ever-improving magazine which covers football in the North-west, the *Berger Isthmian News*, and the *Kingsmead Athenian News* last season. We received some excellent handbooks and club magazines during the season including the *Stafford Rangers Handbook* (20p), Dagenham's *Dagger* magazine (10p), the Sussex County League Review *Score* (20p), the *Northwood F.C. Handbook*, the very original Wealdstone F.C. Supporters' club magazine *Long Ball Down the Middle* (15p), Harlow Town's *Centenary Newspaper*, Leatherhead's 1978 *Cup Final Souvenir* and Hungerford Town's *Berks and Bucks Cup Final Souvenir*.

If you are interested in receiving information concerning non-league programme clubs, the availability of programmes, non-league periodicals and club handbooks, you may like to join The Non-League Football Fellowship publicised elsewhere in this Annual. The club will do all in its power to give an up-to-date and efficient information service on all non-league matters and will have many journalists and programme experts working to provide a first-class nationwide service.

F.A. PUBLICATIONS 1979-80

The following publications are all available from:
The Football Association, 16 Lancaster Gate, London, W2 3LW.
The 1979-80 F.A. Diary Containing the Football League fixtures; International, Representative and Cup dates for 1979–80, results and useful addresses £1.00 inclusive of post and V.A.T.
The F.A. Guide to Training and Coaching £4.95 (hardback) plus 54p post and packing
Coach Yourself Association Football
£2.95 (softback) plus 22p post and packing (also available as individual booklets: Goalkeepers, Back Defenders, Midfield Players, Strikers 95p per copy plus 10p postage and packing
Tactics and Teamwork (softback) £2.95 plus 19p post and packing
The 1979-80 Referees Chart Now Contains alterations to the laws of the game agreed upon at this year's International Board Meeting, advice to referees and linesmen. 60p plus 10p post and packing
Was That Player Off-side Find the answer and test your knowledge of the laws of the game with the Referee's *Quiz Book 2*. Questions and answers prepared by Football Association Referees' Secretary, Reg Paine. 70p plus 10p post and packing (available October 1979). Copies of *Quiz Book 1* are still available. 50p plus 10p post and packing
The 1978 World Cup Report by F.A. Director of Education and Training, Allen Wade. A comprehensive technical report of every game played in the 1978 World Cup finals, complete with detailed diagrams. £1.00 (inclusive of post and packing). Copies of the 1974 *World Cup Report* also available. 50p inclusive of post and packing.
F.A. Today The new official Football Association magazine.
64 pages of official views, stimulating articles and exciting reviews of F.A. matches. Incorporates the F.A. coaching magazine *Insight*. Four editions per year – first edition available October 1979. Available only on subscription. £2.50 for four issues inclusive of post and packing.

TAKE UP YOUR SUBSCRIPTION TODAY
To: The Subscriptions Department,
      The Football Association,
      16 Lancaster Gate,
      London, W2 3LW.
Please send me the first four editions of *F.A. Today*
I enclose my Cheque/Postal Order No. _____
for £2.50
Name _____
      (Block letters)
Address _____
_____
_____
_____

Date Ordered _____

INTER-SERVICES RESULTS 1978-79

Royal Navy 0 Army 0	7 March 1979	H.M.S. Chatham
Royal Air Force 0 Royal Navy 0	14 March 1979	R.A.F. Cosford
Army 0 Royal Air Force 1	21 March 1979	Aldershot

Goalscorer for Royal Air Force: Off./Cadet J. Lazzarri, after 73 minutes.

Inter-services final positions
1. Royal Air Force (champions)
2. Royal Navy
3. Army

KENTISH CUP 1978-79
Army 0   French Armed Forces 3 (in France)
Army 0   Belgian Armed Forces 3 (Aldershot)
Note: It has been proposed that Combined Services UK fulfil this fixture next season as opposed to the Army only.

COMBINED SERVICES F.A. 1978-79

Selected squad:	S/Ldr. C. Riley	team manager	R.A.F.
	Chief/Tech. J. Lamb	team coach	R.A.F.
	Sgt. R. Clare	team trainer	R.A.F.

Players:	Sgt. T. Thompson	L/Cpl. G. Torrence
	Lt. T. Miklinski	P.O. B. Reed
	Pt. G. Holden	P.O. T. Johnston
	P.O. A. Carlisle	Sgt. D. Woods
	Cpl. G. Corkish	P.O. L. Tongue
	Cpl. D. Dodds	Sgt. J. Woodward
	Cpl. G. Hern	P.O. L. Ashmore
	Cp. A. Hamilton	P.O. K. Maddox

Combined Services played the England F.A. at Aldershot on 11 April 1979. Result: 1–1 draw. Scorer for Combined Services: G. Corkish.

COMBINED SERVICES TOUR TO HONG KONG 15–30 APRIL 1979
Opening fixture v Combined Services HK: Combined Services UK 7 Combined Services HK 0 (Ashmore, Reed, Maddox, Woods 2, Woodward 2).
2nd fixture v HK Police: Combined Services UK 1 HK Police 1 (Ashmore).
3rd fixture v HK F.A.: Combined Services UK 3 HK F.A. 0 (Woodward, Hern, Maddox). Attendance at this match totalled 10,000. HK F.A. team had narrowly failed to qualify for the 1978 World Cup finals in Argentina.
4th fixture v Combined Leagues HK: Combined Services *UK* 0 HK Combined Leagues 1.

ROTHMANS NATIONAL
XI TOURS 1978 AND 1979

1978 Touring Party Dave Collyer (Kingstonian), Rod Oland (Newbury Town), Dave Curry (Spennymoor United), Ronnie Dicks (Welton Rovers), Bob Perrott (Glastonbury), Brian Faulkes (Hungerford Town), Dave Lesbirel (Vale Recreation), Bobby Green (Tooting & Mitcham), John Cooper (*capt.*) (Leatherhead), Fred Hissett (Tow Law Town), Alan Hurford (Bridgwater Town), Colin Shepherd (Moreton Town), Mal Harkins (Dagenham), Tommy Holden (Wellington), Alan Shoulder (Bishop Auckland), Rory Crick (First Tower United), Joe Scott (Falmouth Town). *Tour guest:* Geoff Hurst.

Las Palmas U-23 v Rothmans XI (*6–3 – Holden 3, Shoulder 2, Cooper*). *Team:* Oland, Faulkes (Dicks), Hurford, Hissett, Perrott, Cooper, Green, Shoulder, Hawkins (Lesbirel), Crick (Scott), Holden.

Las Palmas League XI v Rothmans XI (*2–1 – Lesbirel, Crick*). *Team:* Collyer, Curry, Dicks, Lesbirel, Hurford, Hissett, Shoulder, Green, Holden (Hurst), Crick, Scott (Hawkins).

Tenerife U-23 v Rothmans XI (*1–1 – Holden. R.XI lost 8–9 on penalties*). *Team:* Collyer, Curry, Hurford, Hissett, Perrott, Cooper, Green, Shoulder (Hawkins), Scott, Holden, Crick.

Las Palmas League XI v Rothmans XI (*4–1 – Scott 3, Green*). *Team:* Collyer, Dicks, Hurford, Hissett, Faulkes, Cooper, Lesbirel, Shoulder (Green), Scott, Crick (Holden), Hawkins (Perrott).

Dave Clarke (Blyth Spartans), Barry Breuilly (St Pauls, Jersey), Steve Foster (Cheltenham Town), John Crossley (Barton Rovers), Keith Manley (Falmouth Town), Colin Hallimond (Brandon United), Bobby Green (*capt.*) (Tooting & Mitcham), Phil Buck (Thame United), Paul Sussams (Corinthian Casuals), David Ingram (Hungerford Town), Mick King (Newbury Town), Tommy Holden (Brandon United), John Evans (Gloucester City), Derek Hampton (Whitby Town), Ian Farr (Hungerford Town), *coach:* Jim Kelman. *Tour guest:* Bobby Charlton.

Tenerife v Rothmans XI (*2–1 – Hampton, Evans*). *Team:* Clarke, Foster, Crassley, Manley, Hallimond, Green (capt.), Buck, Ingram, Holden, Evans, Hampton, King, Sussams, Farr, Breuilly.

Las Palmas v Rothmans XI (*0–1*). *Team:* Clarke, Foster, Crossley, Manley, Hallimond, Green (capt.), Buck, Ingram, King, Farr, Holden, Sussams, Evans, Breuilly.

Telde v Rothmans XI (*1–1 – Evans*). *Team:* Breuilly, Crossley, Green, Foster, Hanley, Sussams, Buck, Ingram, Holden, Evans, Clark.

PHILIPS FLOODLIGHTING
COMPETITION 1978-79

The eight national finalists had qualified by scoring the most goals in their respective groups (approximately 30 clubs). Only clubs who had entered the F.A. Vase took part, and the groups' winners were decided by totalling the goals scored by each club in 12 league fixtures played after 1 November 1978. The competition was held at Alexander Stadium, Birmingham on 6 May 1979, and was organised by Alan Reville (Sales Link Ltd.). The referees were from the Birmingham Referees' Association. The presentation was made by Mike Goodwin (Philips Lighting Division director) and Alec Smith (F.A. Challenge Vase Committee chairman).

Group 1	WD	BS	AU	LW	Goals
Waterloo Dock	–	4–2	8–5	5–1	17–8
Blue Star	2–4	–	4–2	7–1	14–7
Ash United	5–8	2–4	–	6–1	13–13
Leyton-Wingate	1–5	1–7	1–6	–	3–18

Group 2	SCW	SM	BAC	BSo	Goals
Seeham CW. RS.	–	5–6	7–0	3–2	15–8
St Martins	6–5	–	1–5	5–2	12–12
BAC (Weybridge)	0–7	5–1	–	2–2	7–10
Billingham Soc.	2–3	2–5	2–2	–	6–10

Final: Seeham C.W. Red Star 5   Waterloo Dock 1

Southern Amateur Football League
Final Tables 1978-79
SENIOR SECTION

FIRST DIVISION

	P	W	D	L	F	A	Pts.
Catford Wanderers	22	15	4	3	58	22	34
West Wickham	22	12	5	5	52	33	29
Kew Association	21	8	8	5	41	34	24
Norsemen	22	10	4	8	37	35	24
National Westminster Bank	22	6	10	6	33	30	22
Old Esthameians	22	8	6	8	30	29	22
Midland Bank	22	5	10	7	20	28	20
Winchmore Hill	21	6	8	7	22	31	20
Barclays Bank	22	7	5	10	25	37	19
Lloyds Bank	22	6	6	10	26	32	18
Carshalton	22	4	7	11	21	35	15
Southgate Olympic	22	4	7	11	24	43	15

SECOND DIVISION

	P	W	D	L	F	A	Pts.
East Barnet Old Gram. ...	22	15	5	2	54	27	35
Crouch End Vampires	22	14	3	5	60	20	31
Polytechnic.....................	22	12	6	4	34	25	30
Merton	22	12	4	6	42	33	28
Old Actonians Association	22	9	5	8	38	31	23
Civil Service	22	7	6	9	42	42	20
Broomfield	22	9	2	11	31	32	20
Lensbury	22	8	4	10	28	35	20
South Bank Polytechnic ...	22	8	3	11	43	39	19
Old Parkonians	22	7	5	10	26	35	19
Old Stationers	22	5	2	15	32	58	12
Old Bromleians	22	2	3	17	17	70	7

THIRD DIVISION

	P	W	D	L	F	A	Pts.
Old Westminster Citizens...	22	18	3	1	65	24	39
Old Lyonians	22	12	6	4	50	36	30
Alleyn Old Boys	22	10	5	7	62	37	25
Britannic House	22	9	4	9	40	48	22
Bank of England	22	9	3	10	36	31	21
Old Latymerians	22	8	5	9	44	40	21
Alexandra Park	22	10	1	11	40	42	21
Ibis	22	9	3	10	27	39	21
Brentham	22	5	8	9	29	35	18
Cuaco	22	6	6	10	25	34	18
Pearl Assurance..............	22	4	8	10	20	34	16
Reigate Priory	22	4	4	14	26	64	12

SENIOR CUP RESULTS

A.F.A. Senior Cup	Lloyds Bank 2	Carshalton 0
A.F.A. Middlesex Senior Cup	East Barnet O. Grams 2	Old Ignatians 1
A.F.A. Surrey Senior Cup	Clapham Old Xaverians 4	Old Josephians 1
A.F.A. Essex Senior Cup	Old Fairlopians 1	Old Buckwellians 0
Arthur Dunn Cup	Old Aldenhamians 1	Old Brentwoods 0

VARSITY MATCH 1978

Cambridge University 2 (*Cox, McGuire*)
B. Jones (Prescot GS/St Catharine's); Nick McNay (Allerton Grange Comp./Clare); G. Little (Stratford GS/St Catharine's); P. Roberts (Yale VI Form College/St John's); L. Watson (Isleworth GS/Christ's); A. Smith (Guthlaxton College/Sidney Sussex); M. Cox (Torquay GS/Christ's); S. Evans (West Park GS/Trinity Hall); P. Dinkenor (*capt.*) (Manchester GS/Sidney Sussex); J. Wilks (Slough GS/Trinity Hall); S. Buck (Gosforth HS/Fitzwilliam); *Subs:* M. McGuire (St Patrick's College/Christ's); P. Horne (Preston Lodge HS/Sidney Sussex).

Oxford University 1 (*Hannon*)
M. Power (Devonport HS/St Edmund Hall); D. Chambers (Bemrose, Derby/Corpus Christi); I. Barr (Gosford Hill School, Kidlington/Lincoln); N. Morrill (Millfield/Lincoln); M. Mrowiec (*capt.*) (Northgate GS, Ipswich/Christ Church); C. Walton (Matthew Humberstone Comp/Oriel); V. Boyle (St Ignatius College/Magdalen); R. Nugent (Birkenhead School/Queen's); J. Dorrian (St Malachys College/Christ Church); M. Hall (Bournemouth School/Mansfield); P. Hannon (St Mary's College, Crosby/Queen's); *Subs:* M. Shapley (Drayton Manor HS/Trinity); N. Rogers (Manchester GS/Oriel).

THE OFFICIAL F.A. CUP REVIEW 1979

including

reports, results, photographs and features
on the F.A. Cup in general

and

the 1978-79 competition in particular

from

THE PRELIMINARY ROUND TO THE CUP FINAL
FEATURED IN WELL OVER 100 PHOTOGRAPHS ARE

ALTRINCHAM	MACCLESFIELD T.	RUNCORN
CROYDON	MARCH TOWN U.	SOUTHPORT
DULWICH HAMLET	MARGATE	WITTON ALBION
EASTWOOD TOWN	MARINE	WOKING
GRAVESEND &	NORTHWICH VIC.	WORKSOP TOWN
NORTHFLEET	PORTHMADOC	YEOVIL TOWN
HUNGERFORD TOWN		

A SPECIAL FEATURE ON ALTRINCHAM
F.A. CUP 'RESULT OF THE ROUNDS' 1978-79 INCLUDES

Preliminary Round	Bangor City	1	Leek Town	2
1st Qualifying Round	Telford United	0	Halesowen Town	1
2nd Qualifying Round	Atherstone Town	1	Irthlingborough D.	3
3rd Qualifying Round	Eastbourne United	2	Hastings United	1
4th Qualifying Round	Margate	1	Woking	7
1st Round Proper	Rochdale	0	Droylsden	1
2nd Round Proper	Swansea	2	Worthing	1
3rd Round Proper	Woking	3	Swansea City	5
4th Round Proper	Tottenham H.	1	Altrincham	1

*The book (98 pages) is available from Tony Williams (Football Promotions)
Ltd., 130 High Street, Hungerford, Berkshire.*

QUALITY, PRICE, DELIVERY

We have a comprehensive range of football jerseys, shorts and socks AVAILABLE NOW FROM STOCK in combinations of the eleven Barralan colours.

Special lines can be made to order.

Athletics/Sportswear, Leotards & Regulation Swimwear also available.

Barralan Sportswear

Barralan Leicester Limited LE9 7FP
Wenton Street, Earl Shilton (0455) 42007
Telephone:, Earl Shilton

294

CHANNEL ISLANDS FOOTBALL

ROTHMANS JERSEY FOOTBALL COMBINATION

Final Table 1978-79
FIRST DIVISION

	P	W	D	L	F	A	Pts.	C	D
Oaklands	18	12	4	2	40	21	40	1	0
First Tower	18	11	6	1	41	20	39	3	8
Wanderers	18	10	2	6	45	33	32	1	0
St Pauls	18	9	3	6	48	33	30	4	0
St Peter	18	8	5	5	35	28	29	0	0
St Saviour	18	6	4	8	26	31	22	6	4
Beeches Old Boys	18	6	3	9	21	34	21	0	0
St Owen	18	5	2	11	27	35	17	2	4
Anglos & Springfield	18	2	6	10	20	38	12	4	4
Rozel Rovers	18	1	5	12	19	52	8	2	4

Promoted – Georgetown and Old Victorians.

ROTHMANS GUERNSEY PRIAULX LEAGUE

Final Table 1978-79

	P	W	D	L	F	A	Pts.
St Martin's	21	19	1	1	99	21	58
Rangers	21	17	1	3	71	13	52
Vale Rec.	21	9	4	8	95	35	31
Northerners	21	9	4	8	49	35	31
Rovers	21	8	5	8	42	43	29
Belgrave Wanderers	21	6	5	10	40	60	23
Sylvans	21	3	5	13	30	63	14
Centrals	21	0	1	20	9	165	1

LEADING GOALSCORERS
(League, Cup and Island representative matches)

	Total
C. Fallaize (St Martin's)	47
N. Hunter (Rangers)	35
P. Blondel (Vale Rec.)	28

MURATTI CUP FINAL
(Channel Islands 'international' championship)
Guernsey 5 Jersey 0 (attendance: 2,500)

Guernsey: R. Froome; K. Allen, P. Blondel, R. Despres, C. Hargreaves; C. Fallaize, K. Le Gallez, M. Loveridge; W. Kennedy, N. Le Page, R. Webb. *Substitutes*: A. Le Page and C. Le Page for Fallaize and N. Le Page.
Jersey: D. Matthews; D. A'Court, A. Williams, A. Herbert, A. Pitman; J. Murphy, M. Matthews; A. Cunningham, R. Crick, P. Fleury, B. Pitman. *Substitute*: G. Pinel for M. Matthews.

Goalscorers: Le Gallez, Kennedy, Fallaize, Blondel (pen.), Webb.
Referee: A. Robinson (Waterlooville, Hants.)

This was the biggest win ever recorded by either island in a Guernsey-Jersey final. Guernsey has now won the cup 31 times to Jersey's 30. It was Guernsey's first home win over Jersey for 10 years.

In the semi-final, Jersey beat Alderney 8-0 with P. Fleury and B. Pitman each scoring a hat-trick.

UPTON PARK CUP
(Jersey League champions v Guernsey League champions)
Oaklands (Jersey) 2 St Martin's (Guernsey) 3 (attendance: 900)

Oaklands: D. Cramsie; J. McFarlane, I. Corfield, M. Cooper, G. Bryce; I. Farley, C. Lumsden, T. Smith; A. Cunningham, S. Dewhurst, B. McDonald. *Substitute*: G. White for McFarlane.

St Martin's: R. Froome; K. Allen, N. Thoume, G. Rowe, S. Le Lerre; R. Avery, K. Le Gallez, M. Loveridge; W. Kennedy, C. Fallaize, R. Webb. *Substitute*: H. Davey for Fallaize.

Goalscorers: Oaklands: Dewhurst and Smith; St Martin's: Corfield (o.g.), Fallaize, Kennedy.
Referee: R. Challis (Tonbridge, Kent).

JERSEY WHEWAY CUP FINAL
Oaklands 0 St Martin's (Guernsey) 2

GUERNSEY JEREMIE CUP FINAL
St Martin's 2 Northerners 0

Guernsey Island XI results in the 'build-up' for the Muratti final included a 5-0 win over Royal Naval Air Command; a 1-1 draw with Oxford United (Football League); a 5-0 win over Kew Association; a 4-1 win over Manchester Polytechnic and a 0-0 draw with Abingdon Town. No match was lost. During the season one of Guernsey's star players, Craig Allen, the Rangers forward, turned professional with NASL club California Surf.

ISLE OF MAN FOOTBALL

Final Table 1978-79

FIRST DIVISION

	P	W	D	L	F	A	Pts.
Rushen	19	16	2	1	83	25	34
Castletown	20	15	3	2	75	27	33
Peel	20	13	3	4	61	39	29
Pulrose	19	11	3	5	68	37	25
Ramsey	18	11	1	6	49	28	23
Gymns	20	10	3	7	51	60	23
Malew	19	6	2	11	28	37	14
St John's	20	4	2	14	30	65	10
Old Boys	20	4	2	14	35	74	10
St Mary's	20	3	3	14	27	72	9
Laxey	19	0	4	15	25	68	4

Not every team completed the total of 20 games, including champions Rushen, who retained the title, because of an F.A. decision to terminate the season prematurely as bad weather had resulted in so many match postponements during the winter.

SENIOR CUP WINNERS

Railway Cup	Rushen
F.A. Cup	Ramsey
Hospital Cup	Castletown
Woods Cup	Onchan

Teams promoted to the First Division were Corinthians and Braddan.

POST-WAR ENGLAND AMATEUR INTERNATIONALS

Adams, D. W
Adams, J.
Agar, R.
Alexander, F.
Amor, W.
Amos, A.
Andrews, D.
Ardrey, R.
Ashworth, J.
Aston, P.

Banks, K.
Barker, C.
Barker, M.
Bass A.
Bassett, D.
Bates, P.
Beardsley, E.
Bell, R.
Bennett, E.
Biggs, A.
Bladon, T.
Bradley, W.
Bridges, A. J.
Bromilow, G. J.
Brooks, J.
Broomfield, W.
Brown, B. R.
Brown, G.
Brown, G. R.
Brown, L.
Brown, L. G.
Brown, R. H.
Browning, M.
Bumpstead, D.
Bunce, G.
Bunker, E.
Burchell, G. S.
Burns, M.
Butterfield, J.

Candey, M.
Carr, R. B.
Champelovier, L.
Charles, J.
Charlton, S.
Childs, A. R.
Childs, E.

Clark, F.
Clarke, D.
Clements, P.
Coates, A.
Coates, J.
Cobb, D.
Connell, R.
Cooper, M.
Cowan, R.
Creasey, W.
Cresswell, C.
Crosbie, T.
Cross, E.
Cruse, P.
Cutbush, D.

D'Arcy, A.
D'Arcy, D.
Darey, J.
Davison, R.
Day, R.
Deadman, P.
Delaney, J.
Dickin, E.
Diwell, P.
Dodkins, H. E.
Dougall, J.
Doyle, M.
Duggan, C.
Dutchman, J.

Eason, L.
Eaton, R.
Edelston, M.
Edwards, D.
Evans, D.

Farrer, L. T.
Feely, P.
Figg, R.
Flanagan, D.
Fletcher, J.
Frankish, P.
Friend, B.
Fright, E. G.
Fry, P.
Fryer, R.
Fuller, C. E.

Fuschillo, P.

Gadsden, R. F.
Gamblin, D.
Garbutt, P.
Gardener, D.
Goodwin, H.
Gradi, D.
Gray, K.
Greene, P.
Greenwood, M. M.
Griffin, D. J.
Groves, V.

Haider, R.
Hamm, G.
Hammond, P.
Hardcastle, P.
Harding, A.
Harding, J.
Hardisty, J. R. E.
Harlow, J.
Harris, J.
Harrison, K.
Harvey, B.
Heckman, R.
Hodges, P.
Hogwood, D.
Holden, G.
Holmes, W.
Hopper, A. H.
Howard, T.
Hunt, L.
Hyde, D.

Ives, A.

Jackson, R. F.
Jarvis, D. H.
Jeffrey, A.
Jelly, K.
Joseph, L.

Kavanagh, J. J. M.
Kelly, C.
Kelly, M.
King, A.
King, B.
Kippax, F. P.
Knox, A.

Lailey, J.
Law, R. K.
Lawrence, T.

Laybourne. J S.,
Lee, E. G.
Lewin, D. J.
Lewis, J. L.
Lindsay, H. M.
Littlejohn, R.
Lunn, R. G.

McGhee, T.
McIlvenny, H. J.
McKenna, F.
McKinna, G. H.
McMillan, J.
Mahon, M.
Major, J.
Marshall, D.
Martin, B.
Martin, C. L.
Martin, J.
Mason, J.
Mead, K.
Mellows, M.
Mendrum, A.
Merritt, R.
Mills, D. J.
Moffat, B.
Moore, D.
Mortimore, C. T.
Mortimore, J.
Moxon, H.

Neale, C. R.
Neale, M.
Neil, P. T.
Noble, A. W.

O'Connell, S.
Oliver, R.

Page, R.
Parr, H.
Paviour, J. S.
Pawson, H. A.
Payne, J.
Peel, A. M.
Phillips, P.
Phipps, R. W.
Picking, L.
Pinner, M. J.
Potts, H. J.
Powell, E.
Pragg, M.
Preston, M.
Prince, S. T.

Pritchard, L.

Randall, D.
Rawlings, J. W.
Reardon, T.
Reid, I.
Ritchie, J.
Ritchie, J.
Robb, G.
Robertson, J. D.
Robinson, T. H.
Robinson, W.
Rosethorn, A.
Roughley, W.
Rowe, R. G.
Rowlands, L. C.
Russell, W.
Rutherford, D.
Rutherford, S.

Sadler, D.
Saunders, D. F.
Saunders, D. W.
Sharratt, H.
Shaw, M.
Shepherd, W.
Shewring, D.
Shippey, J.
Shuttleworth, G. M.
Slater, W. J.
Sleap, R. W.
Smith, A. C.
Smith, D.
Smith, N. L.
Smith, P.
Smith, W.
Spector, M.
Stacey, T.
Stewart, M. J.
Stoker, D.
Stratton, L.
Stratton, R.
Streten, B.
Stroud, R. W.
Studley, D.
Suddaby, P.
Sutcliffe, R.
Swannell, J.

Tanner, J. D. P.
Taylor, J. R.
Teasdale, H.
Terry, P.
Thompson, P.
Thompson, T.
Thursby, R.
Tilley, L.
Topp, L.
Townsend, C.
Tracey, M.
Trimby, R. W.
Turley, A.
Turner, J.
Twissell, C.

Unsworth, J.

Valentine, J. H.
Vaughan, C.
Veart, R.
Venables, T.
Vowells, R. C.

Waiters, A. K.
Walby, M.
Wallis, L. J.
Walton, D.
Walton, J. A.
Ward, G.
Ward, J. R.
West, L.
Whittall, A.
Williams, A.
Wilson, J. J.
Wilson, P.
Windsor, A.
Wolstenholme, I.
Wood, P.
Woods, D.
Worley, L.
Worswick, M.
Wright, D.

Yenson, K.
Young, D.

NON-LEAGUE CLUB EXEMPTIONS IN F.A. COMPETITIONS 1979-80

F.A. Cup

4 *to First Round Proper:* Altrincham (A.P.L.), Scarborough (A.P.L.), Kettering Town (A.P.L.), Stafford Rangers (A.P.L.).

20 *to Fourth Qualifying Round:* Barnet (A.P.L.), Blyth Spartans (D.N.), Dagenham (B.I.L.), Dartford (S.L.S.), Enfield (B.I.L.), Hitchin Town (B.I.L.), A. P. Leamington (A.P.L.), Leatherhead (B.I.L.), Maidstone United (A.P.L.), Minehead (S.L.M.), Morecambe (N.P.L.), Nuneaton Borough (A.P.L.), Runcorn (N.P.L.), Southport (N.P.L.), Tooting and Mitcham United (B.I.L.), Wealdstone (A.P.L.), Weymouth (A.P.L.), Worcester City (A.P.L.), Workington (A.P.L.). Wycombe Wanderers (B.I.L.).

F.A. Trophy:

32 *clubs to First Round Proper:* Altrincham, Atherstone Town, Bangor City, Barking, Bedford Town, Bishop Auckland, Blyth Spartans, Boston United, Cheltenham Town, Chorley, Dagenham, Enfield, Hendon, Kettering Town, Lancaster City, Leatherhead, Maidstone United, Marine, Matlock Town, Mossley, Runcorn, Scarborough, Slough Town, Spennymoor United, Stafford Rangers, Telford United, Tooting and Mitcham United, Weymouth, Winsford United, Worcester City, Wycombe Wanderers, Yeovil Town.

32 *clubs to Third Qualifying Round:* Ashington, Bath City, Consett, Crook Town, Dartford, Dover, Dulwich Hamlet, Enderby Town, Falmouth Town, Frome Town, Gainsborough Trinity, Goole Town, Grantham, Hayes, Harrow Borough, Hastings United, Hednesford Town, Hillingdon Borough, Horwich R.M.I., Kidderminster Harriers, Margate, Merthyr Tydfil, Minehead, Morecambe, Northwich Victoria, Nuneaton Borough, Southport, Sutton United, Walthamstow Avenue, Whitby Town, Witton Albion, Woking.

NON-LEAGUE CHAMPIONS TROPHY
1978 to 1979

Northern Premier & Southern Premier

1971-72   Chelmsford City beat Stafford Rangers 3-2 agg.
1972-73   Boston United beat Kettering Town 6-2 agg.
1973-74   Dartford beat Boston United 3-2 agg.
1974-75   Wimbledon beat Wigan Athletic 3-0 agg.
1975-76   Wimbledon beat Runcorn 3-2 agg.
1976-77   Boston United beat Wimbledon 2-1 agg.
1977-78   Bath City beat Boston United 4-3 agg.

1st Leg Wednesday, 6 December 1978 (*Attendance: 1,343*) **Boston United 2** (Kabia, Callery) **Bath City 0**

Boston United: Stewart, Simmonite, Towle, Moyes, Adamson, Thompson, Phelan, Hector, Welch, Kabia, Callery. *Sub:* Brown.

Bath City: Book, Ryan, M. Rogers, Burns, Bourne, Broom, Wheeler, Tavener, Jenkins, T. Rogers, Higgins, Gibbs.

2nd Leg Monday, 11 December 1978 (*Attendance: 694*) **Bath City 4** (Bourne 2, Bryant, Jenkins) **Boston United 1** (Brown)

Bath City: Book, Ryan, M. Rogers, Burns, Bourne, Broom, Gover, Wheeler, Tavener, Jenkins, T. Rogers, Bryant, Gibbs.

Boston United: Stewart, Phelan, Simmonite, Poplar, Adamson, Thompson, Welch, Hector, Brown, Kabia, Callery *Sub:* Towle.

THE F.A. SEASON 1979-80

1 Sept 1979	Challenge Cup	Preliminary Round
8 Sept 1979	Challenge Trophy	Preliminary Round
8 Sept 1979	Challenge Vase	Extra Preliminary Round
15 Sept 1979	Challenge Cup	First Qualifying Round
29 Sept 1979	Challenge Vase	Preliminary Round
6 Oct 1979	Challenge Cup	Second Qualifying Round
13 Oct 1979	Challenge Trophy	First Qualifying Round
20 Oct 1979	Challenge Cup	Third Qualifying Round
27 Oct 1979	Challenge Vase	First Round
3 Nov 1979	Challenge Cup	Fourth Qualifying Round
10 Nov 1979	Challenge Trophy	Second Qualifying Round
24 Nov 1979	Challenge Cup	First Round Proper
24 Nov 1979	Challenge Vase	Second Round
1 Dec 1979	Challenge Trophy	Third Qualifying Round
15 Dec 1979	Challenge Cup	Second Round Proper
15 Dec 1979	Challenge Vase	Third Round
5 Jan 1980	Challenge Cup	Third Round Proper
12 Jan 1980	Challenge Trophy	First Round Proper
19 Jan 1980	Challenge Vase	Fourth Round
26 Jan 1980	Challenge Cup	Fourth Round Proper
2 Feb 1980	Challenge Trophy	Second Round Proper
9 Feb 1980	Challenge Vase	Fifth Round
16 Feb 1980	Challenge Cup	Fifth Round Proper
23 Feb 1980	Challenge Trophy	Third Round Proper
1 Mar 1980	Challenge Vase	Sixth Round
8 Mar 1980	Challenge Cup	Sixth Round Proper
15 Mar 1980	Challenge Trophy	Fourth Round Proper
22 Mar 1980	Challenge Vase	Semi-final first leg
29 Mar 1980	Challenge Vase	Semi-final second leg
12 Apr 1980	Challenge Cup	Semi-final
12 Apr 1980	Challenge Trophy	Semi-final first leg
19 Apr 1980	Challenge Trophy	Semi-final second leg
26 Apr 1980	Challenge Vase	Final
10 May 1980	Challenge Cup	Final
17 May 1980	Challenge Trophy	Final